Table of Contents

CONFIDEN

CASE CLOSED

Volume 22 • VIZ Media Edition

GOSHO AOYAMA

Translation
Tetsuichiro Miyaki

Touch-up & Lettering
Freeman Wong

Cover & Graphics Design
Andrea Rice

Editor
Shaenon K. Garrity

Editor in Chief, Books **Alvin Lu**
Editor in Chief, Magazines **Marc Weidenbaum**
VP of Publishing Licensing **Rika Inouye**
VP of Sales **Gonzalo Ferreyra**
Sr. VP of Marketing **Liza Coppola**
Publisher **Hyoe Narita**

store.viz.com

RATED
T+
FOR OLDER
TEEN

PARENTAL ADVISORY
CASE CLOSED is rated T+ for Older Teen and
is recommended for ages 16 and up. This vol-
ume contains realistic and graphic violence.

ratings.viz.com

VIZ
MEDIA

www.viz.com

Printed in the U.S.A.
Published by VIZ Media, LLC
P.O. Box 77010
San Francisco, CA 94107

10 9 8 7 6 5 4 3 2 1
First printing, March 2008

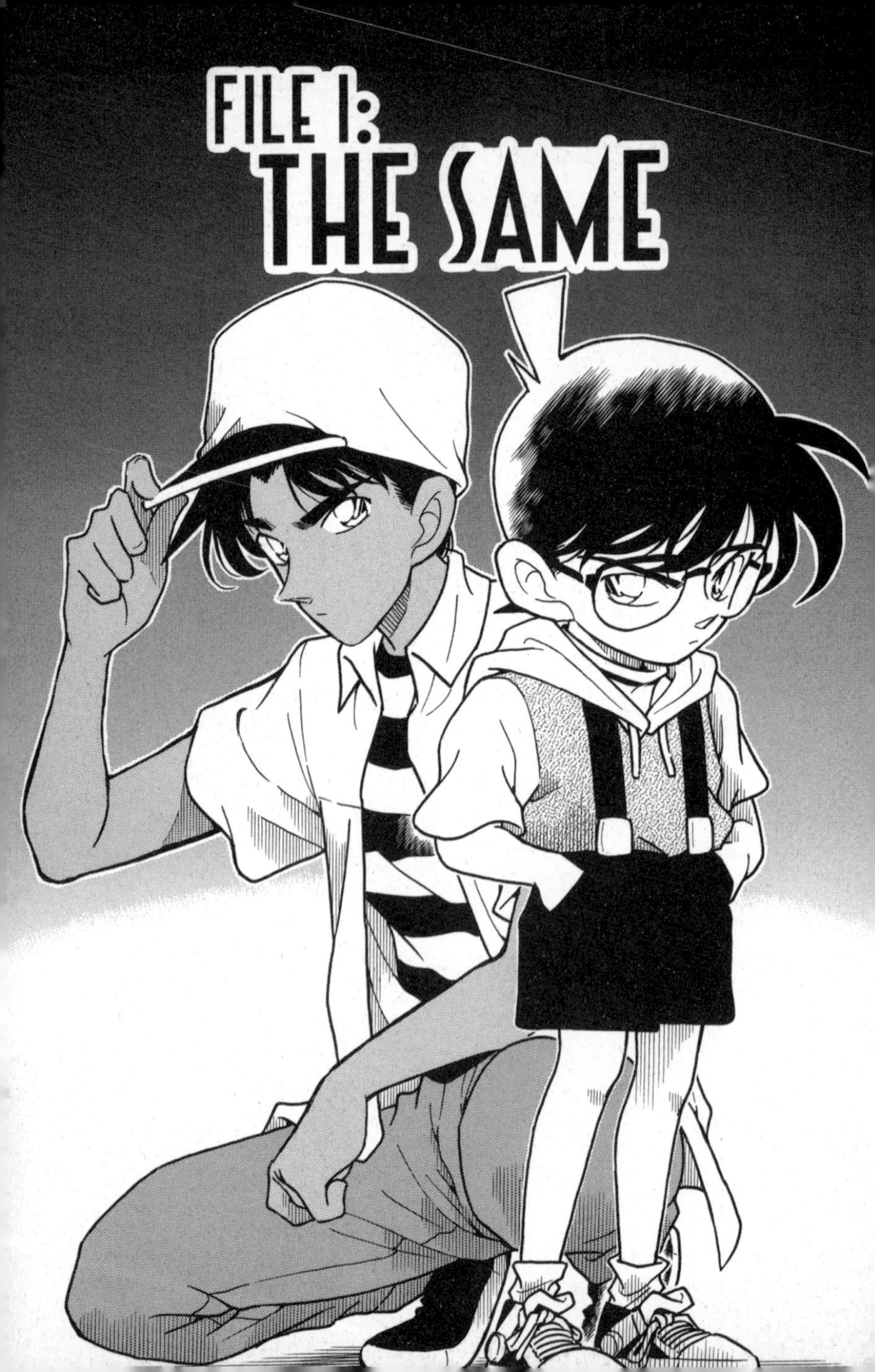
FILE 1:
THE SAME

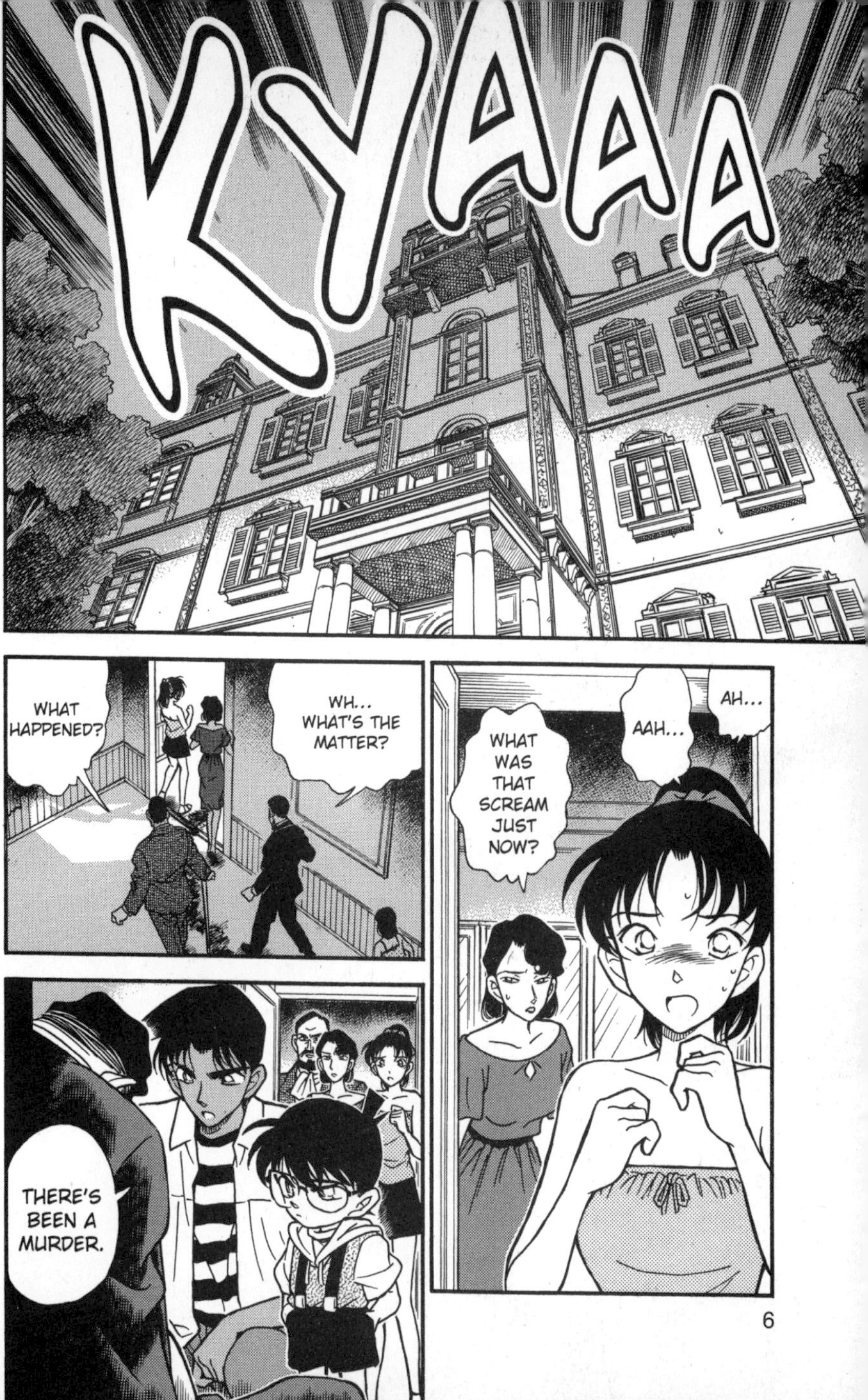
KYAAA
AH...
AAH...
WHAT WAS THAT SCREAM JUST NOW?
WH... WHAT'S THE MATTER?
WHAT HAPPENED?
THERE'S BEEN A MURDER.

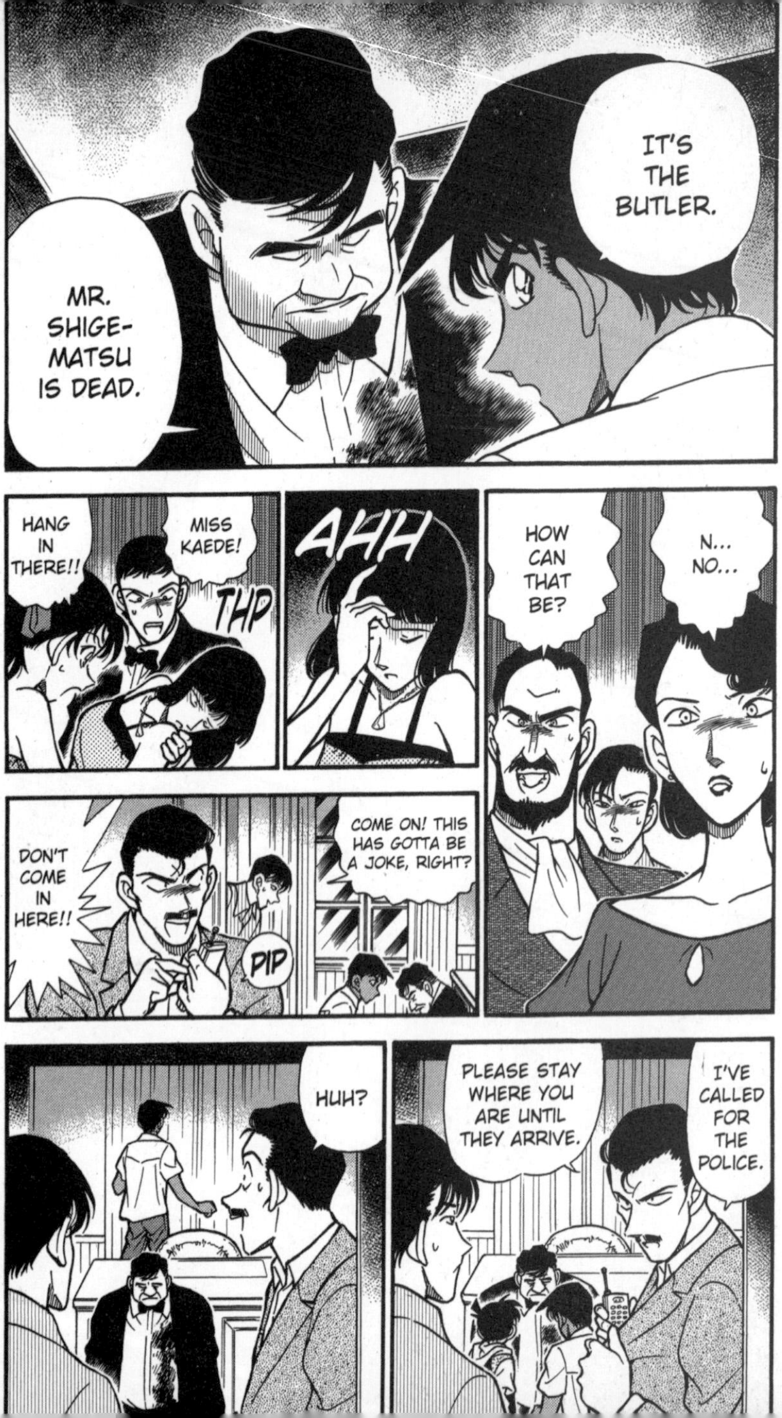
IT'S THE BUTLER.
MR. SHIGE-MATSU IS DEAD.
N... NO...
HOW CAN THAT BE?
AHH
MISS KAEDE!
THP
HANG IN THERE!!
COME ON! THIS HAS GOTTA BE A JOKE, RIGHT?
PIP
DON'T COME IN HERE!!
I'VE CALLED FOR THE POLICE.
PLEASE STAY WHERE YOU ARE UNTIL THEY ARRIVE.
HUH?

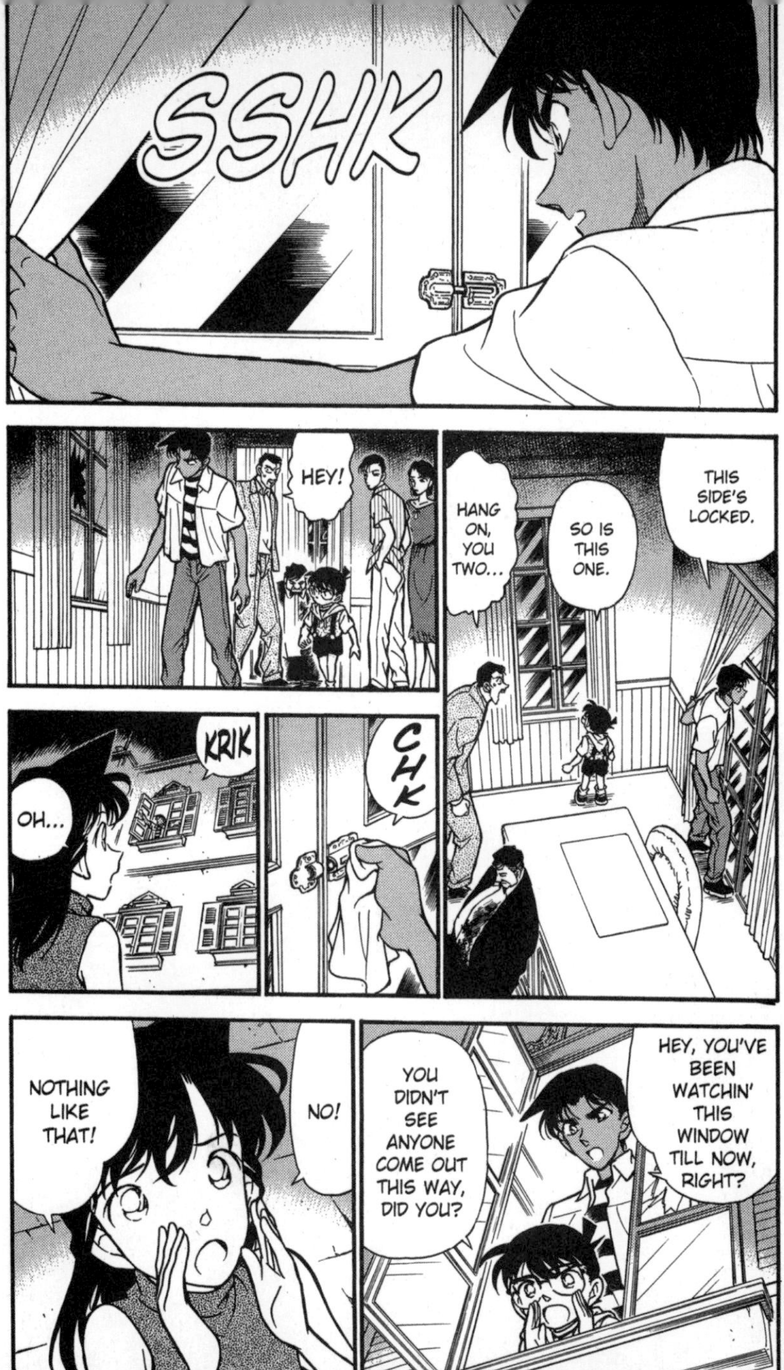
SSHK
THIS SIDE'S LOCKED.
SO IS THIS ONE.
HANG ON, YOU TWO...
HEY!
CHK
KRIK
OH...
HEY, YOU'VE BEEN WATCHIN' THIS WINDOW TILL NOW, RIGHT?
YOU DIDN'T SEE ANYONE COME OUT THIS WAY, DID YOU?
NO!
NOTHING LIKE THAT!

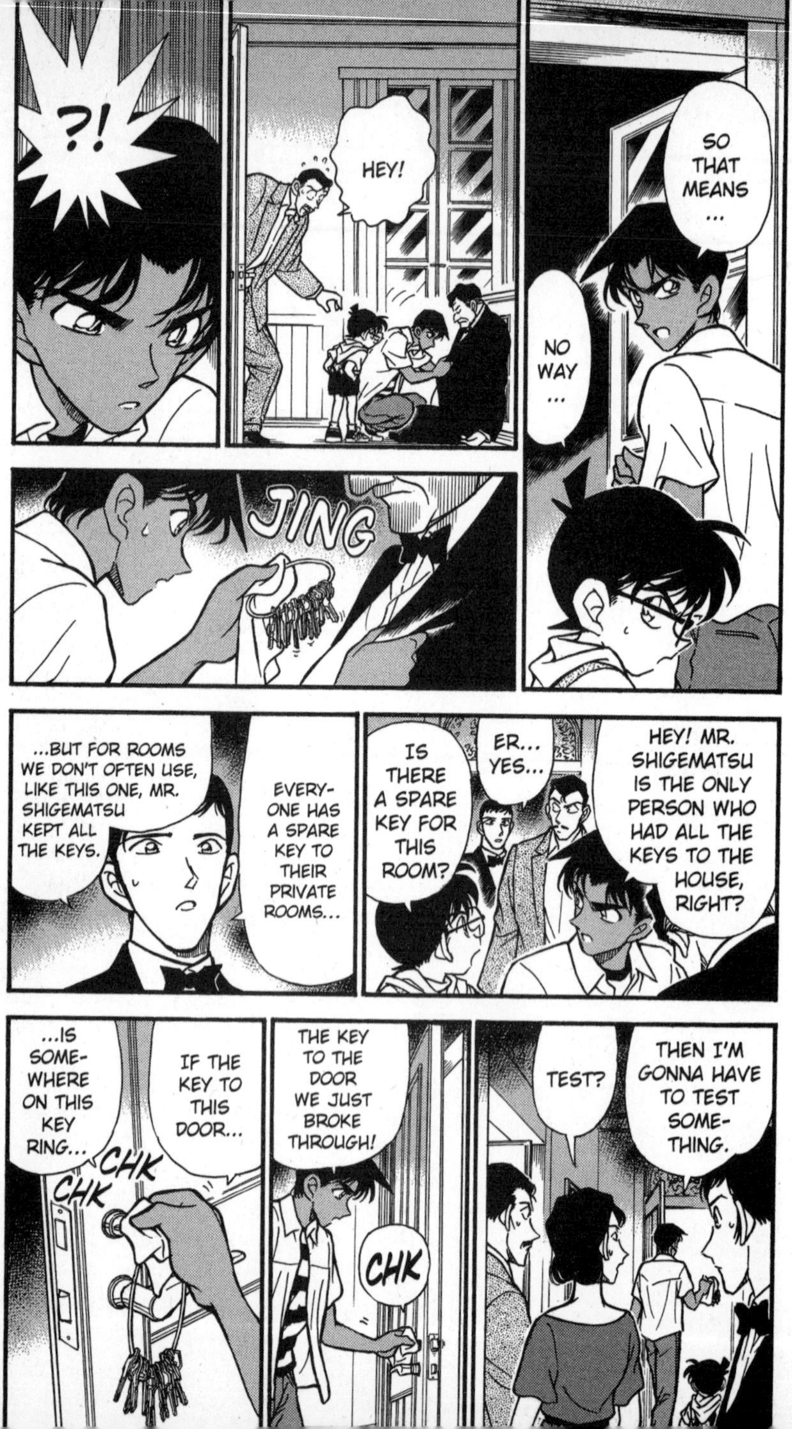
SO THAT MEANS ...
NO WAY ...
HEY!
?!
JING
HEY! MR. SHIGEMATSU IS THE ONLY PERSON WHO HAD ALL THE KEYS TO THE HOUSE, RIGHT?
ER... YES...
IS THERE A SPARE KEY FOR THIS ROOM?
EVERY-ONE HAS A SPARE KEY TO THEIR PRIVATE ROOMS...
...BUT FOR ROOMS WE DON'T OFTEN USE, LIKE THIS ONE, MR. SHIGEMATSU KEPT ALL THE KEYS.
THEN I'M GONNA HAVE TO TEST SOME-THING.
TEST?
THE KEY TO THE DOOR WE JUST BROKE THROUGH!
CHK
IF THE KEY TO THIS DOOR...
...IS SOME-WHERE ON THIS KEY RING...
CHK CHK

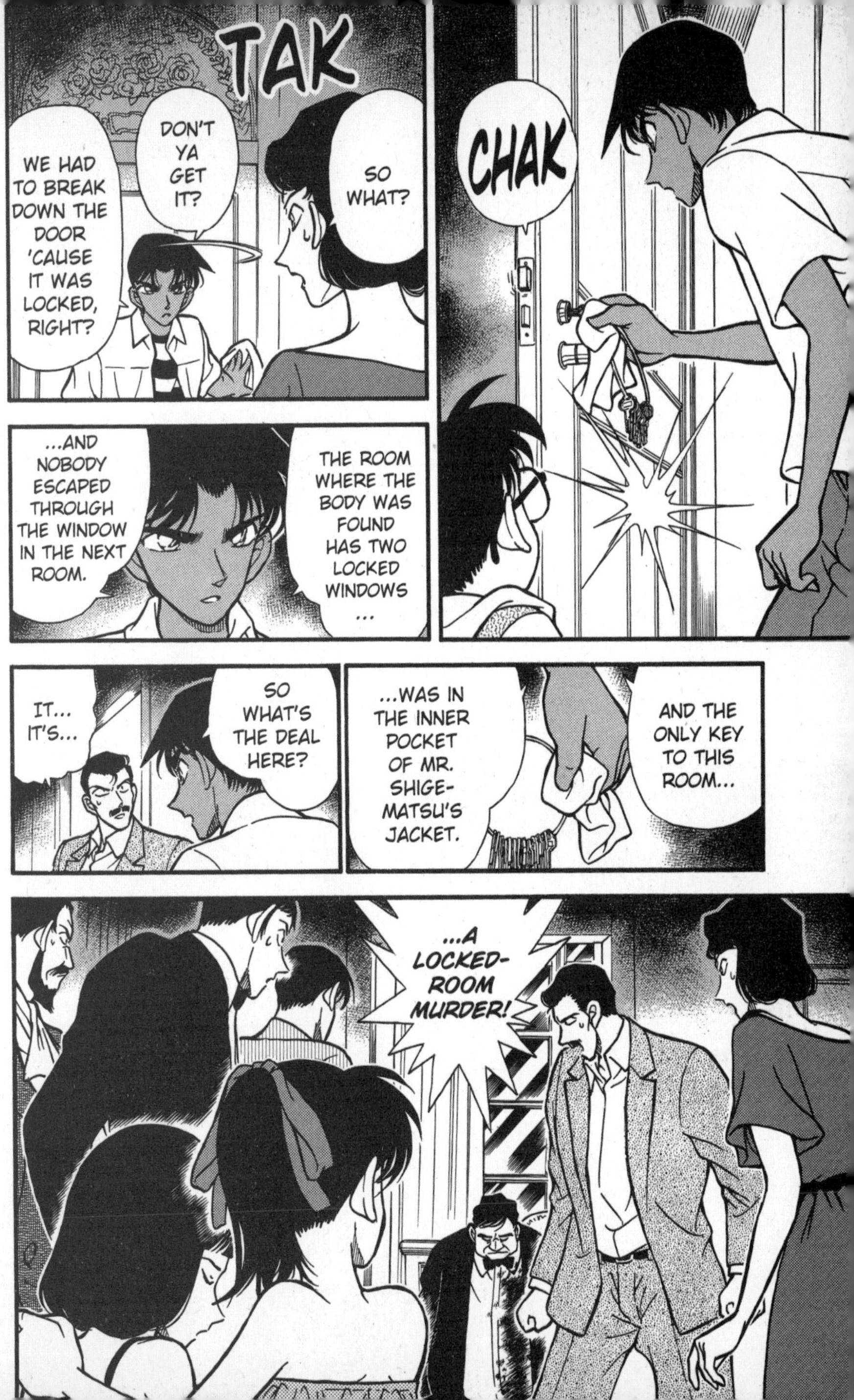
CHAK
TAK
SO WHAT?
DON'T YA GET IT?
WE HAD TO BREAK DOWN THE DOOR 'CAUSE IT WAS LOCKED, RIGHT?
THE ROOM WHERE THE BODY WAS FOUND HAS TWO LOCKED WINDOWS ...
...AND NOBODY ESCAPED THROUGH THE WINDOW IN THE NEXT ROOM.
AND THE ONLY KEY TO THIS ROOM...
...WAS IN THE INNER POCKET OF MR. SHIGE-MATSU'S JACKET.
SO WHAT'S THE DEAL HERE?
IT... IT'S...
...A LOCKED-ROOM MURDER!

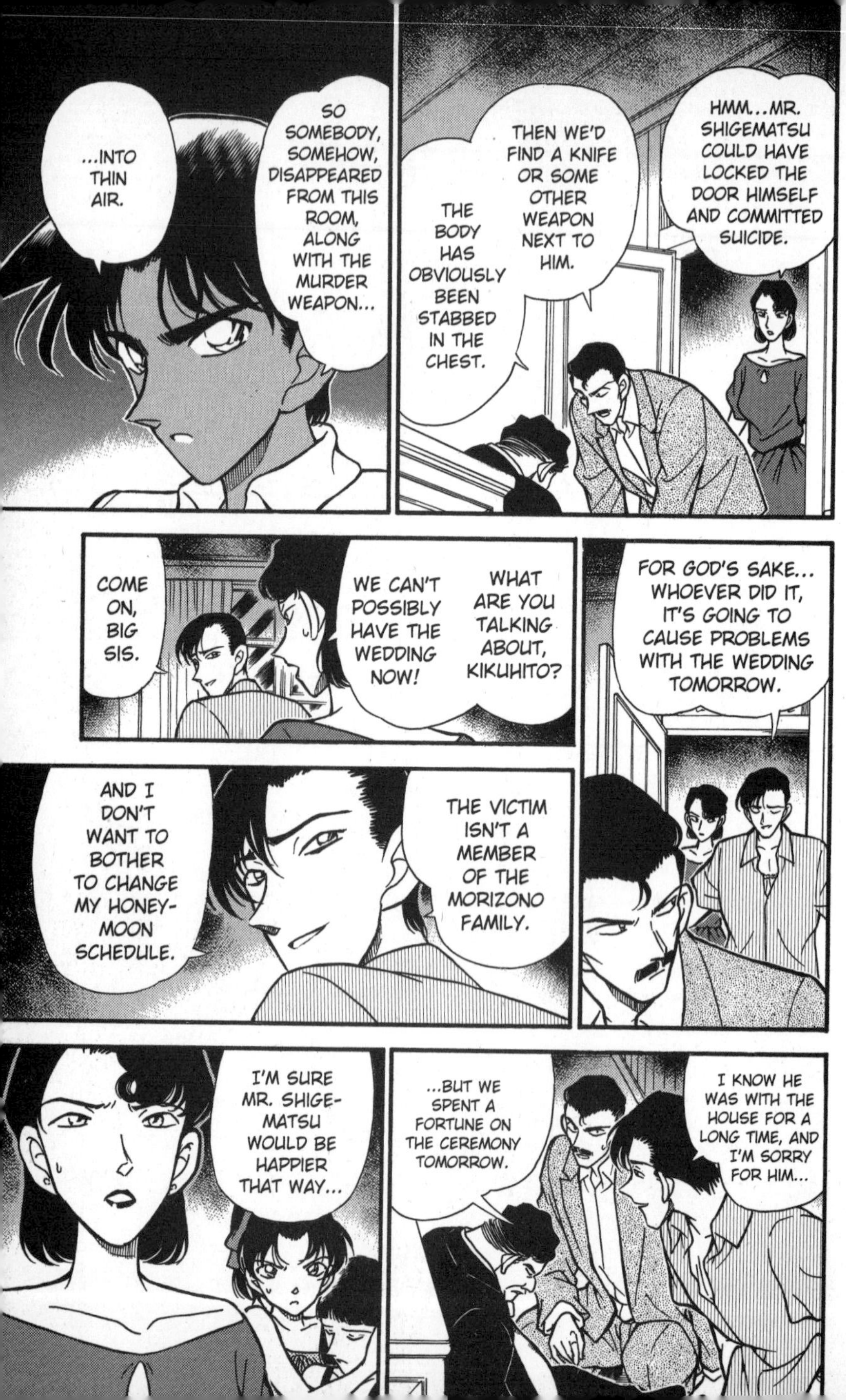

HMM...MR. SHIGEMATSU COULD HAVE LOCKED THE DOOR HIMSELF AND COMMITTED SUICIDE.
THEN WE'D FIND A KNIFE OR SOME OTHER WEAPON NEXT TO HIM.
THE BODY HAS OBVIOUSLY BEEN STABBED IN THE CHEST.
SO SOMEBODY, SOMEHOW, DISAPPEARED FROM THIS ROOM, ALONG WITH THE MURDER WEAPON...
...INTO THIN AIR.
FOR GOD'S SAKE... WHOEVER DID IT, IT'S GOING TO CAUSE PROBLEMS WITH THE WEDDING TOMORROW.
WHAT ARE YOU TALKING ABOUT, KIKUHITO?
WE CAN'T POSSIBLY HAVE THE WEDDING NOW!
COME ON, BIG SIS.
THE VICTIM ISN'T A MEMBER OF THE MORIZONO FAMILY.
AND I DON'T WANT TO BOTHER TO CHANGE MY HONEY-MOON SCHEDULE.
I KNOW HE WAS WITH THE HOUSE FOR A LONG TIME, AND I'M SORRY FOR HIM...
...BUT WE SPENT A FORTUNE ON THE CEREMONY TOMORROW.
I'M SURE MR. SHIGE-MATSU WOULD BE HAPPIER THAT WAY...

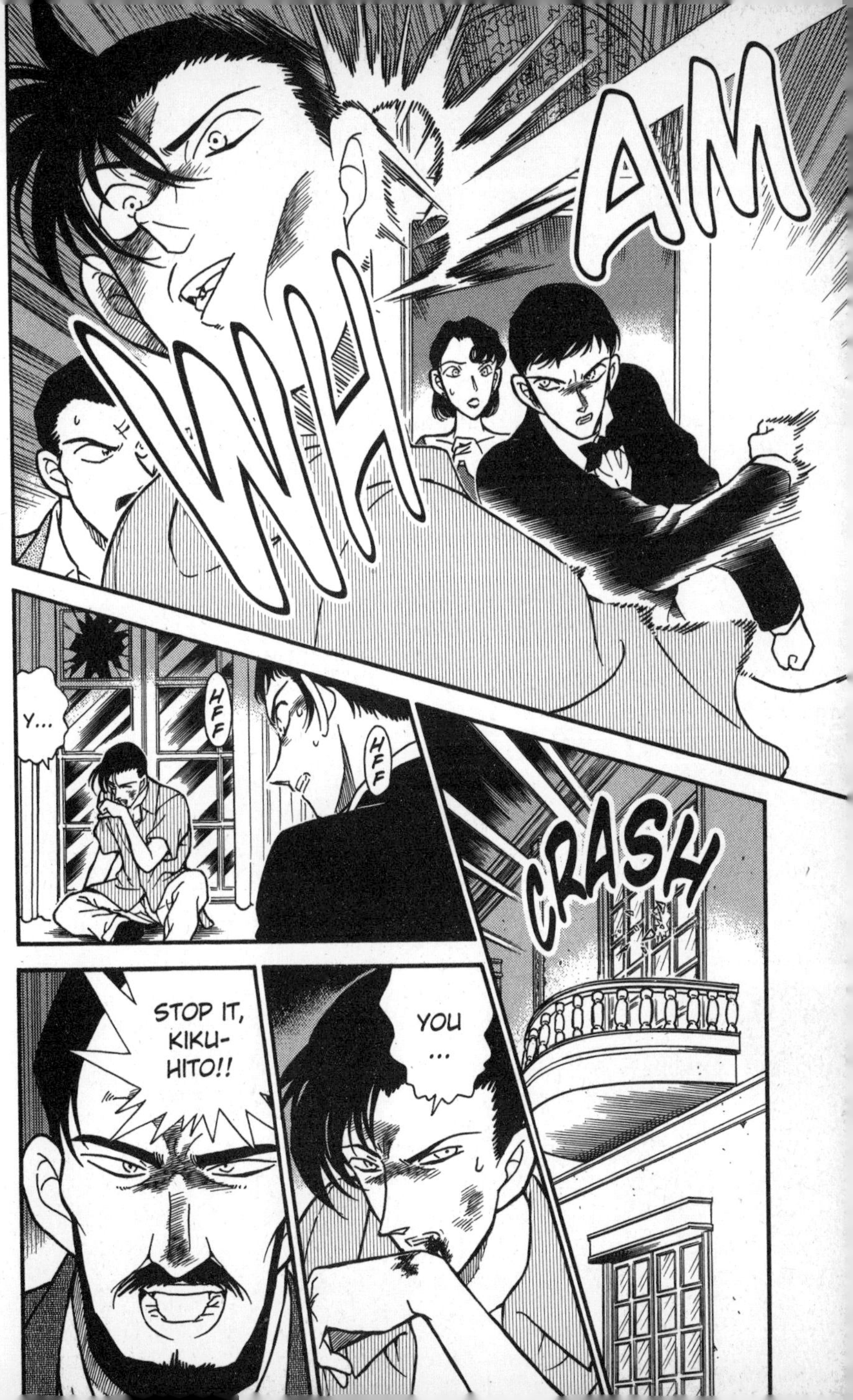
WHAM
CRASH
HFF
HFF
Y...
YOU ...
STOP IT, KIKU-HITO!!

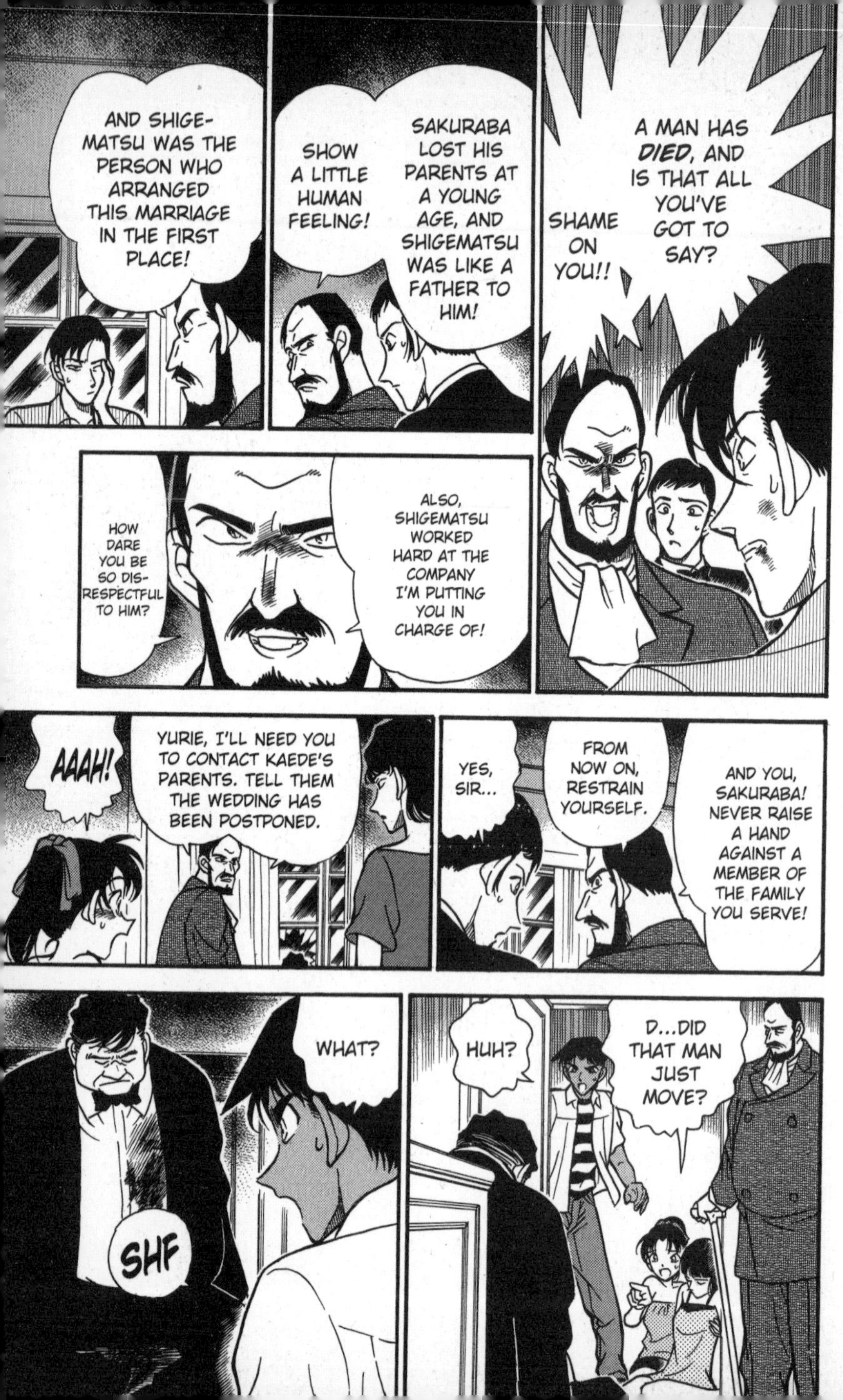
A MAN HAS *DIED*, AND IS THAT ALL YOU'VE GOT TO SAY?
SHAME ON YOU!!
SAKURABA LOST HIS PARENTS AT A YOUNG AGE, AND SHIGEMATSU WAS LIKE A FATHER TO HIM!
SHOW A LITTLE HUMAN FEELING!
AND SHIGE-MATSU WAS THE PERSON WHO ARRANGED THIS MARRIAGE IN THE FIRST PLACE!
ALSO, SHIGEMATSU WORKED HARD AT THE COMPANY I'M PUTTING YOU IN CHARGE OF!
HOW DARE YOU BE SO DIS-RESPECTFUL TO HIM?
AND YOU, SAKURABA! NEVER RAISE A HAND AGAINST A MEMBER OF THE FAMILY YOU SERVE!
FROM NOW ON, RESTRAIN YOURSELF.
YES, SIR...
YURIE, I'LL NEED YOU TO CONTACT KAEDE'S PARENTS. TELL THEM THE WEDDING HAS BEEN POSTPONED.
AAAH!
D...DID THAT MAN JUST MOVE?
HUH?
WHAT?
SHF

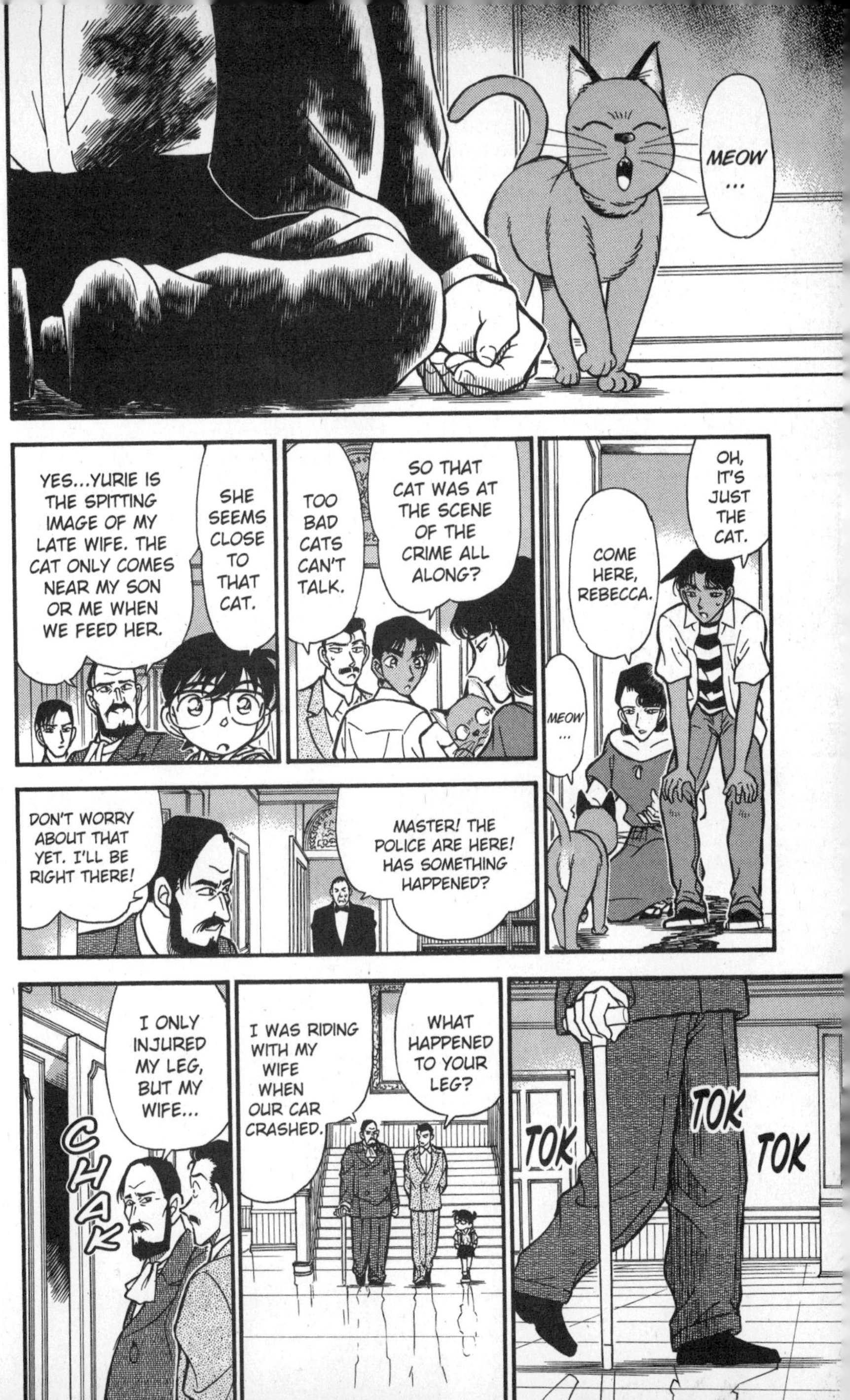
MEOW ...
OH, IT'S JUST THE CAT.
COME HERE, REBECCA.
MEOW ...
SO THAT CAT WAS AT THE SCENE OF THE CRIME ALL ALONG?
TOO BAD CATS CAN'T TALK.
SHE SEEMS CLOSE TO THAT CAT.
YES...YURIE IS THE SPITTING IMAGE OF MY LATE WIFE. THE CAT ONLY COMES NEAR MY SON OR ME WHEN WE FEED HER.
MASTER! THE POLICE ARE HERE! HAS SOMETHING HAPPENED?
DON'T WORRY ABOUT THAT YET. I'LL BE RIGHT THERE!
TOK
TOK
TOK
WHAT HAPPENED TO YOUR LEG?
I WAS RIDING WITH MY WIFE WHEN OUR CAR CRASHED.
I ONLY INJURED MY LEG, BUT MY WIFE...
CHAK

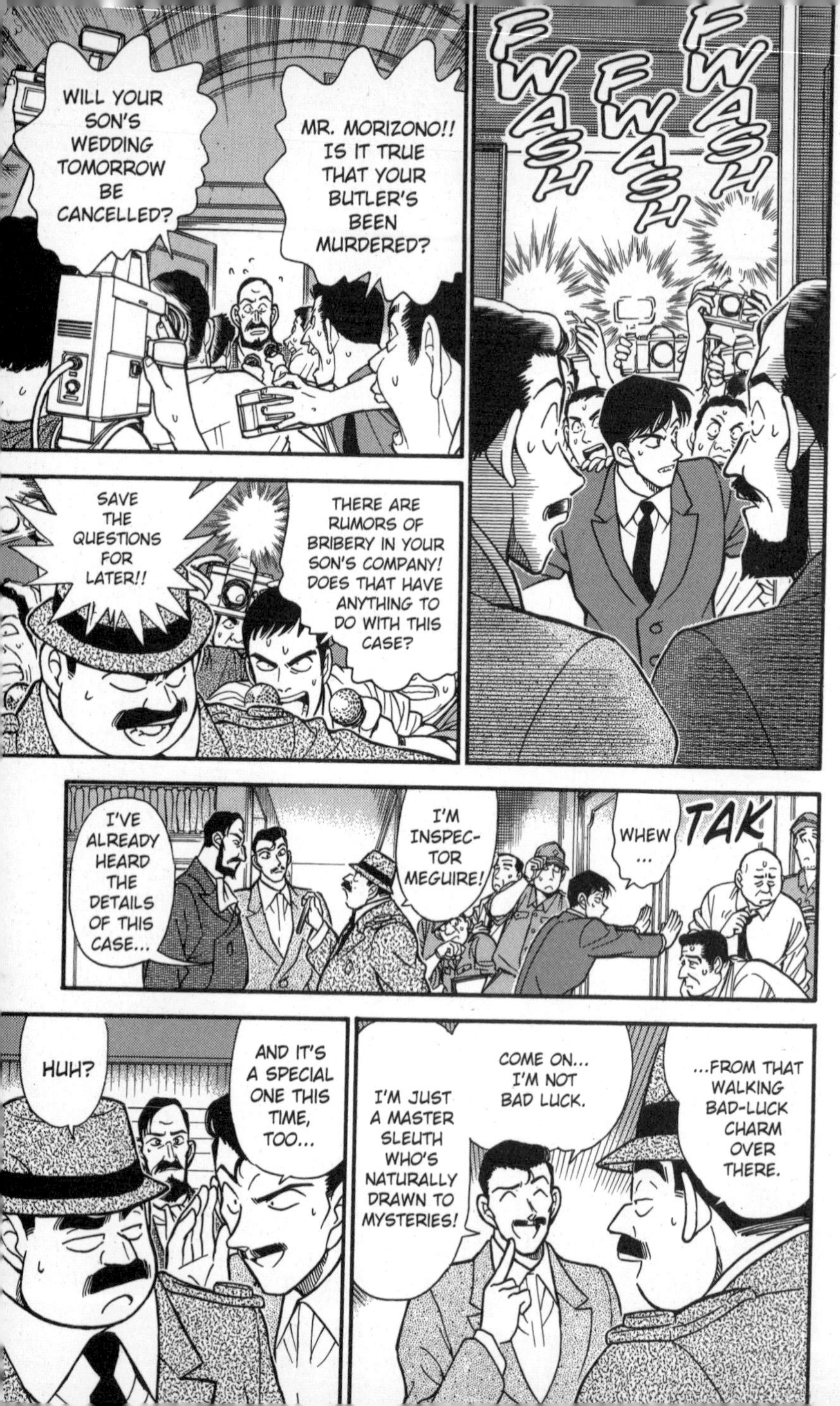
FWASH FWASH FWASH
MR. MORIZONO!! IS IT TRUE THAT YOUR BUTLER'S BEEN MURDERED?
WILL YOUR SON'S WEDDING TOMORROW BE CANCELLED?
THERE ARE RUMORS OF BRIBERY IN YOUR SON'S COMPANY! DOES THAT HAVE ANYTHING TO DO WITH THIS CASE?
SAVE THE QUESTIONS FOR LATER!!
TAK
WHEW...
I'M INSPEC-TOR MEGUIRE!
I'VE ALREADY HEARD THE DETAILS OF THIS CASE...
...FROM THAT WALKING BAD-LUCK CHARM OVER THERE.
COME ON... I'M NOT BAD LUCK.
I'M JUST A MASTER SLEUTH WHO'S NATURALLY DRAWN TO MYSTERIES!
AND IT'S A SPECIAL ONE THIS TIME, TOO...
HUH?

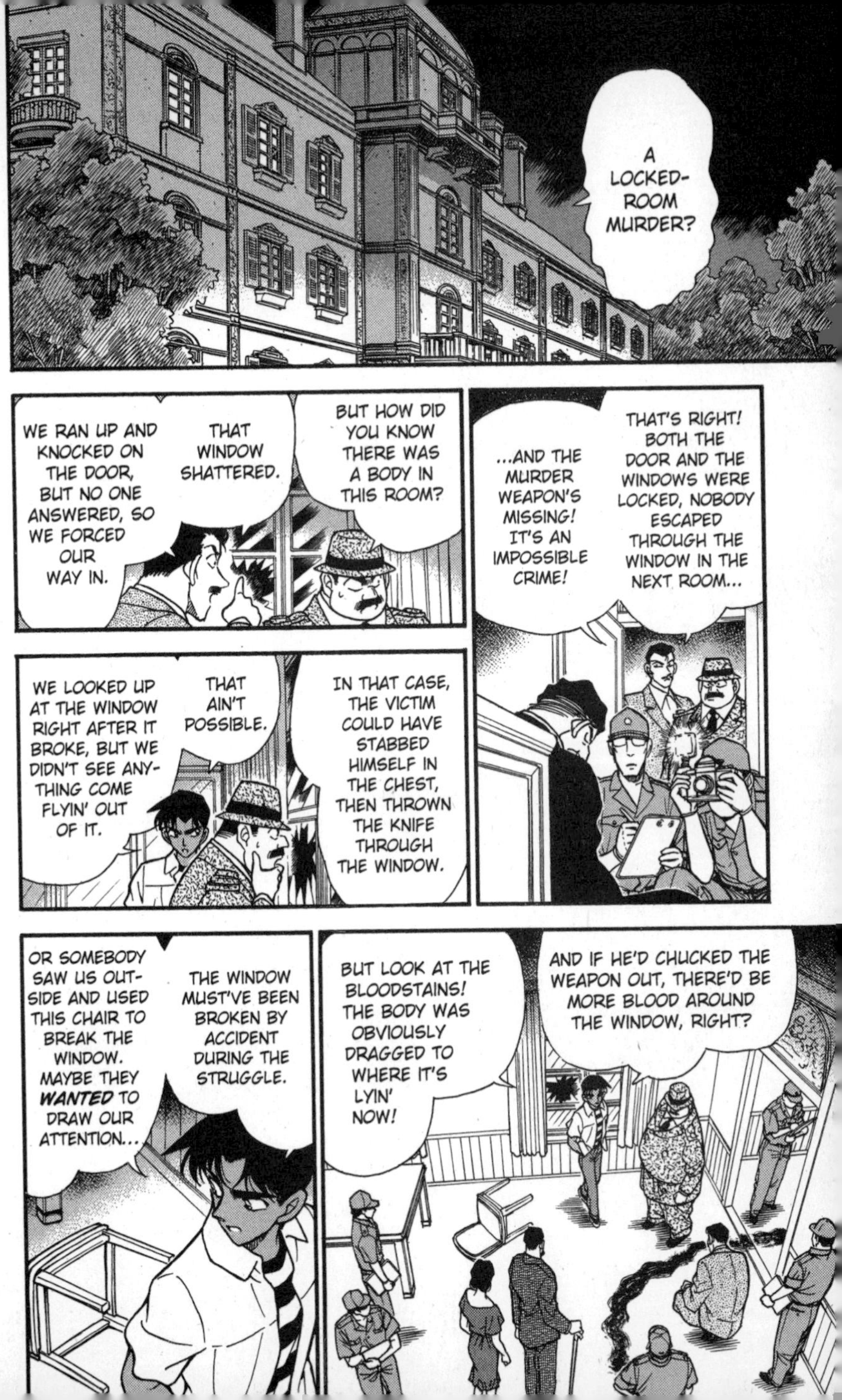
A LOCKED-ROOM MURDER?
THAT'S RIGHT! BOTH THE DOOR AND THE WINDOWS WERE LOCKED, NOBODY ESCAPED THROUGH THE WINDOW IN THE NEXT ROOM...
...AND THE MURDER WEAPON'S MISSING! IT'S AN IMPOSSIBLE CRIME!
BUT HOW DID YOU KNOW THERE WAS A BODY IN THIS ROOM?
THAT WINDOW SHATTERED.
WE RAN UP AND KNOCKED ON THE DOOR, BUT NO ONE ANSWERED, SO WE FORCED OUR WAY IN.
IN THAT CASE, THE VICTIM COULD HAVE STABBED HIMSELF IN THE CHEST, THEN THROWN THE KNIFE THROUGH THE WINDOW.
THAT AIN'T POSSIBLE.
WE LOOKED UP AT THE WINDOW RIGHT AFTER IT BROKE, BUT WE DIDN'T SEE ANY-THING COME FLYIN' OUT OF IT.
AND IF HE'D CHUCKED THE WEAPON OUT, THERE'D BE MORE BLOOD AROUND THE WINDOW, RIGHT?
BUT LOOK AT THE BLOODSTAINS! THE BODY WAS OBVIOUSLY DRAGGED TO WHERE IT'S LYIN' NOW!
THE WINDOW MUST'VE BEEN BROKEN BY ACCIDENT DURING THE STRUGGLE.
OR SOMEBODY SAW US OUT-SIDE AND USED THIS CHAIR TO BREAK THE WINDOW. MAYBE THEY *WANTED* TO DRAW OUR ATTENTION...

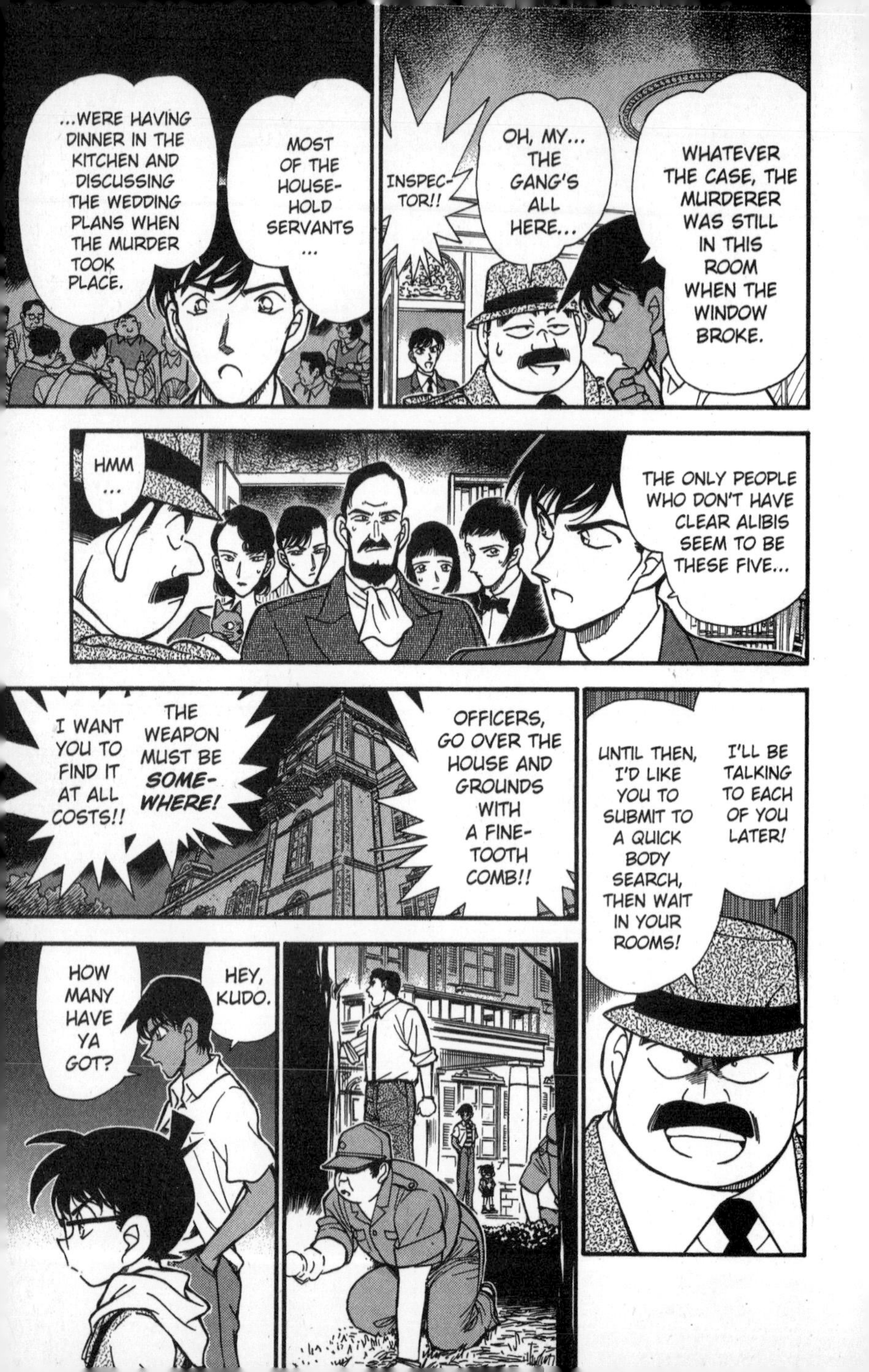
WHATEVER THE CASE, THE MURDERER WAS STILL IN THIS ROOM WHEN THE WINDOW BROKE.
OH, MY... THE GANG'S ALL HERE...
INSPEC-TOR!!
MOST OF THE HOUSE-HOLD SERVANTS ...
...WERE HAVING DINNER IN THE KITCHEN AND DISCUSSING THE WEDDING PLANS WHEN THE MURDER TOOK PLACE.
THE ONLY PEOPLE WHO DON'T HAVE CLEAR ALIBIS SEEM TO BE THESE FIVE...
HMM ...
I'LL BE TALKING TO EACH OF YOU LATER!
UNTIL THEN, I'D LIKE YOU TO SUBMIT TO A QUICK BODY SEARCH, THEN WAIT IN YOUR ROOMS!
OFFICERS, GO OVER THE HOUSE AND GROUNDS WITH A FINE-TOOTH COMB!!
THE WEAPON MUST BE *SOME-WHERE!*
I WANT YOU TO FIND IT AT ALL COSTS!!
HEY, KUDO.
HOW MANY HAVE YA GOT?

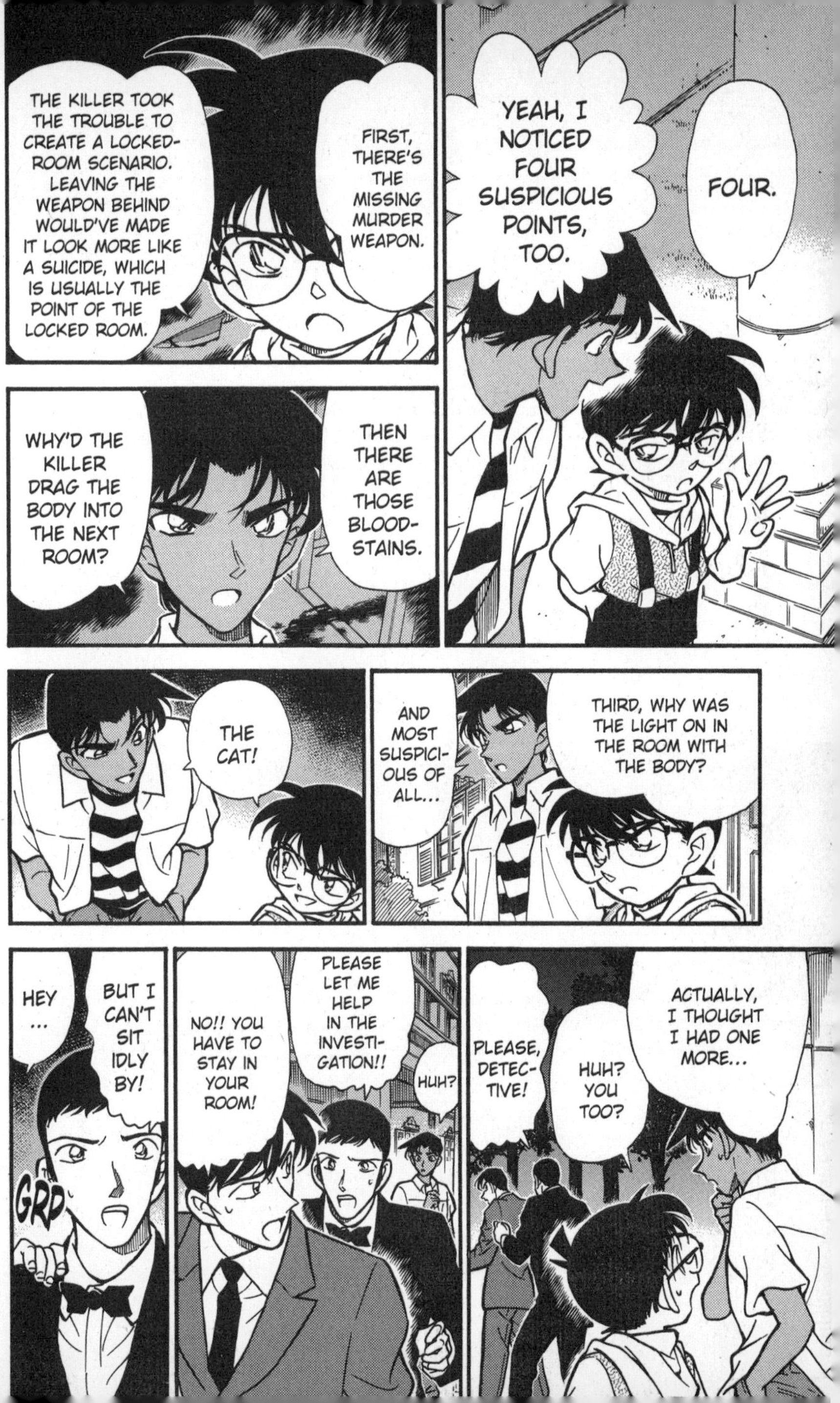
FOUR.
YEAH, I NOTICED FOUR SUSPICIOUS POINTS, TOO.
FIRST, THERE'S THE MISSING MURDER WEAPON.
THE KILLER TOOK THE TROUBLE TO CREATE A LOCKED-ROOM SCENARIO. LEAVING THE WEAPON BEHIND WOULD'VE MADE IT LOOK MORE LIKE A SUICIDE, WHICH IS USUALLY THE POINT OF THE LOCKED ROOM.
THEN THERE ARE THOSE BLOOD-STAINS.
WHY'D THE KILLER DRAG THE BODY INTO THE NEXT ROOM?
THIRD, WHY WAS THE LIGHT ON IN THE ROOM WITH THE BODY?
AND MOST SUSPICI-OUS OF ALL...
THE CAT!
ACTUALLY, I THOUGHT I HAD ONE MORE...
HUH? YOU TOO?
PLEASE, DETEC-TIVE!
HUH?
PLEASE LET ME HELP IN THE INVESTI-GATION!!
NO!! YOU HAVE TO STAY IN YOUR ROOM!
BUT I CAN'T SIT IDLY BY!
HEY ...
GRD

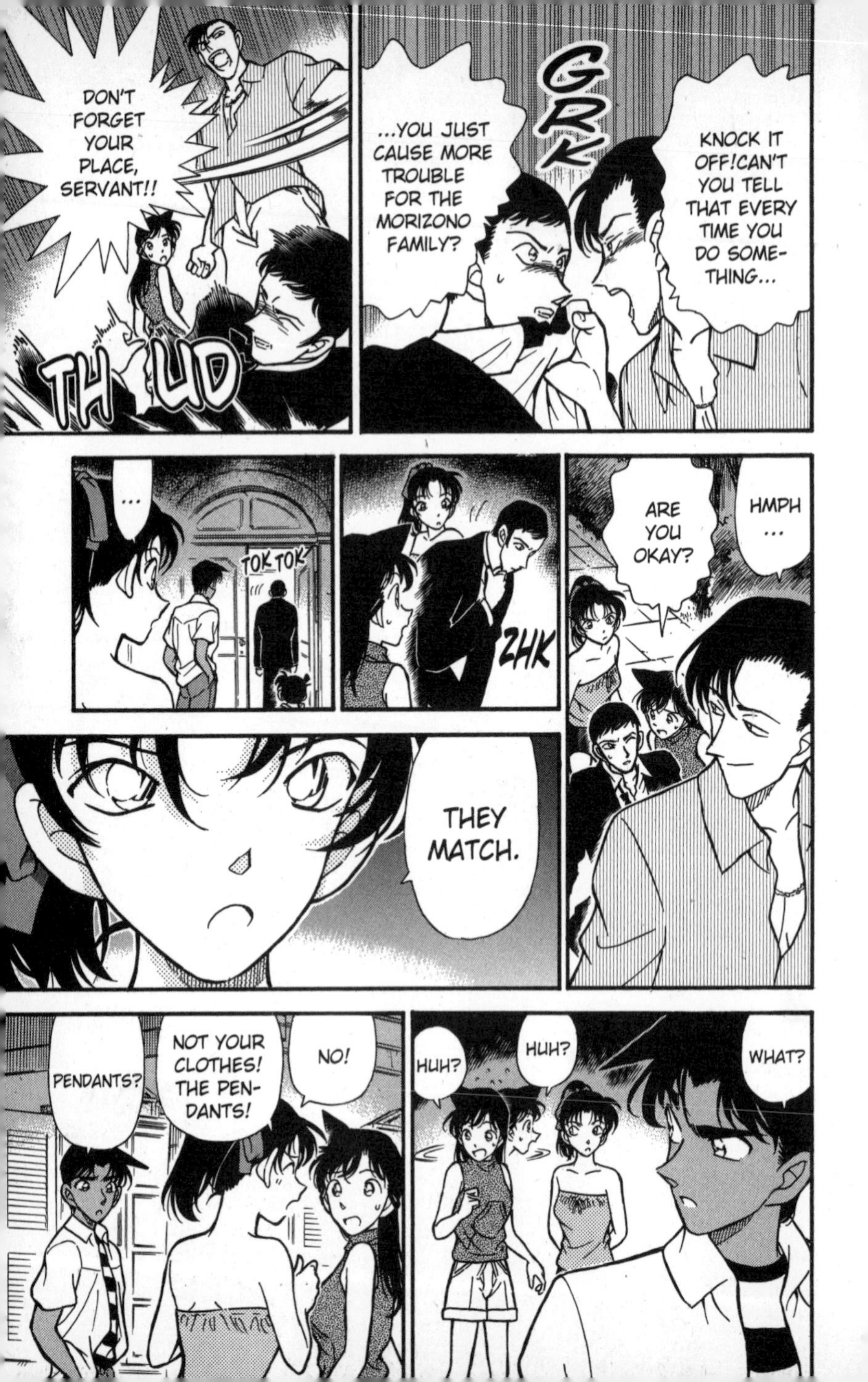
GRK
KNOCK IT OFF! CAN'T YOU TELL THAT EVERY TIME YOU DO SOME-THING...
...YOU JUST CAUSE MORE TROUBLE FOR THE MORIZONO FAMILY?
DON'T FORGET YOUR PLACE, SERVANT!!
THUD
HMPH ...
ARE YOU OKAY?
ZHK
...
TOK TOK
THEY MATCH.
WHAT?
HUH?
HUH?
NO!
NOT YOUR CLOTHES! THE PEN-DANTS!
PENDANTS?

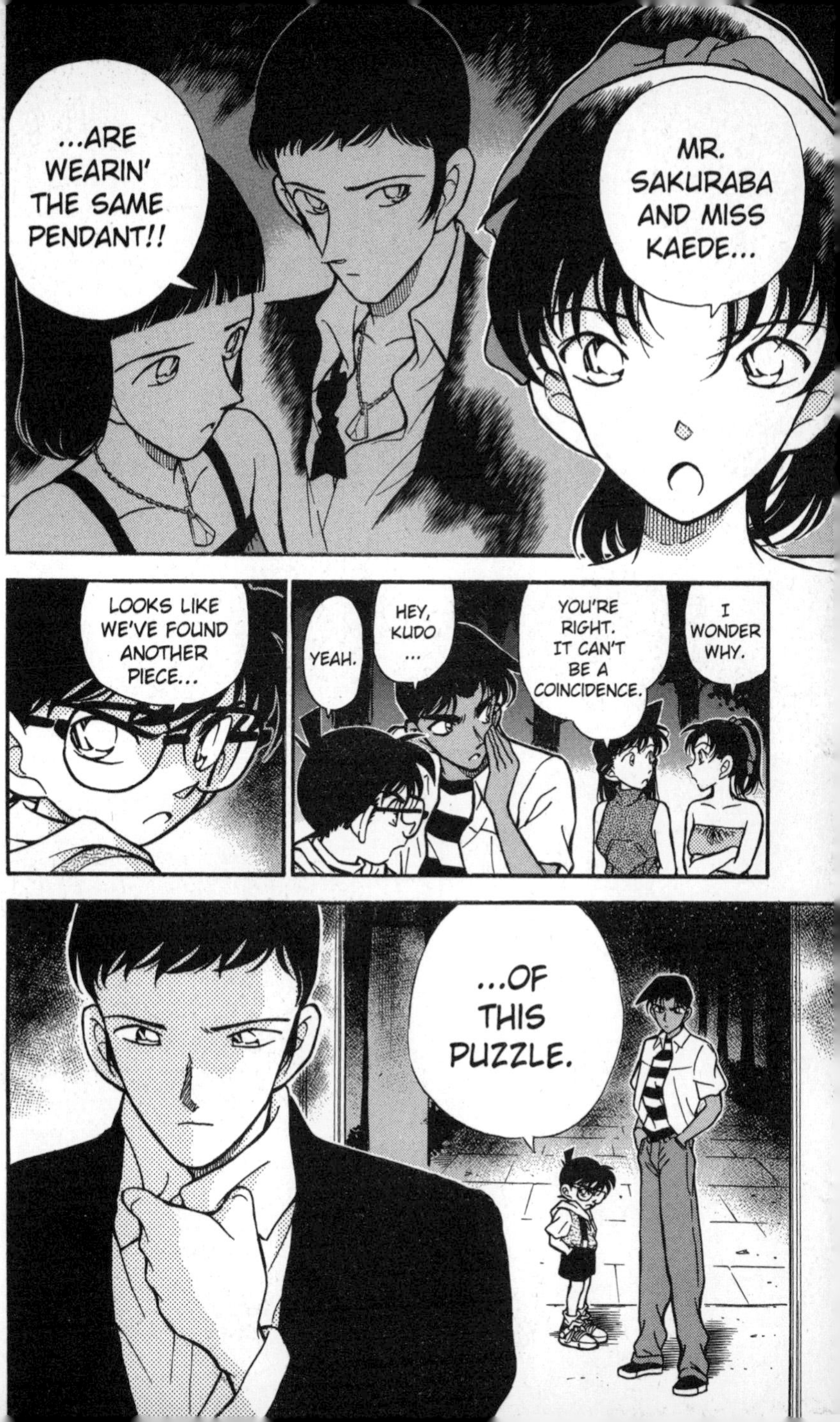
MR. SAKURABA AND MISS KAEDE...
...ARE WEARIN' THE SAME PENDANT!!
I WONDER WHY.
YOU'RE RIGHT. IT CAN'T BE A COINCIDENCE.
HEY, KUDO ...
YEAH.
LOOKS LIKE WE'VE FOUND ANOTHER PIECE...
...OF THIS PUZZLE.

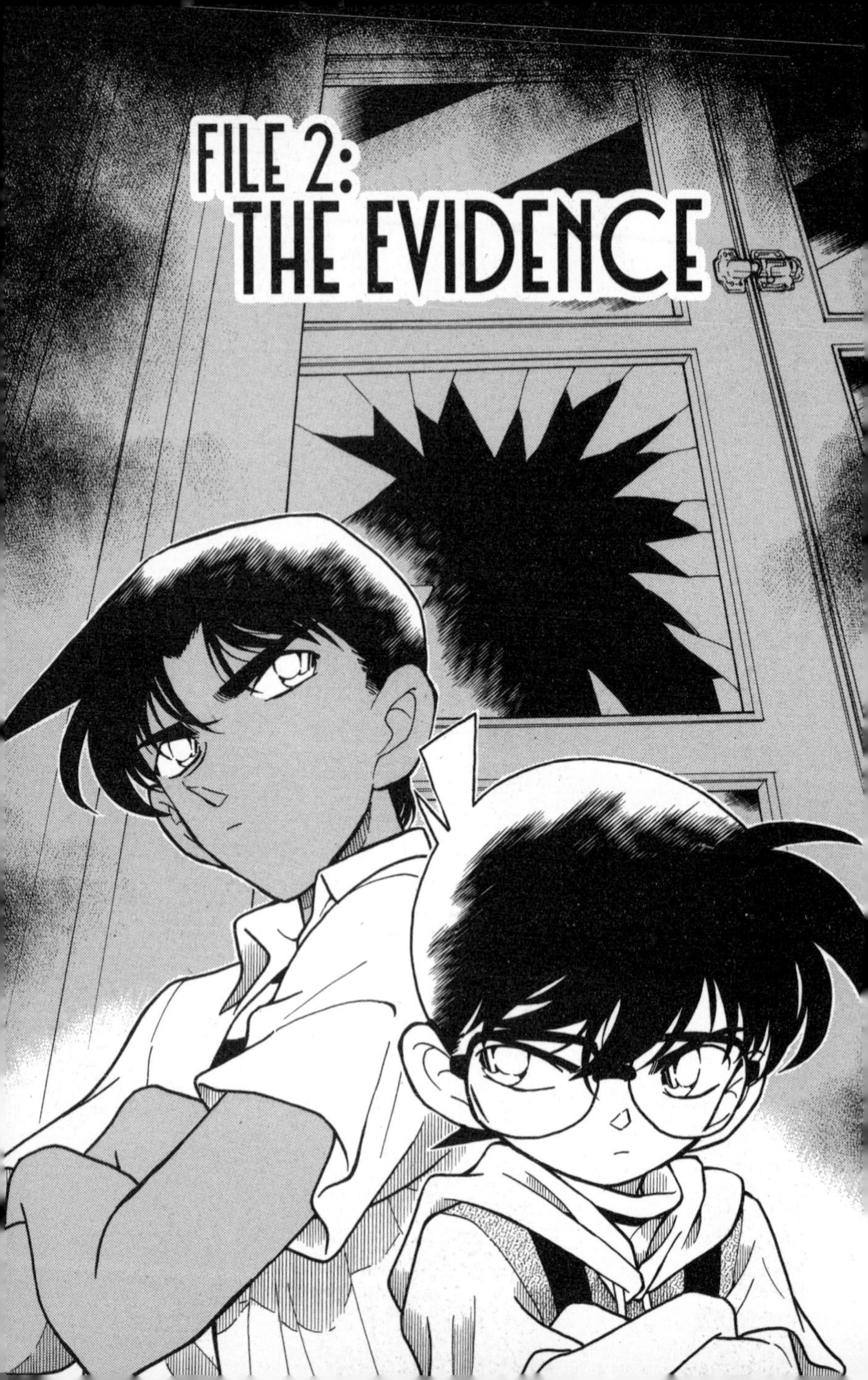
FILE 2:
THE EVIDENCE

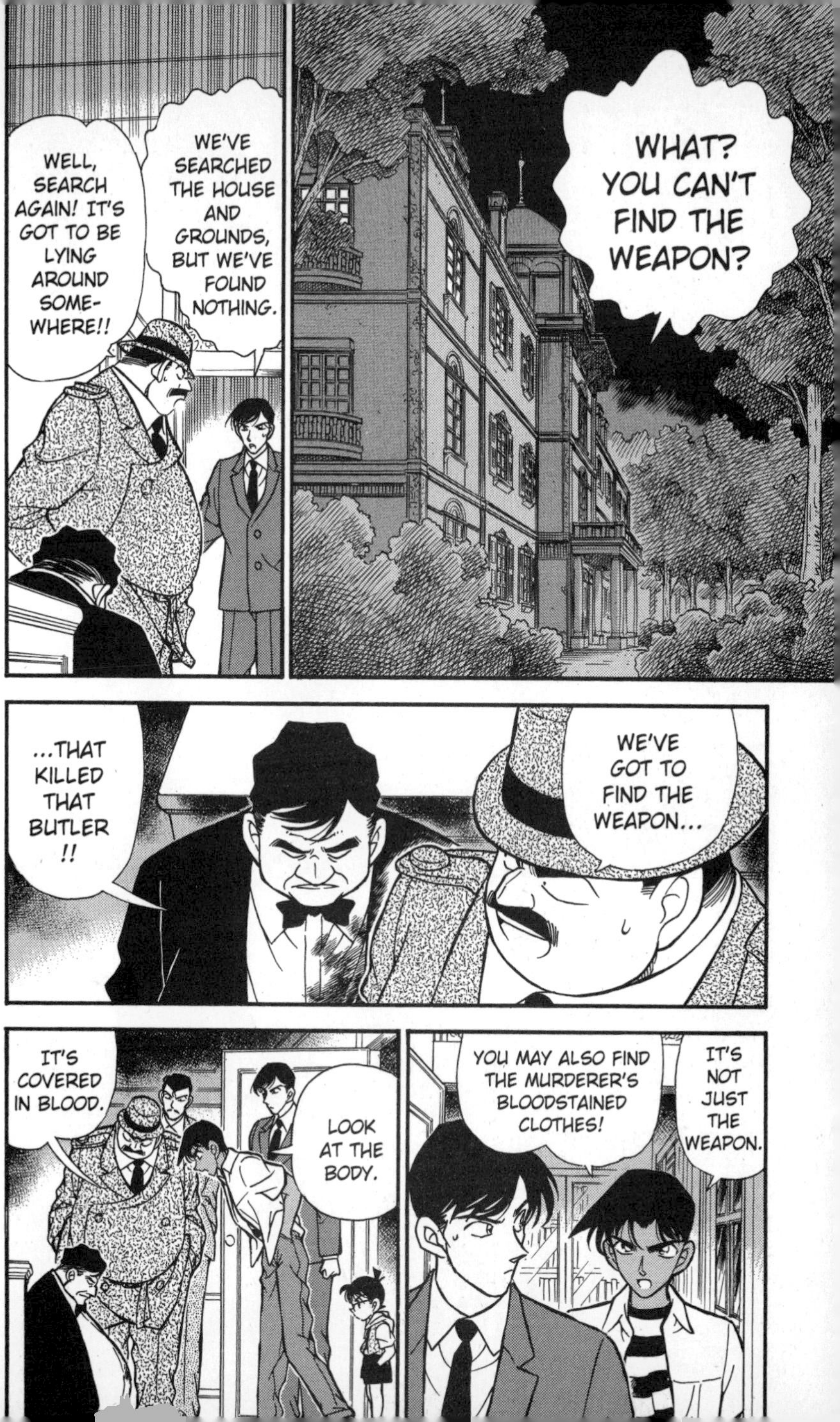
WHAT? YOU CAN'T FIND THE WEAPON?
WE'VE SEARCHED THE HOUSE AND GROUNDS, BUT WE'VE FOUND NOTHING.
WELL, SEARCH AGAIN! IT'S GOT TO BE LYING AROUND SOME-WHERE!!
WE'VE GOT TO FIND THE WEAPON...
...THAT KILLED THAT BUTLER !!
IT'S NOT JUST THE WEAPON.
YOU MAY ALSO FIND THE MURDERER'S BLOODSTAINED CLOTHES!
LOOK AT THE BODY.
IT'S COVERED IN BLOOD.

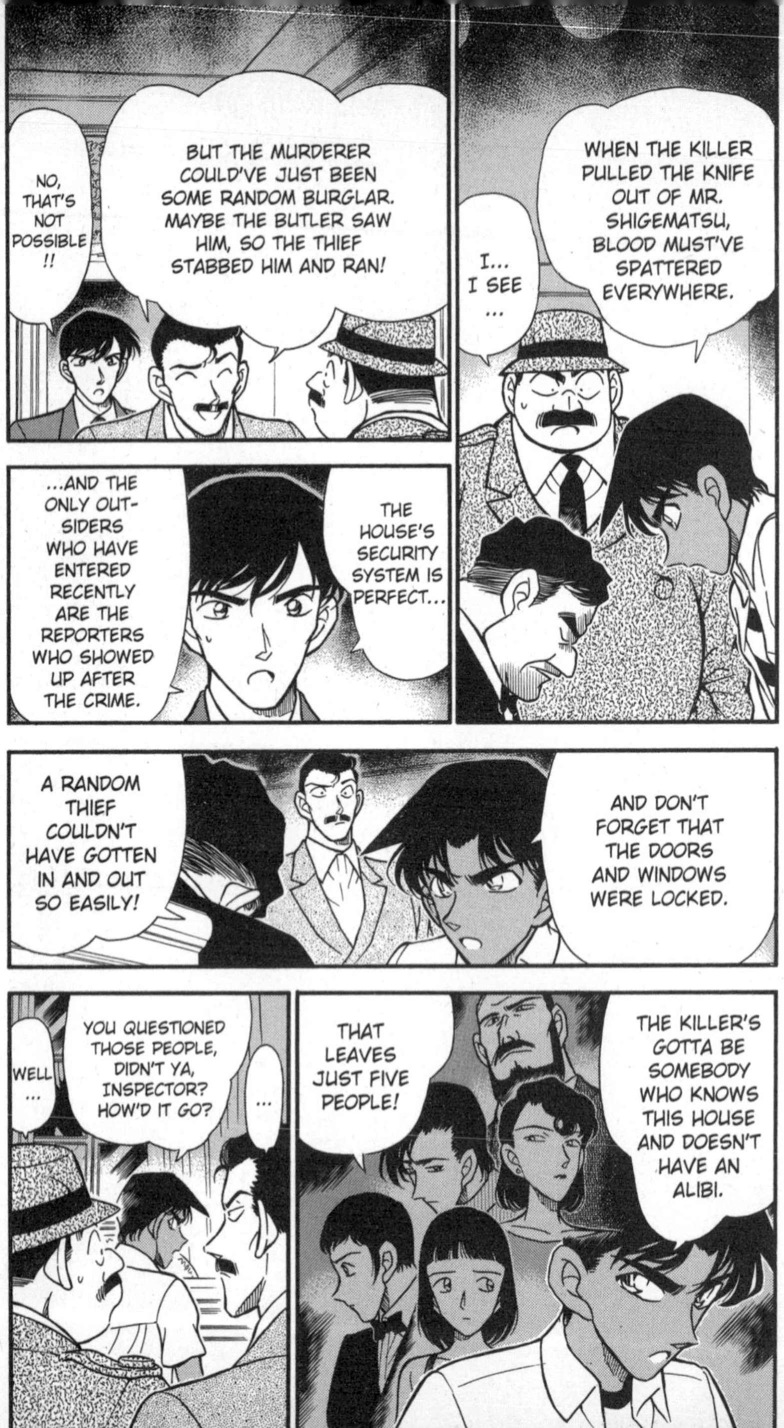
WHEN THE KILLER PULLED THE KNIFE OUT OF MR. SHIGEMATSU, BLOOD MUST'VE SPATTERED EVERYWHERE.
I... I SEE ...
BUT THE MURDERER COULD'VE JUST BEEN SOME RANDOM BURGLAR. MAYBE THE BUTLER SAW HIM, SO THE THIEF STABBED HIM AND RAN!
NO, THAT'S NOT POSSIBLE !!
THE HOUSE'S SECURITY SYSTEM IS PERFECT...
...AND THE ONLY OUT-SIDERS WHO HAVE ENTERED RECENTLY ARE THE REPORTERS WHO SHOWED UP AFTER THE CRIME.
AND DON'T FORGET THAT THE DOORS AND WINDOWS WERE LOCKED.
A RANDOM THIEF COULDN'T HAVE GOTTEN IN AND OUT SO EASILY!
THE KILLER'S GOTTA BE SOMEBODY WHO KNOWS THIS HOUSE AND DOESN'T HAVE AN ALIBI.
THAT LEAVES JUST FIVE PEOPLE!
...
YOU QUESTIONED THOSE PEOPLE, DIDN'T YA, INSPECTOR? HOW'D IT GO?
WELL ...

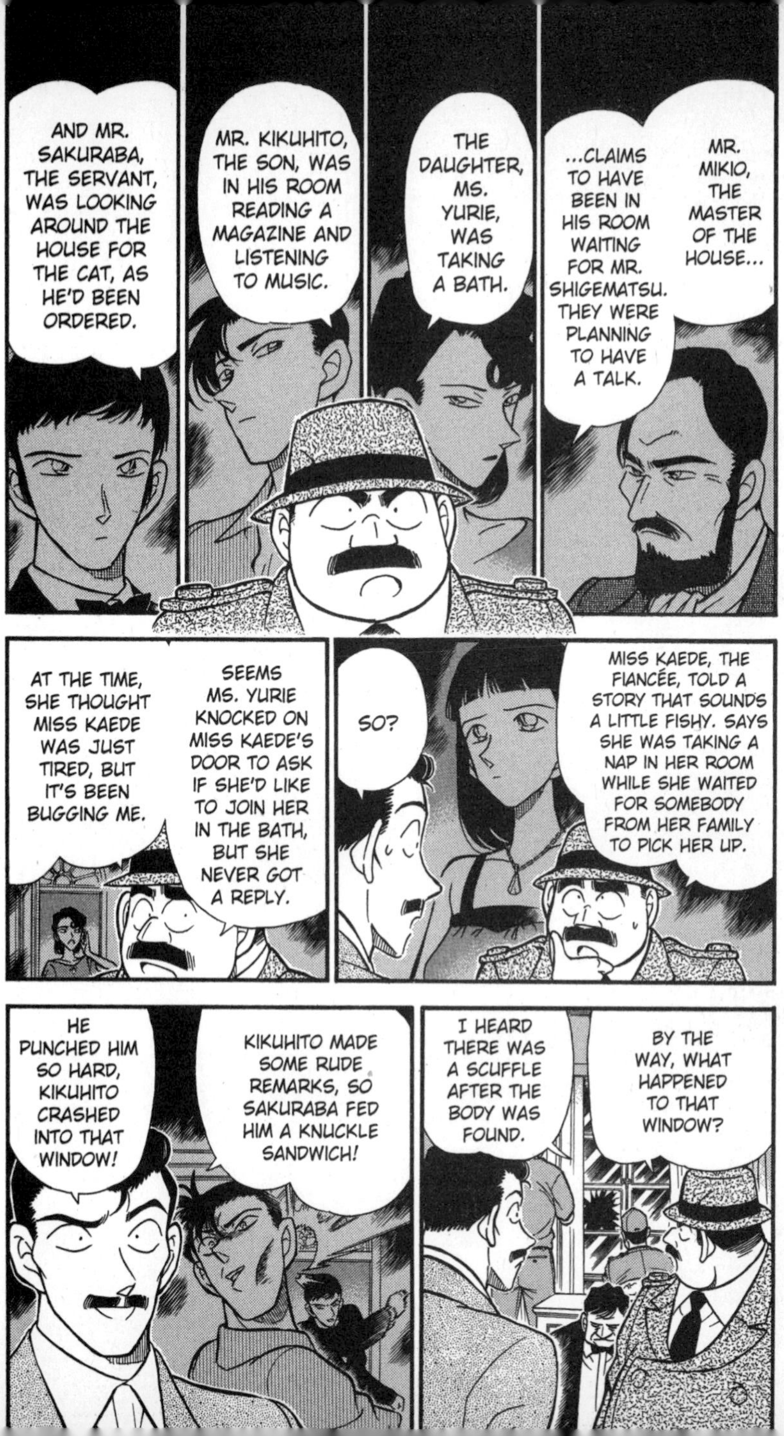
MR. MIKIO, THE MASTER OF THE HOUSE...
...CLAIMS TO HAVE BEEN IN HIS ROOM WAITING FOR MR. SHIGEMATSU. THEY WERE PLANNING TO HAVE A TALK.
THE DAUGHTER, MS. YURIE, WAS TAKING A BATH.
MR. KIKUHITO, THE SON, WAS IN HIS ROOM READING A MAGAZINE AND LISTENING TO MUSIC.
AND MR. SAKURABA, THE SERVANT, WAS LOOKING AROUND THE HOUSE FOR THE CAT, AS HE'D BEEN ORDERED.
MISS KAEDE, THE FIANCÉE, TOLD A STORY THAT SOUNDS A LITTLE FISHY. SAYS SHE WAS TAKING A NAP IN HER ROOM WHILE SHE WAITED FOR SOMEBODY FROM HER FAMILY TO PICK HER UP.
SO?
SEEMS MS. YURIE KNOCKED ON MISS KAEDE'S DOOR TO ASK IF SHE'D LIKE TO JOIN HER IN THE BATH, BUT SHE NEVER GOT A REPLY.
AT THE TIME, SHE THOUGHT MISS KAEDE WAS JUST TIRED, BUT IT'S BEEN BUGGING ME.
BY THE WAY, WHAT HAPPENED TO THAT WINDOW?
I HEARD THERE WAS A SCUFFLE AFTER THE BODY WAS FOUND.
KIKUHITO MADE SOME RUDE REMARKS, SO SAKURABA FED HIM A KNUCKLE SANDWICH!
HE PUNCHED HIM SO HARD, KIKUHITO CRASHED INTO THAT WINDOW!

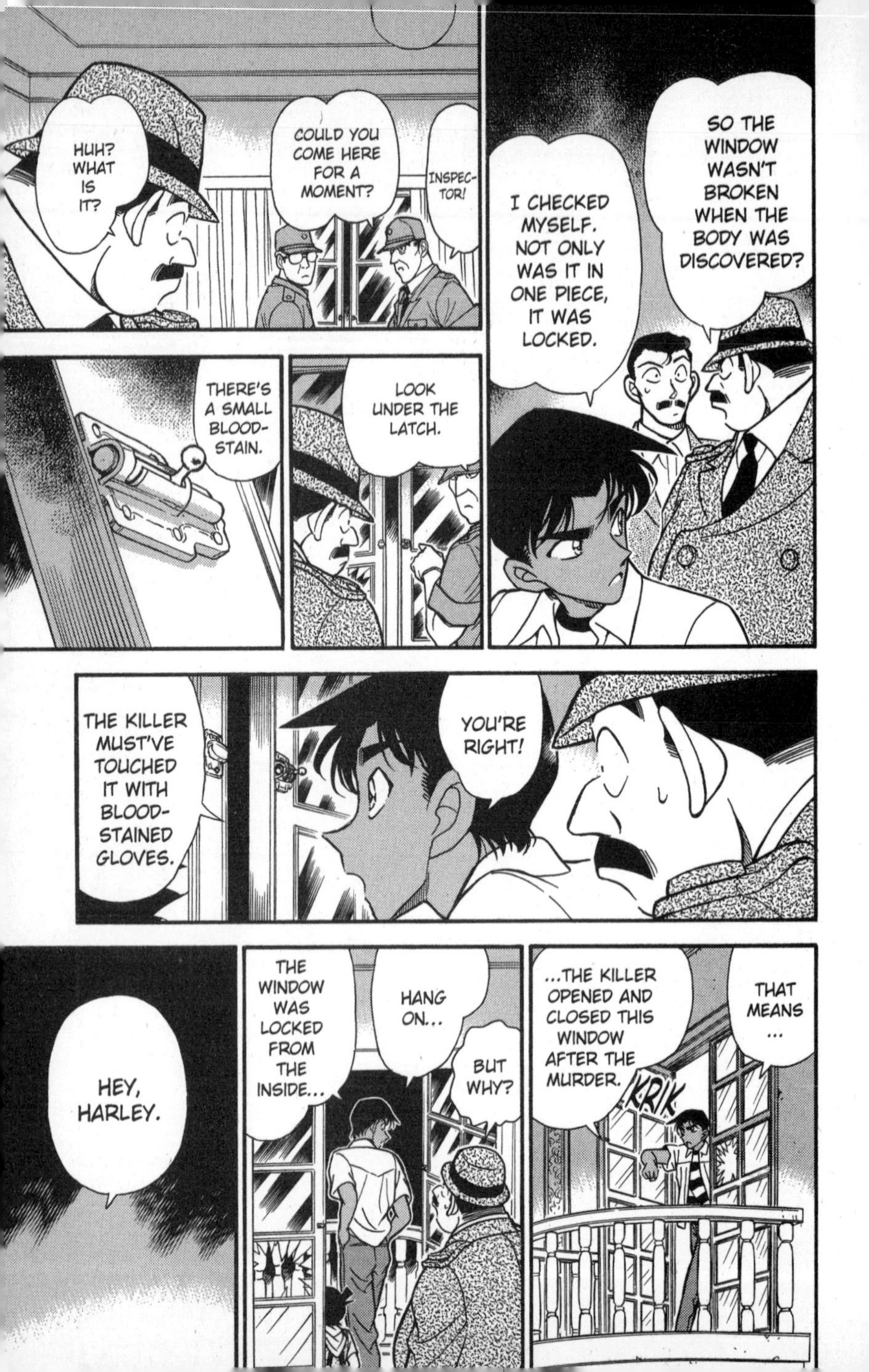
SO THE WINDOW WASN'T BROKEN WHEN THE BODY WAS DISCOVERED?
I CHECKED MYSELF. NOT ONLY WAS IT IN ONE PIECE, IT WAS LOCKED.
INSPECTOR!
COULD YOU COME HERE FOR A MOMENT?
HUH? WHAT IS IT?
LOOK UNDER THE LATCH.
THERE'S A SMALL BLOOD-STAIN.
YOU'RE RIGHT!
THE KILLER MUST'VE TOUCHED IT WITH BLOOD-STAINED GLOVES.
THAT MEANS ...
...THE KILLER OPENED AND CLOSED THIS WINDOW AFTER THE MURDER.
KRIK
HANG ON...
BUT WHY?
THE WINDOW WAS LOCKED FROM THE INSIDE...
HEY, HARLEY.

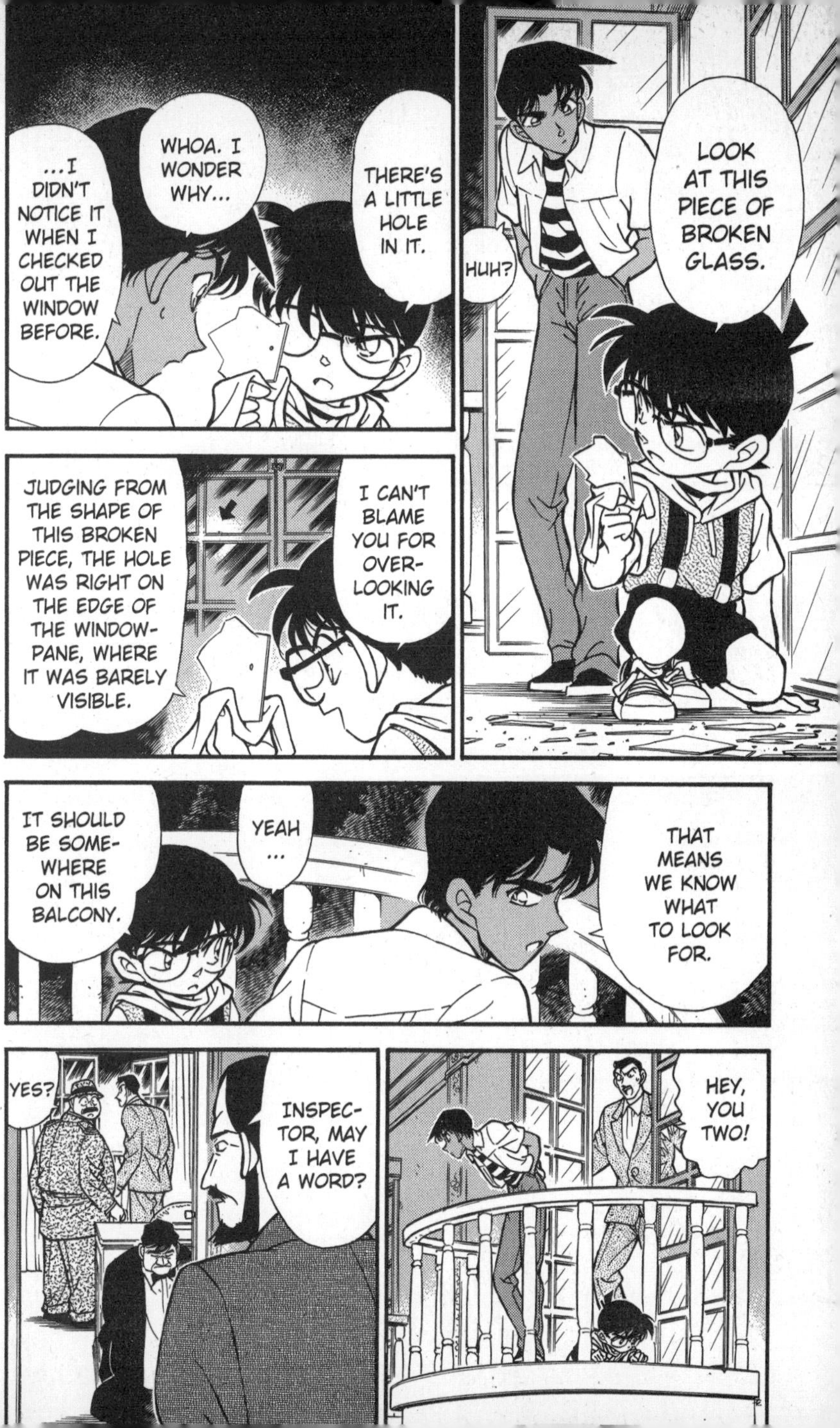
LOOK AT THIS PIECE OF BROKEN GLASS.
HUH?
THERE'S A LITTLE HOLE IN IT.
WHOA. I WONDER WHY...
...I DIDN'T NOTICE IT WHEN I CHECKED OUT THE WINDOW BEFORE.
I CAN'T BLAME YOU FOR OVER-LOOKING IT.
JUDGING FROM THE SHAPE OF THIS BROKEN PIECE, THE HOLE WAS RIGHT ON THE EDGE OF THE WINDOW-PANE, WHERE IT WAS BARELY VISIBLE.
THAT MEANS WE KNOW WHAT TO LOOK FOR.
YEAH ...
IT SHOULD BE SOME-WHERE ON THIS BALCONY.
HEY, YOU TWO!
INSPEC-TOR, MAY I HAVE A WORD?
YES?

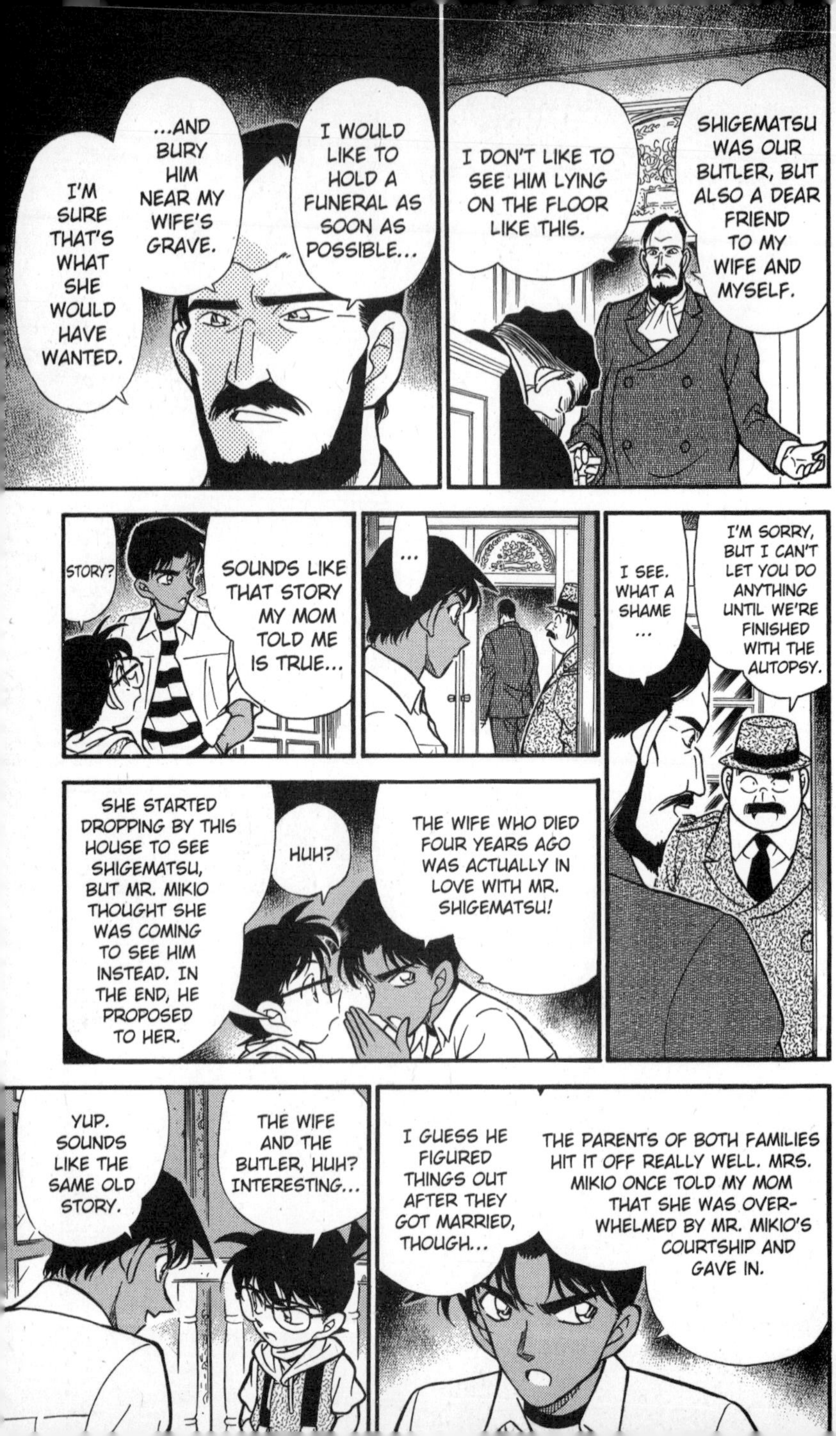
SHIGEMATSU WAS OUR BUTLER, BUT ALSO A DEAR FRIEND TO MY WIFE AND MYSELF.
I DON'T LIKE TO SEE HIM LYING ON THE FLOOR LIKE THIS.
I WOULD LIKE TO HOLD A FUNERAL AS SOON AS POSSIBLE...
...AND BURY HIM NEAR MY WIFE'S GRAVE.
I'M SURE THAT'S WHAT SHE WOULD HAVE WANTED.
I'M SORRY, BUT I CAN'T LET YOU DO ANYTHING UNTIL WE'RE FINISHED WITH THE AUTOPSY.
I SEE. WHAT A SHAME...
...
SOUNDS LIKE THAT STORY MY MOM TOLD ME IS TRUE...
STORY?
THE WIFE WHO DIED FOUR YEARS AGO WAS ACTUALLY IN LOVE WITH MR. SHIGEMATSU!
HUH?
SHE STARTED DROPPING BY THIS HOUSE TO SEE SHIGEMATSU, BUT MR. MIKIO THOUGHT SHE WAS COMING TO SEE HIM INSTEAD. IN THE END, HE PROPOSED TO HER.
THE PARENTS OF BOTH FAMILIES HIT IT OFF REALLY WELL. MRS. MIKIO ONCE TOLD MY MOM THAT SHE WAS OVER-WHELMED BY MR. MIKIO'S COURTSHIP AND GAVE IN.
I GUESS HE FIGURED THINGS OUT AFTER THEY GOT MARRIED, THOUGH...
THE WIFE AND THE BUTLER, HUH? INTERESTING...
YUP. SOUNDS LIKE THE SAME OLD STORY.

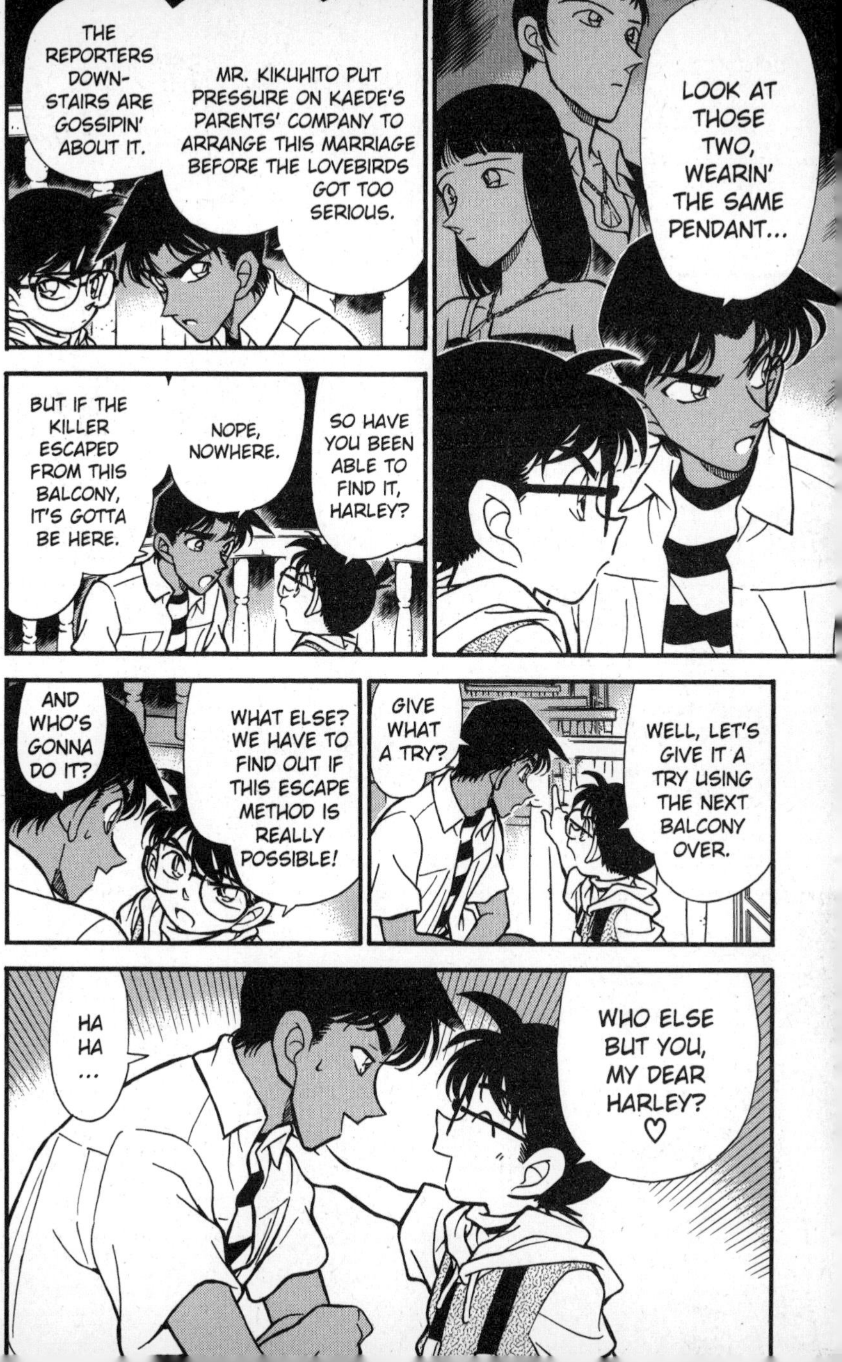
LOOK AT THOSE TWO, WEARIN' THE SAME PENDANT...
MR. KIKUHITO PUT PRESSURE ON KAEDE'S PARENTS' COMPANY TO ARRANGE THIS MARRIAGE BEFORE THE LOVEBIRDS GOT TOO SERIOUS.
THE REPORTERS DOWN-STAIRS ARE GOSSIPIN' ABOUT IT.
SO HAVE YOU BEEN ABLE TO FIND IT, HARLEY?
NOPE, NOWHERE.
BUT IF THE KILLER ESCAPED FROM THIS BALCONY, IT'S GOTTA BE HERE.
WELL, LET'S GIVE IT A TRY USING THE NEXT BALCONY OVER.
GIVE WHAT A TRY?
WHAT ELSE? WE HAVE TO FIND OUT IF THIS ESCAPE METHOD IS REALLY POSSIBLE!
AND WHO'S GONNA DO IT?
WHO ELSE BUT YOU, MY DEAR HARLEY? ♡
HA HA ...

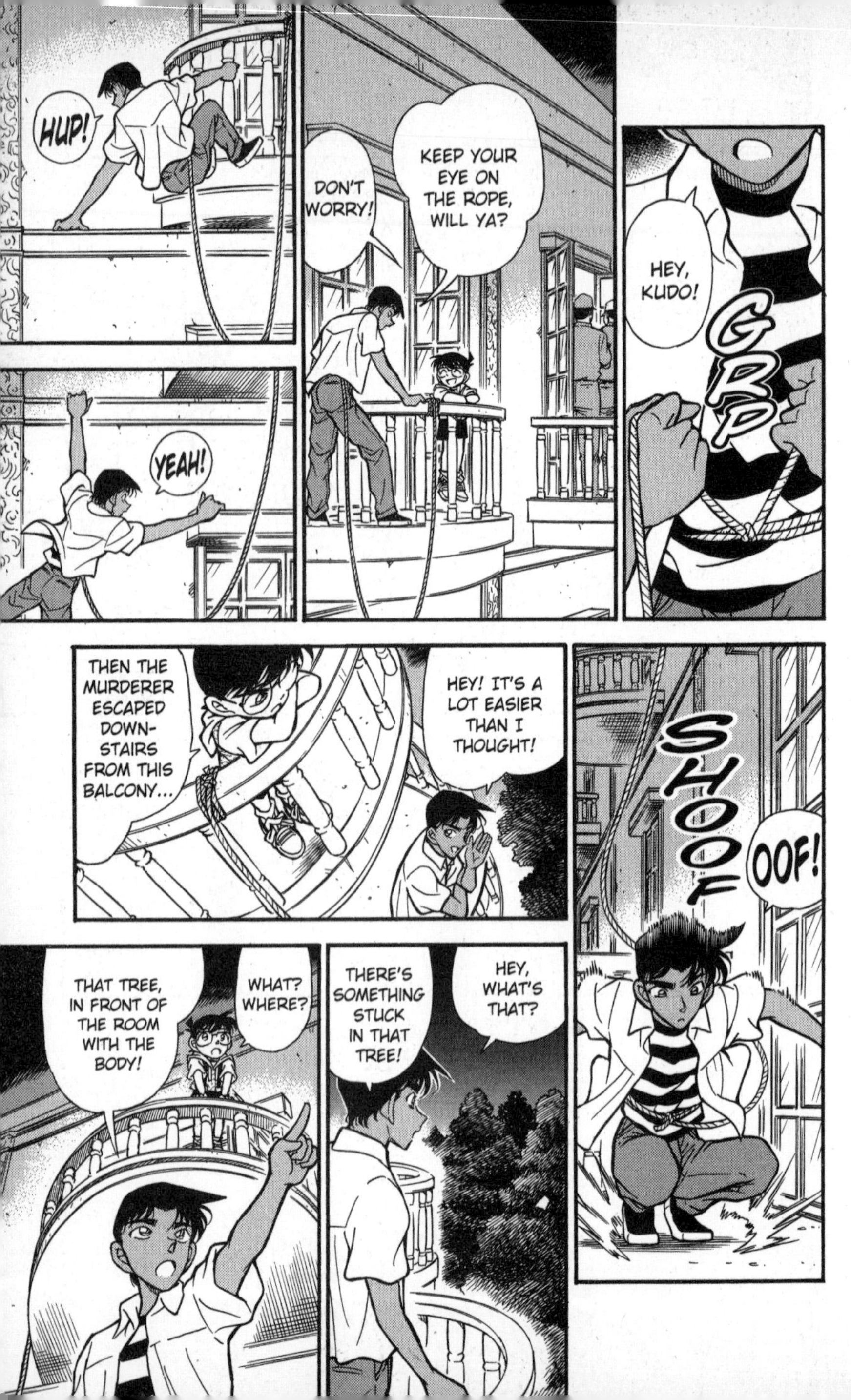
HEY, KUDO!
GRP
KEEP YOUR EYE ON THE ROPE, WILL YA?
DON'T WORRY!
HUP!
YEAH!
SHOOF
OOF!
HEY! IT'S A LOT EASIER THAN I THOUGHT!
THEN THE MURDERER ESCAPED DOWN-STAIRS FROM THIS BALCONY...
HEY, WHAT'S THAT?
THERE'S SOMETHING STUCK IN THAT TREE!
WHAT? WHERE?
THAT TREE, IN FRONT OF THE ROOM WITH THE BODY!

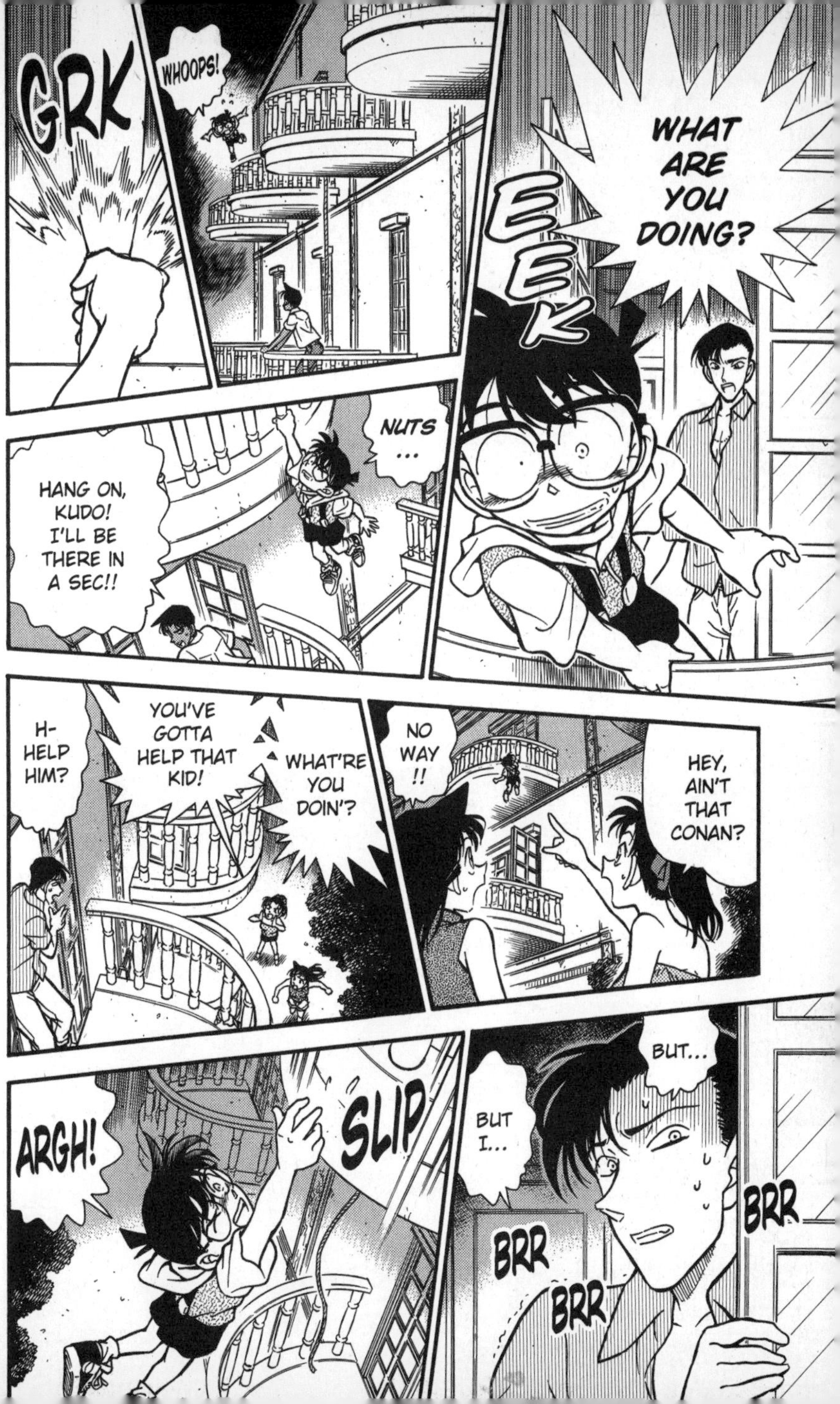
WHAT ARE YOU DOING?
EEK
WHOOPS!
GRK
NUTS...
HANG ON, KUDO! I'LL BE THERE IN A SEC!!
HEY, AIN'T THAT CONAN?
NO WAY!!
WHAT'RE YOU DOIN'?
YOU'VE GOTTA HELP THAT KID!
H-HELP HIM?
BUT...
BUT I...
BRR
BRR
BRR
SLIP
ARGH!

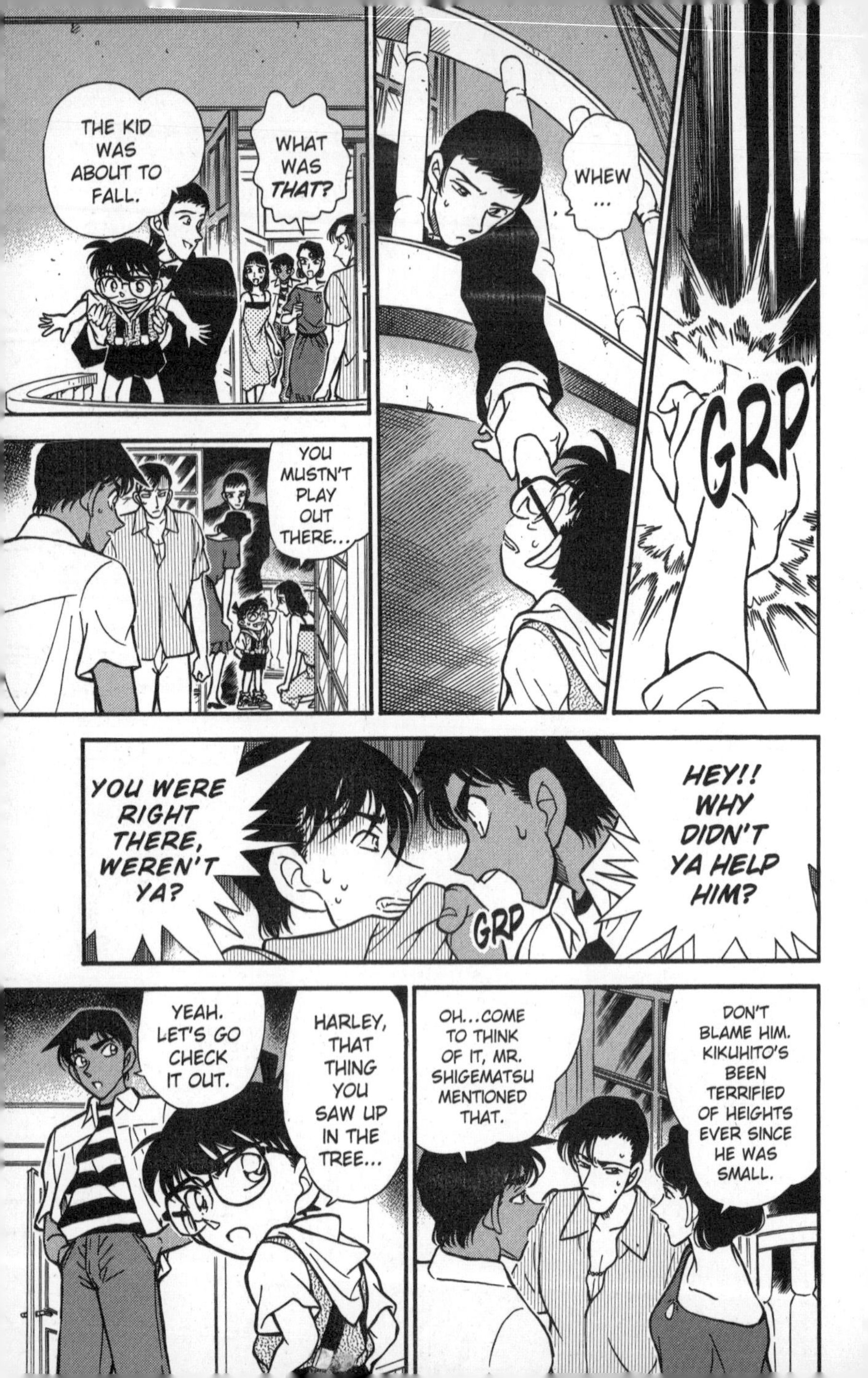
GRP
WHEW ...
WHAT WAS THAT?
THE KID WAS ABOUT TO FALL.
YOU MUSTN'T PLAY OUT THERE...
HEY!! WHY DIDN'T YA HELP HIM?
YOU WERE RIGHT THERE, WEREN'T YA?
GRP
DON'T BLAME HIM. KIKUHITO'S BEEN TERRIFIED OF HEIGHTS EVER SINCE HE WAS SMALL.
OH...COME TO THINK OF IT, MR. SHIGEMATSU MENTIONED THAT.
HARLEY, THAT THING YOU SAW UP IN THE TREE...
YEAH. LET'S GO CHECK IT OUT.

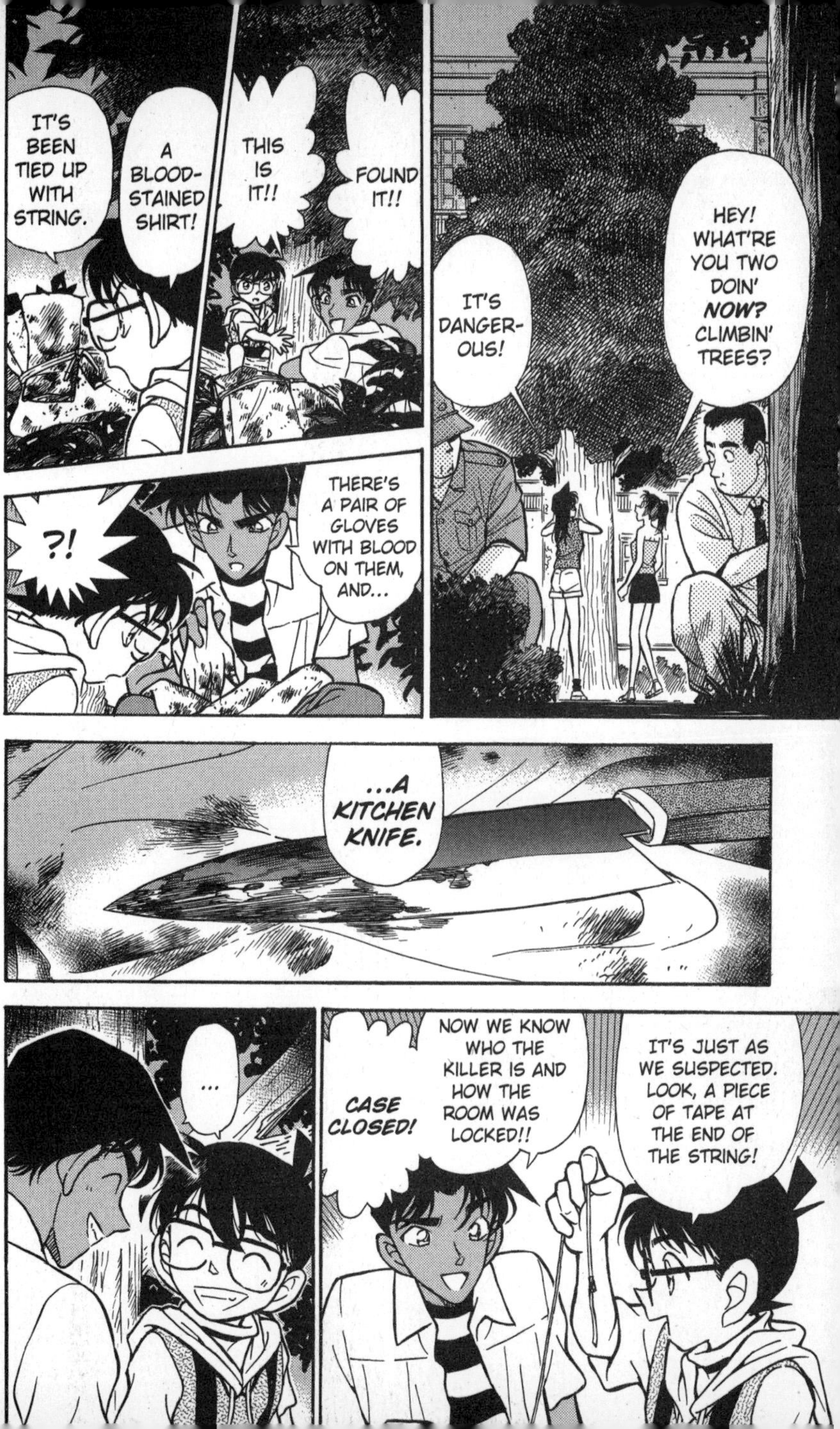
HEY! WHAT'RE YOU TWO DOIN' NOW? CLIMBIN' TREES?
IT'S DANGER-OUS!
FOUND IT!!
THIS IS IT!!
A BLOOD-STAINED SHIRT!
IT'S BEEN TIED UP WITH STRING.
THERE'S A PAIR OF GLOVES WITH BLOOD ON THEM, AND...
?!
...A KITCHEN KNIFE.
IT'S JUST AS WE SUSPECTED. LOOK, A PIECE OF TAPE AT THE END OF THE STRING!
NOW WE KNOW WHO THE KILLER IS AND HOW THE ROOM WAS LOCKED!!
CASE CLOSED!
...

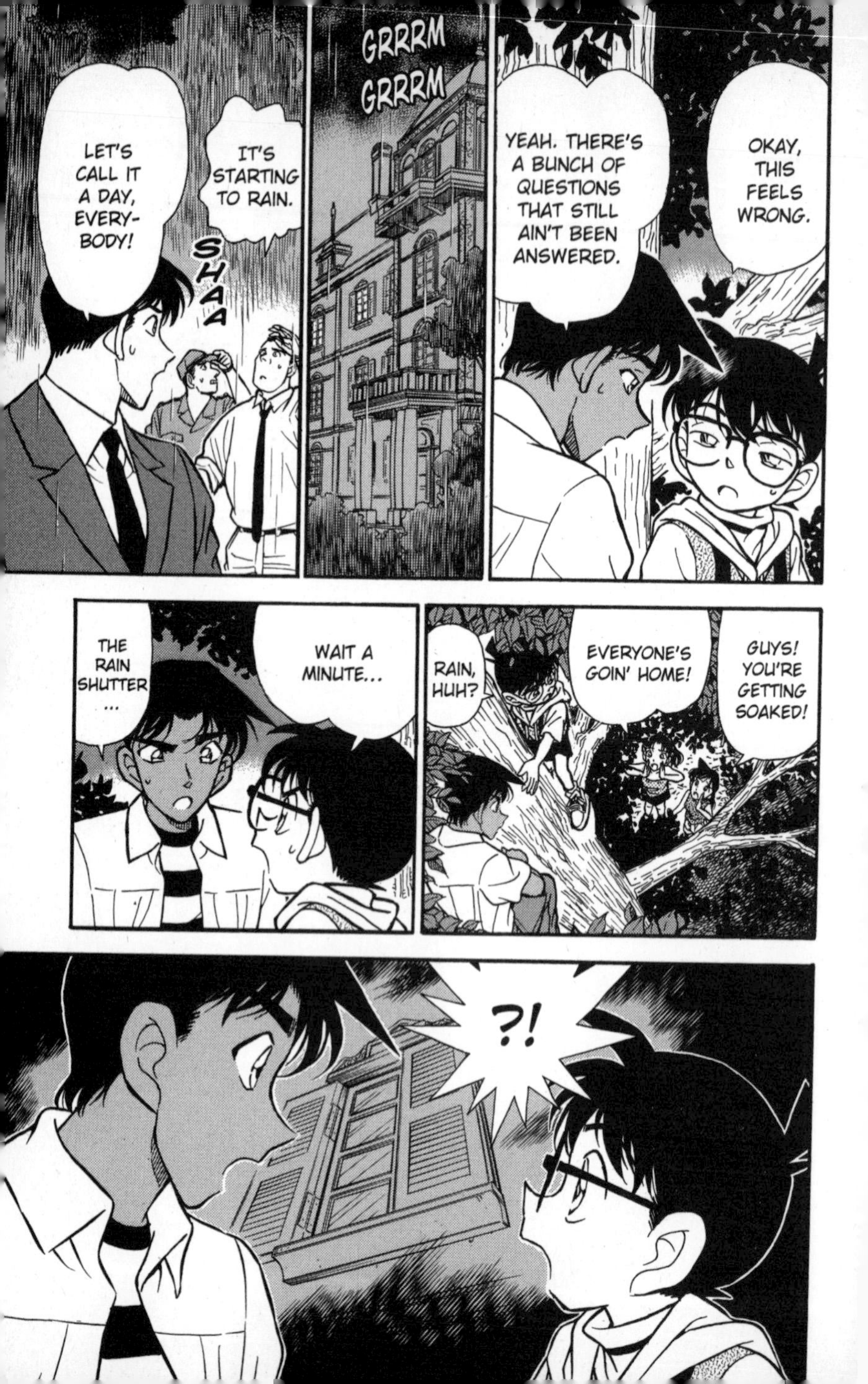
OKAY, THIS FEELS WRONG.
YEAH. THERE'S A BUNCH OF QUESTIONS THAT STILL AIN'T BEEN ANSWERED.
GRRRM GRRRM
IT'S STARTING TO RAIN.
LET'S CALL IT A DAY, EVERY-BODY!
SHAA
GUYS! YOU'RE GETTING SOAKED!
EVERYONE'S GOIN' HOME!
RAIN, HUH?
WAIT A MINUTE...
THE RAIN SHUTTER...
?!

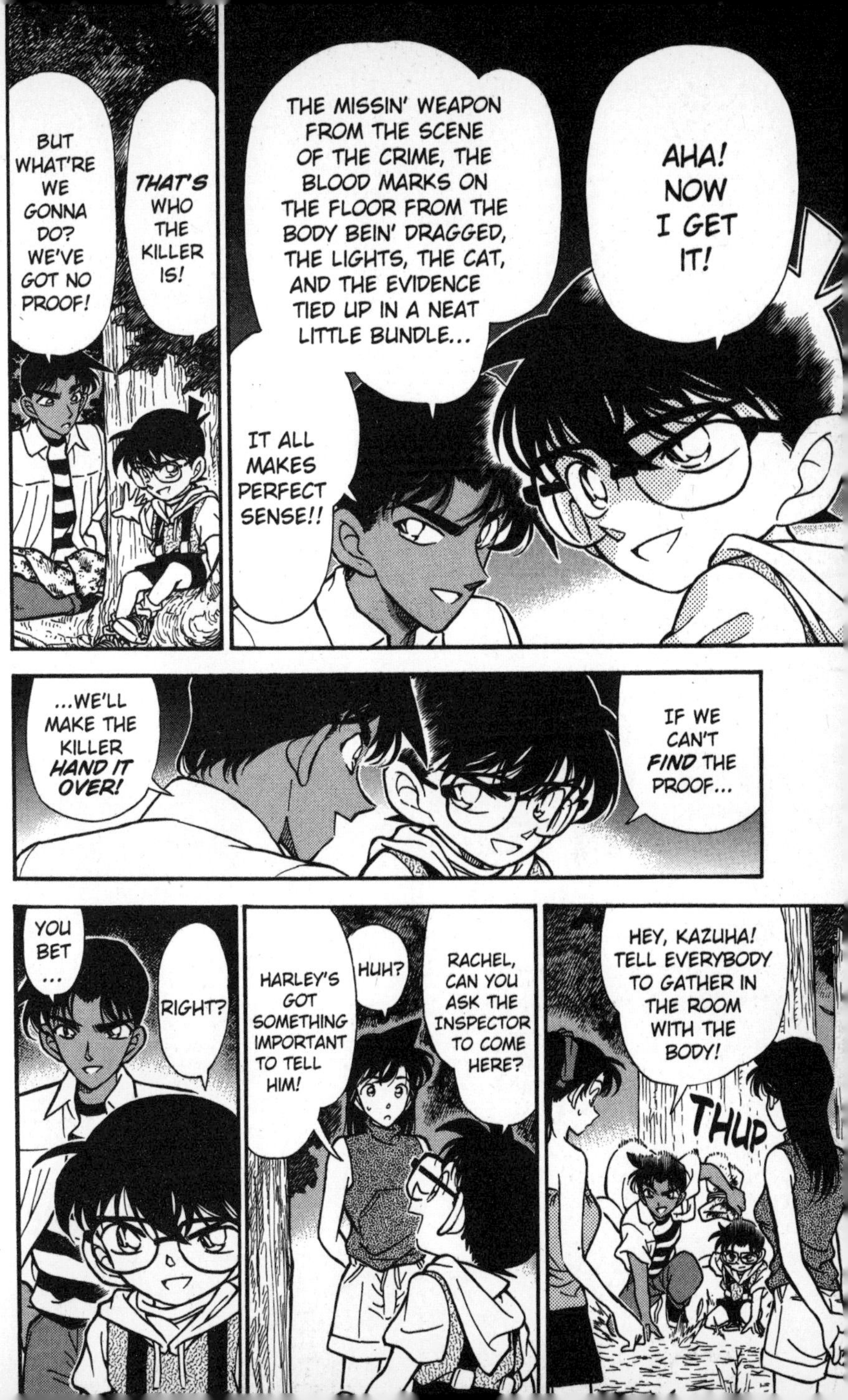
AHA! NOW I GET IT!
THE MISSIN' WEAPON FROM THE SCENE OF THE CRIME, THE BLOOD MARKS ON THE FLOOR FROM THE BODY BEIN' DRAGGED, THE LIGHTS, THE CAT, AND THE EVIDENCE TIED UP IN A NEAT LITTLE BUNDLE...
IT ALL MAKES PERFECT SENSE!!
THAT'S WHO THE KILLER IS!
BUT WHAT'RE WE GONNA DO? WE'VE GOT NO PROOF!
IF WE CAN'T *FIND* THE PROOF...
...WE'LL MAKE THE KILLER *HAND IT OVER!*
HEY, KAZUHA! TELL EVERYBODY TO GATHER IN THE ROOM WITH THE BODY!
THUP
RACHEL, CAN YOU ASK THE INSPECTOR TO COME HERE?
HUH?
HARLEY'S GOT SOMETHING IMPORTANT TO TELL HIM!
RIGHT?
YOU BET...

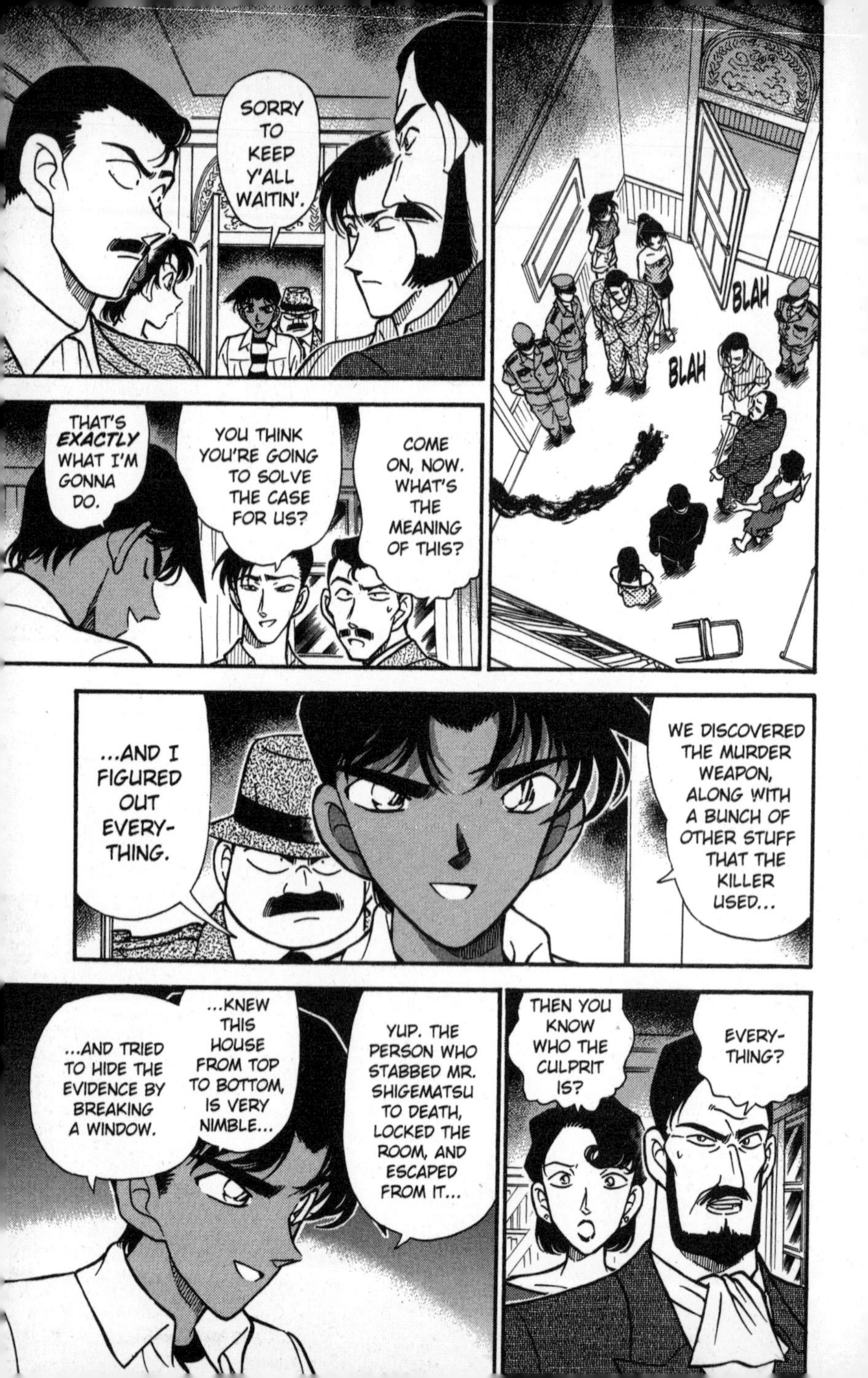
BLAH
BLAH
SORRY TO KEEP Y'ALL WAITIN'.
COME ON, NOW. WHAT'S THE MEANING OF THIS?
YOU THINK YOU'RE GOING TO SOLVE THE CASE FOR US?
THAT'S *EXACTLY* WHAT I'M GONNA DO.
WE DISCOVERED THE MURDER WEAPON, ALONG WITH A BUNCH OF OTHER STUFF THAT THE KILLER USED...
...AND I FIGURED OUT EVERYTHING.
EVERYTHING?
THEN YOU KNOW WHO THE CULPRIT IS?
YUP. THE PERSON WHO STABBED MR. SHIGEMATSU TO DEATH, LOCKED THE ROOM, AND ESCAPED FROM IT...
...KNEW THIS HOUSE FROM TOP TO BOTTOM, IS VERY NIMBLE...
...AND TRIED TO HIDE THE EVIDENCE BY BREAKING A WINDOW.

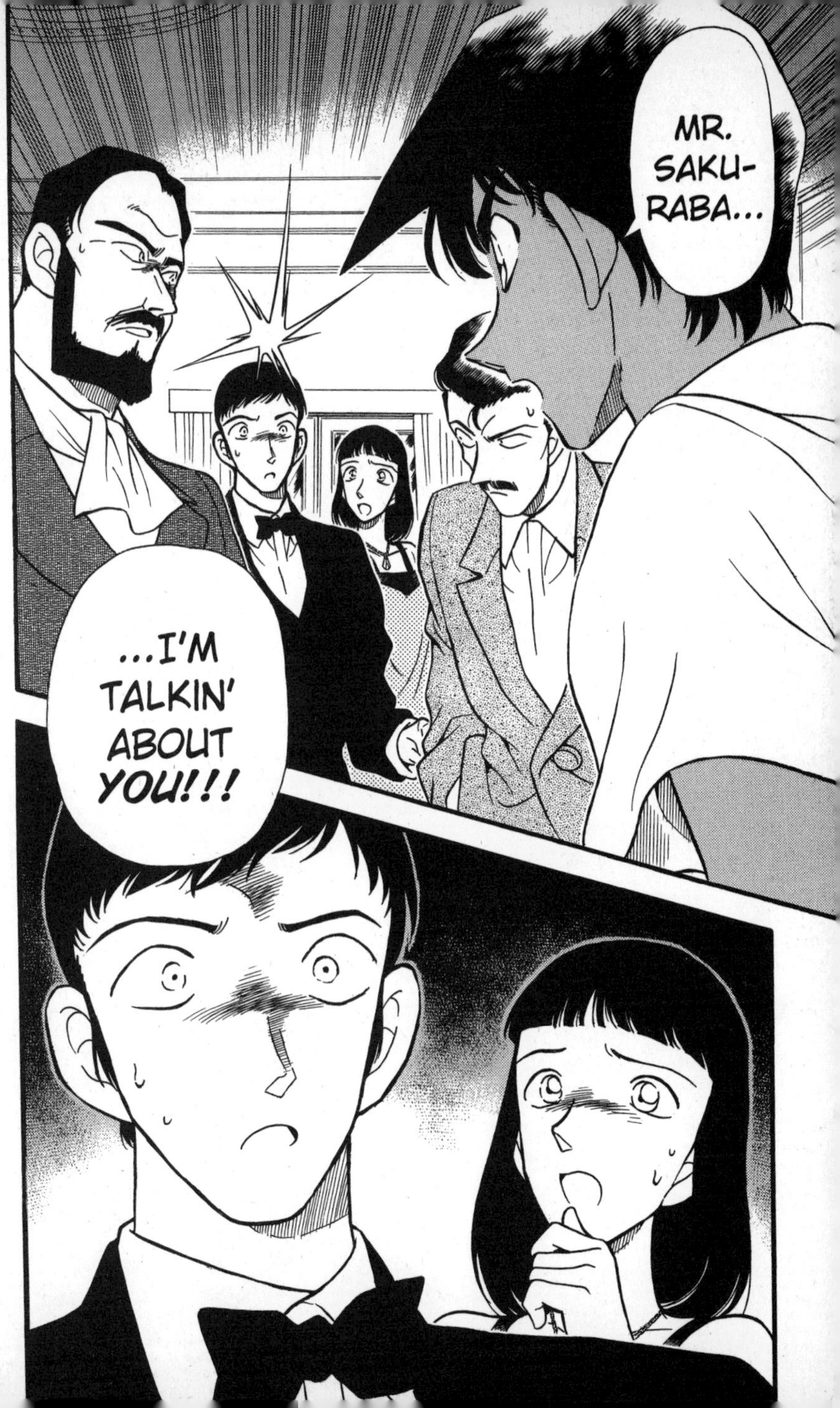
MR. SAKU-RABA...
...I'M TALKIN' ABOUT YOU!!!

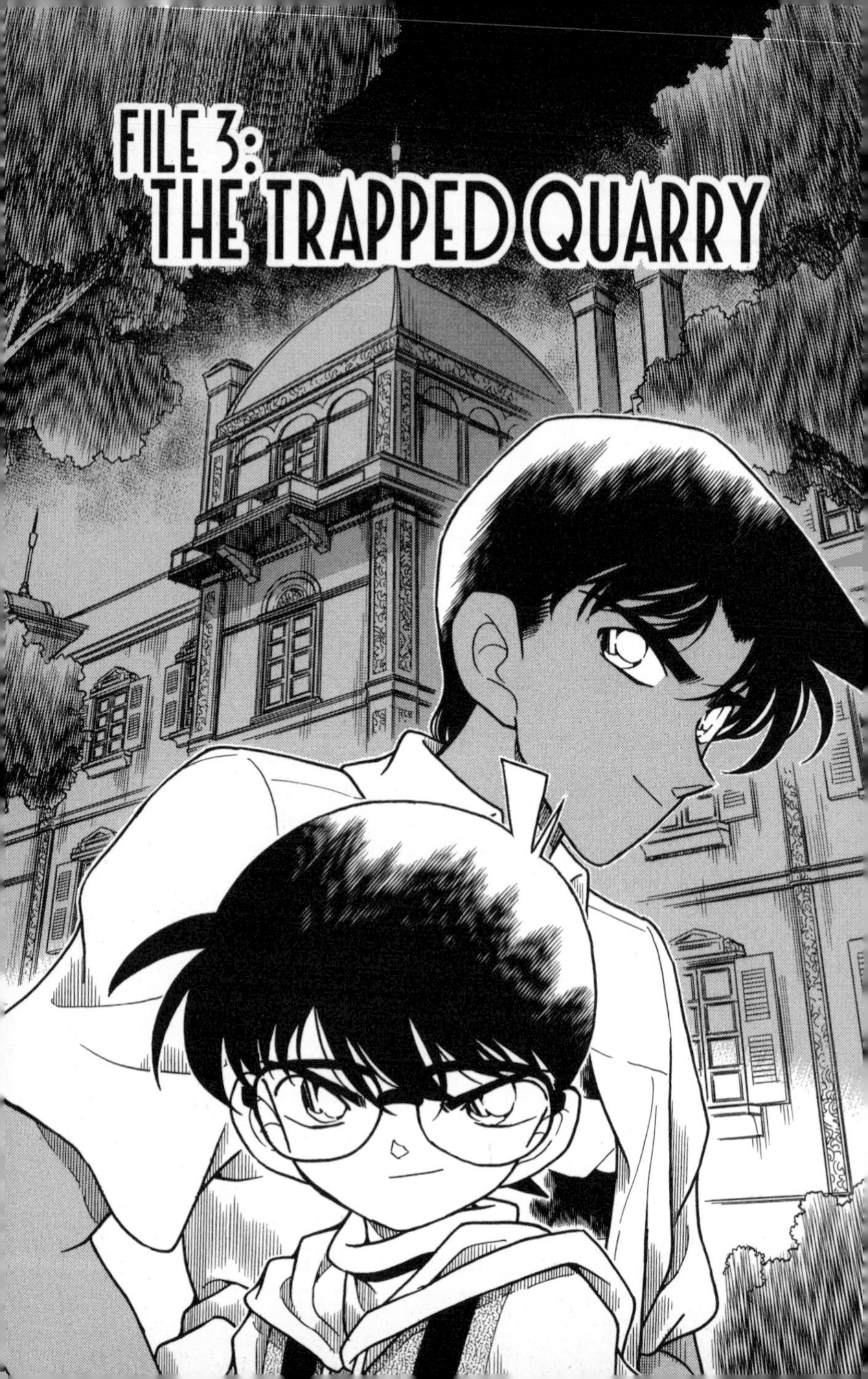
FILE 3:
THE TRAPPED QUARRY

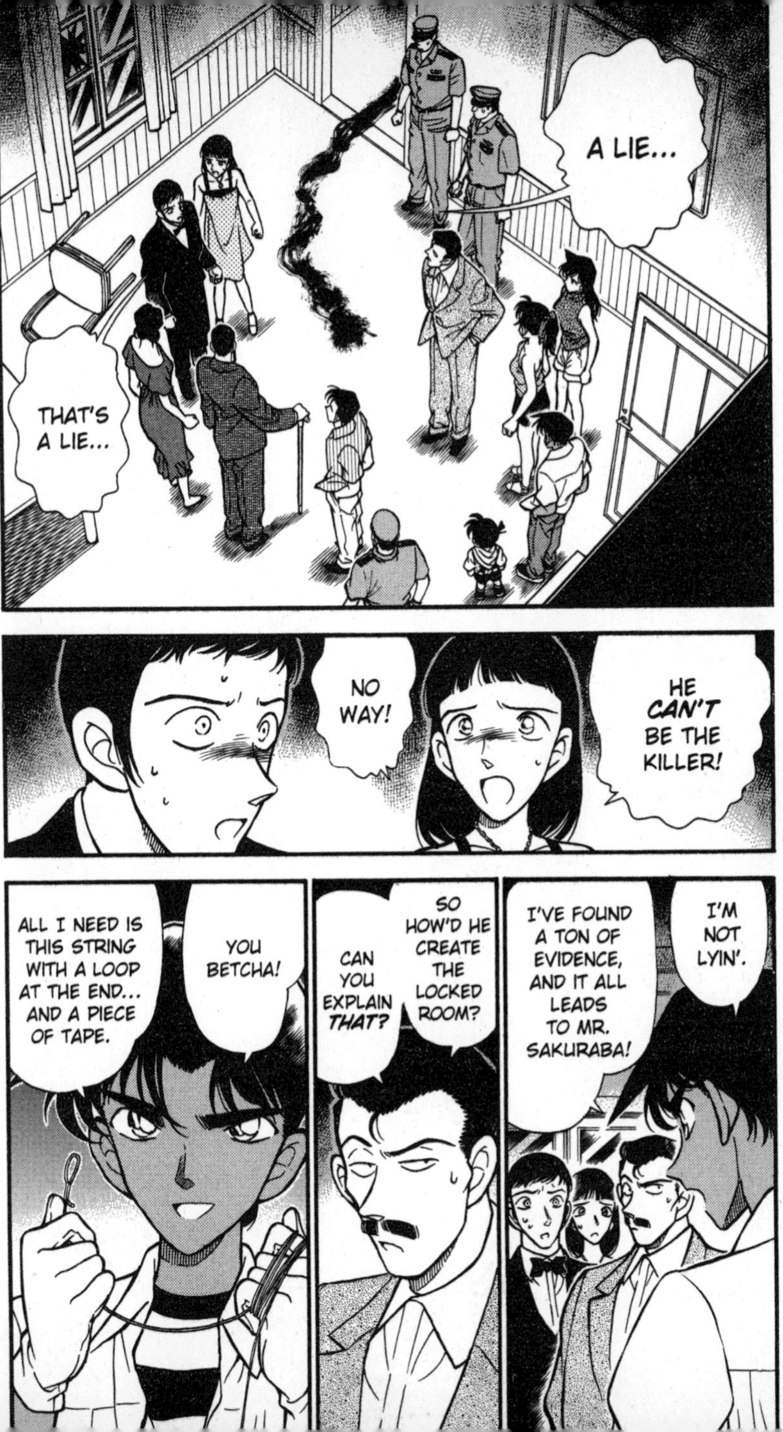

A LIE...
THAT'S A LIE...
HE *CAN'T* BE THE KILLER!
NO WAY!
I'M NOT LYIN'.
I'VE FOUND A TON OF EVIDENCE, AND IT ALL LEADS TO MR. SAKURABA!
SO HOW'D HE CREATE THE LOCKED ROOM?
CAN YOU EXPLAIN *THAT?*
YOU BETCHA!
ALL I NEED IS THIS STRING WITH A LOOP AT THE END... AND A PIECE OF TAPE.

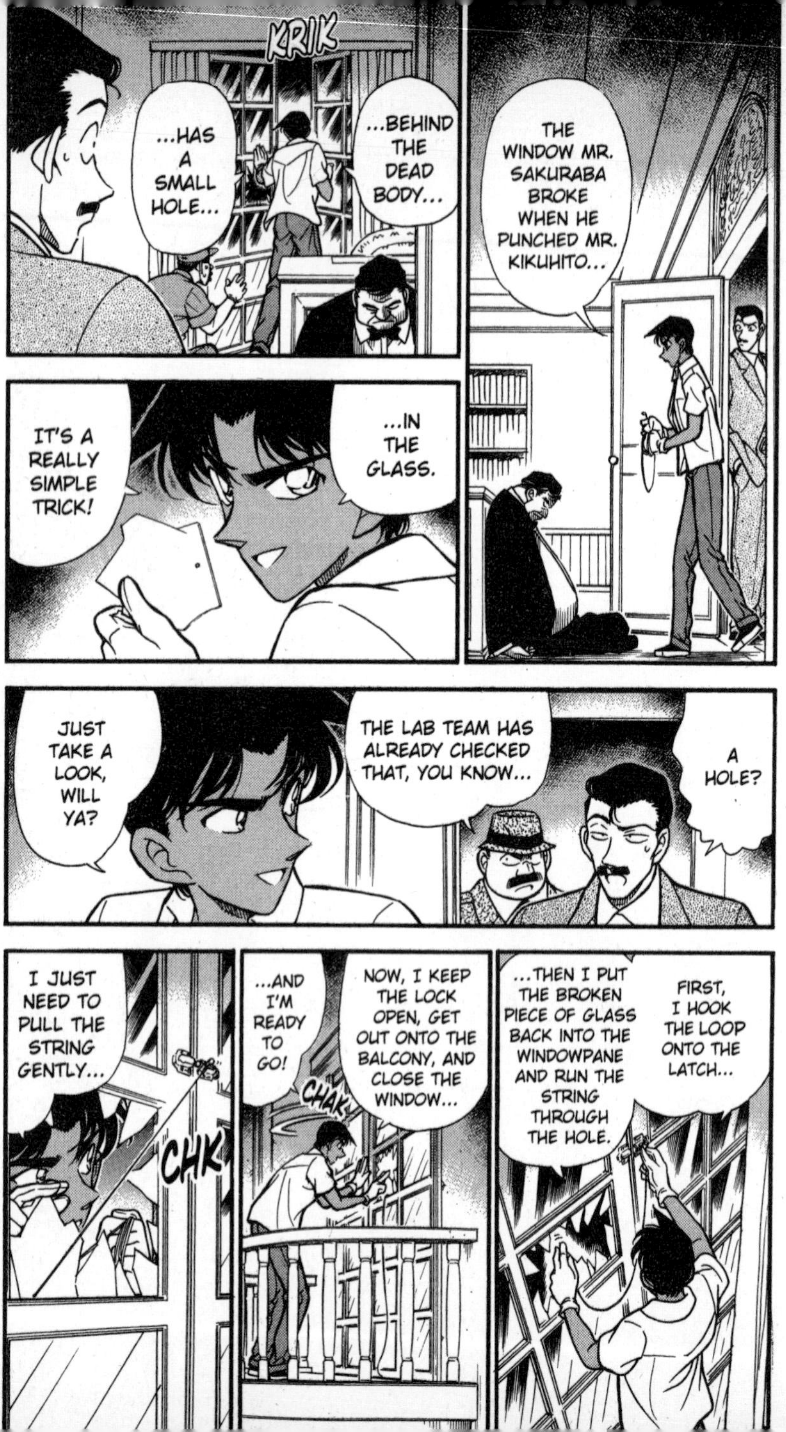
THE WINDOW MR. SAKURABA BROKE WHEN HE PUNCHED MR. KIKUHITO...
...BEHIND THE DEAD BODY...
KRIK
...HAS A SMALL HOLE...
...IN THE GLASS.
IT'S A REALLY SIMPLE TRICK!
A HOLE?
THE LAB TEAM HAS ALREADY CHECKED THAT, YOU KNOW...
JUST TAKE A LOOK, WILL YA?
FIRST, I HOOK THE LOOP ONTO THE LATCH...
...THEN I PUT THE BROKEN PIECE OF GLASS BACK INTO THE WINDOWPANE AND RUN THE STRING THROUGH THE HOLE.
NOW, I KEEP THE LOCK OPEN, GET OUT ONTO THE BALCONY, AND CLOSE THE WINDOW...
CHAK
...AND I'M READY TO GO!
I JUST NEED TO PULL THE STRING GENTLY...
CHK

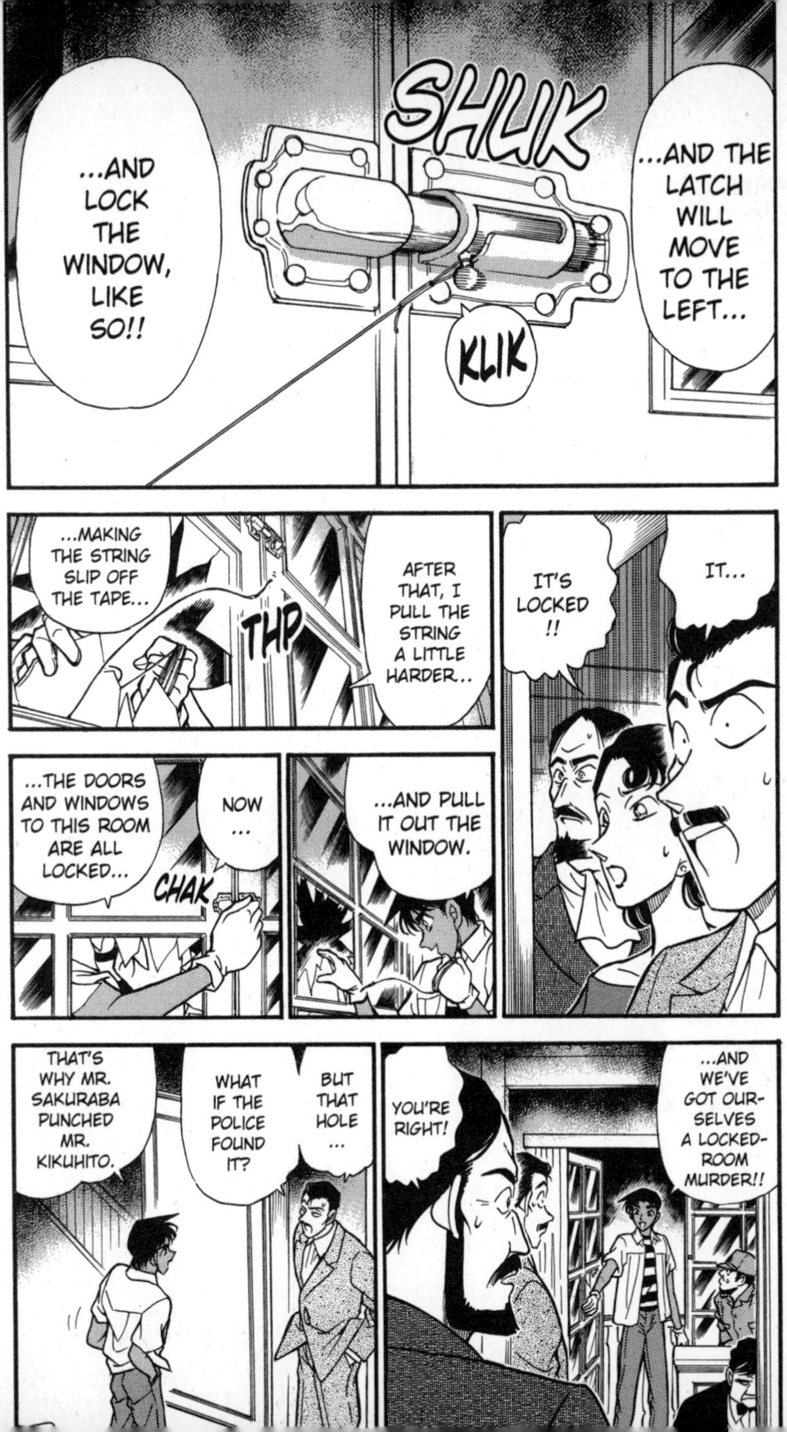
SHUK
...AND THE LATCH WILL MOVE TO THE LEFT...
KLIK
...AND LOCK THE WINDOW, LIKE SO!!
IT...
IT'S LOCKED!!
AFTER THAT, I PULL THE STRING A LITTLE HARDER...
THP
...MAKING THE STRING SLIP OFF THE TAPE...
...AND PULL IT OUT THE WINDOW.
NOW...
...THE DOORS AND WINDOWS TO THIS ROOM ARE ALL LOCKED...
CHAK
...AND WE'VE GOT OURSELVES A LOCKED-ROOM MURDER!!
YOU'RE RIGHT!
BUT THAT HOLE...
WHAT IF THE POLICE FOUND IT?
THAT'S WHY MR. SAKURABA PUNCHED MR. KIKUHITO.

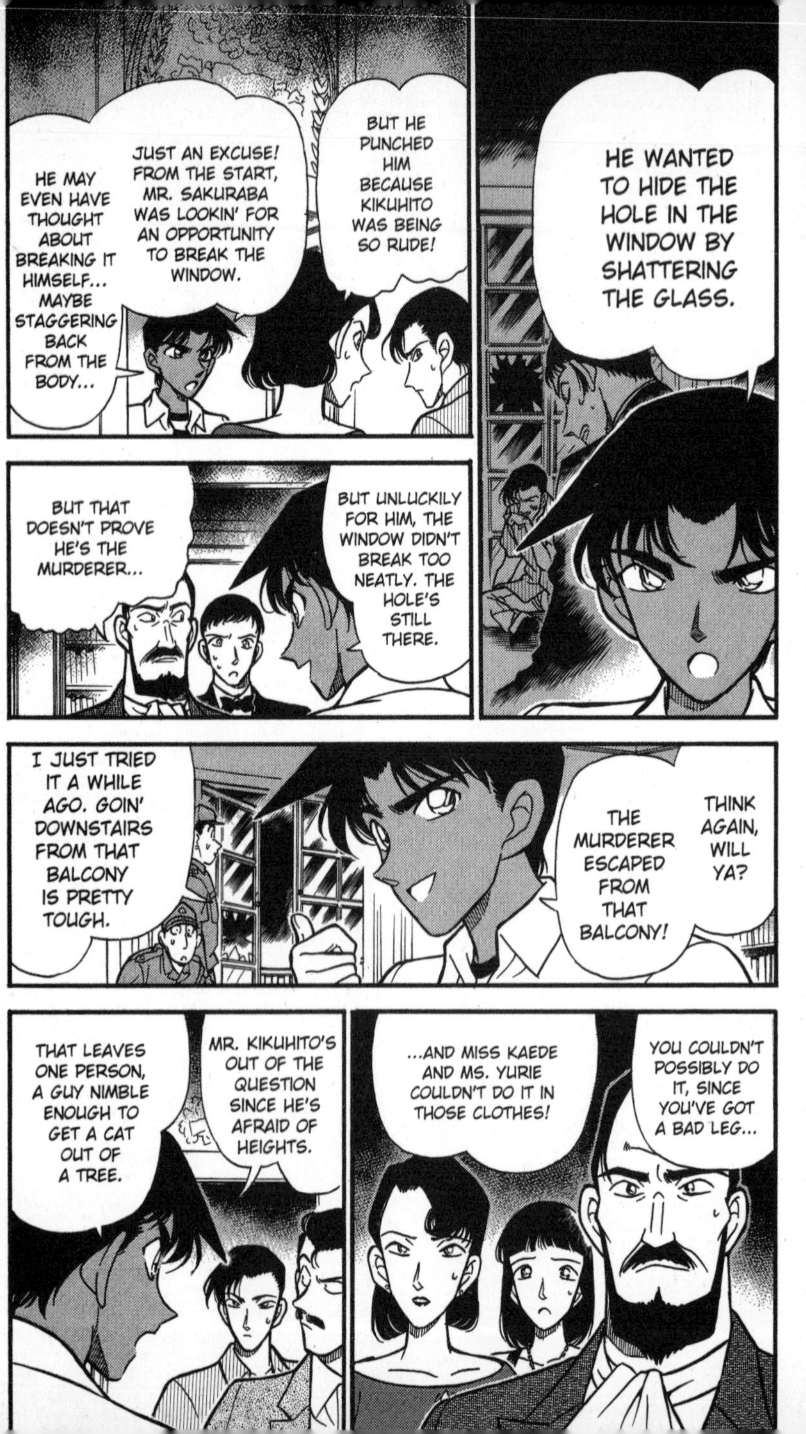
HE WANTED TO HIDE THE HOLE IN THE WINDOW BY SHATTERING THE GLASS.
BUT HE PUNCHED HIM BECAUSE KIKUHITO WAS BEING SO RUDE!
JUST AN EXCUSE! FROM THE START, MR. SAKURABA WAS LOOKIN' FOR AN OPPORTUNITY TO BREAK THE WINDOW.
HE MAY EVEN HAVE THOUGHT ABOUT BREAKING IT HIMSELF... MAYBE STAGGERING BACK FROM THE BODY...
BUT UNLUCKILY FOR HIM, THE WINDOW DIDN'T BREAK TOO NEATLY. THE HOLE'S STILL THERE.
BUT THAT DOESN'T PROVE HE'S THE MURDERER...
THINK AGAIN, WILL YA?
THE MURDERER ESCAPED FROM THAT BALCONY!
I JUST TRIED IT A WHILE AGO. GOIN' DOWNSTAIRS FROM THAT BALCONY IS PRETTY TOUGH.
YOU COULDN'T POSSIBLY DO IT, SINCE YOU'VE GOT A BAD LEG...
...AND MISS KAEDE AND MS. YURIE COULDN'T DO IT IN THOSE CLOTHES!
MR. KIKUHITO'S OUT OF THE QUESTION SINCE HE'S AFRAID OF HEIGHTS.
THAT LEAVES ONE PERSON, A GUY NIMBLE ENOUGH TO GET A CAT OUT OF A TREE.

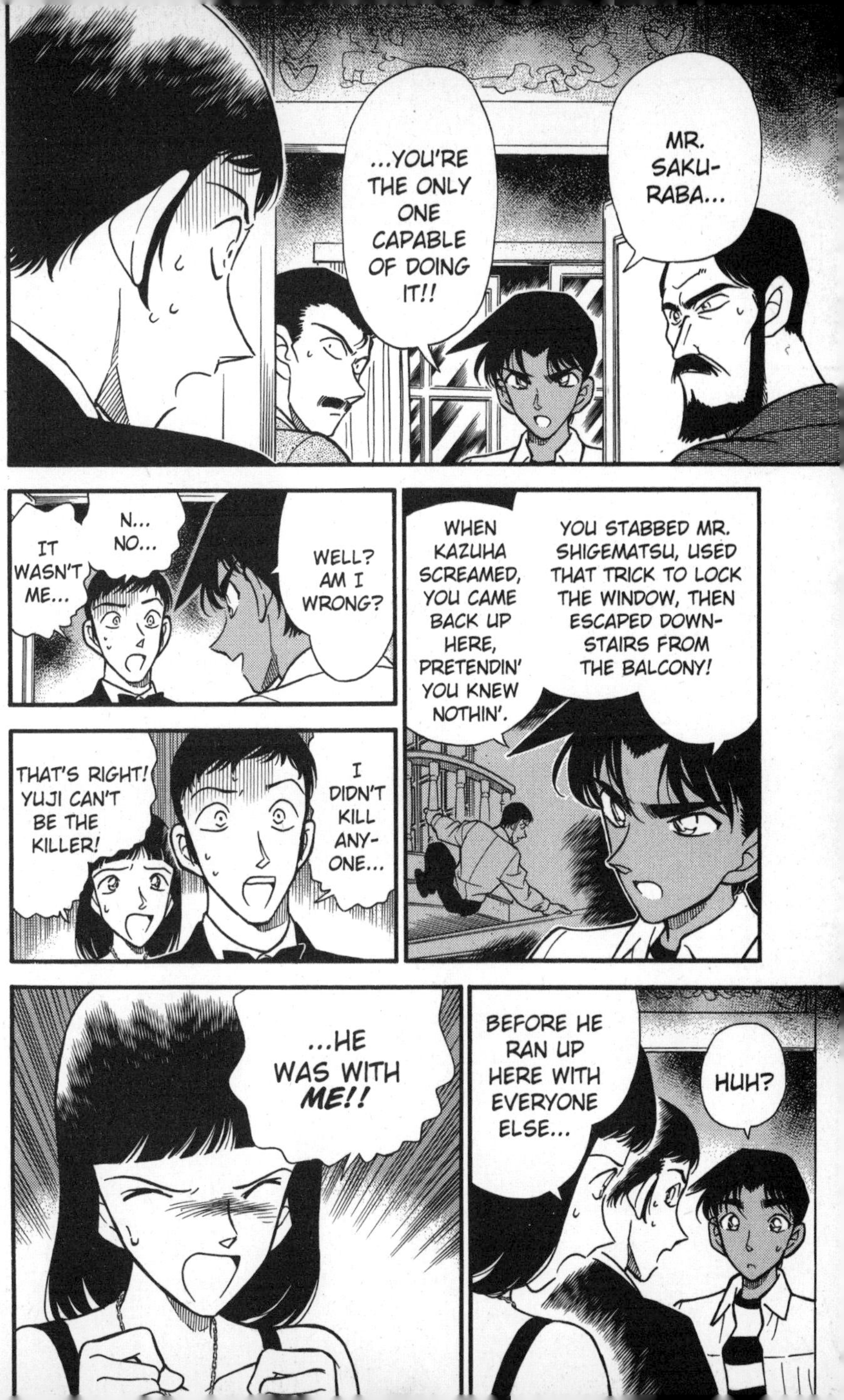
MR. SAKU-RABA...
...YOU'RE THE ONLY ONE CAPABLE OF DOING IT!!
YOU STABBED MR. SHIGEMATSU, USED THAT TRICK TO LOCK THE WINDOW, THEN ESCAPED DOWN-STAIRS FROM THE BALCONY!
WHEN KAZUHA SCREAMED, YOU CAME BACK UP HERE, PRETENDIN' YOU KNEW NOTHIN'.
WELL? AM I WRONG?
N... NO...
IT WASN'T ME...
I DIDN'T KILL ANY-ONE...
THAT'S RIGHT! YUJI CAN'T BE THE KILLER!
HUH?
BEFORE HE RAN UP HERE WITH EVERYONE ELSE...
...HE WAS WITH ***ME!!***

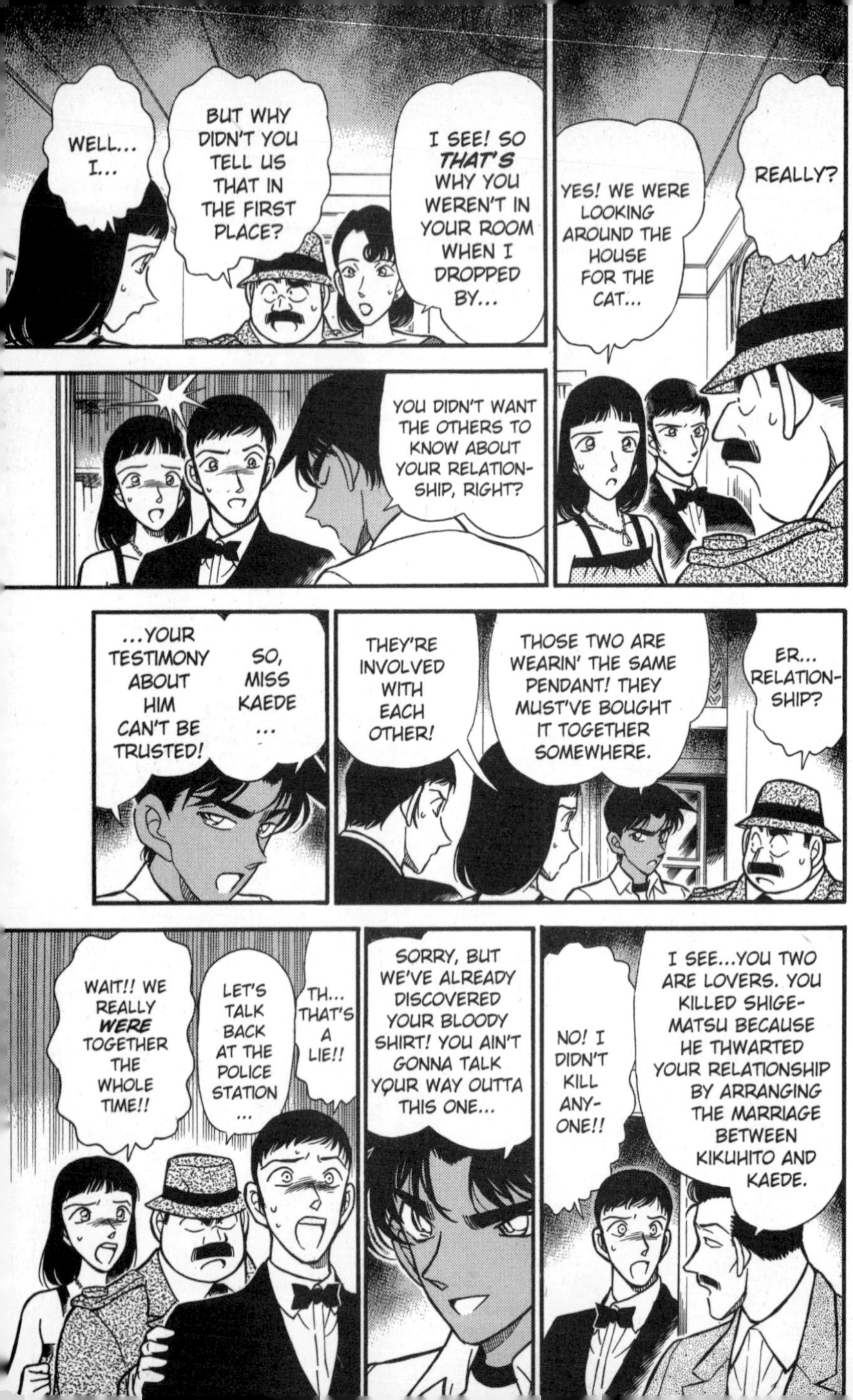
REALLY?
YES! WE WERE LOOKING AROUND THE HOUSE FOR THE CAT...
I SEE! SO *THAT'S* WHY YOU WEREN'T IN YOUR ROOM WHEN I DROPPED BY...
BUT WHY DIDN'T YOU TELL US THAT IN THE FIRST PLACE?
WELL... I...
YOU DIDN'T WANT THE OTHERS TO KNOW ABOUT YOUR RELATIONSHIP, RIGHT?
ER... RELATIONSHIP?
THOSE TWO ARE WEARIN' THE SAME PENDANT! THEY MUST'VE BOUGHT IT TOGETHER SOMEWHERE.
THEY'RE INVOLVED WITH EACH OTHER!
SO, MISS KAEDE...
...YOUR TESTIMONY ABOUT HIM CAN'T BE TRUSTED!
I SEE...YOU TWO ARE LOVERS. YOU KILLED SHIGEMATSU BECAUSE HE THWARTED YOUR RELATIONSHIP BY ARRANGING THE MARRIAGE BETWEEN KIKUHITO AND KAEDE.
NO! I DIDN'T KILL ANYONE!!
SORRY, BUT WE'VE ALREADY DISCOVERED YOUR BLOODY SHIRT! YOU AIN'T GONNA TALK YOUR WAY OUTTA THIS ONE...
TH... THAT'S A LIE!!
LET'S TALK BACK AT THE POLICE STATION...
WAIT!! WE REALLY *WERE* TOGETHER THE WHOLE TIME!!

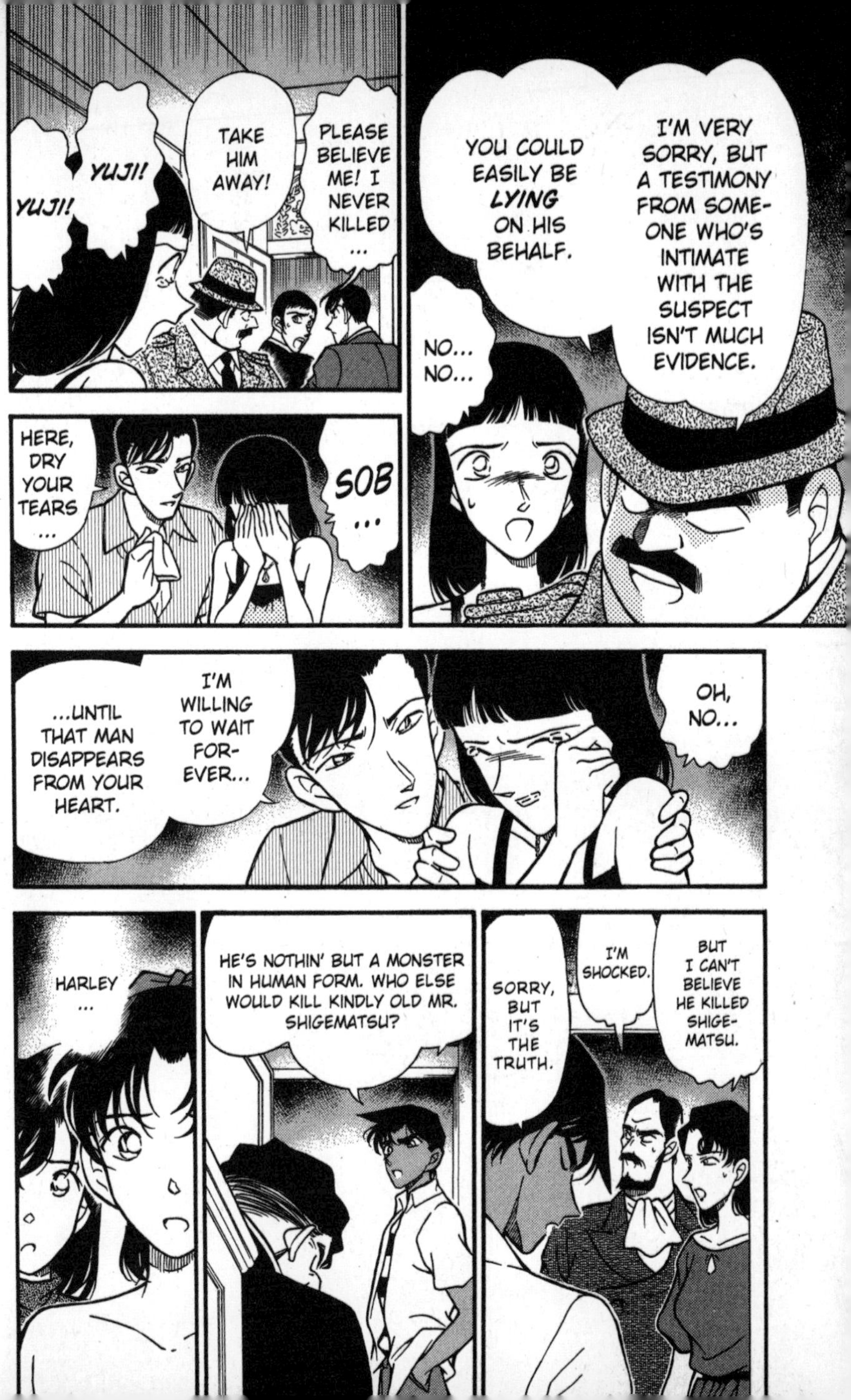
I'M VERY SORRY, BUT A TESTIMONY FROM SOME-ONE WHO'S INTIMATE WITH THE SUSPECT ISN'T MUCH EVIDENCE.
YOU COULD EASILY BE *LYING* ON HIS BEHALF.
NO... NO...
PLEASE BELIEVE ME! I NEVER KILLED ...
TAKE HIM AWAY!
YUJI!
YUJI!
SOB ...
HERE, DRY YOUR TEARS ...
OH, NO...
I'M WILLING TO WAIT FOR-EVER...
...UNTIL THAT MAN DISAPPEARS FROM YOUR HEART.
BUT I CAN'T BELIEVE HE KILLED SHIGE-MATSU.
I'M SHOCKED.
SORRY, BUT IT'S THE TRUTH.
HE'S NOTHIN' BUT A MONSTER IN HUMAN FORM. WHO ELSE WOULD KILL KINDLY OLD MR. SHIGEMATSU?
HARLEY ...

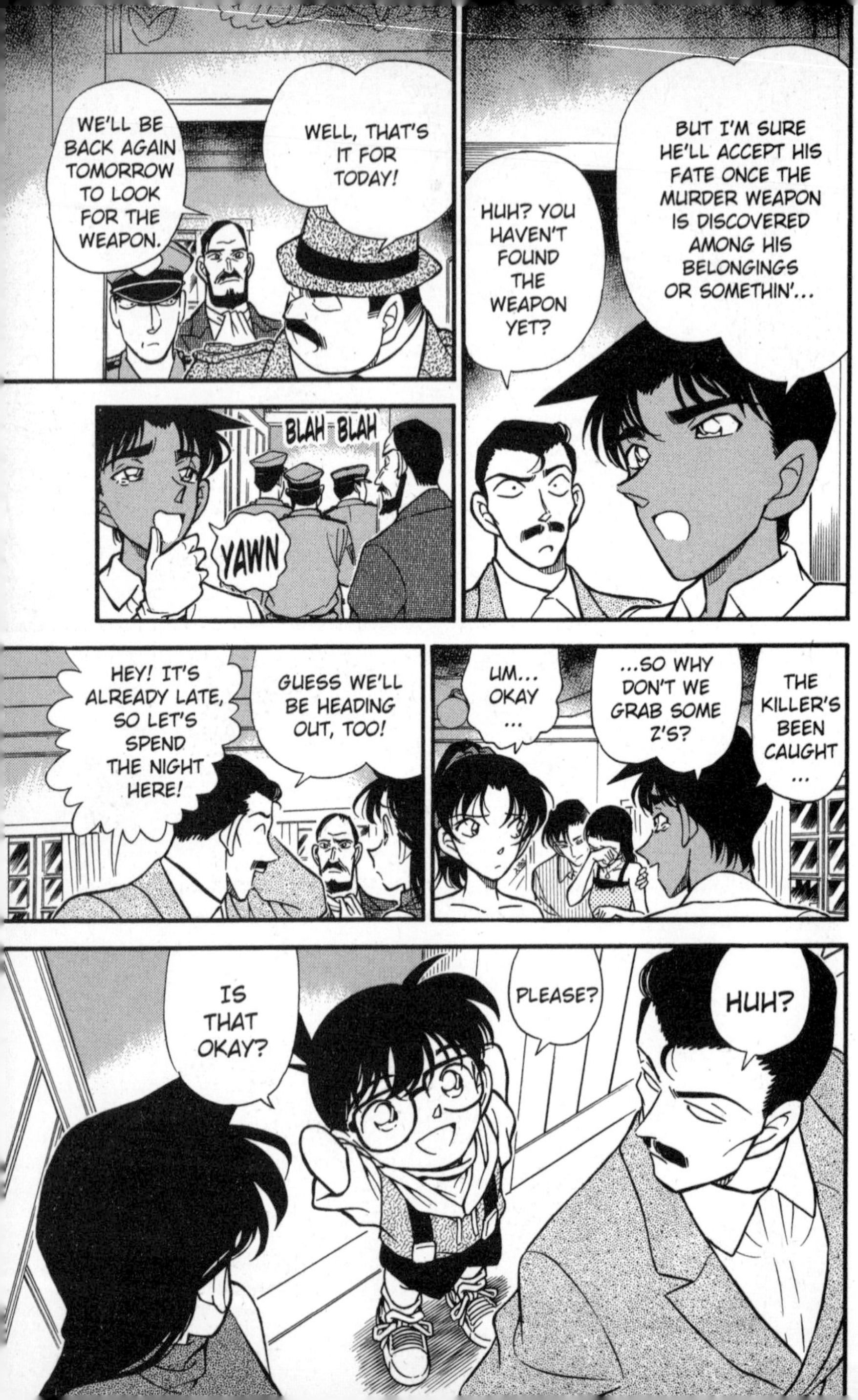

BUT I'M SURE HE'LL ACCEPT HIS FATE ONCE THE MURDER WEAPON IS DISCOVERED AMONG HIS BELONGINGS OR SOMETHIN'...
HUH? YOU HAVEN'T FOUND THE WEAPON YET?
WELL, THAT'S IT FOR TODAY!
WE'LL BE BACK AGAIN TOMORROW TO LOOK FOR THE WEAPON.
BLAH BLAH
YAWN
THE KILLER'S BEEN CAUGHT ...
...SO WHY DON'T WE GRAB SOME Z'S?
UM... OKAY ...
GUESS WE'LL BE HEADING OUT, TOO!
HEY! IT'S ALREADY LATE, SO LET'S SPEND THE NIGHT HERE!
HUH?
PLEASE?
IS THAT OKAY?

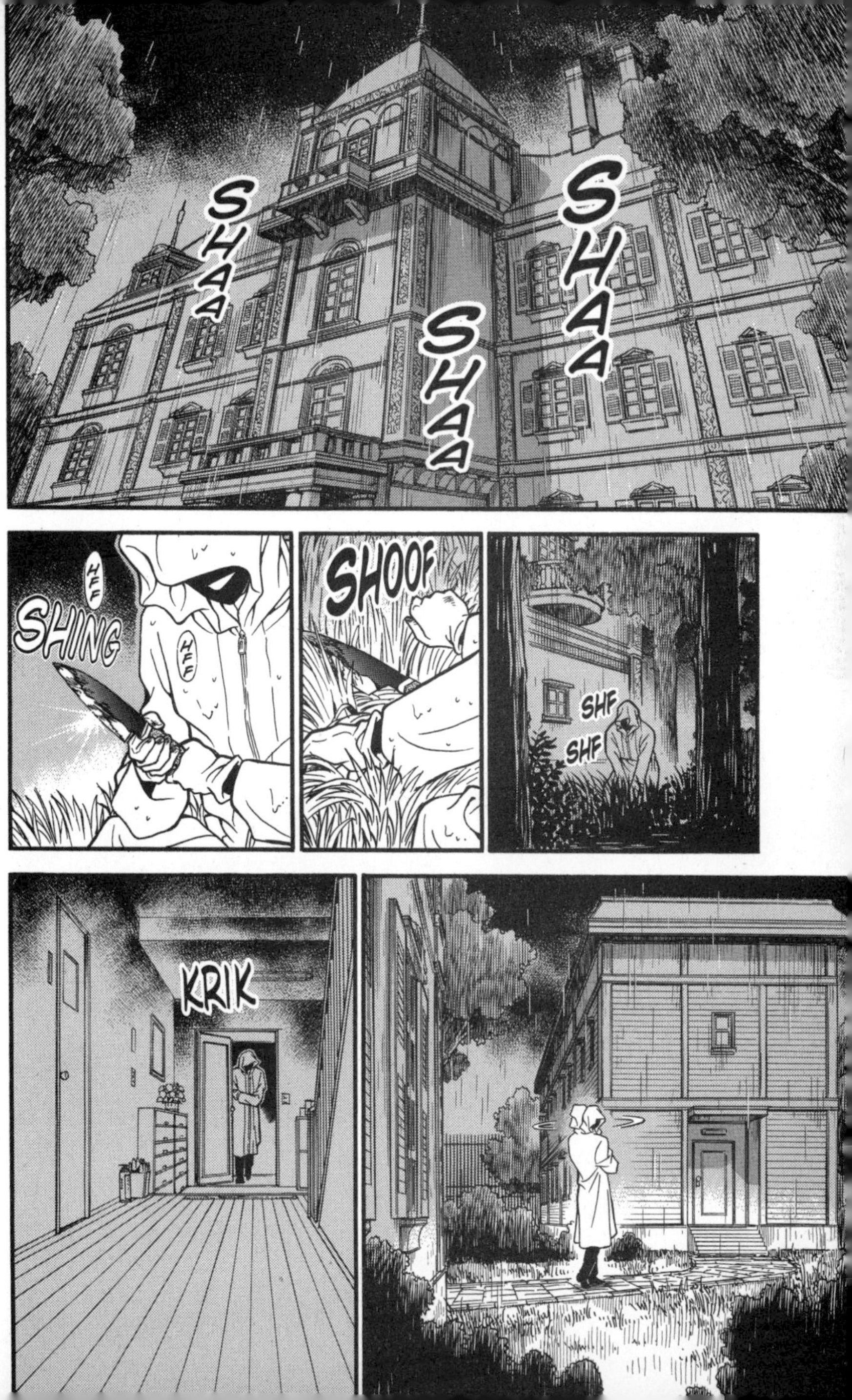
SHAA
SHAA
SHAA
SHF
SHF
SHOOF
HFF
SHING
HFF
KRIK

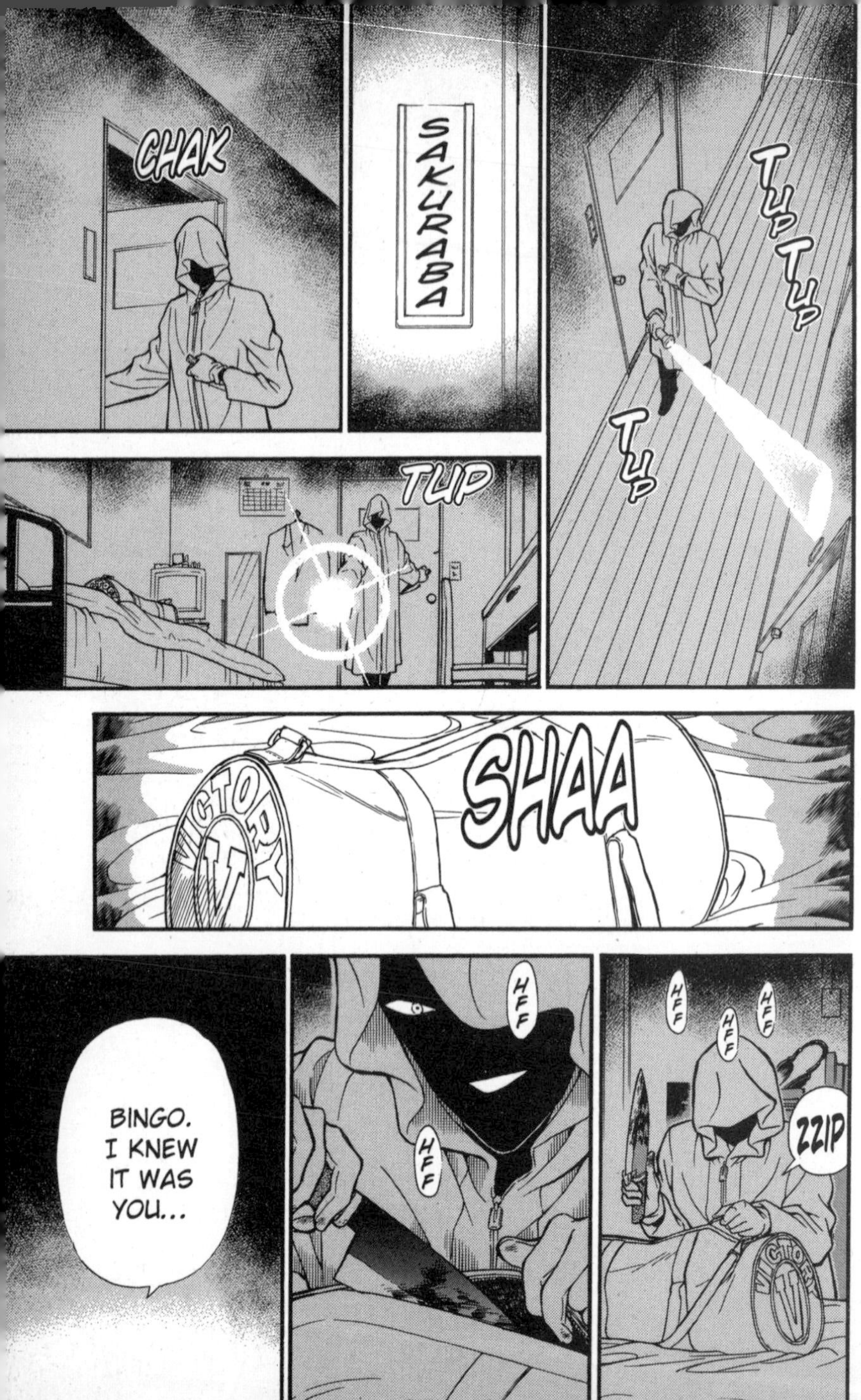
TUP TUP
TUP
SAKURABA
CHAK
TUP
SHAA
HFF
HFF
HFF
ZZIP
HFF
HFF
BINGO. I KNEW IT WAS YOU...

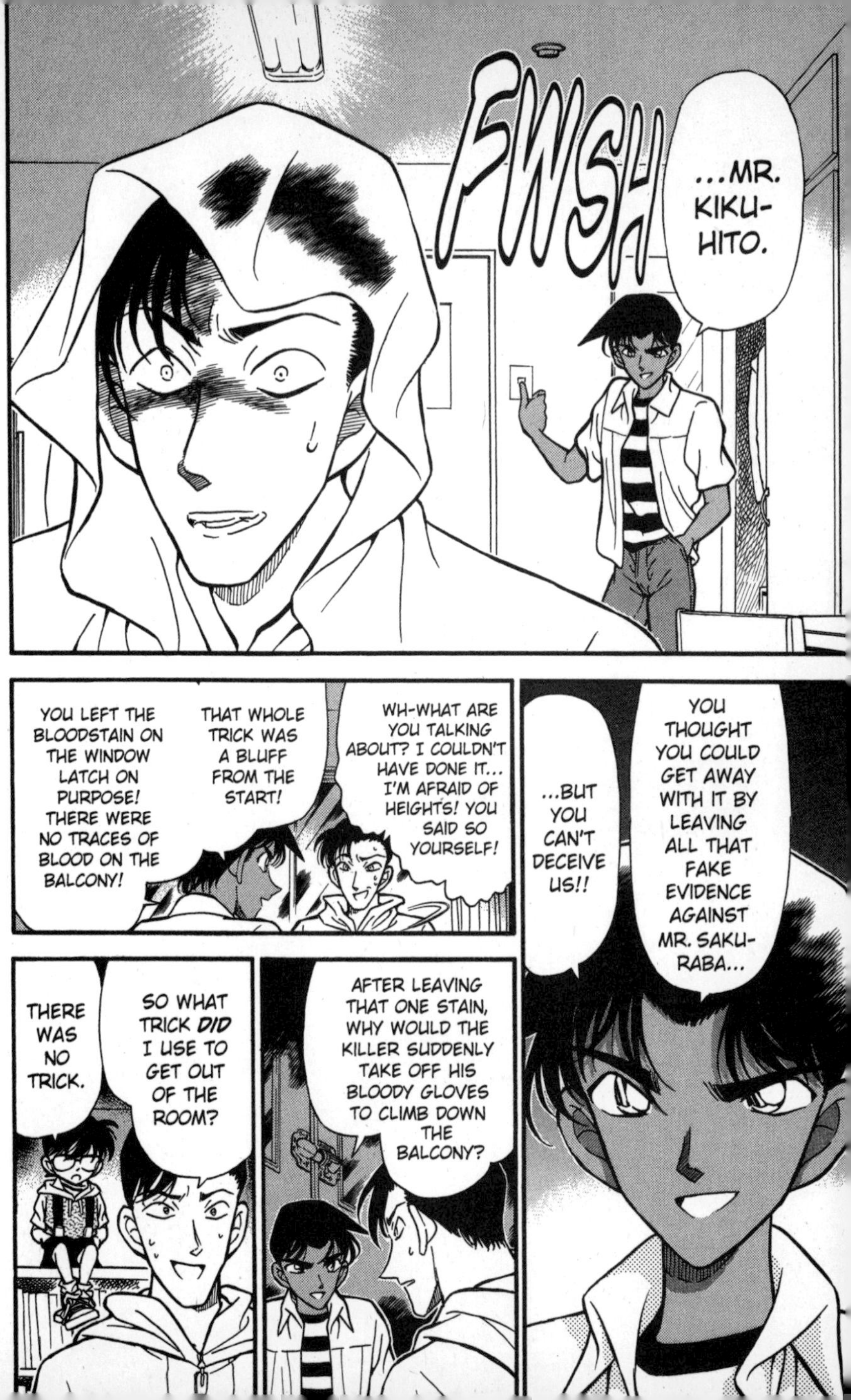
FWSH
...MR. KIKU-HITO.
YOU THOUGHT YOU COULD GET AWAY WITH IT BY LEAVING ALL THAT FAKE EVIDENCE AGAINST MR. SAKU-RABA...
...BUT YOU CAN'T DECEIVE US!!
WH-WHAT ARE YOU TALKING ABOUT? I COULDN'T HAVE DONE IT... I'M AFRAID OF HEIGHTS! YOU SAID SO YOURSELF!
THAT WHOLE TRICK WAS A BLUFF FROM THE START!
YOU LEFT THE BLOODSTAIN ON THE WINDOW LATCH ON PURPOSE! THERE WERE NO TRACES OF BLOOD ON THE BALCONY!
AFTER LEAVING THAT ONE STAIN, WHY WOULD THE KILLER SUDDENLY TAKE OFF HIS BLOODY GLOVES TO CLIMB DOWN THE BALCONY?
SO WHAT TRICK *DID* I USE TO GET OUT OF THE ROOM?
THERE WAS NO TRICK.

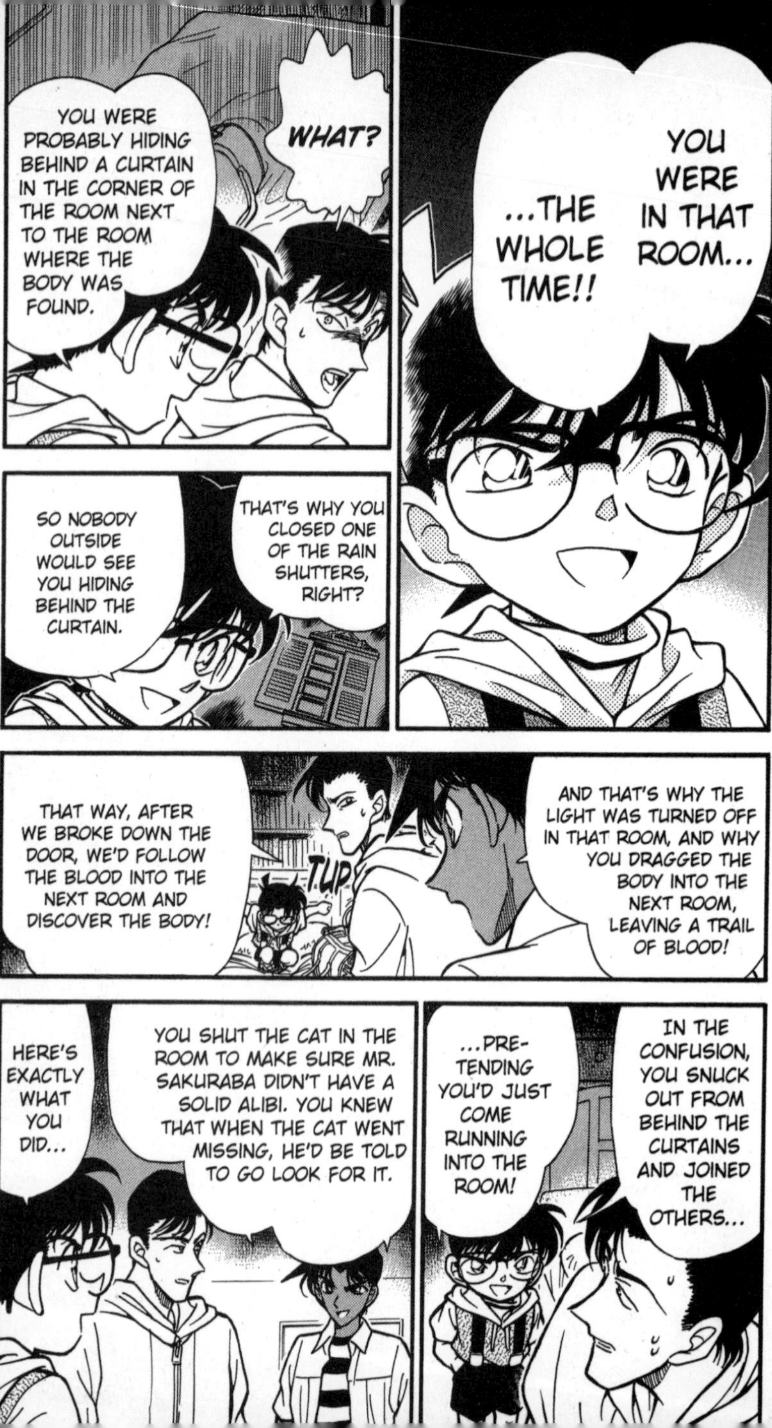
YOU WERE IN THAT ROOM...
...THE WHOLE TIME!!
WHAT?
YOU WERE PROBABLY HIDING BEHIND A CURTAIN IN THE CORNER OF THE ROOM NEXT TO THE ROOM WHERE THE BODY WAS FOUND.
THAT'S WHY YOU CLOSED ONE OF THE RAIN SHUTTERS, RIGHT?
SO NOBODY OUTSIDE WOULD SEE YOU HIDING BEHIND THE CURTAIN.
AND THAT'S WHY THE LIGHT WAS TURNED OFF IN THAT ROOM, AND WHY YOU DRAGGED THE BODY INTO THE NEXT ROOM, LEAVING A TRAIL OF BLOOD!
TUP
THAT WAY, AFTER WE BROKE DOWN THE DOOR, WE'D FOLLOW THE BLOOD INTO THE NEXT ROOM AND DISCOVER THE BODY!
IN THE CONFUSION, YOU SNUCK OUT FROM BEHIND THE CURTAINS AND JOINED THE OTHERS...
...PRE-TENDING YOU'D JUST COME RUNNING INTO THE ROOM!
YOU SHUT THE CAT IN THE ROOM TO MAKE SURE MR. SAKURABA DIDN'T HAVE A SOLID ALIBI. YOU KNEW THAT WHEN THE CAT WENT MISSING, HE'D BE TOLD TO GO LOOK FOR IT.
HERE'S EXACTLY WHAT YOU DID...

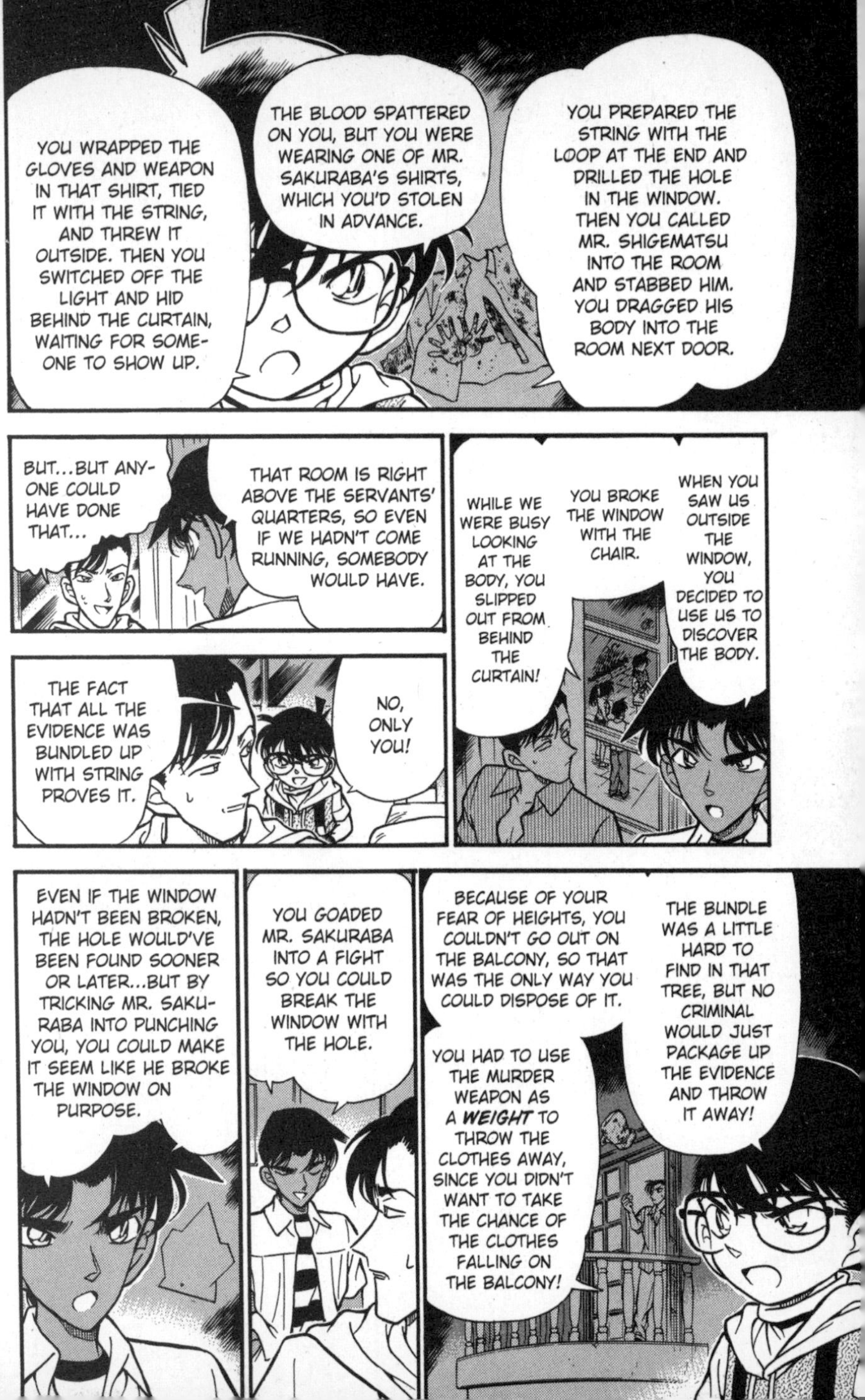
YOU PREPARED THE STRING WITH THE LOOP AT THE END AND DRILLED THE HOLE IN THE WINDOW. THEN YOU CALLED MR. SHIGEMATSU INTO THE ROOM AND STABBED HIM. YOU DRAGGED HIS BODY INTO THE ROOM NEXT DOOR.
THE BLOOD SPATTERED ON YOU, BUT YOU WERE WEARING ONE OF MR. SAKURABA'S SHIRTS, WHICH YOU'D STOLEN IN ADVANCE.
YOU WRAPPED THE GLOVES AND WEAPON IN THAT SHIRT, TIED IT WITH THE STRING, AND THREW IT OUTSIDE. THEN YOU SWITCHED OFF THE LIGHT AND HID BEHIND THE CURTAIN, WAITING FOR SOME-ONE TO SHOW UP.
WHEN YOU SAW US OUTSIDE THE WINDOW, YOU DECIDED TO USE US TO DISCOVER THE BODY.
YOU BROKE THE WINDOW WITH THE CHAIR.
WHILE WE WERE BUSY LOOKING AT THE BODY, YOU SLIPPED OUT FROM BEHIND THE CURTAIN!
THAT ROOM IS RIGHT ABOVE THE SERVANTS' QUARTERS, SO EVEN IF WE HADN'T COME RUNNING, SOMEBODY WOULD HAVE.
BUT...BUT ANY-ONE COULD HAVE DONE THAT...
NO, ONLY YOU!
THE FACT THAT ALL THE EVIDENCE WAS BUNDLED UP WITH STRING PROVES IT.
THE BUNDLE WAS A LITTLE HARD TO FIND IN THAT TREE, BUT NO CRIMINAL WOULD JUST PACKAGE UP THE EVIDENCE AND THROW IT AWAY!
BECAUSE OF YOUR FEAR OF HEIGHTS, YOU COULDN'T GO OUT ON THE BALCONY, SO THAT WAS THE ONLY WAY YOU COULD DISPOSE OF IT.
YOU HAD TO USE THE MURDER WEAPON AS A ***WEIGHT*** TO THROW THE CLOTHES AWAY, SINCE YOU DIDN'T WANT TO TAKE THE CHANCE OF THE CLOTHES FALLING ON THE BALCONY!
YOU GOADED MR. SAKURABA INTO A FIGHT SO YOU COULD BREAK THE WINDOW WITH THE HOLE.
EVEN IF THE WINDOW HADN'T BEEN BROKEN, THE HOLE WOULD'VE BEEN FOUND SOONER OR LATER...BUT BY TRICKING MR. SAKU-RABA INTO PUNCHING YOU, YOU COULD MAKE IT SEEM LIKE HE BROKE THE WINDOW ON PURPOSE.

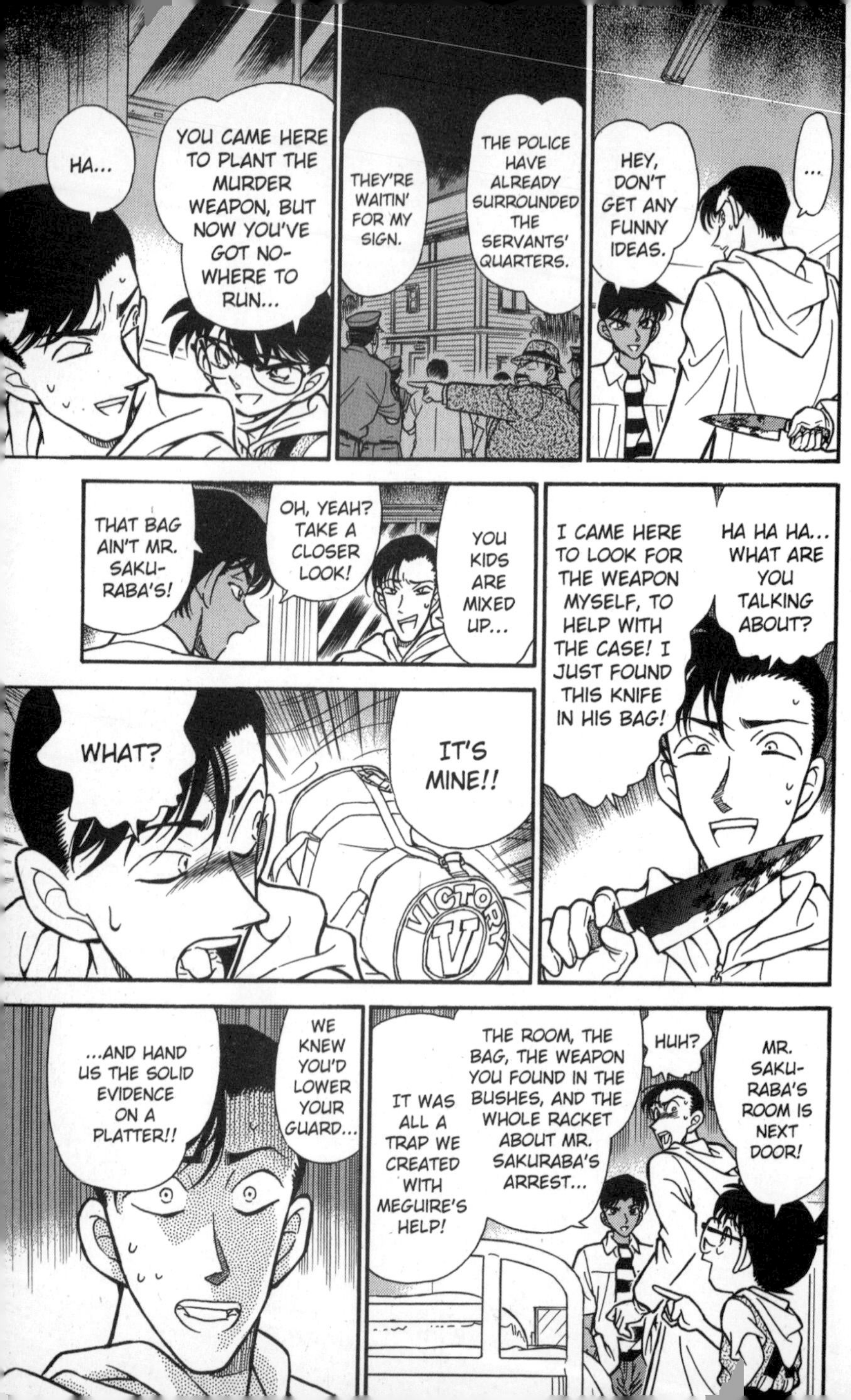
...
HEY, DON'T GET ANY FUNNY IDEAS.
THE POLICE HAVE ALREADY SURROUNDED THE SERVANTS' QUARTERS.
THEY'RE WAITIN' FOR MY SIGN.
YOU CAME HERE TO PLANT THE MURDER WEAPON, BUT NOW YOU'VE GOT NO-WHERE TO RUN...
HA...
HA HA HA... WHAT ARE YOU TALKING ABOUT?
I CAME HERE TO LOOK FOR THE WEAPON MYSELF, TO HELP WITH THE CASE! I JUST FOUND THIS KNIFE IN HIS BAG!
YOU KIDS ARE MIXED UP...
OH, YEAH? TAKE A CLOSER LOOK!
THAT BAG AIN'T MR. SAKURABA'S!
IT'S MINE!!
VICTORY V
WHAT?
MR. SAKURABA'S ROOM IS NEXT DOOR!
HUH?
THE ROOM, THE BAG, THE WEAPON YOU FOUND IN THE BUSHES, AND THE WHOLE RACKET ABOUT MR. SAKURABA'S ARREST...
IT WAS ALL A TRAP WE CREATED WITH MEGUIRE'S HELP!
WE KNEW YOU'D LOWER YOUR GUARD...
...AND HAND US THE SOLID EVIDENCE ON A PLATTER!!

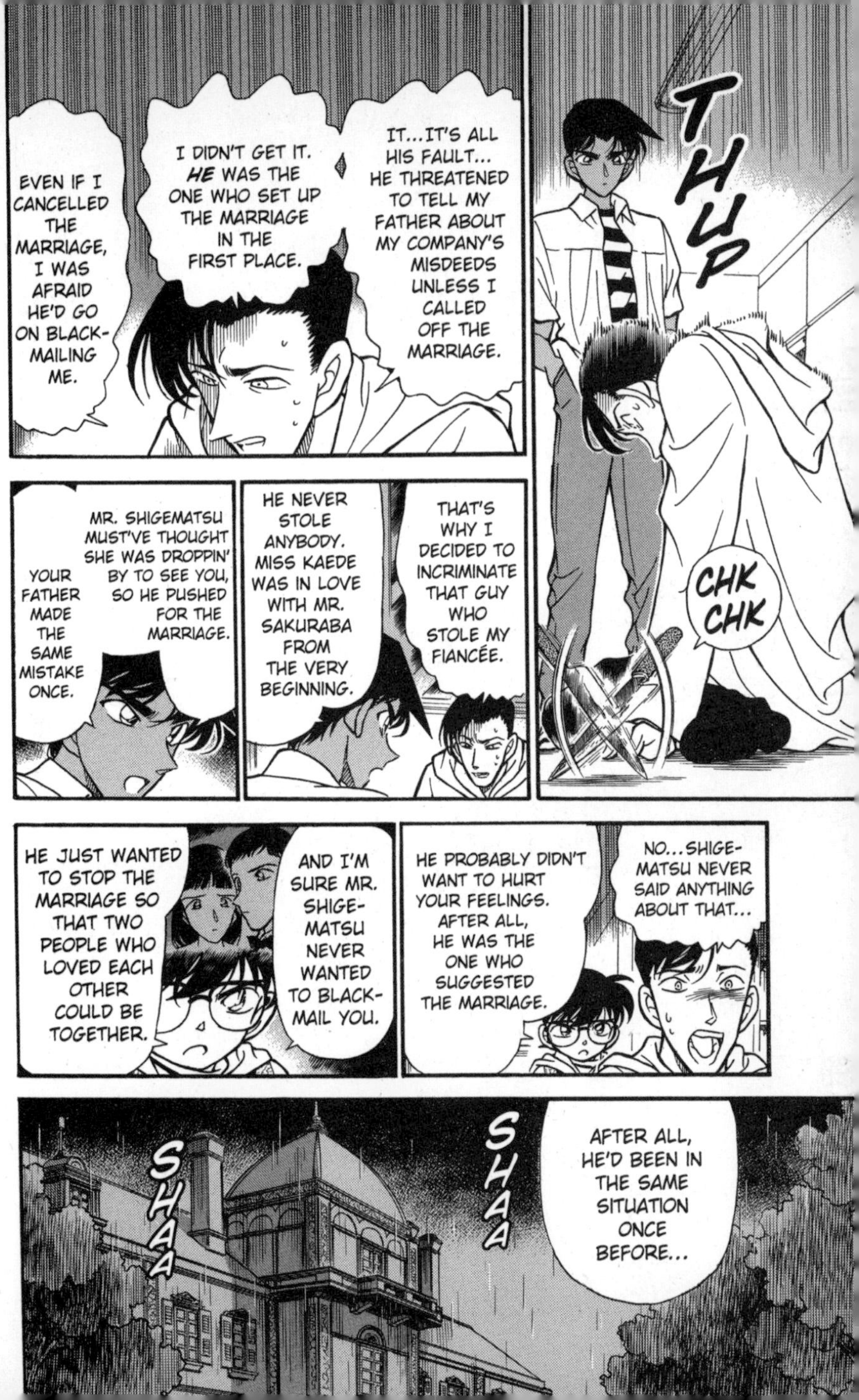
THUP
CHK CHK
IT...IT'S ALL HIS FAULT... HE THREATENED TO TELL MY FATHER ABOUT MY COMPANY'S MISDEEDS UNLESS I CALLED OFF THE MARRIAGE.
I DIDN'T GET IT. HE WAS THE ONE WHO SET UP THE MARRIAGE IN THE FIRST PLACE.
EVEN IF I CANCELLED THE MARRIAGE, I WAS AFRAID HE'D GO ON BLACK-MAILING ME.
THAT'S WHY I DECIDED TO INCRIMINATE THAT GUY WHO STOLE MY FIANCÉE.
HE NEVER STOLE ANYBODY. MISS KAEDE WAS IN LOVE WITH MR. SAKURABA FROM THE VERY BEGINNING.
MR. SHIGEMATSU MUST'VE THOUGHT SHE WAS DROPPIN' BY TO SEE YOU, SO HE PUSHED FOR THE MARRIAGE.
YOUR FATHER MADE THE SAME MISTAKE ONCE.
NO...SHIGE-MATSU NEVER SAID ANYTHING ABOUT THAT...
HE PROBABLY DIDN'T WANT TO HURT YOUR FEELINGS. AFTER ALL, HE WAS THE ONE WHO SUGGESTED THE MARRIAGE.
AND I'M SURE MR. SHIGE-MATSU NEVER WANTED TO BLACK-MAIL YOU.
HE JUST WANTED TO STOP THE MARRIAGE SO THAT TWO PEOPLE WHO LOVED EACH OTHER COULD BE TOGETHER.
AFTER ALL, HE'D BEEN IN THE SAME SITUATION ONCE BEFORE...
SHAA
SHAA

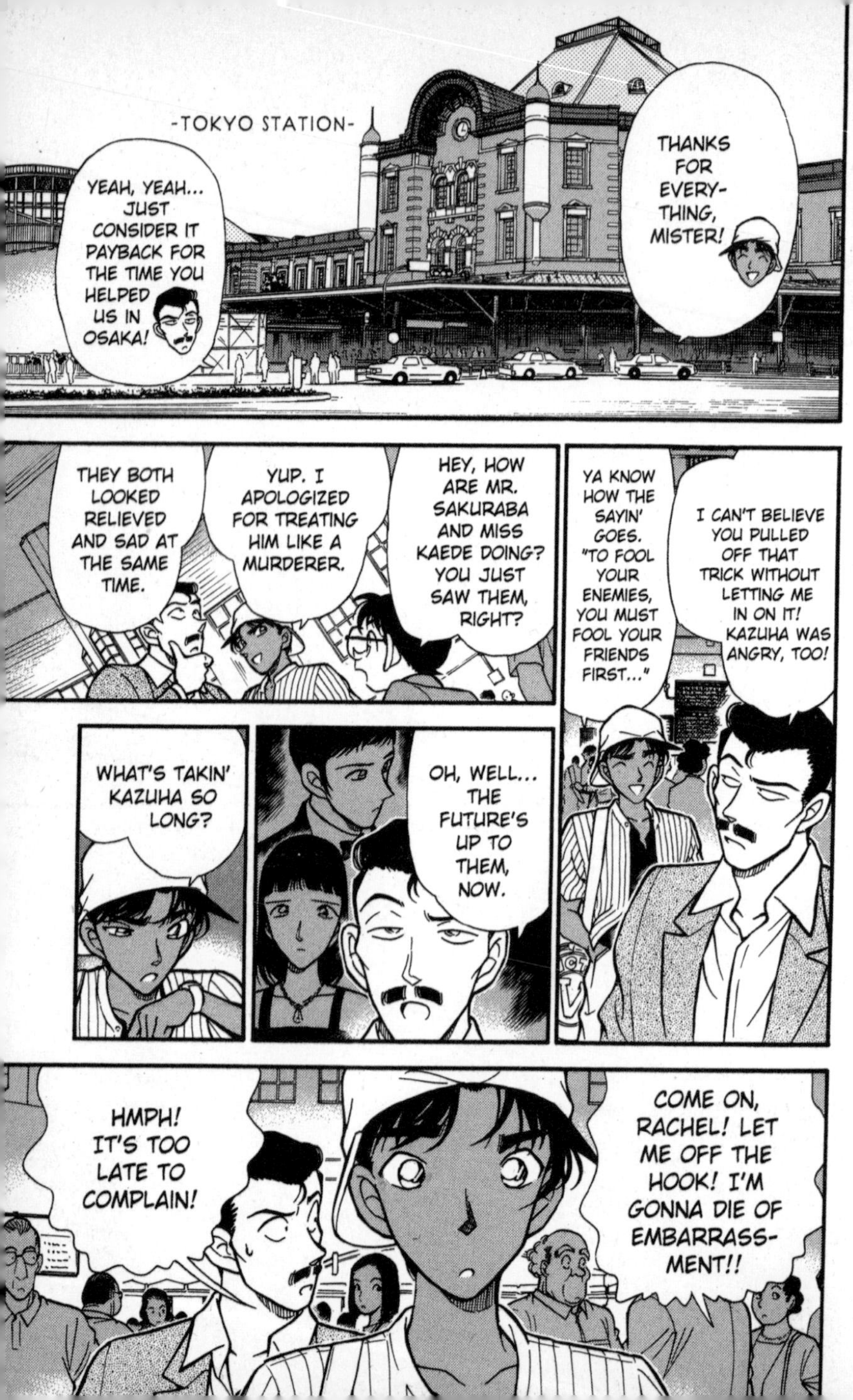
-TOKYO STATION-
THANKS FOR EVERY-THING, MISTER!
YEAH, YEAH... JUST CONSIDER IT PAYBACK FOR THE TIME YOU HELPED US IN OSAKA!
I CAN'T BELIEVE YOU PULLED OFF THAT TRICK WITHOUT LETTING ME IN ON IT! KAZUHA WAS ANGRY, TOO!
YA KNOW HOW THE SAYIN' GOES. "TO FOOL YOUR ENEMIES, YOU MUST FOOL YOUR FRIENDS FIRST..."
HEY, HOW ARE MR. SAKURABA AND MISS KAEDE DOING? YOU JUST SAW THEM, RIGHT?
YUP. I APOLOGIZED FOR TREATING HIM LIKE A MURDERER.
THEY BOTH LOOKED RELIEVED AND SAD AT THE SAME TIME.
OH, WELL... THE FUTURE'S UP TO THEM, NOW.
WHAT'S TAKIN' KAZUHA SO LONG?
COME ON, RACHEL! LET ME OFF THE HOOK! I'M GONNA DIE OF EMBARRASS-MENT!!
HMPH! IT'S TOO LATE TO COMPLAIN!

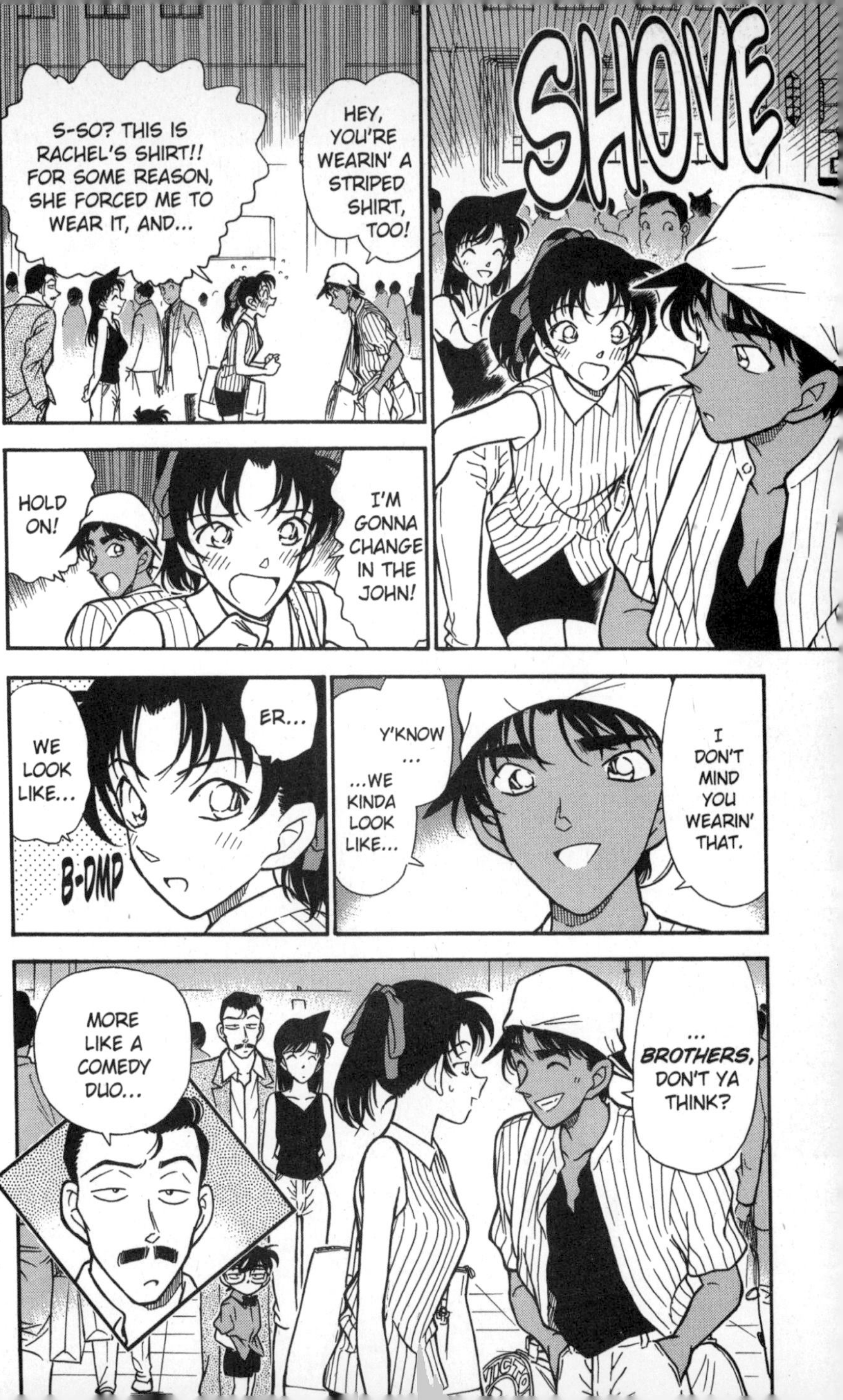
SHOVE
HEY, YOU'RE WEARIN' A STRIPED SHIRT, TOO!
S-SO? THIS IS RACHEL'S SHIRT!! FOR SOME REASON, SHE FORCED ME TO WEAR IT, AND...
I'M GONNA CHANGE IN THE JOHN!
HOLD ON!
I DON'T MIND YOU WEARIN' THAT.
Y'KNOW ... ...WE KINDA LOOK LIKE...
ER...
WE LOOK LIKE...
B-DMP
... BROTHERS, DON'T YA THINK?
MORE LIKE A COMEDY DUO...

THE NORTHERN STAR

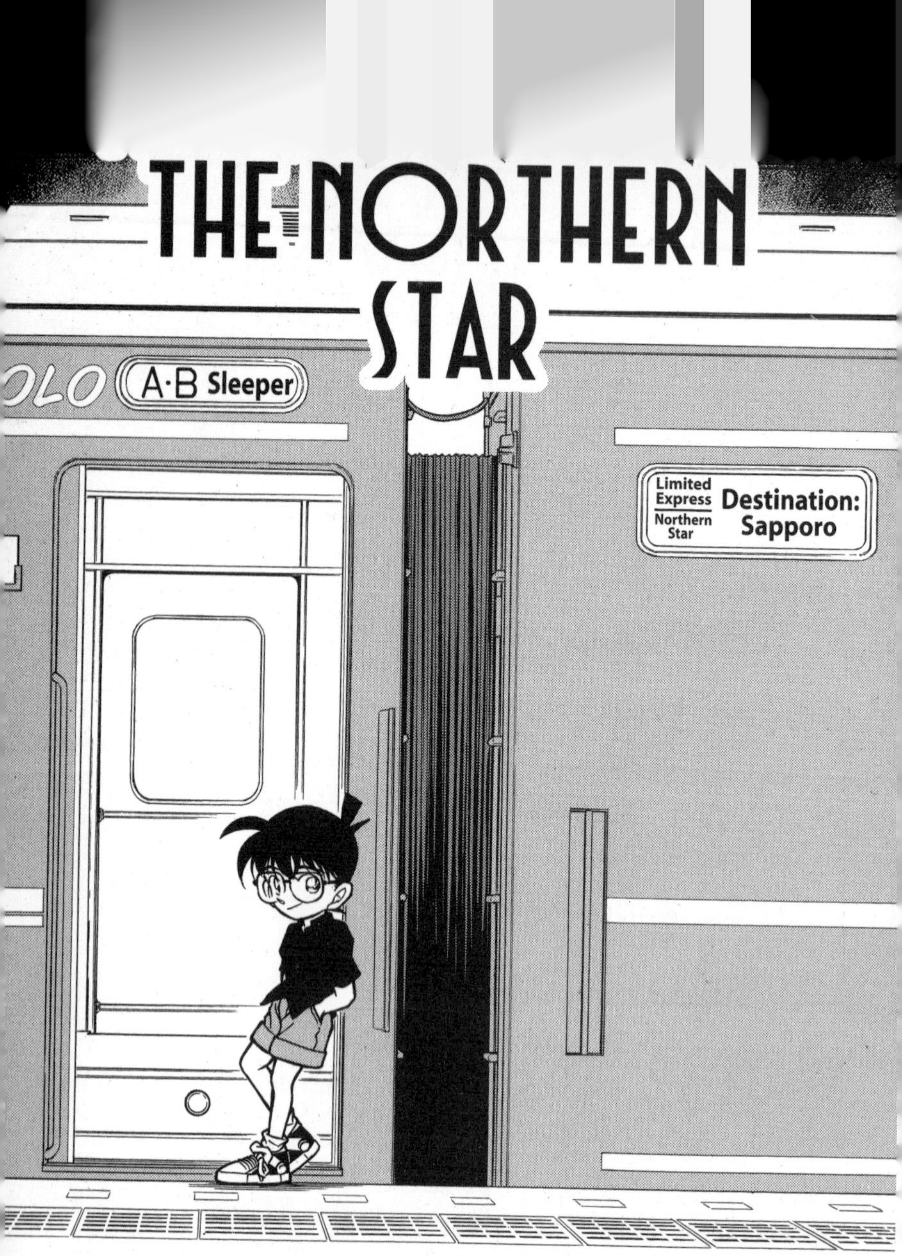
A·B Sleeper
Limited Express Northern Star
Destination: Sapporo

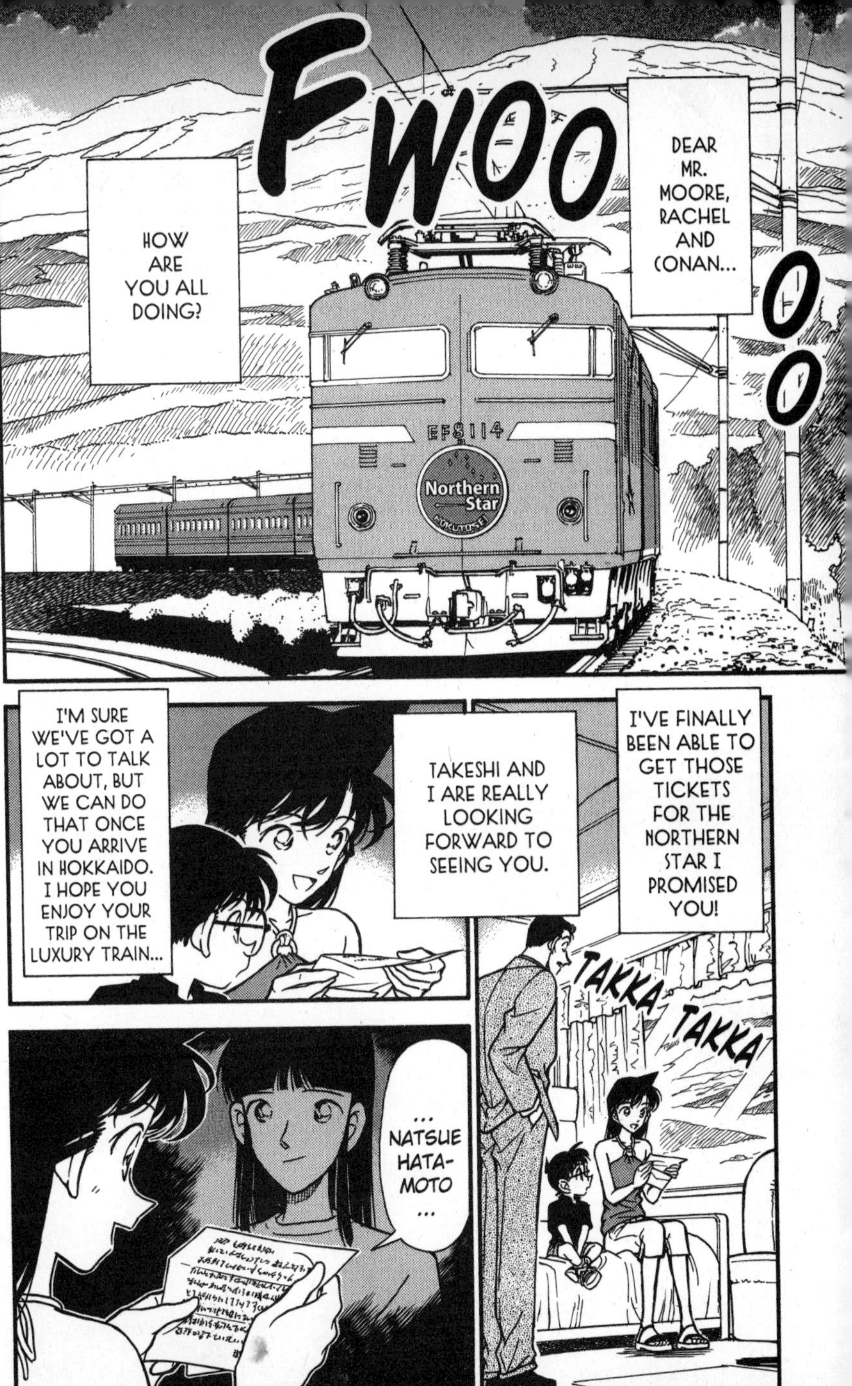

DEAR MR. MOORE, RACHEL AND CONAN...
FWOOOOO
HOW ARE YOU ALL DOING?
Northern Star
I'VE FINALLY BEEN ABLE TO GET THOSE TICKETS FOR THE NORTHERN STAR I PROMISED YOU!
TAKKA TAKKA
TAKESHI AND I ARE REALLY LOOKING FORWARD TO SEEING YOU.
I'M SURE WE'VE GOT A LOT TO TALK ABOUT, BUT WE CAN DO THAT ONCE YOU ARRIVE IN HOKKAIDO. I HOPE YOU ENJOY YOUR TRIP ON THE LUXURY TRAIN...
... NATSUE HATA-MOTO ...

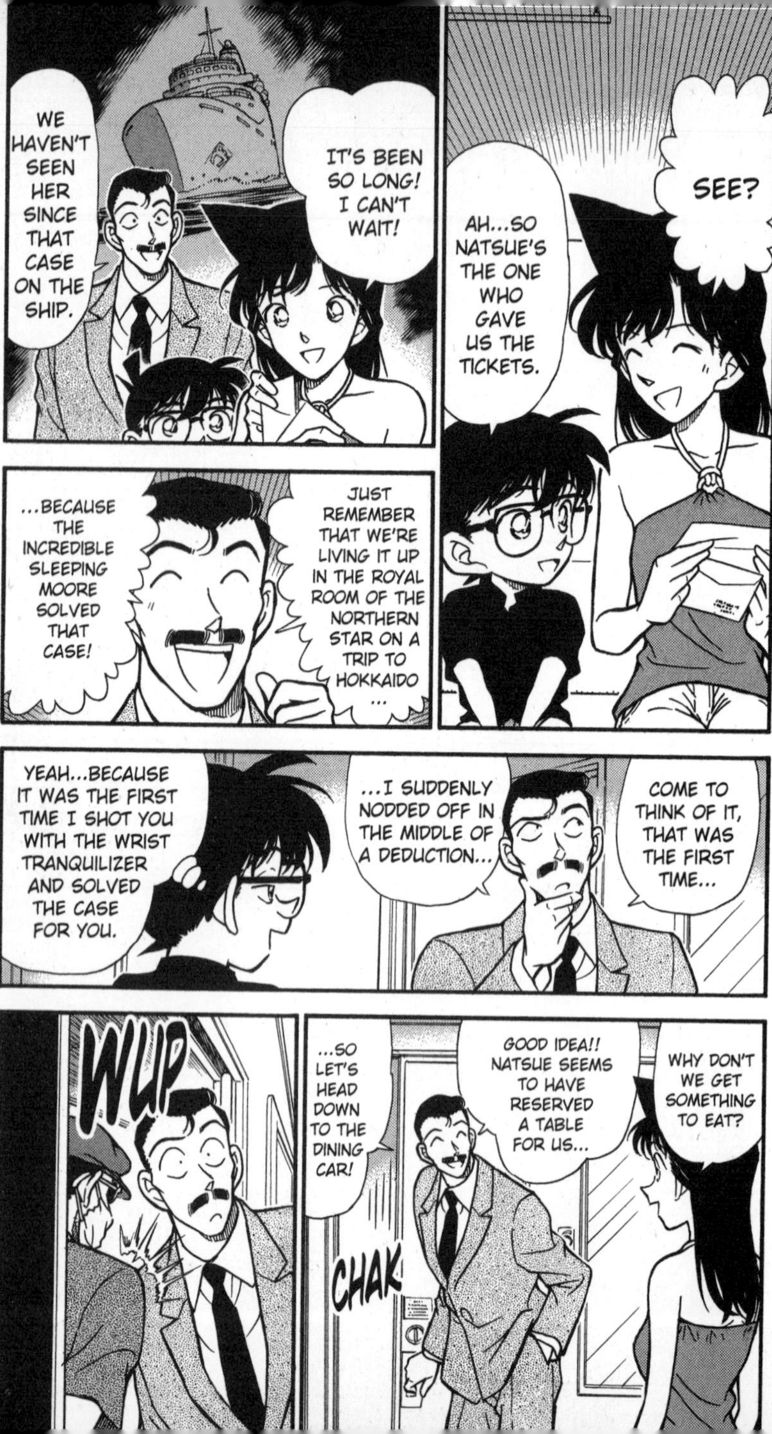
SEE?
AH...SO NATSUE'S THE ONE WHO GAVE US THE TICKETS.
IT'S BEEN SO LONG! I CAN'T WAIT!
WE HAVEN'T SEEN HER SINCE THAT CASE ON THE SHIP.
JUST REMEMBER THAT WE'RE LIVING IT UP IN THE ROYAL ROOM OF THE NORTHERN STAR ON A TRIP TO HOKKAIDO ...
...BECAUSE THE INCREDIBLE SLEEPING MOORE SOLVED THAT CASE!
COME TO THINK OF IT, THAT WAS THE FIRST TIME...
...I SUDDENLY NODDED OFF IN THE MIDDLE OF A DEDUCTION...
YEAH...BECAUSE IT WAS THE FIRST TIME I SHOT YOU WITH THE WRIST TRANQUILIZER AND SOLVED THE CASE FOR YOU.
WHY DON'T WE GET SOMETHING TO EAT?
GOOD IDEA!! NATSUE SEEMS TO HAVE RESERVED A TABLE FOR US...
...SO LET'S HEAD DOWN TO THE DINING CAR!
CHAK
WUP

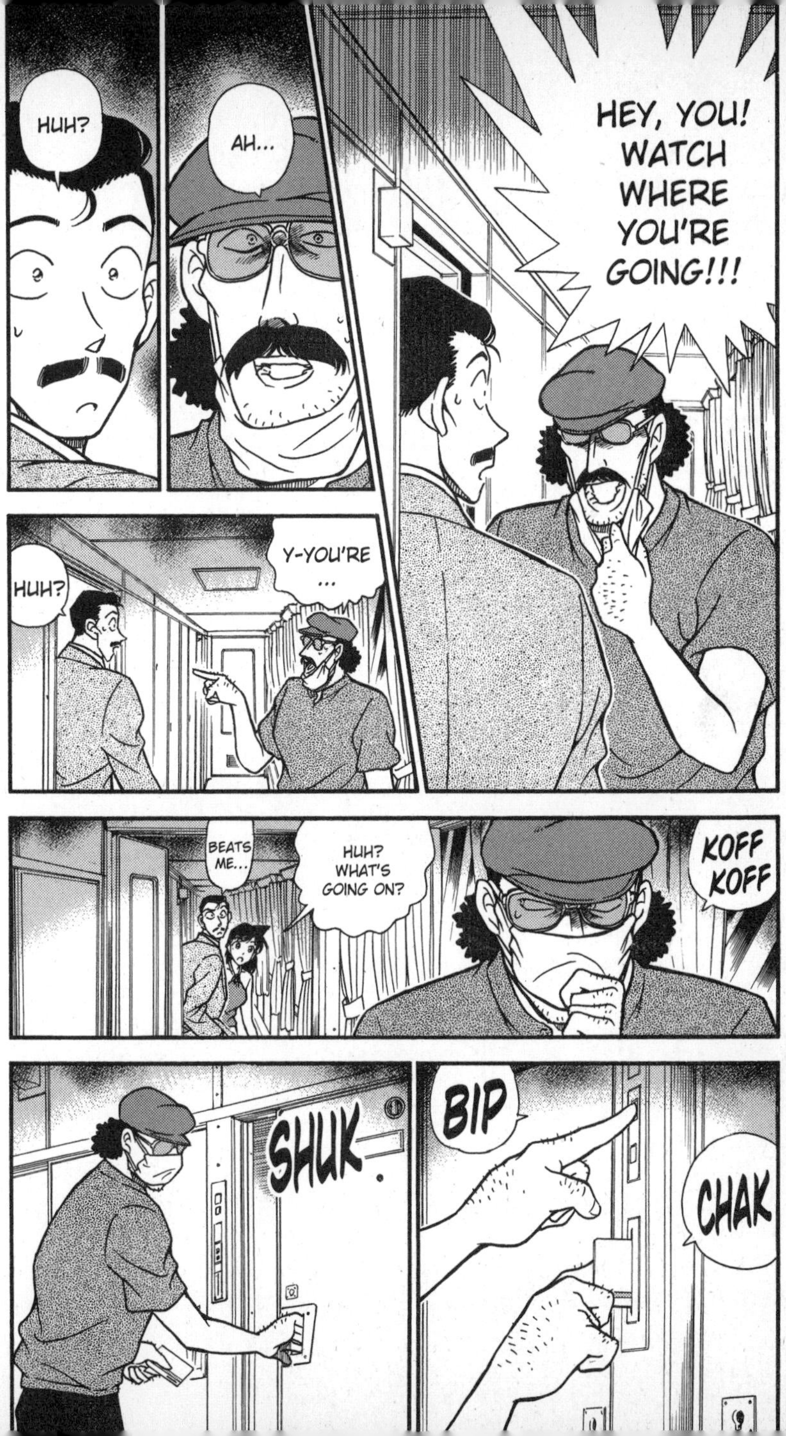
HEY, YOU! WATCH WHERE YOU'RE GOING!!!
AH...
HUH?
Y-YOU'RE ...
HUH?
KOFF KOFF
HUH? WHAT'S GOING ON?
BEATS ME...
BIP
CHAK
SHUK

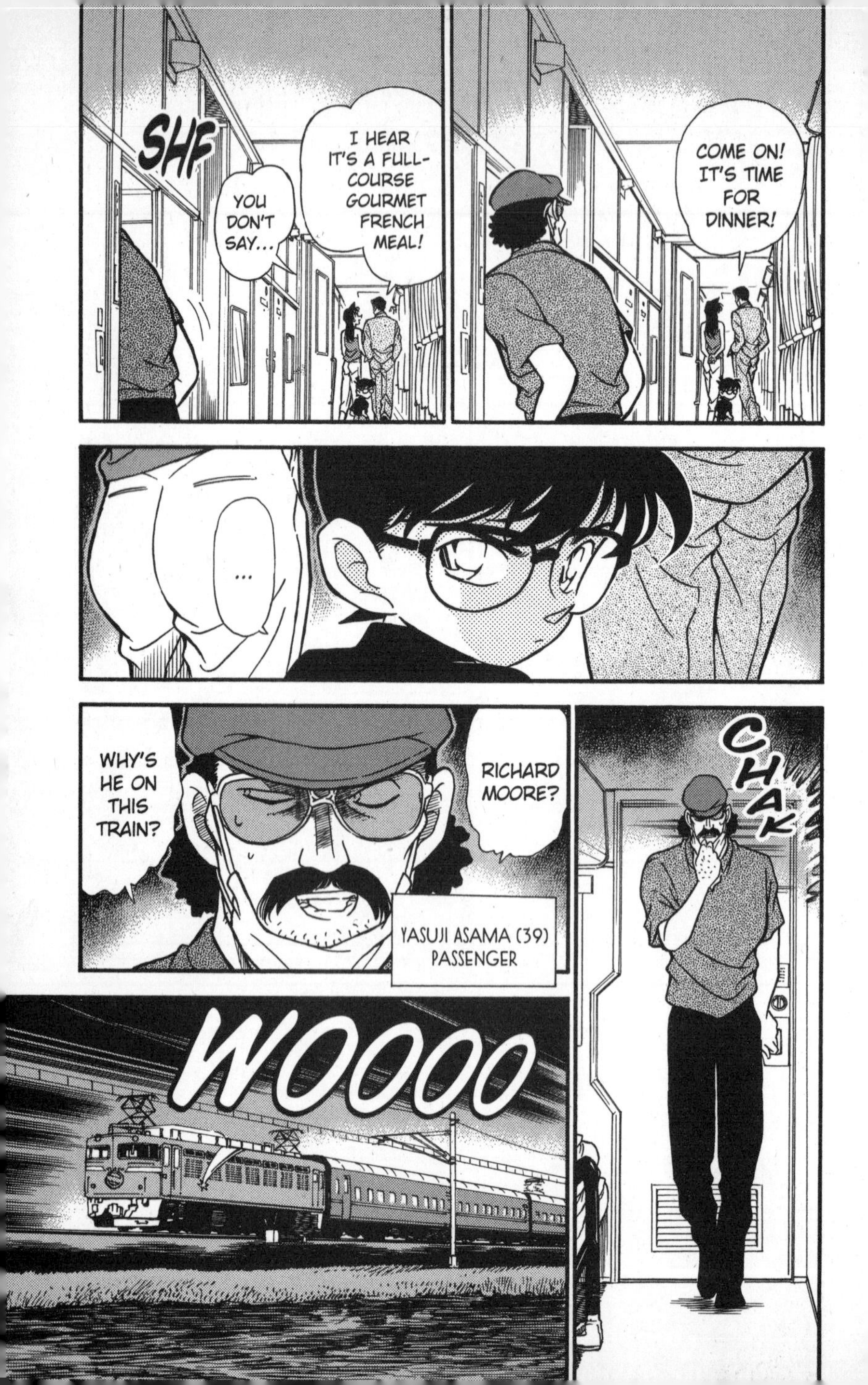
COME ON! IT'S TIME FOR DINNER!
I HEAR IT'S A FULL-COURSE GOURMET FRENCH MEAL!
YOU DON'T SAY...
SHF
...
CHAK
RICHARD MOORE?
WHY'S HE ON THIS TRAIN?
YASUJI ASAMA (39) PASSENGER
WOOOO

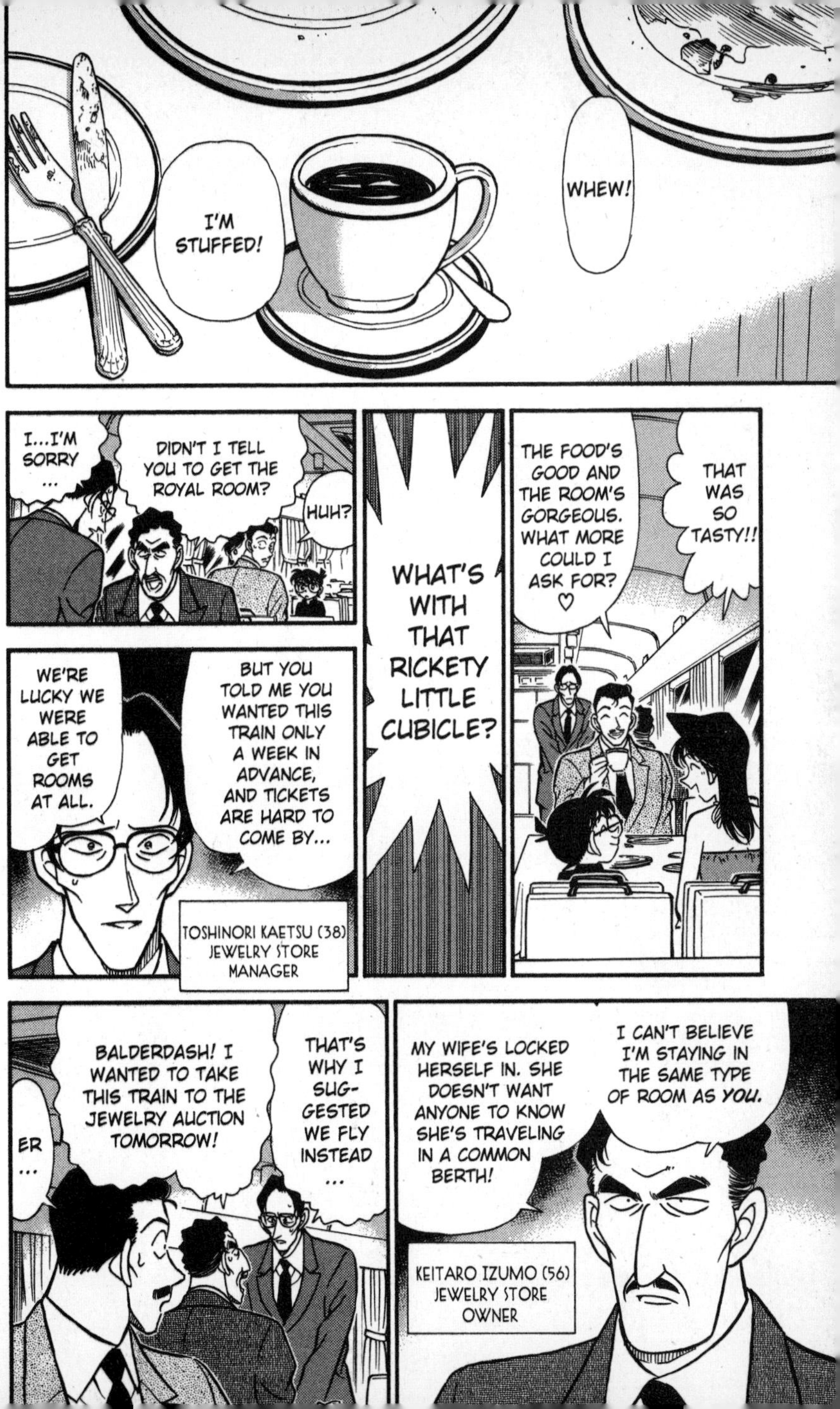
WHEW!
I'M STUFFED!
THAT WAS SO TASTY!!
THE FOOD'S GOOD AND THE ROOM'S GORGEOUS. WHAT MORE COULD I ASK FOR? ♡
WHAT'S WITH THAT RICKETY LITTLE CUBICLE?
HUH?
DIDN'T I TELL YOU TO GET THE ROYAL ROOM?
I...I'M SORRY...
BUT YOU TOLD ME YOU WANTED THIS TRAIN ONLY A WEEK IN ADVANCE, AND TICKETS ARE HARD TO COME BY...
WE'RE LUCKY WE WERE ABLE TO GET ROOMS AT ALL.
TOSHINORI KAETSU (38) JEWELRY STORE MANAGER
I CAN'T BELIEVE I'M STAYING IN THE SAME TYPE OF ROOM AS *YOU*.
MY WIFE'S LOCKED HERSELF IN. SHE DOESN'T WANT ANYONE TO KNOW SHE'S TRAVELING IN A COMMON BERTH!
KEITARO IZUMO (56) JEWELRY STORE OWNER
THAT'S WHY I SUG-GESTED WE FLY INSTEAD...
BALDERDASH! I WANTED TO TAKE THIS TRAIN TO THE JEWELRY AUCTION TOMORROW!
ER...

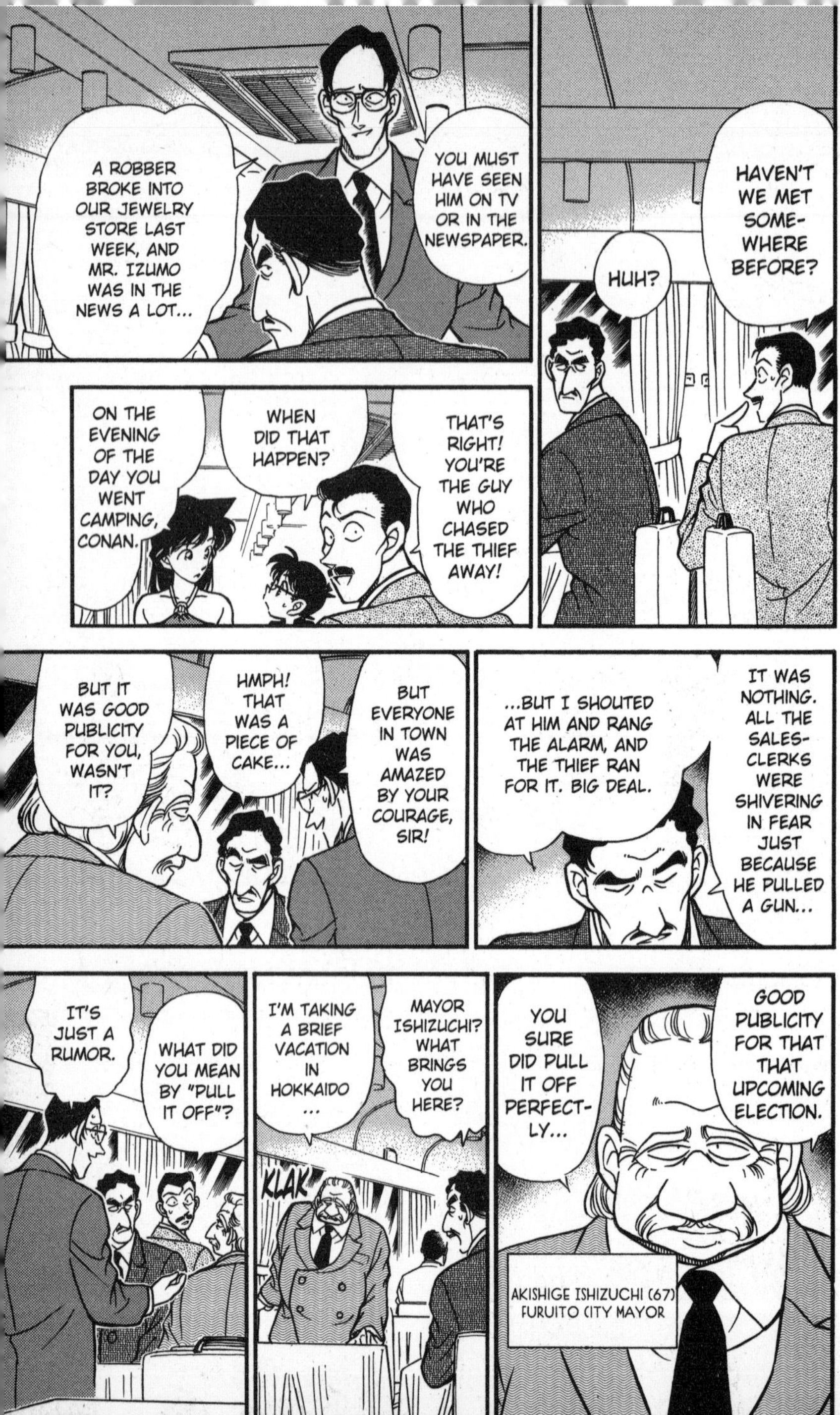
HAVEN'T WE MET SOME-WHERE BEFORE?
HUH?
YOU MUST HAVE SEEN HIM ON TV OR IN THE NEWSPAPER.
A ROBBER BROKE INTO OUR JEWELRY STORE LAST WEEK, AND MR. IZUMO WAS IN THE NEWS A LOT...
THAT'S RIGHT! YOU'RE THE GUY WHO CHASED THE THIEF AWAY!
WHEN DID THAT HAPPEN?
ON THE EVENING OF THE DAY YOU WENT CAMPING, CONAN.
IT WAS NOTHING. ALL THE SALES-CLERKS WERE SHIVERING IN FEAR JUST BECAUSE HE PULLED A GUN...
...BUT I SHOUTED AT HIM AND RANG THE ALARM, AND THE THIEF RAN FOR IT. BIG DEAL.
BUT EVERYONE IN TOWN WAS AMAZED BY YOUR COURAGE, SIR!
HMPH! THAT WAS A PIECE OF CAKE...
BUT IT WAS GOOD PUBLICITY FOR YOU, WASN'T IT?
GOOD PUBLICITY FOR THAT UPCOMING ELECTION.
YOU SURE DID PULL IT OFF PERFECT-LY...
AKISHIGE ISHIZUCHI (67) FURUITO CITY MAYOR
KLAK
MAYOR ISHIZUCHI? WHAT BRINGS YOU HERE?
I'M TAKING A BRIEF VACATION IN HOKKAIDO ...
WHAT DID YOU MEAN BY "PULL IT OFF"?
IT'S JUST A RUMOR.

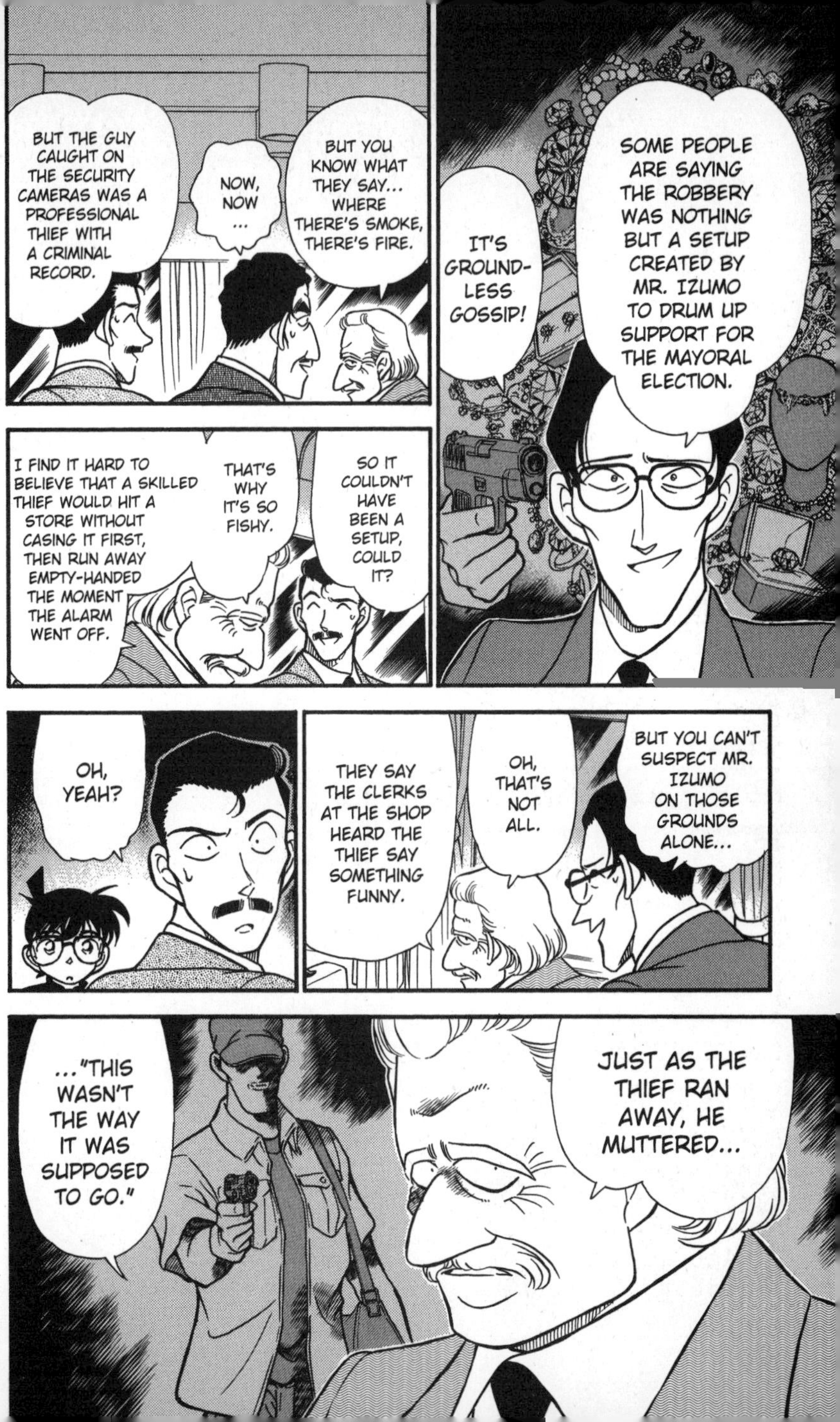
SOME PEOPLE ARE SAYING THE ROBBERY WAS NOTHING BUT A SETUP CREATED BY MR. IZUMO TO DRUM UP SUPPORT FOR THE MAYORAL ELECTION.
IT'S GROUNDLESS GOSSIP!
BUT YOU KNOW WHAT THEY SAY... WHERE THERE'S SMOKE, THERE'S FIRE.
NOW, NOW ...
BUT THE GUY CAUGHT ON THE SECURITY CAMERAS WAS A PROFESSIONAL THIEF WITH A CRIMINAL RECORD.
SO IT COULDN'T HAVE BEEN A SETUP, COULD IT?
THAT'S WHY IT'S SO FISHY.
I FIND IT HARD TO BELIEVE THAT A SKILLED THIEF WOULD HIT A STORE WITHOUT CASING IT FIRST, THEN RUN AWAY EMPTY-HANDED THE MOMENT THE ALARM WENT OFF.
BUT YOU CAN'T SUSPECT MR. IZUMO ON THOSE GROUNDS ALONE...
OH, THAT'S NOT ALL.
THEY SAY THE CLERKS AT THE SHOP HEARD THE THIEF SAY SOMETHING FUNNY.
OH, YEAH?
JUST AS THE THIEF RAN AWAY, HE MUTTERED...
..."THIS WASN'T THE WAY IT WAS SUPPOSED TO GO."

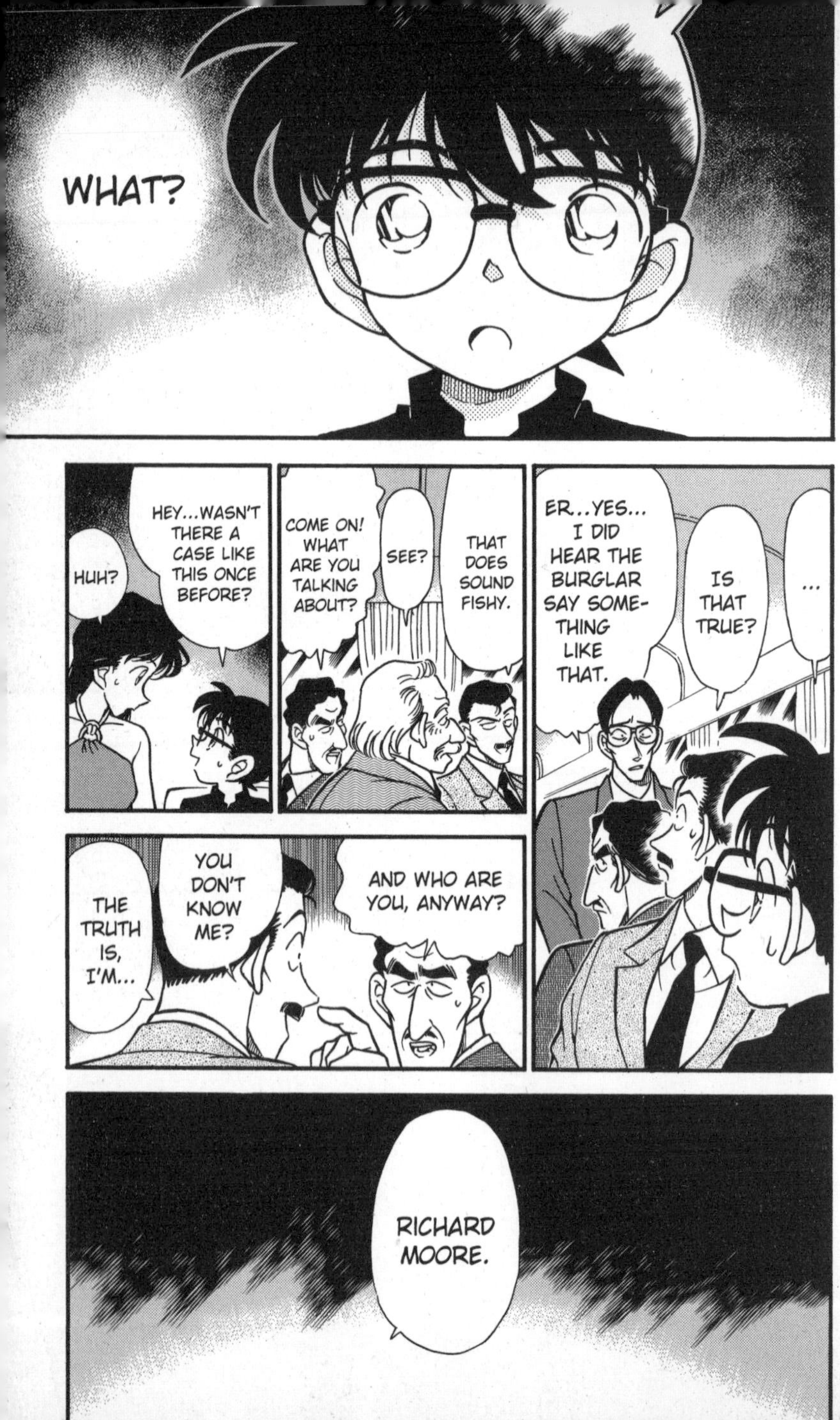
WHAT?
...
IS THAT TRUE?
ER...YES... I DID HEAR THE BURGLAR SAY SOME-THING LIKE THAT.
THAT DOES SOUND FISHY.
SEE?
COME ON! WHAT ARE YOU TALKING ABOUT?
HEY...WASN'T THERE A CASE LIKE THIS ONCE BEFORE?
HUH?
AND WHO ARE YOU, ANYWAY?
YOU DON'T KNOW ME?
THE TRUTH IS, I'M...
RICHARD MOORE.

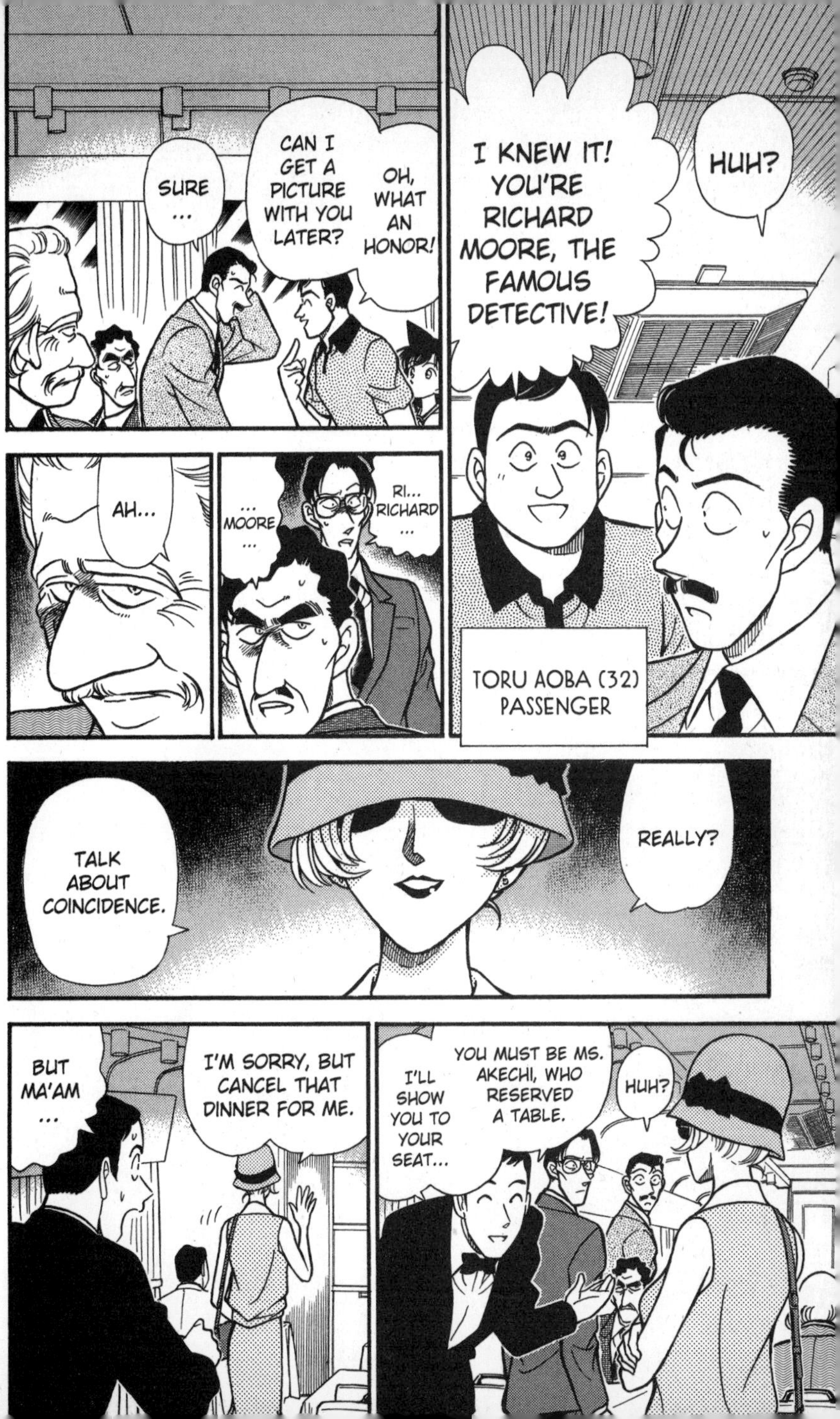
HUH?
I KNEW IT! YOU'RE RICHARD MOORE, THE FAMOUS DETECTIVE!
TORU AOBA (32) PASSENGER
OH, WHAT AN HONOR!
CAN I GET A PICTURE WITH YOU LATER?
SURE ...
RI... RICHARD ...
... MOORE ...
AH...
REALLY?
TALK ABOUT COINCIDENCE.
HUH?
YOU MUST BE MS. AKECHI, WHO RESERVED A TABLE.
I'LL SHOW YOU TO YOUR SEAT...
I'M SORRY, BUT CANCEL THAT DINNER FOR ME.
BUT MA'AM ...

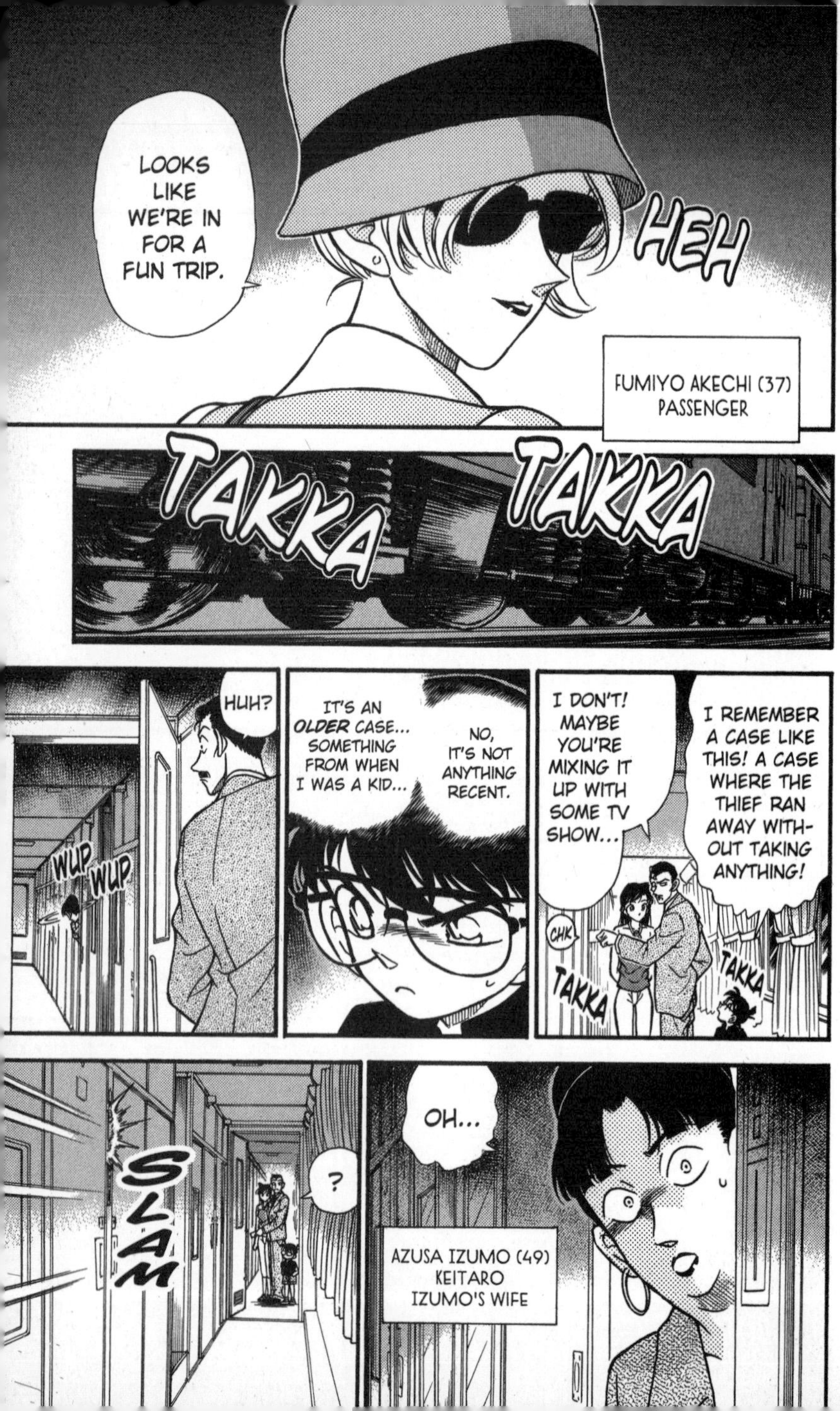
LOOKS LIKE WE'RE IN FOR A FUN TRIP.
HEH
FUMIYO AKECHI (37)
PASSENGER
TAKKA
TAKKA
I REMEMBER A CASE LIKE THIS! A CASE WHERE THE THIEF RAN AWAY WITHOUT TAKING ANYTHING!
I DON'T! MAYBE YOU'RE MIXING IT UP WITH SOME TV SHOW...
CHK
TAKKA
TAKKA
NO, IT'S NOT ANYTHING RECENT.
IT'S AN OLDER CASE... SOMETHING FROM WHEN I WAS A KID...
HUH?
WUP
WUP
OH...
?
AZUSA IZUMO (49)
KEITARO IZUMO'S WIFE
SLAM

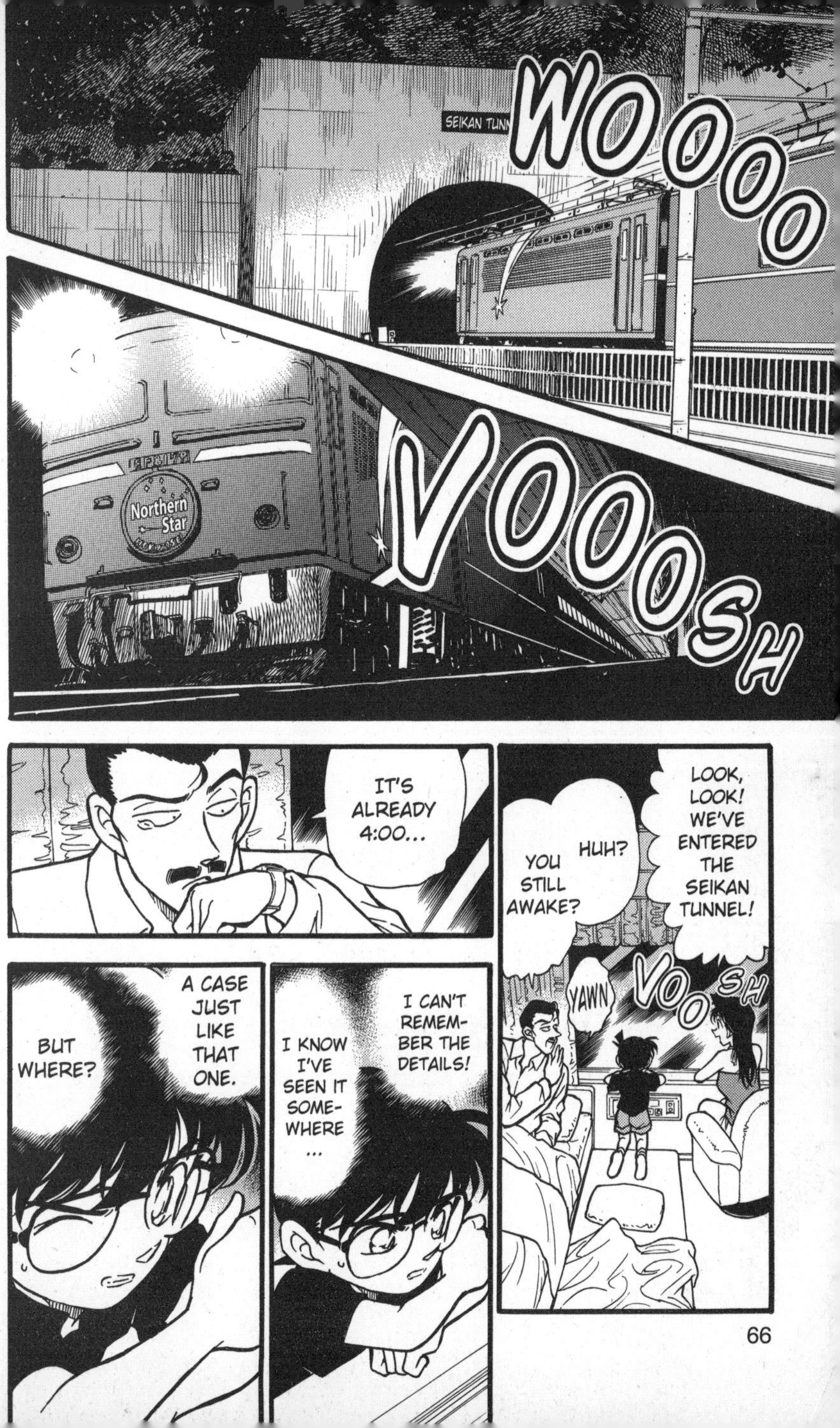
SEIKAN TUNN
WOOOO
Northern Star
VOOOOSH
LOOK, LOOK! WE'VE ENTERED THE SEIKAN TUNNEL!
HUH?
YOU STILL AWAKE?
VOOSH
YAWN
IT'S ALREADY 4:00...
I CAN'T REMEM- BER THE DETAILS!
I KNOW I'VE SEEN IT SOME- WHERE ...
A CASE JUST LIKE THAT ONE.
BUT WHERE?

THE GUNSHOT AND SCREAM DROWNED OUT THE THUNDERING ROAR INSIDE THE TUNNEL...

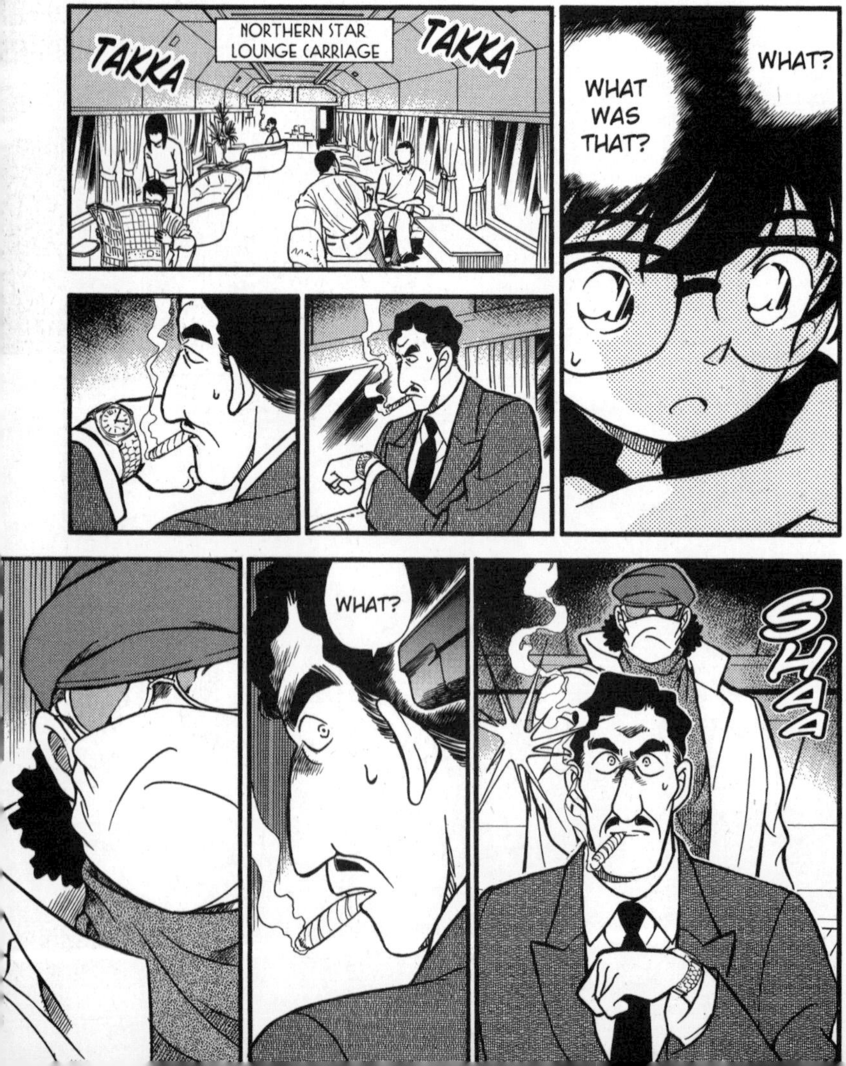
WHAT?
WHAT WAS THAT?
TAKKA
NORTHERN STAR LOUNGE CARRIAGE
TAKKA
SHAA
WHAT?

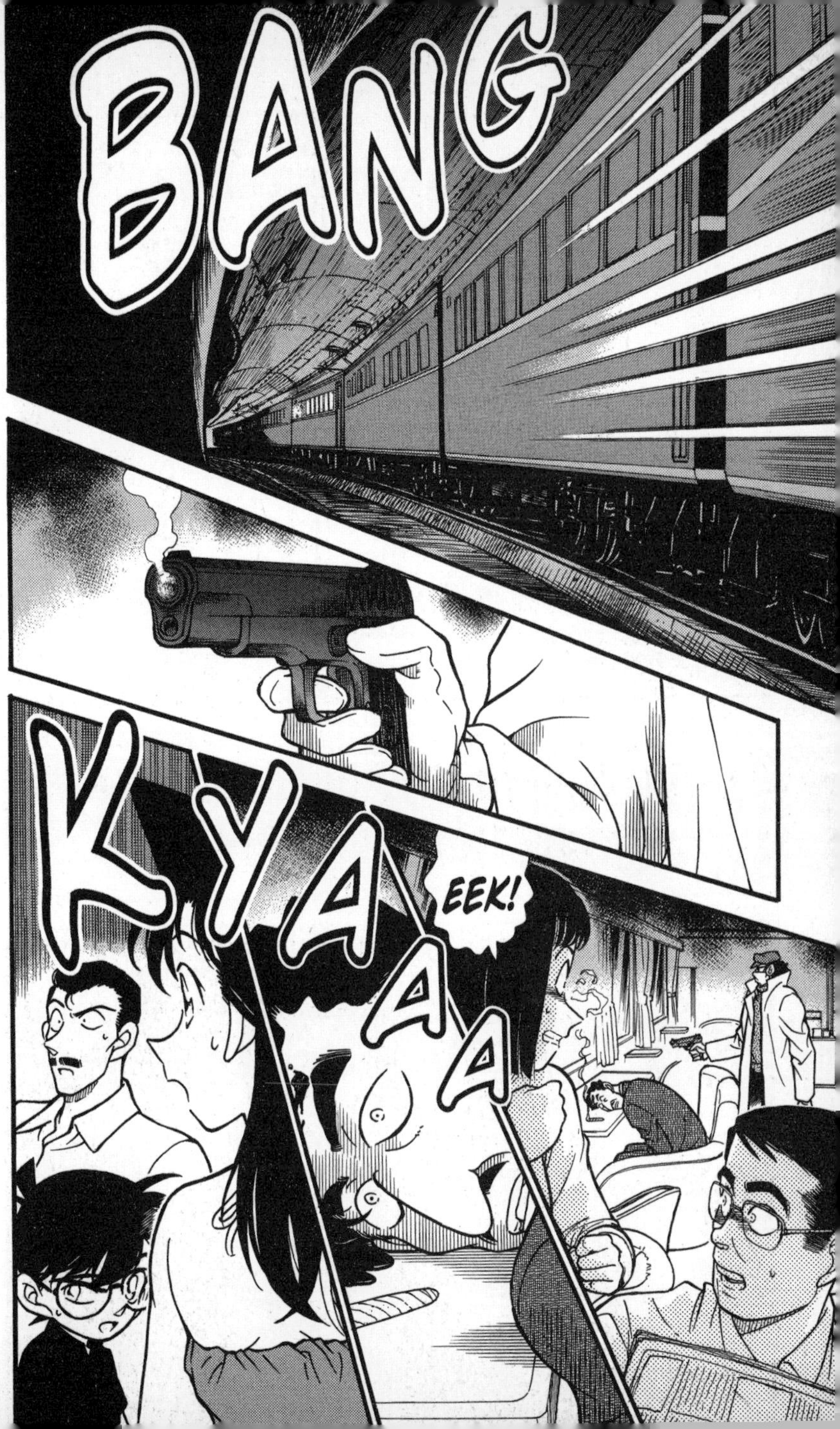
BANG
KYAAAA
EEK!

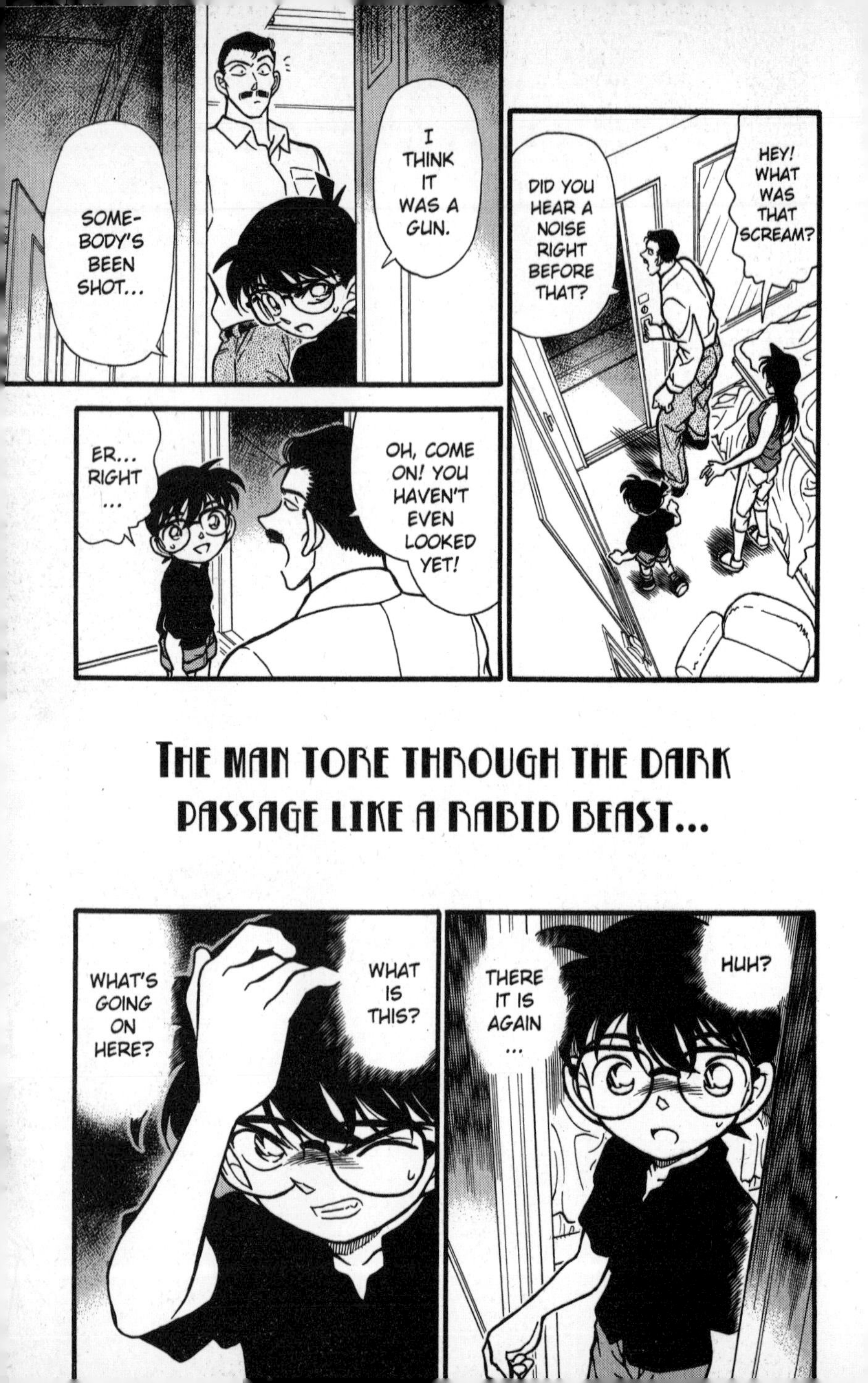
HEY! WHAT WAS THAT SCREAM?
DID YOU HEAR A NOISE RIGHT BEFORE THAT?
I THINK IT WAS A GUN.
SOME-BODY'S BEEN SHOT...
OH, COME ON! YOU HAVEN'T EVEN LOOKED YET!
ER... RIGHT...
THE MAN TORE THROUGH THE DARK PASSAGE LIKE A RABID BEAST...
HUH?
THERE IT IS AGAIN...
WHAT IS THIS?
WHAT'S GOING ON HERE?

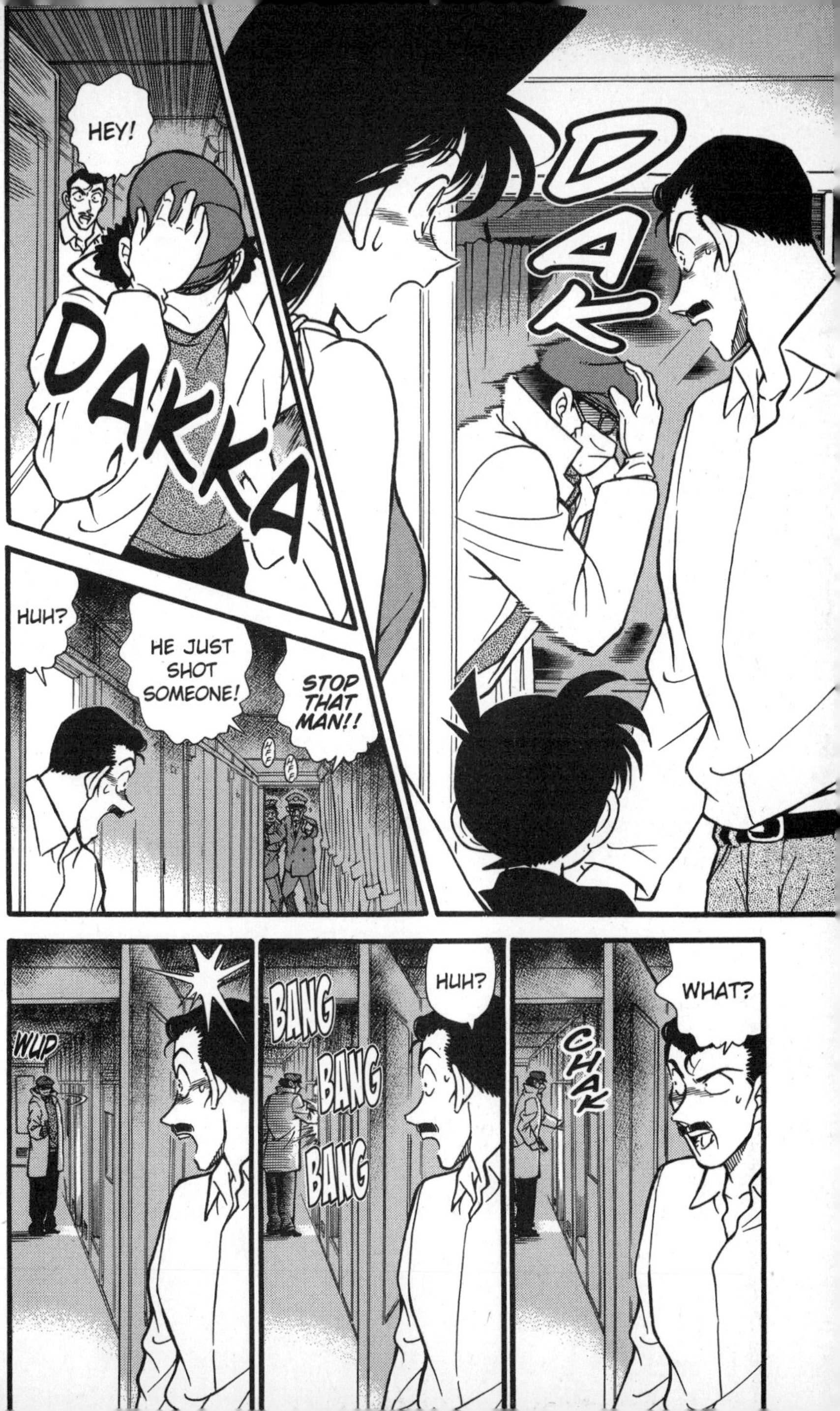
DAK
HEY!
DAKKA
STOP THAT MAN!!
HE JUST SHOT SOMEONE!
HUH?
WHAT?
CHAK
HUH?
BANG
BANG
BANG
WUP

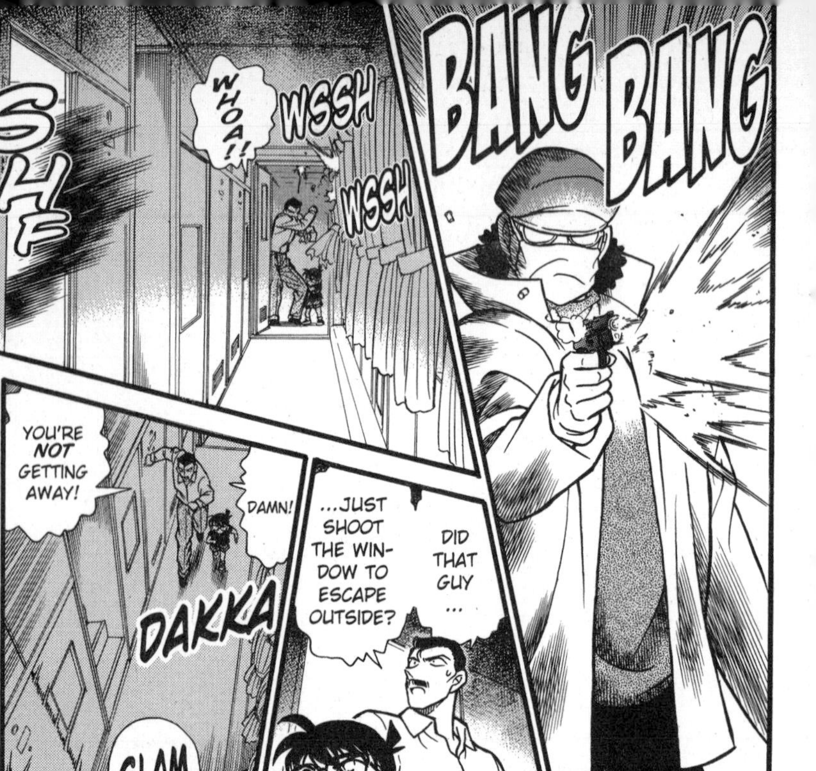
BANG BANG
WSSH
WSSH
WHOA!!
SHF
DID THAT GUY...
...JUST SHOOT THE WIN-DOW TO ESCAPE OUTSIDE?
DAMN!
YOU'RE NOT GETTING AWAY!
DAKKA
SLAM

BUT THE MAN WAS NOWHERE TO BE FOUND...

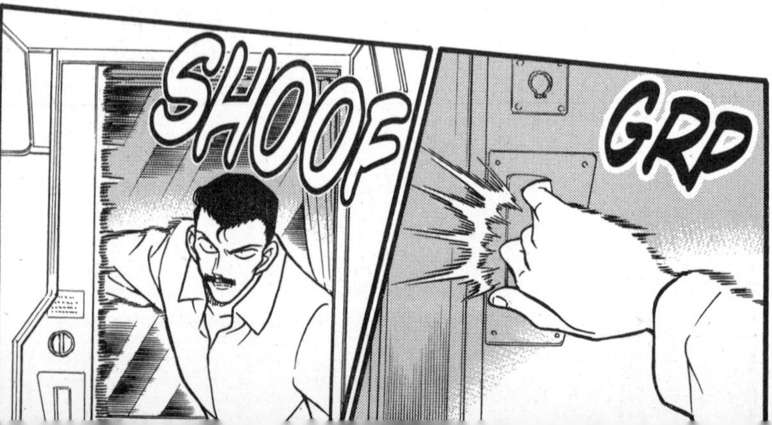
GRD
SHOOF

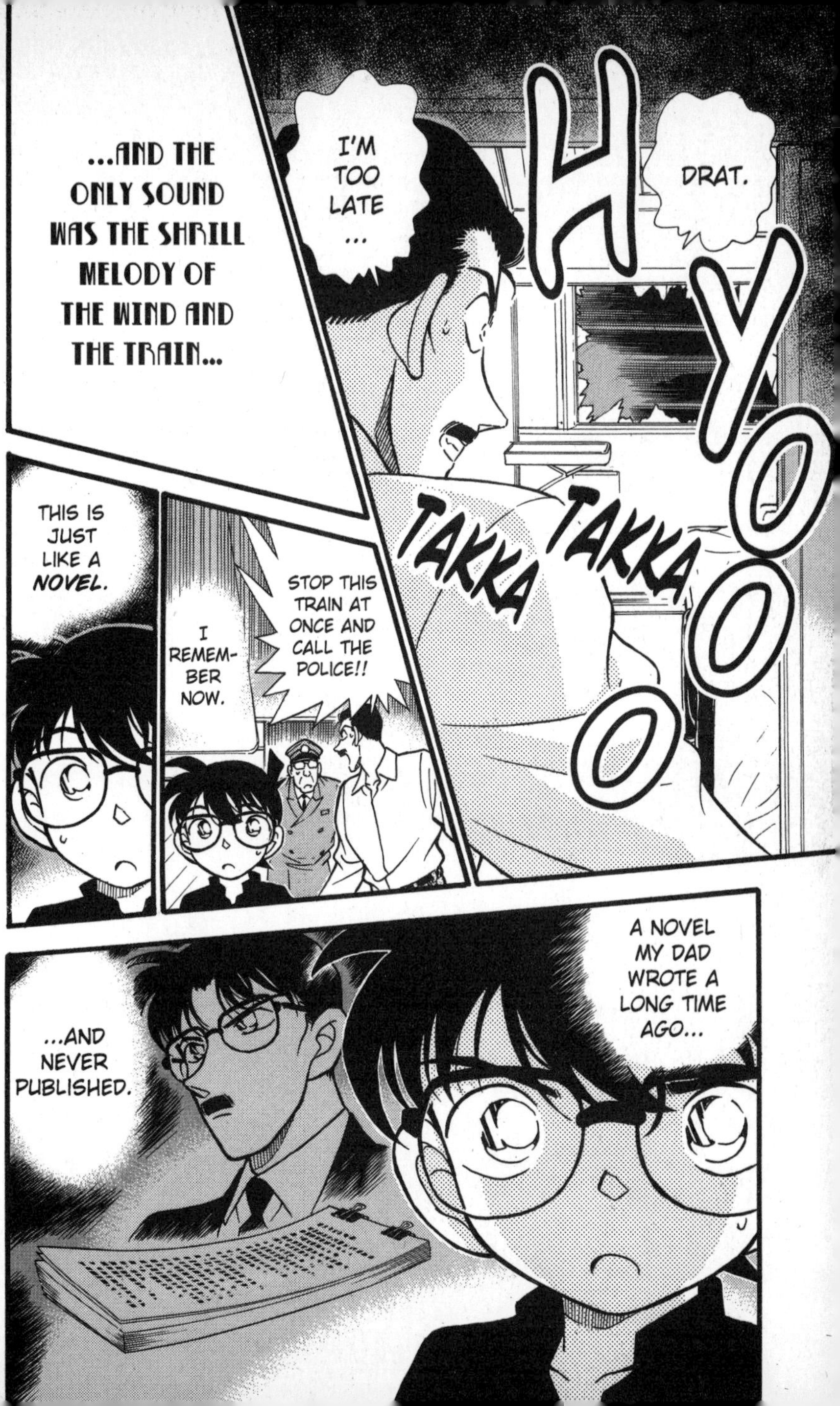
DRAT.
HYOOOO
I'M TOO LATE ...
TAKKA TAKKA
...AND THE ONLY SOUND WAS THE SHRILL MELODY OF THE WIND AND THE TRAIN...
STOP THIS TRAIN AT ONCE AND CALL THE POLICE!!
I REMEMBER NOW.
THIS IS JUST LIKE A ***NOVEL***.
A NOVEL MY DAD WROTE A LONG TIME AGO...
...AND NEVER PUBLISHED.

FILE 5: GIVE YOURSELF AWAY

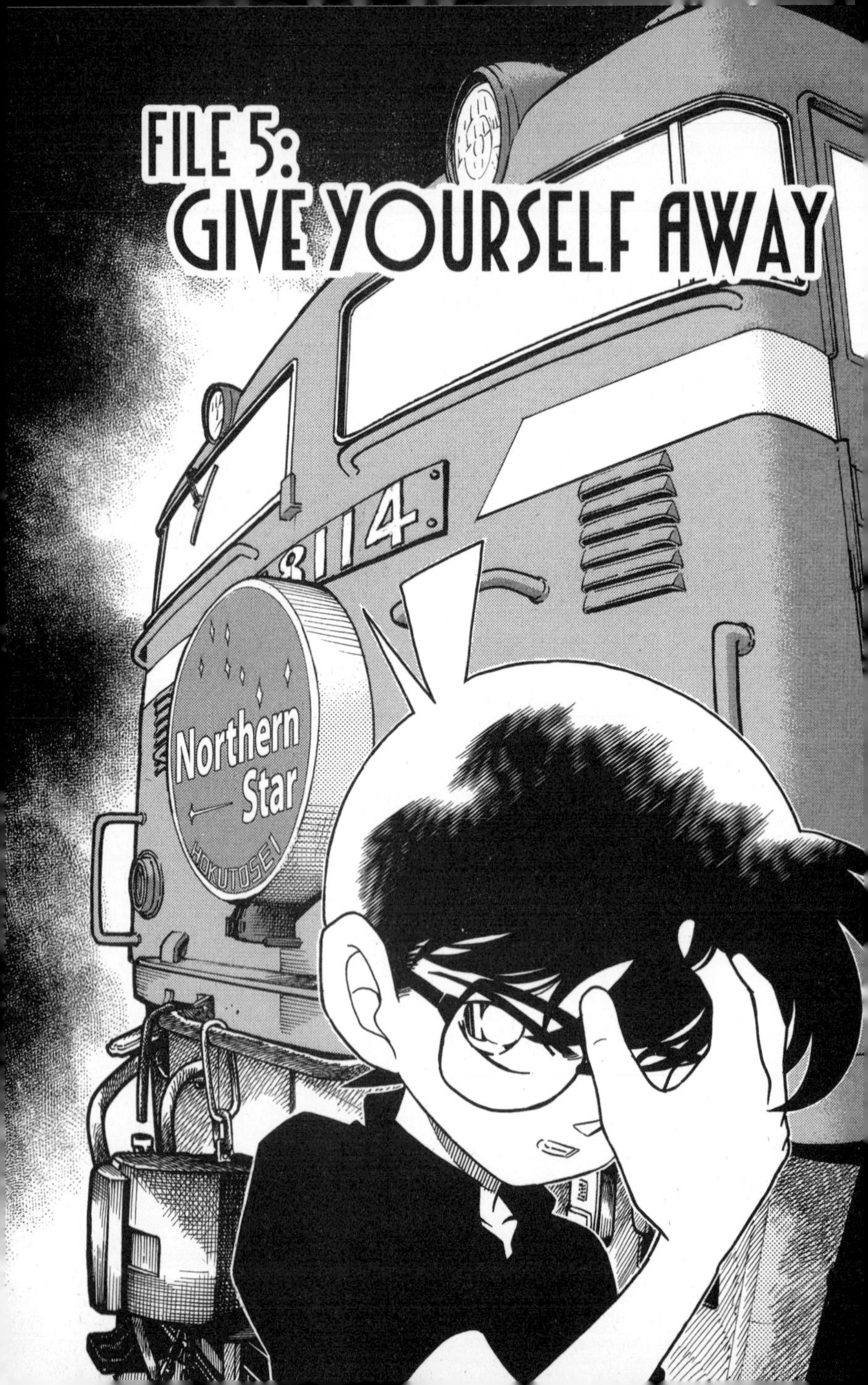
Northern Star
HOKUTOSEI

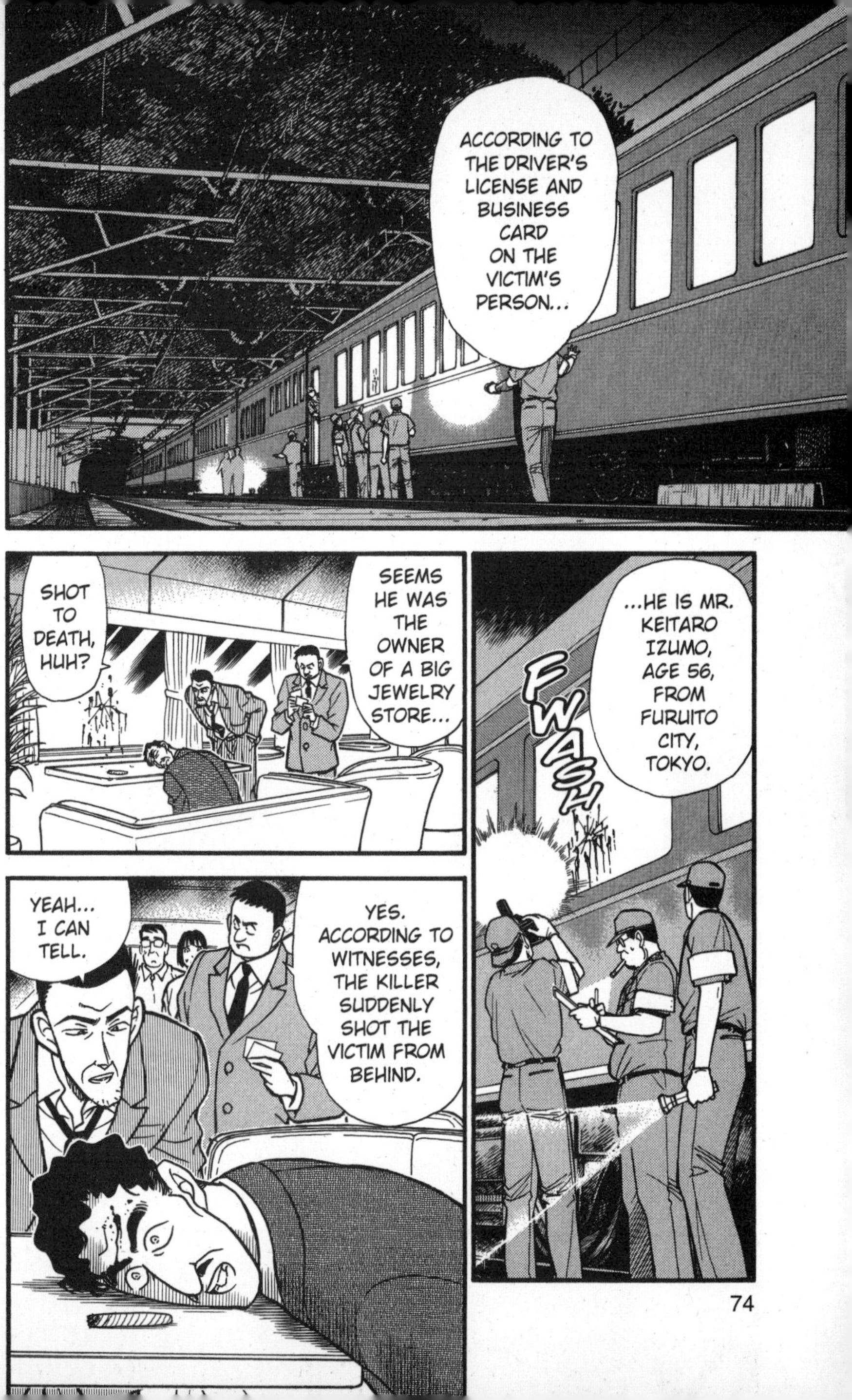
ACCORDING TO THE DRIVER'S LICENSE AND BUSINESS CARD ON THE VICTIM'S PERSON...
...HE IS MR. KEITARO IZUMO, AGE 56, FROM FURUITO CITY, TOKYO.
FWASH
SEEMS HE WAS THE OWNER OF A BIG JEWELRY STORE...
SHOT TO DEATH, HUH?
YES. ACCORDING TO WITNESSES, THE KILLER SUDDENLY SHOT THE VICTIM FROM BEHIND.
YEAH... I CAN TELL.

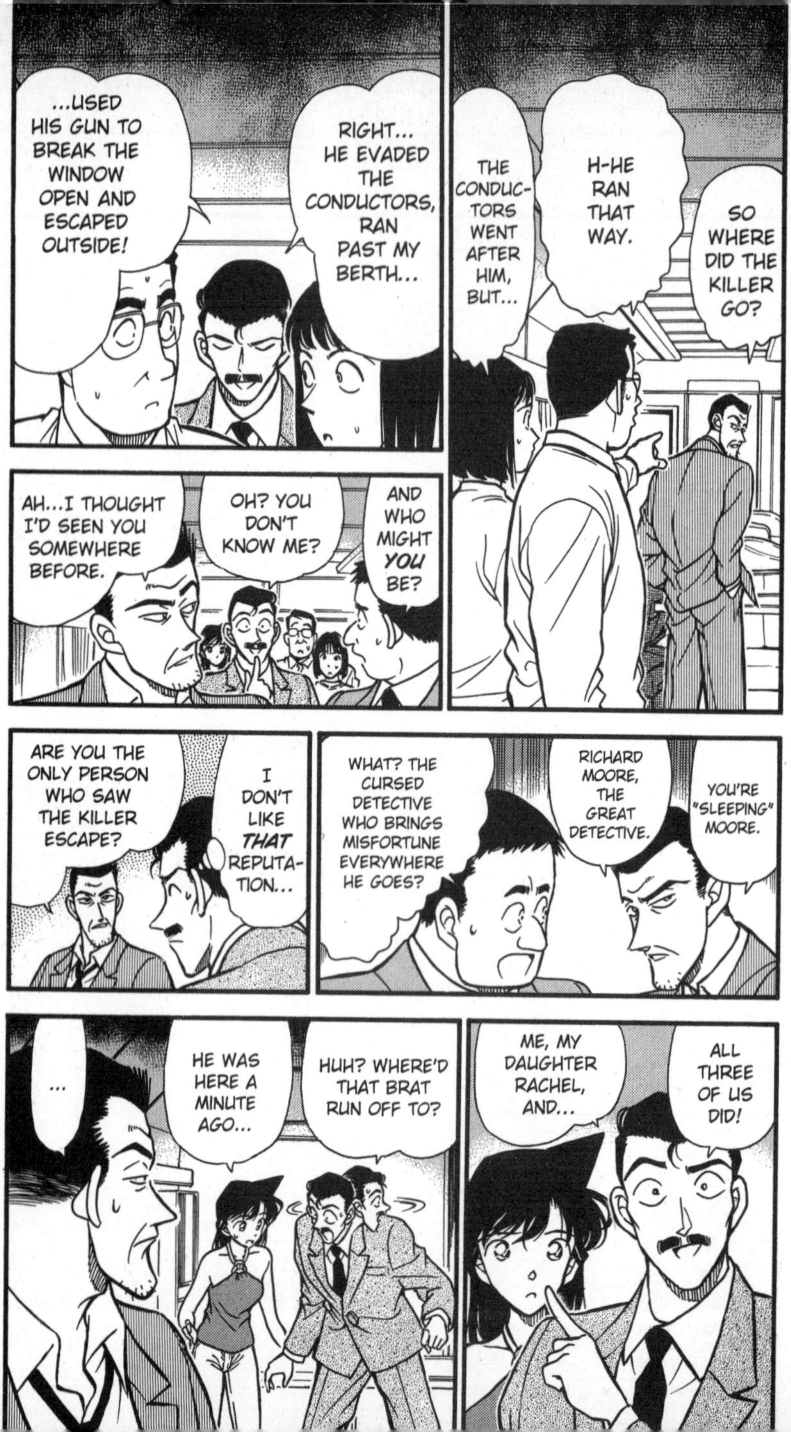
SO WHERE DID THE KILLER GO?
H-HE RAN THAT WAY.
THE CONDUCTORS WENT AFTER HIM, BUT...
RIGHT... HE EVADED THE CONDUCTORS, RAN PAST MY BERTH...
...USED HIS GUN TO BREAK THE WINDOW OPEN AND ESCAPED OUTSIDE!
AND WHO MIGHT *YOU* BE?
OH? YOU DON'T KNOW ME?
AH...I THOUGHT I'D SEEN YOU SOMEWHERE BEFORE.
YOU'RE "SLEEPING" MOORE.
RICHARD MOORE, THE GREAT DETECTIVE.
WHAT? THE CURSED DETECTIVE WHO BRINGS MISFORTUNE EVERYWHERE HE GOES?
I DON'T LIKE *THAT* REPUTATION...
ARE YOU THE ONLY PERSON WHO SAW THE KILLER ESCAPE?
ALL THREE OF US DID!
ME, MY DAUGHTER RACHEL, AND...
HUH? WHERE'D THAT BRAT RUN OFF TO?
HE WAS HERE A MINUTE AGO...
...

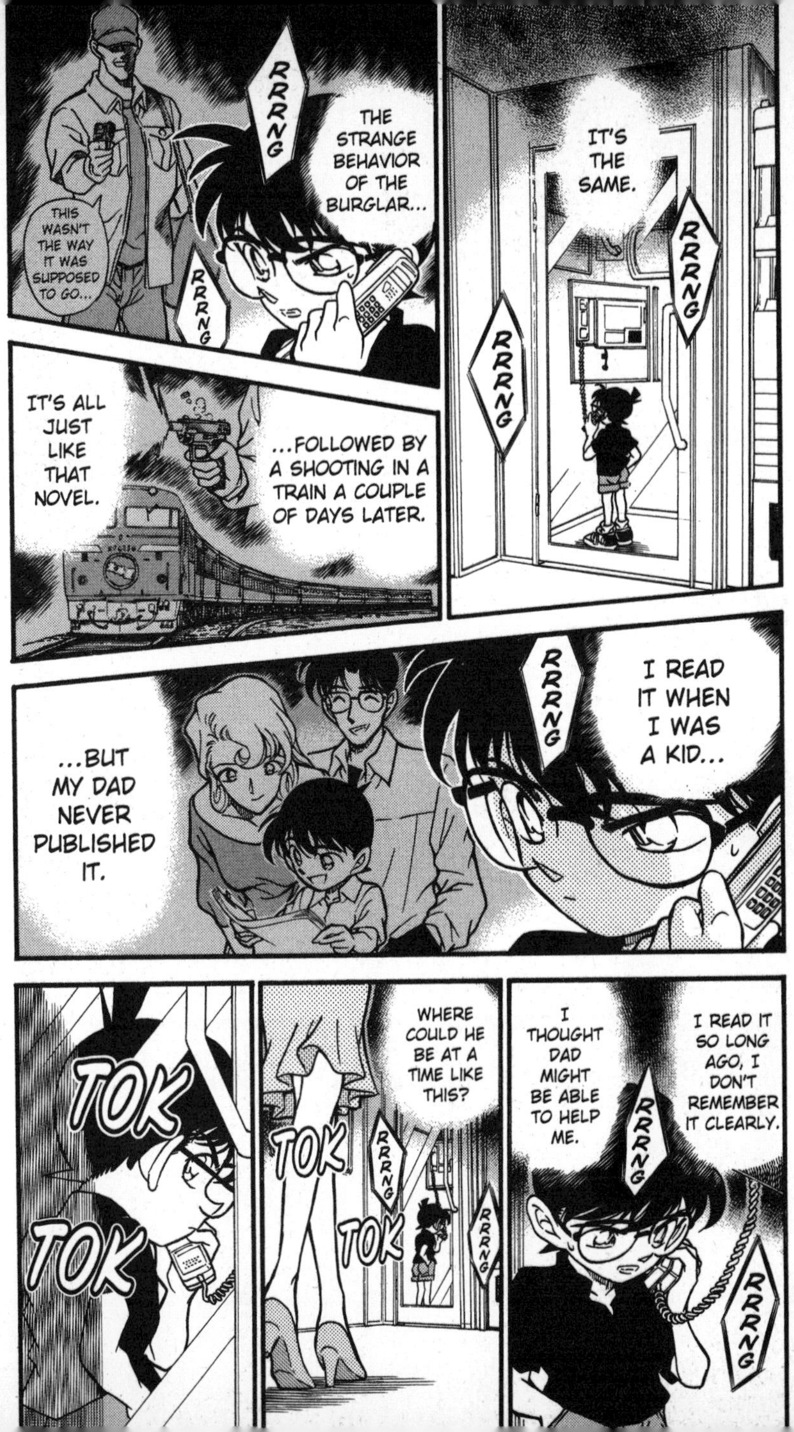

RRRNG
IT'S THE SAME.
RRRNG
RRRNG
THE STRANGE BEHAVIOR OF THE BURGLAR...
THIS WASN'T THE WAY IT WAS SUPPOSED TO GO...
RRRNG
...FOLLOWED BY A SHOOTING IN A TRAIN A COUPLE OF DAYS LATER.
IT'S ALL JUST LIKE THAT NOVEL.
I READ IT WHEN I WAS A KID...
RRRNG
...BUT MY DAD NEVER PUBLISHED IT.
I READ IT SO LONG AGO, I DON'T REMEMBER IT CLEARLY.
I THOUGHT DAD MIGHT BE ABLE TO HELP ME.
RRRNG
RRRNG
WHERE COULD HE BE AT A TIME LIKE THIS?
RRRNG
TOK
RRRNG
TOK
TOK
TOK

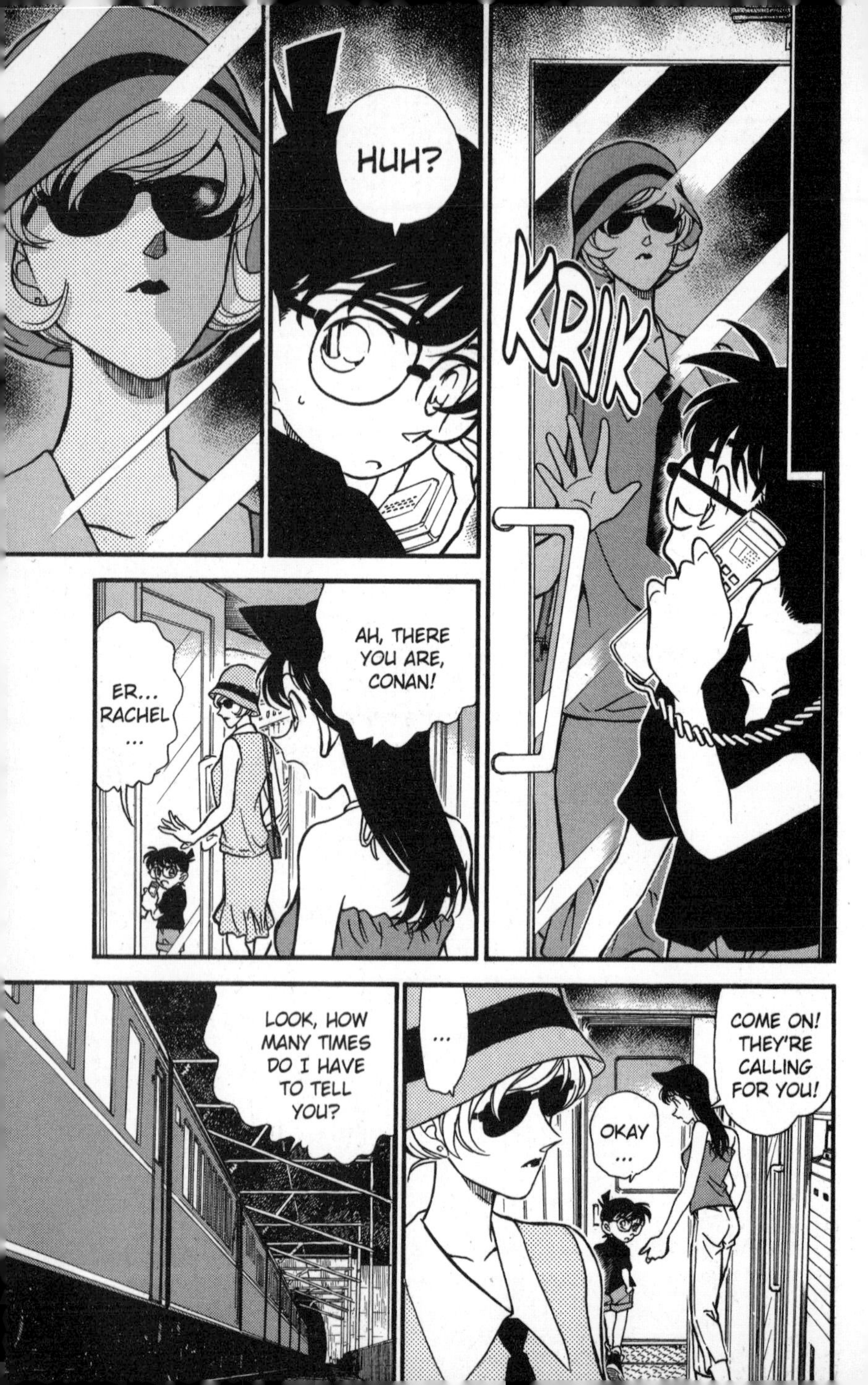
KRIK
HUH?
AH, THERE YOU ARE, CONAN!
ER... RACHEL ...
COME ON! THEY'RE CALLING FOR YOU!
OKAY ...
...
LOOK, HOW MANY TIMES DO I HAVE TO TELL YOU?

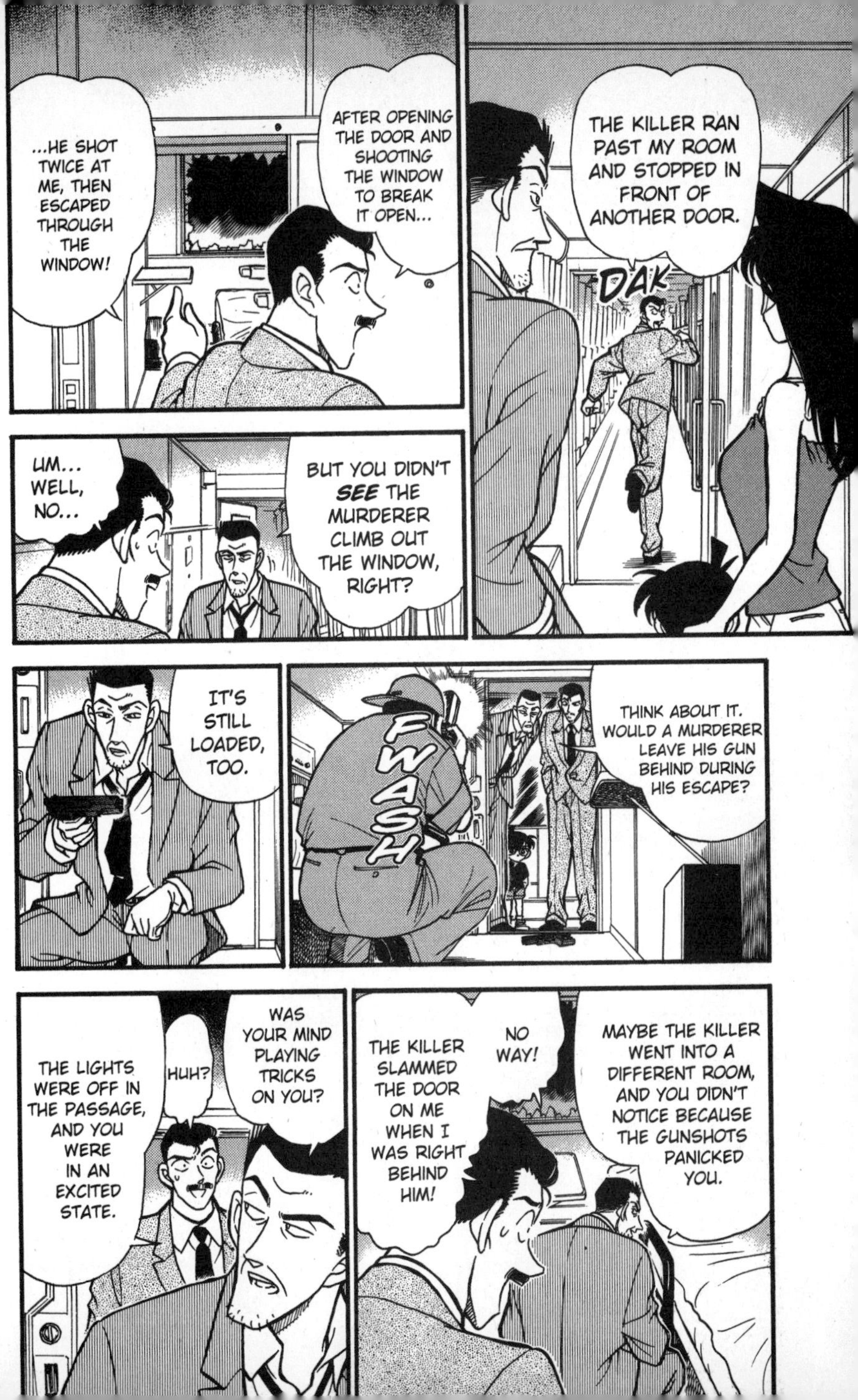
THE KILLER RAN PAST MY ROOM AND STOPPED IN FRONT OF ANOTHER DOOR.
DAK
AFTER OPENING THE DOOR AND SHOOTING THE WINDOW TO BREAK IT OPEN...
...HE SHOT TWICE AT ME, THEN ESCAPED THROUGH THE WINDOW!
BUT YOU DIDN'T *SEE* THE MURDERER CLIMB OUT THE WINDOW, RIGHT?
UM... WELL, NO...
THINK ABOUT IT. WOULD A MURDERER LEAVE HIS GUN BEHIND DURING HIS ESCAPE?
FWASH
IT'S STILL LOADED, TOO.
MAYBE THE KILLER WENT INTO A DIFFERENT ROOM, AND YOU DIDN'T NOTICE BECAUSE THE GUNSHOTS PANICKED YOU.
NO WAY!
THE KILLER SLAMMED THE DOOR ON ME WHEN I WAS RIGHT BEHIND HIM!
WAS YOUR MIND PLAYING TRICKS ON YOU?
HUH?
THE LIGHTS WERE OFF IN THE PASSAGE, AND YOU WERE IN AN EXCITED STATE.

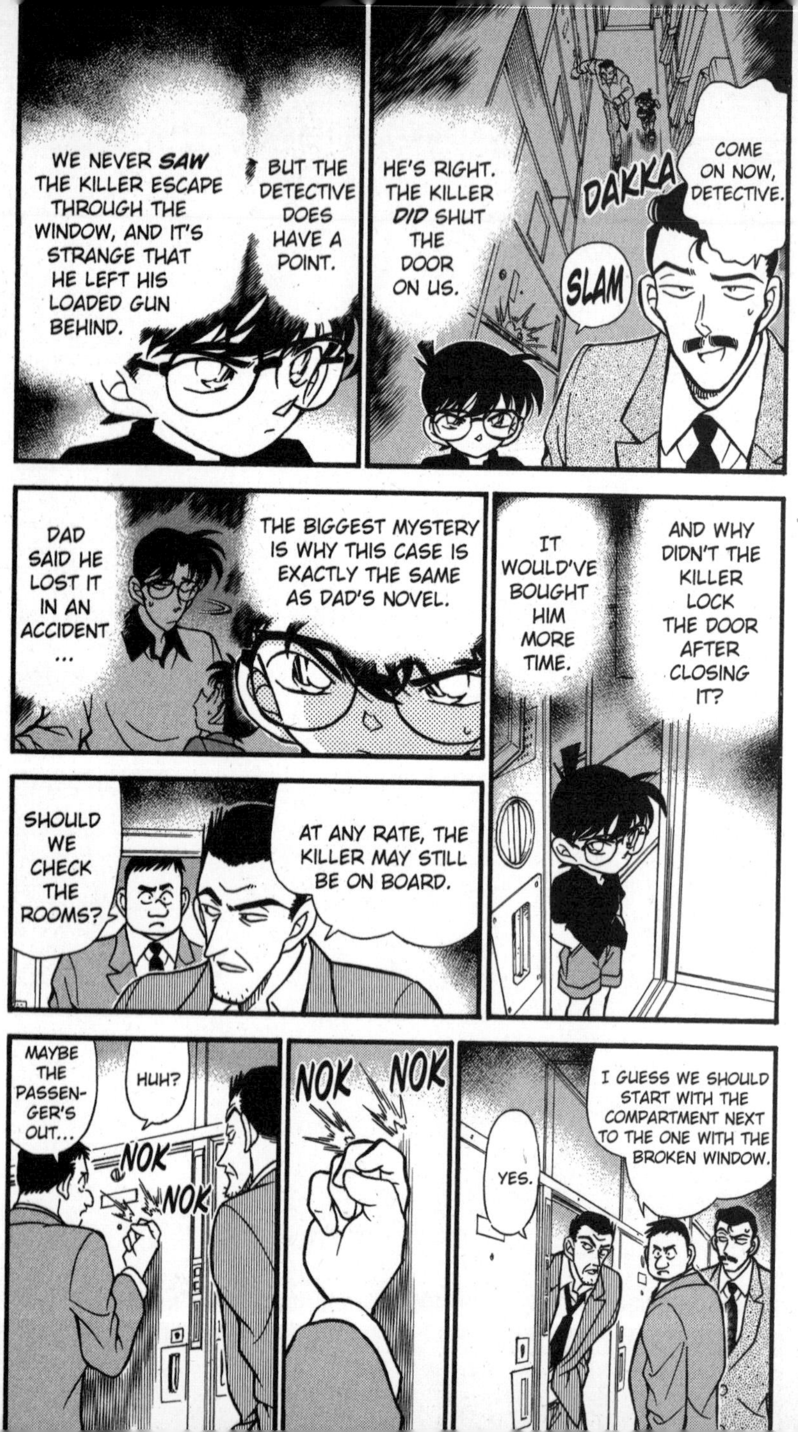
COME ON NOW, DETECTIVE.
DAKKA
SLAM
HE'S RIGHT. THE KILLER *DID* SHUT THE DOOR ON US.
BUT THE DETECTIVE DOES HAVE A POINT.
WE NEVER ***SAW*** THE KILLER ESCAPE THROUGH THE WINDOW, AND IT'S STRANGE THAT HE LEFT HIS LOADED GUN BEHIND.
AND WHY DIDN'T THE KILLER LOCK THE DOOR AFTER CLOSING IT?
IT WOULD'VE BOUGHT HIM MORE TIME.
THE BIGGEST MYSTERY IS WHY THIS CASE IS EXACTLY THE SAME AS DAD'S NOVEL.
DAD SAID HE LOST IT IN AN ACCIDENT...
AT ANY RATE, THE KILLER MAY STILL BE ON BOARD.
SHOULD WE CHECK THE ROOMS?
I GUESS WE SHOULD START WITH THE COMPARTMENT NEXT TO THE ONE WITH THE BROKEN WINDOW.
YES.
NOK NOK
HUH?
NOK NOK
MAYBE THE PASSENGER'S OUT...

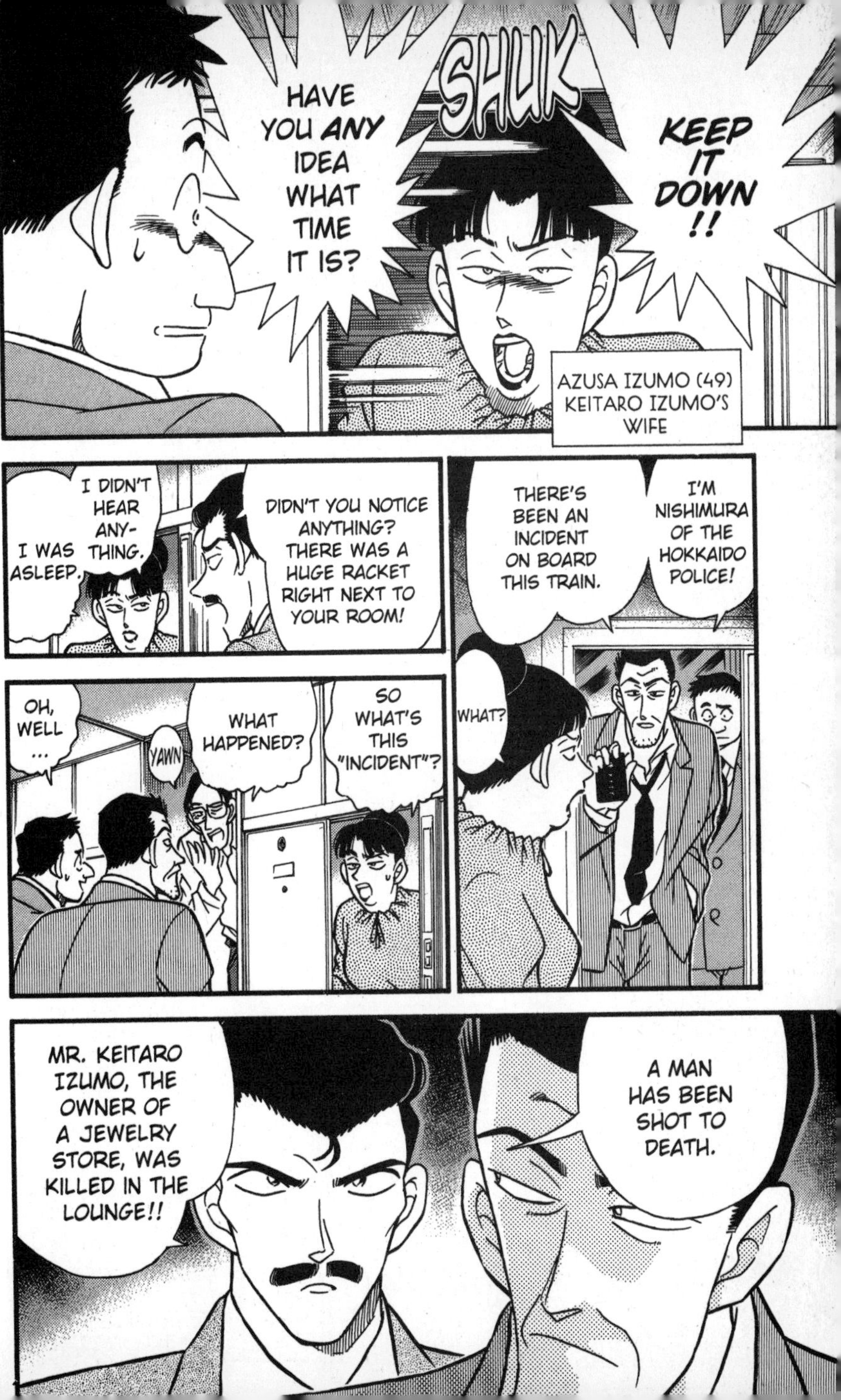
SHUK
KEEP IT DOWN!!
AZUSA IZUMO (49) KEITARO IZUMO'S WIFE
HAVE YOU ANY IDEA WHAT TIME IT IS?
I'M NISHIMURA OF THE HOKKAIDO POLICE!
THERE'S BEEN AN INCIDENT ON BOARD THIS TRAIN.
WHAT?
DIDN'T YOU NOTICE ANYTHING? THERE WAS A HUGE RACKET RIGHT NEXT TO YOUR ROOM!
I DIDN'T HEAR ANY-THING.
I WAS ASLEEP.
SO WHAT'S THIS "INCIDENT"?
WHAT HAPPENED?
YAWN
OH, WELL ...
A MAN HAS BEEN SHOT TO DEATH.
MR. KEITARO IZUMO, THE OWNER OF A JEWELRY STORE, WAS KILLED IN THE LOUNGE!!

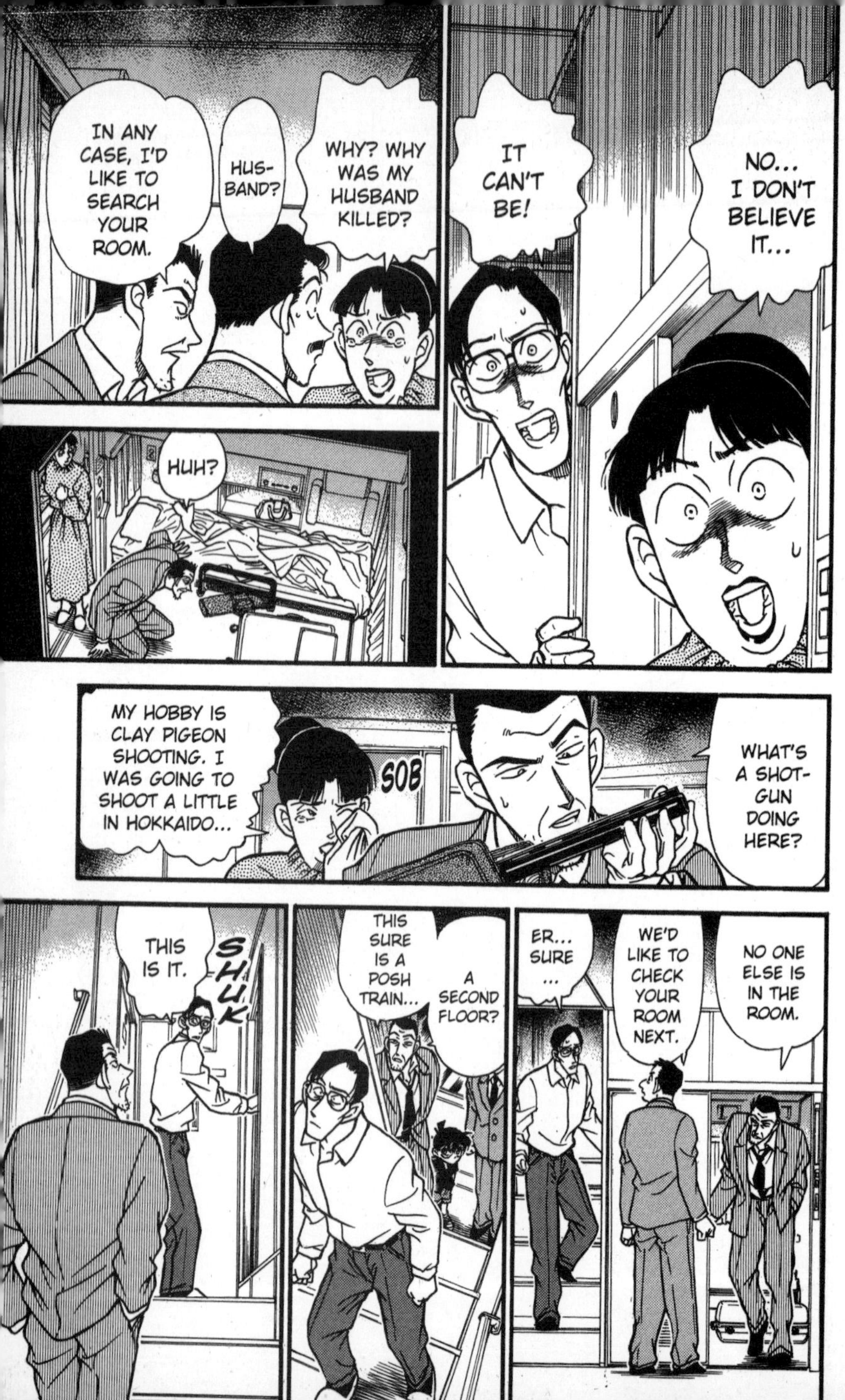
NO... I DON'T BELIEVE IT...
IT CAN'T BE!
WHY? WHY WAS MY HUSBAND KILLED?
HUS-BAND?
IN ANY CASE, I'D LIKE TO SEARCH YOUR ROOM.
HUH?
WHAT'S A SHOT-GUN DOING HERE?
SOB
MY HOBBY IS CLAY PIGEON SHOOTING. I WAS GOING TO SHOOT A LITTLE IN HOKKAIDO...
NO ONE ELSE IS IN THE ROOM.
WE'D LIKE TO CHECK YOUR ROOM NEXT.
ER... SURE...
A SECOND FLOOR?
THIS SURE IS A POSH TRAIN...
SHUK
THIS IS IT.

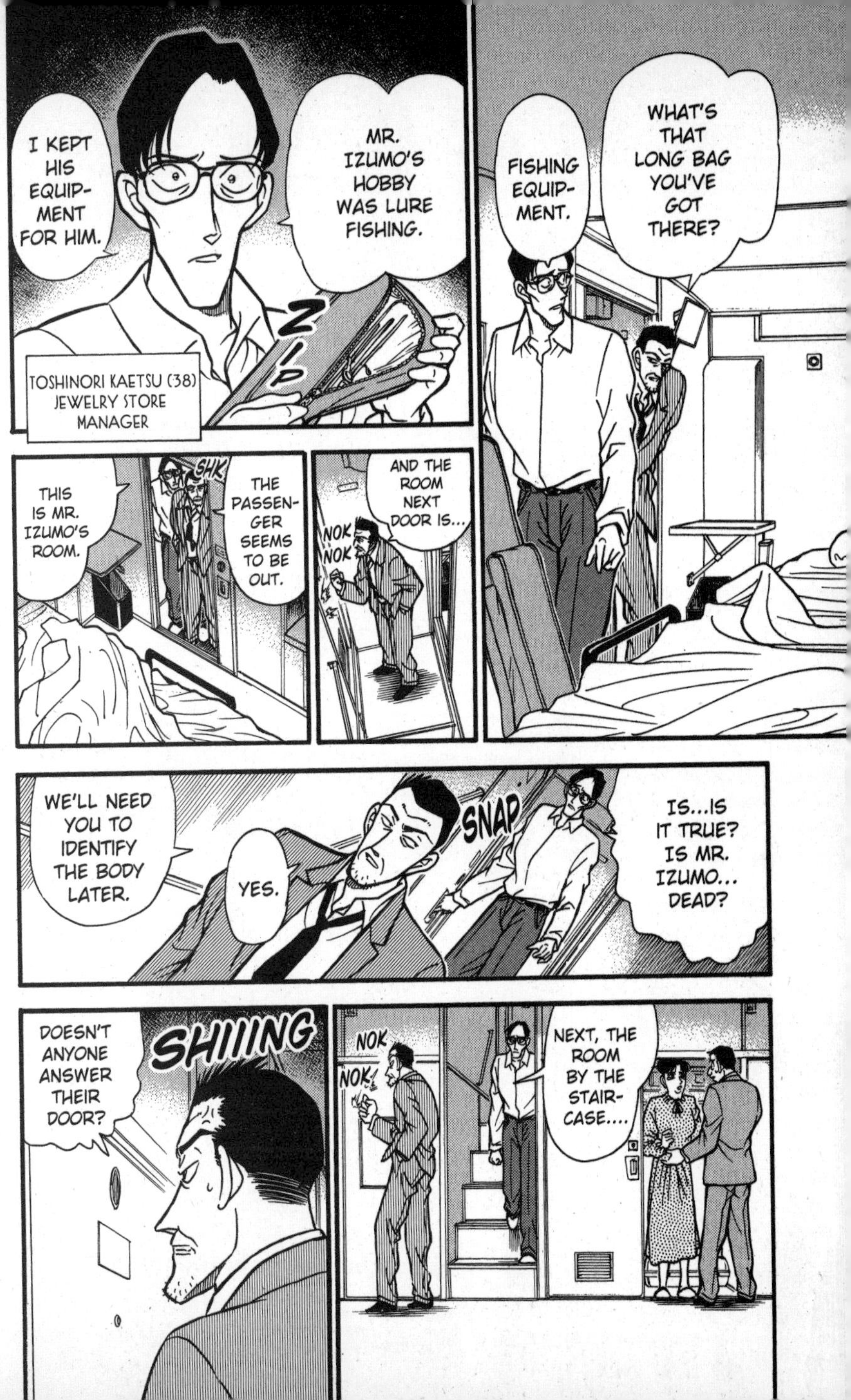
WHAT'S THAT LONG BAG YOU'VE GOT THERE?
FISHING EQUIPMENT.
MR. IZUMO'S HOBBY WAS LURE FISHING.
I KEPT HIS EQUIPMENT FOR HIM.
ZIP
TOSHINORI KAETSU (38) JEWELRY STORE MANAGER
AND THE ROOM NEXT DOOR IS...
NOK NOK
SHK
THE PASSENGER SEEMS TO BE OUT.
THIS IS MR. IZUMO'S ROOM.
IS...IS IT TRUE? IS MR. IZUMO... DEAD?
SNAP
YES.
WE'LL NEED YOU TO IDENTIFY THE BODY LATER.
NEXT, THE ROOM BY THE STAIRCASE....
NOK NOK
SHIIIING
DOESN'T ANYONE ANSWER THEIR DOOR?

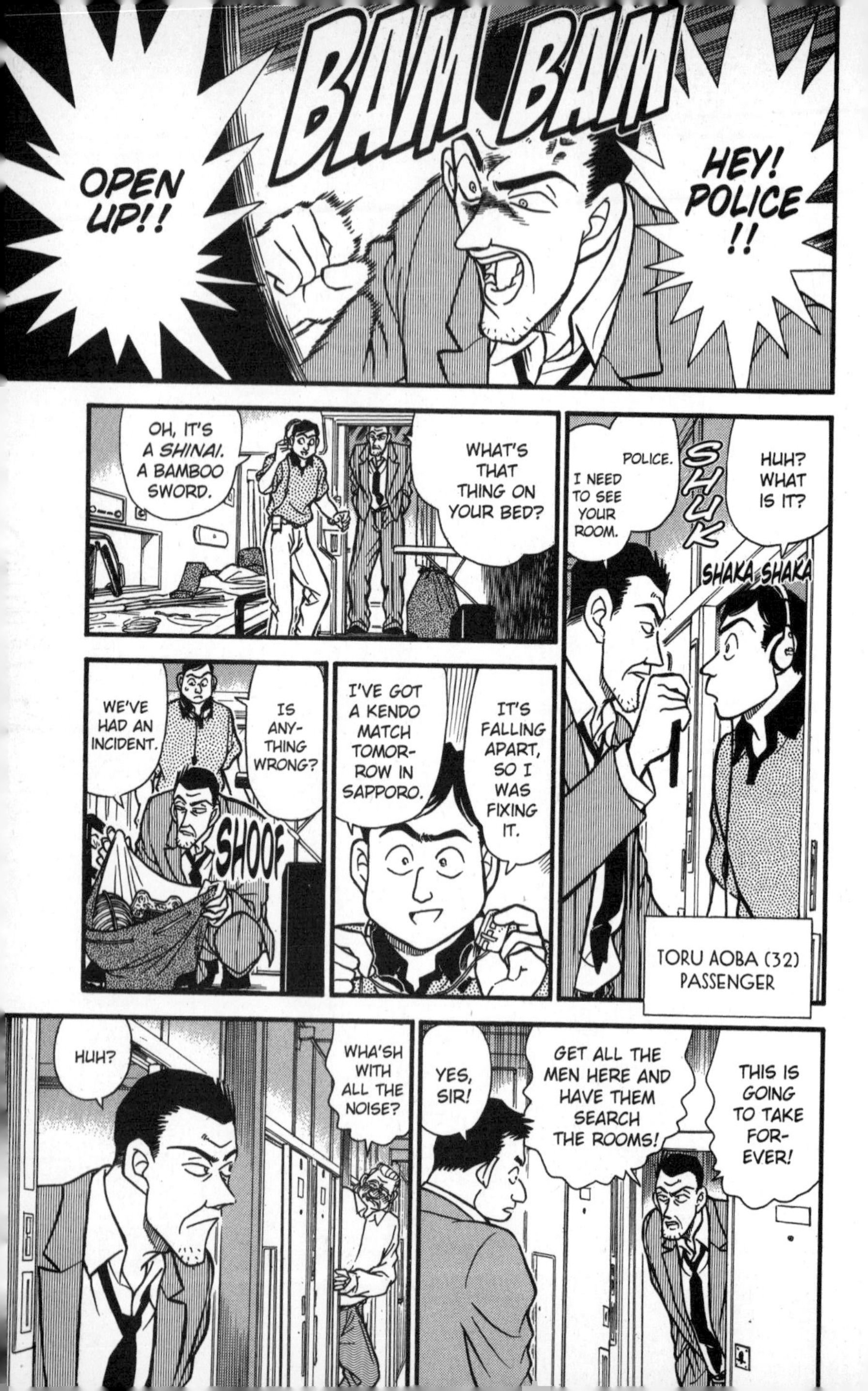
BAM BAM
HEY! POLICE!!
OPEN UP!!
HUH? WHAT IS IT?
SHUK
SHAKA SHAKA
POLICE. I NEED TO SEE YOUR ROOM.
TORU AOBA (32) PASSENGER
WHAT'S THAT THING ON YOUR BED?
OH, IT'S A *SHINAI*. A BAMBOO SWORD.
IT'S FALLING APART, SO I WAS FIXING IT.
I'VE GOT A KENDO MATCH TOMORROW IN SAPPORO.
IS ANYTHING WRONG?
WE'VE HAD AN INCIDENT.
SHOOF
THIS IS GOING TO TAKE FOREVER!
GET ALL THE MEN HERE AND HAVE THEM SEARCH THE ROOMS!
YES, SIR!
WHA'SH WITH ALL THE NOISE?
HUH?

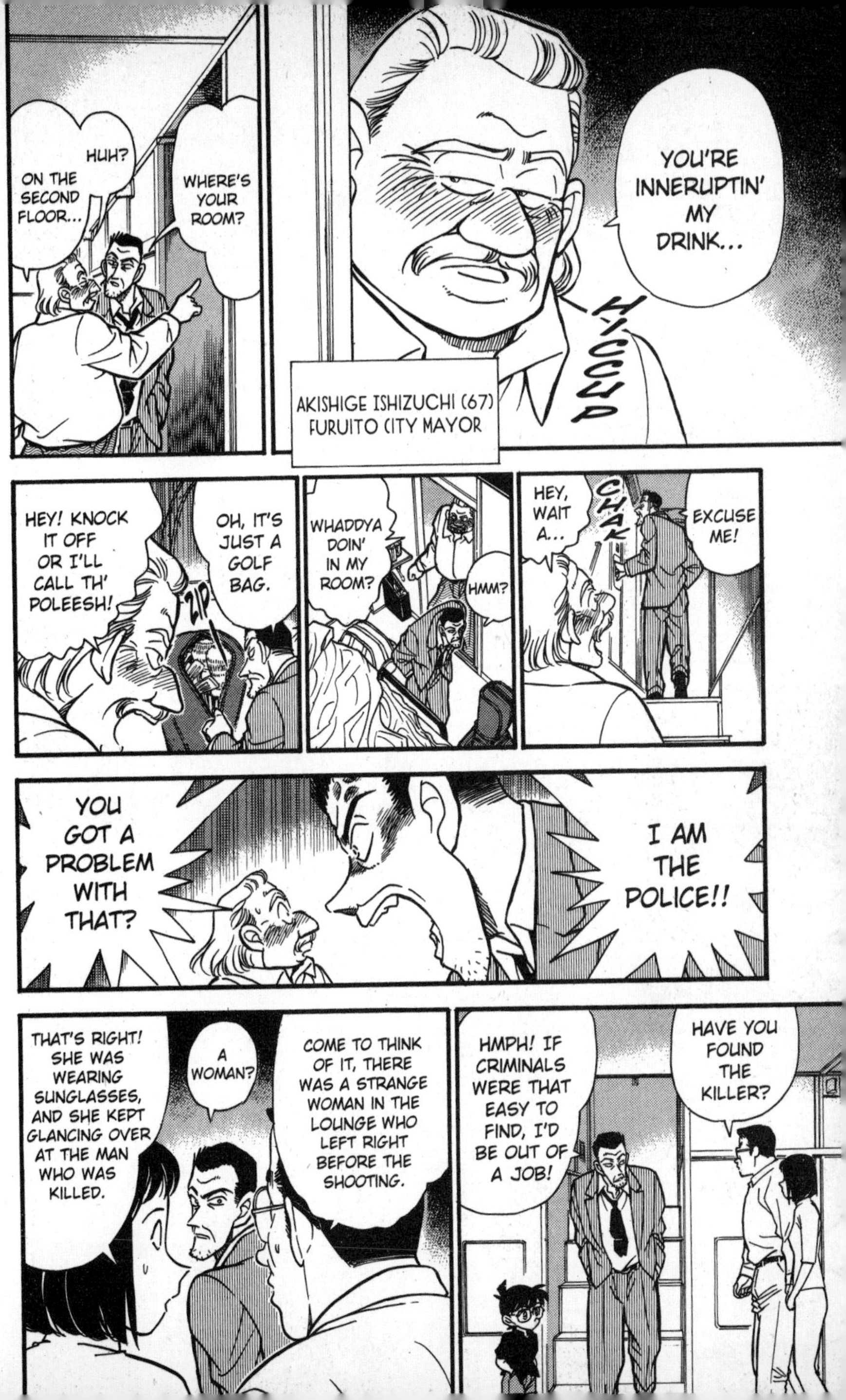
YOU'RE INNERUPTIN' MY DRINK...
HICCUP
AKISHIGE ISHIZUCHI (67) FURUITO CITY MAYOR
WHERE'S YOUR ROOM?
HUH?
ON THE SECOND FLOOR...
EXCUSE ME!
CHAK
HEY, WAIT A...
WHADDYA DOIN' IN MY ROOM?
HMM?
OH, IT'S JUST A GOLF BAG.
ZIP
HEY! KNOCK IT OFF OR I'LL CALL TH' POLEESH!
I AM THE POLICE!!
YOU GOT A PROBLEM WITH THAT?
HAVE YOU FOUND THE KILLER?
HMPH! IF CRIMINALS WERE THAT EASY TO FIND, I'D BE OUT OF A JOB!
COME TO THINK OF IT, THERE WAS A STRANGE WOMAN IN THE LOUNGE WHO LEFT RIGHT BEFORE THE SHOOTING.
A WOMAN?
THAT'S RIGHT! SHE WAS WEARING SUNGLASSES, AND SHE KEPT GLANCING OVER AT THE MAN WHO WAS KILLED.

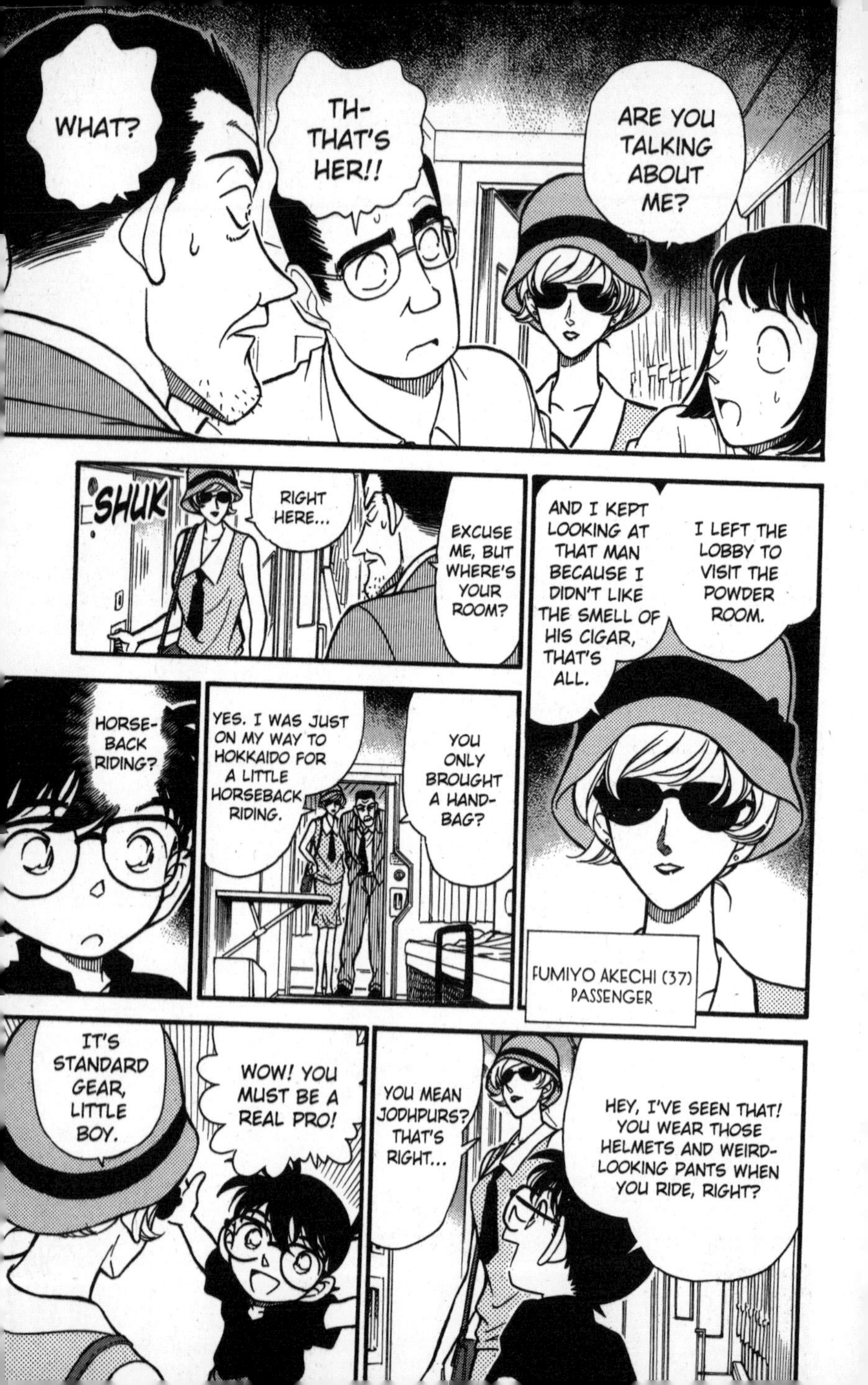
ARE YOU TALKING ABOUT ME?
TH- THAT'S HER!!
WHAT?
I LEFT THE LOBBY TO VISIT THE POWDER ROOM.
AND I KEPT LOOKING AT THAT MAN BECAUSE I DIDN'T LIKE THE SMELL OF HIS CIGAR, THAT'S ALL.
FUMIYO AKECHI (37) PASSENGER
EXCUSE ME, BUT WHERE'S YOUR ROOM?
RIGHT HERE...
SHUK
YOU ONLY BROUGHT A HAND-BAG?
YES. I WAS JUST ON MY WAY TO HOKKAIDO FOR A LITTLE HORSEBACK RIDING.
HORSE-BACK RIDING?
HEY, I'VE SEEN THAT! YOU WEAR THOSE HELMETS AND WEIRD-LOOKING PANTS WHEN YOU RIDE, RIGHT?
YOU MEAN JODHPURS? THAT'S RIGHT...
WOW! YOU MUST BE A REAL PRO!
IT'S STANDARD GEAR, LITTLE BOY.

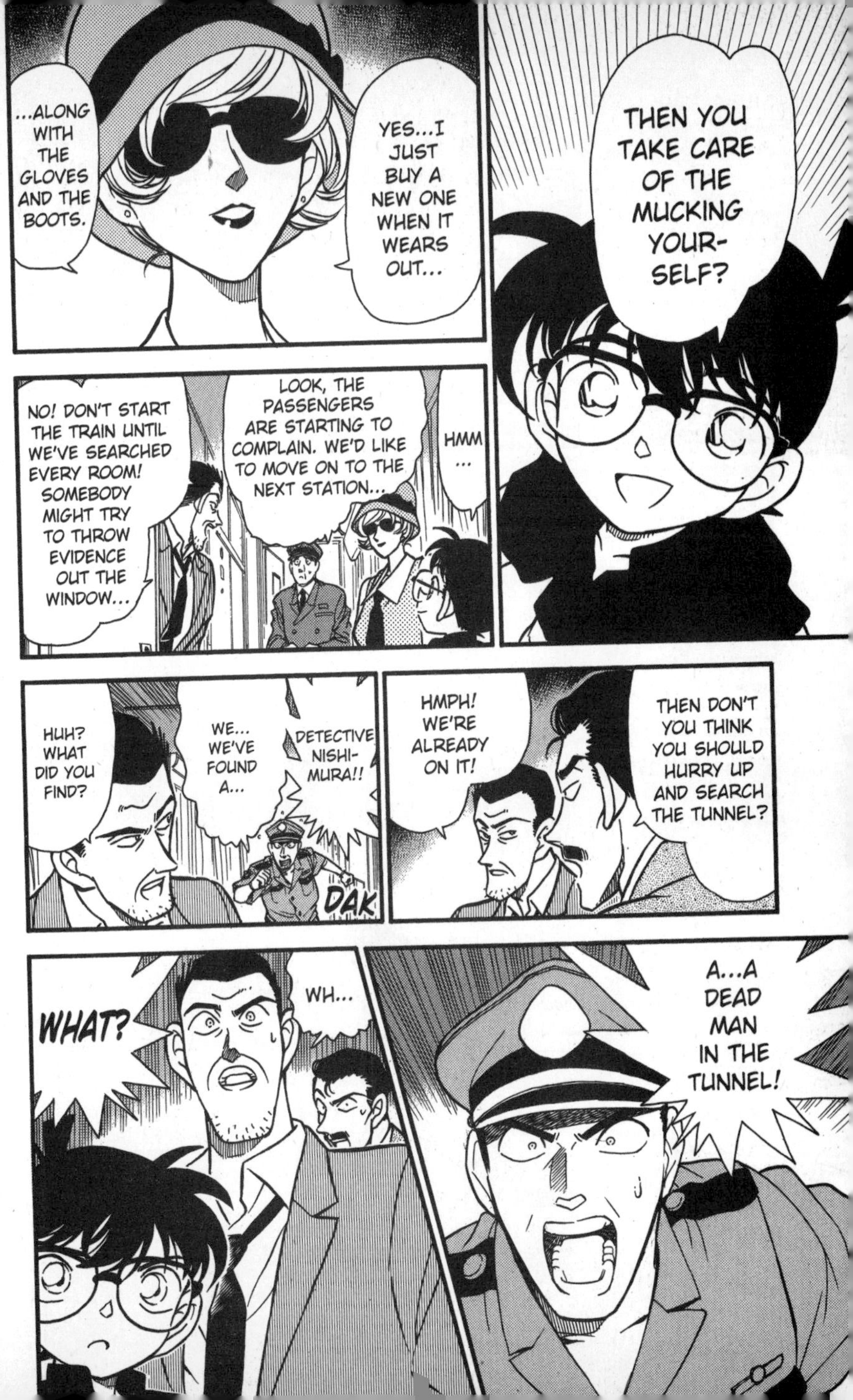
THEN YOU TAKE CARE OF THE MUCKING YOURSELF?
YES...I JUST BUY A NEW ONE WHEN IT WEARS OUT...
...ALONG WITH THE GLOVES AND THE BOOTS.
HMM...
LOOK, THE PASSENGERS ARE STARTING TO COMPLAIN. WE'D LIKE TO MOVE ON TO THE NEXT STATION...
NO! DON'T START THE TRAIN UNTIL WE'VE SEARCHED EVERY ROOM! SOMEBODY MIGHT TRY TO THROW EVIDENCE OUT THE WINDOW...
THEN DON'T YOU THINK YOU SHOULD HURRY UP AND SEARCH THE TUNNEL?
HMPH! WE'RE ALREADY ON IT!
DETECTIVE NISHIMURA!!
DAK
WE... WE'VE FOUND A...
HUH? WHAT DID YOU FIND?
A...A DEAD MAN IN THE TUNNEL!
WH...
WHAT?

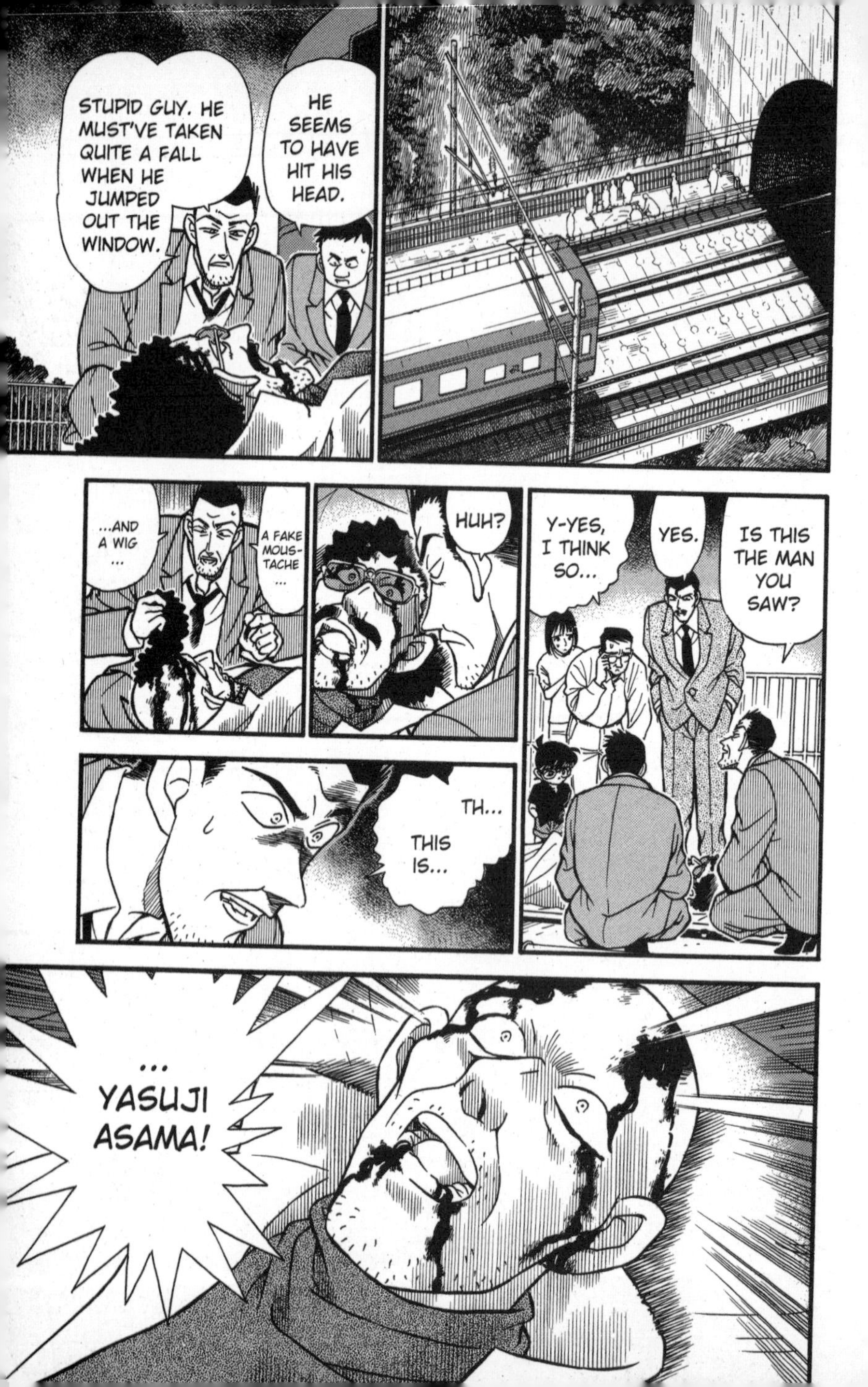
HE SEEMS TO HAVE HIT HIS HEAD.
STUPID GUY. HE MUST'VE TAKEN QUITE A FALL WHEN HE JUMPED OUT THE WINDOW.
IS THIS THE MAN YOU SAW?
YES.
Y-YES, I THINK SO...
HUH?
A FAKE MOUS-TACHE ...
...AND A WIG ...
TH...
THIS IS...
... YASUJI ASAMA!

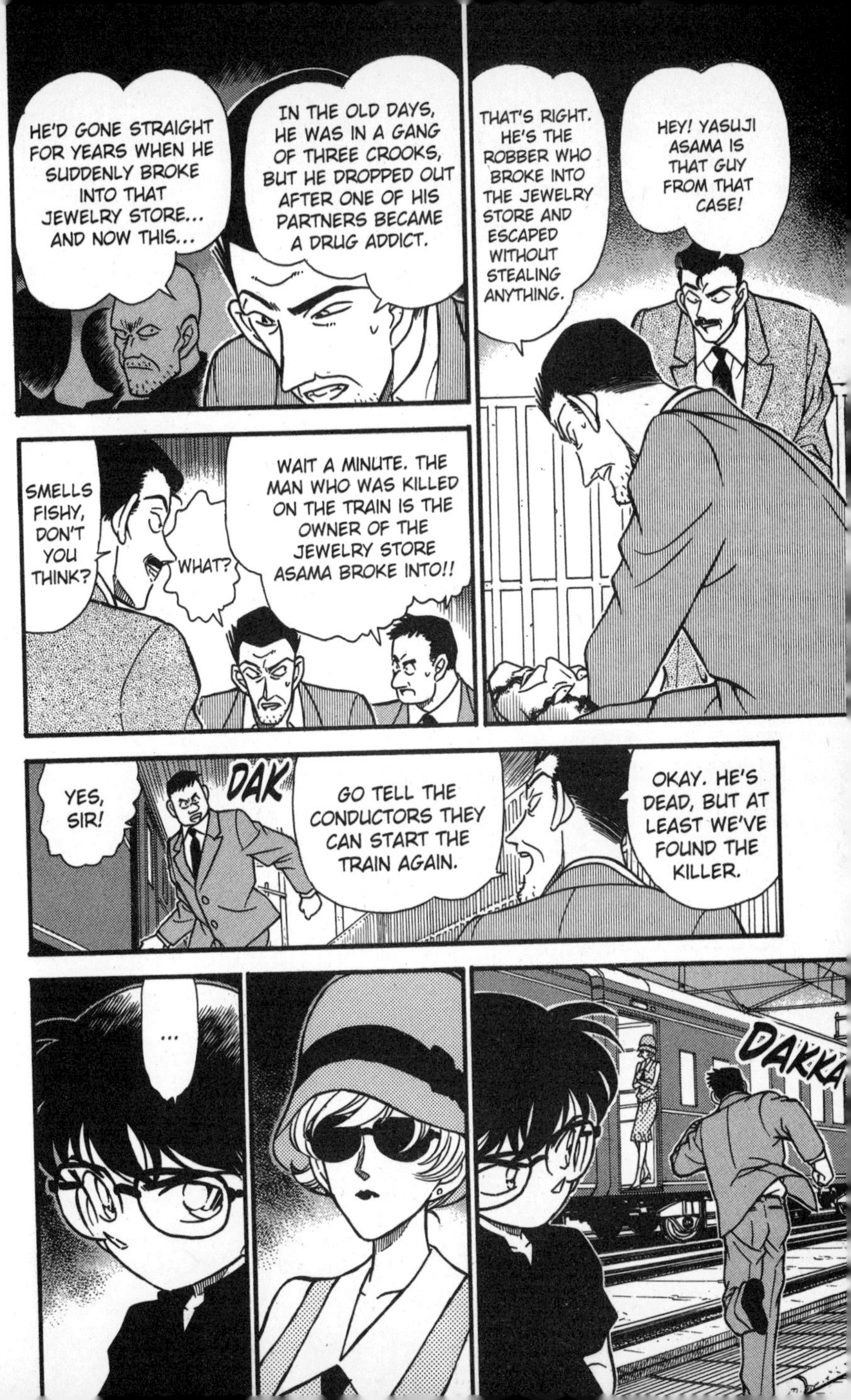
HEY! YASUJI ASAMA IS THAT GUY FROM THAT CASE!
THAT'S RIGHT. HE'S THE ROBBER WHO BROKE INTO THE JEWELRY STORE AND ESCAPED WITHOUT STEALING ANYTHING.
IN THE OLD DAYS, HE WAS IN A GANG OF THREE CROOKS, BUT HE DROPPED OUT AFTER ONE OF HIS PARTNERS BECAME A DRUG ADDICT.
HE'D GONE STRAIGHT FOR YEARS WHEN HE SUDDENLY BROKE INTO THAT JEWELRY STORE... AND NOW THIS...
WAIT A MINUTE. THE MAN WHO WAS KILLED ON THE TRAIN IS THE OWNER OF THE JEWELRY STORE ASAMA BROKE INTO!!
WHAT?
SMELLS FISHY, DON'T YOU THINK?
OKAY. HE'S DEAD, BUT AT LEAST WE'VE FOUND THE KILLER.
GO TELL THE CONDUCTORS THEY CAN START THE TRAIN AGAIN.
DAK
YES, SIR!
DAKKA
...

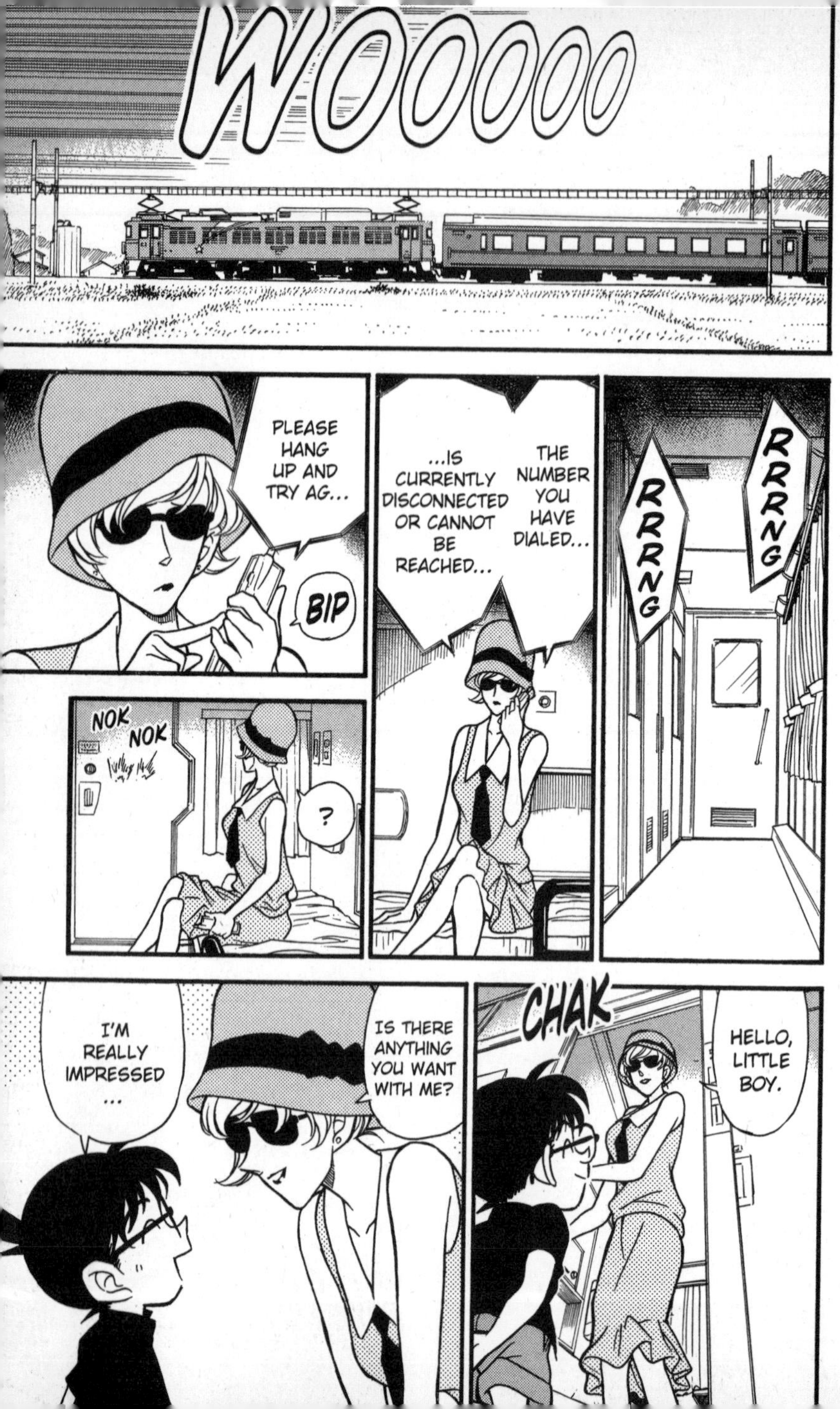
WOOOOO
RRRNG
RRRNG
THE NUMBER YOU HAVE DIALED...
...IS CURRENTLY DISCONNECTED OR CANNOT BE REACHED...
PLEASE HANG UP AND TRY AG...
BIP
NOK NOK
?
CHAK
HELLO, LITTLE BOY.
IS THERE ANYTHING YOU WANT WITH ME?
I'M REALLY IMPRESSED ...

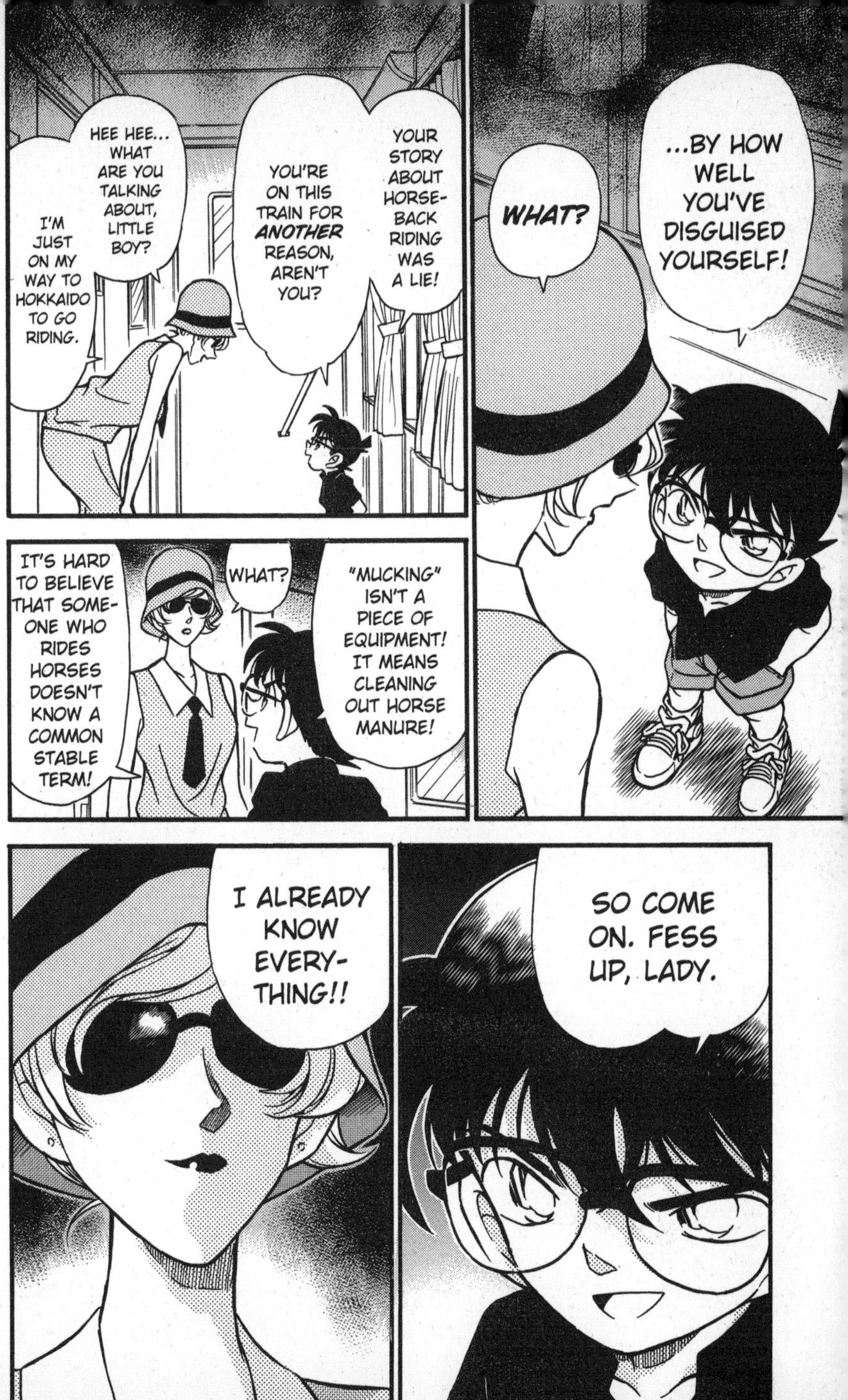
...BY HOW WELL YOU'VE DISGUISED YOURSELF!
WHAT?
YOUR STORY ABOUT HORSE-BACK RIDING WAS A LIE!
YOU'RE ON THIS TRAIN FOR ANOTHER REASON, AREN'T YOU?
HEE HEE... WHAT ARE YOU TALKING ABOUT, LITTLE BOY?
I'M JUST ON MY WAY TO HOKKAIDO TO GO RIDING.
"MUCKING" ISN'T A PIECE OF EQUIPMENT! IT MEANS CLEANING OUT HORSE MANURE!
WHAT?
IT'S HARD TO BELIEVE THAT SOME-ONE WHO RIDES HORSES DOESN'T KNOW A COMMON STABLE TERM!
SO COME ON. FESS UP, LADY.
I ALREADY KNOW EVERY-THING!!

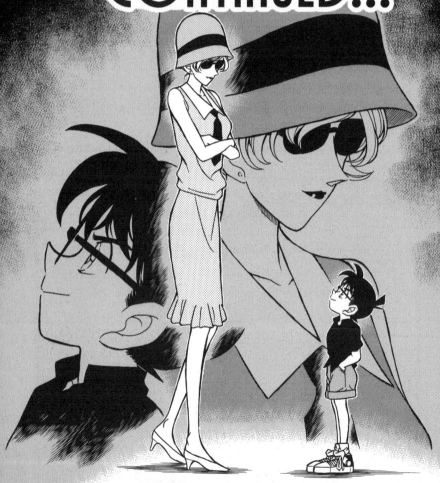

FILE 6:
TO BE
CONTINUED...

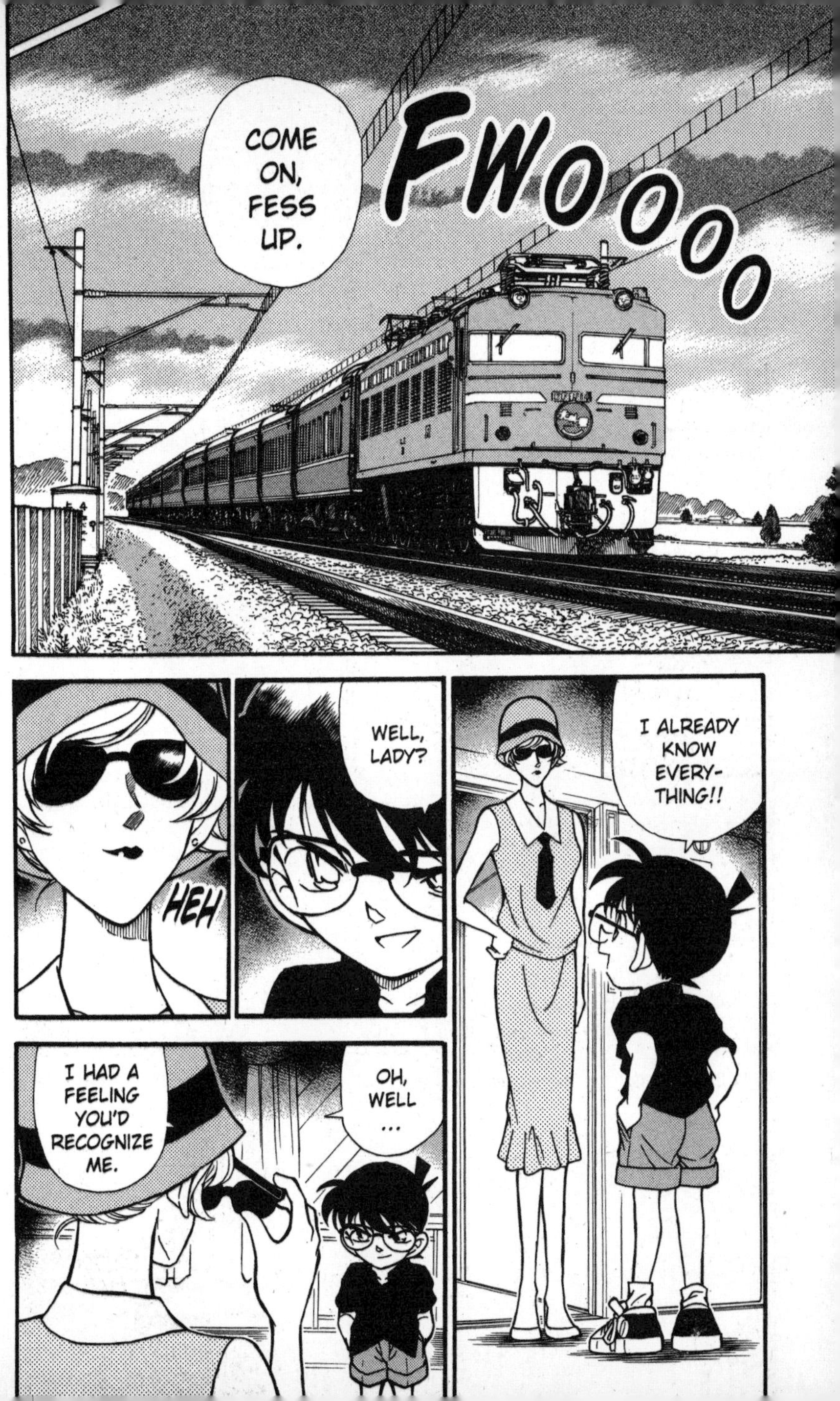
FWOOOO
COME ON, FESS UP.
I ALREADY KNOW EVERY-THING!!
WELL, LADY?
HEH
OH, WELL ...
I HAD A FEELING YOU'D RECOGNIZE ME.

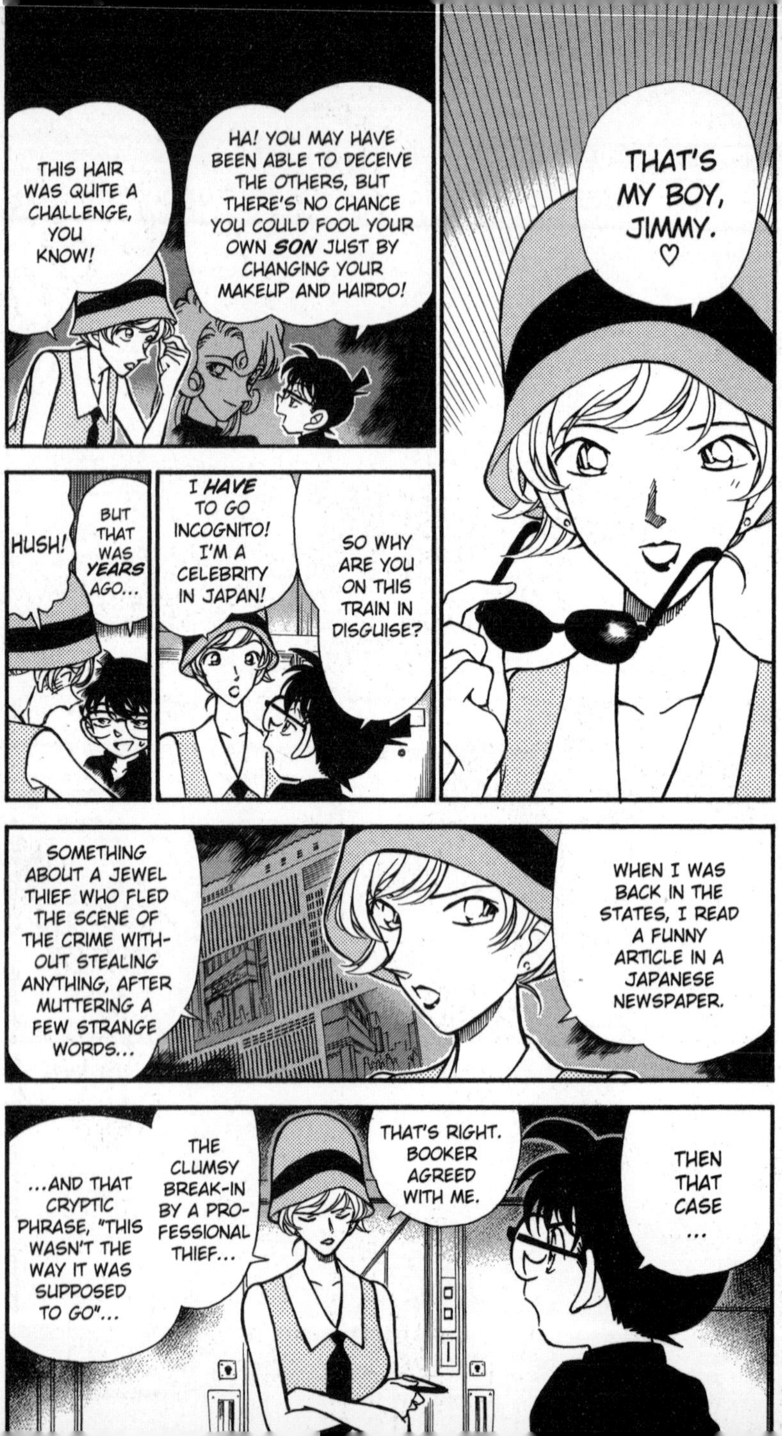
THAT'S MY BOY, JIMMY. ♡
HA! YOU MAY HAVE BEEN ABLE TO DECEIVE THE OTHERS, BUT THERE'S NO CHANCE YOU COULD FOOL YOUR OWN **SON** JUST BY CHANGING YOUR MAKEUP AND HAIRDO!
THIS HAIR WAS QUITE A CHALLENGE, YOU KNOW!
SO WHY ARE YOU ON THIS TRAIN IN DISGUISE?
I **HAVE** TO GO INCOGNITO! I'M A CELEBRITY IN JAPAN!
BUT THAT WAS **YEARS** AGO...
HUSH!
WHEN I WAS BACK IN THE STATES, I READ A FUNNY ARTICLE IN A JAPANESE NEWSPAPER.
SOMETHING ABOUT A JEWEL THIEF WHO FLED THE SCENE OF THE CRIME WITH-OUT STEALING ANYTHING, AFTER MUTTERING A FEW STRANGE WORDS...
THEN THAT CASE...
THAT'S RIGHT. BOOKER AGREED WITH ME.
THE CLUMSY BREAK-IN BY A PRO-FESSIONAL THIEF...
...AND THAT CRYPTIC PHRASE, "THIS WASN'T THE WAY IT WAS SUPPOSED TO GO"...

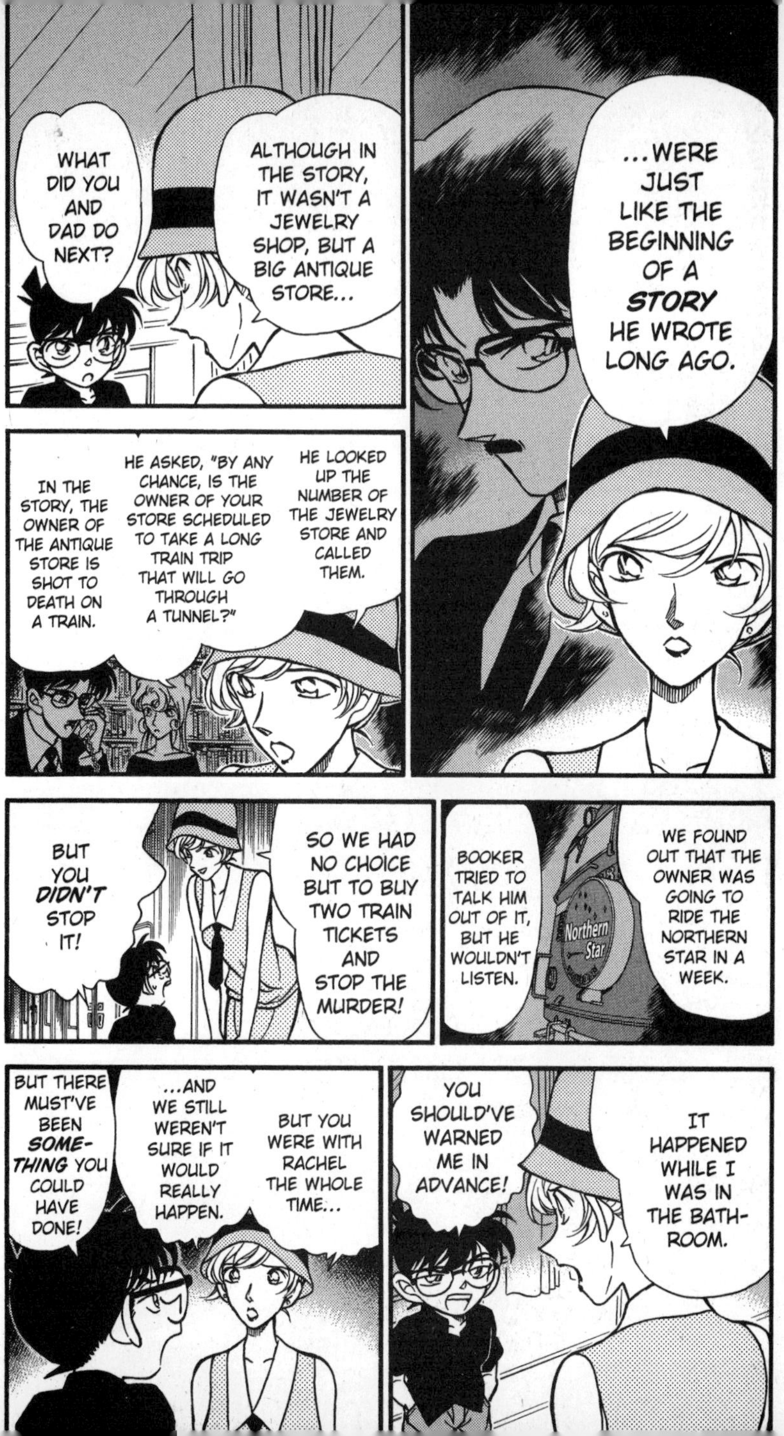
...WERE JUST LIKE THE BEGINNING OF A ***STORY*** HE WROTE LONG AGO.
ALTHOUGH IN THE STORY, IT WASN'T A JEWELRY SHOP, BUT A BIG ANTIQUE STORE...
WHAT DID YOU AND DAD DO NEXT?
HE LOOKED UP THE NUMBER OF THE JEWELRY STORE AND CALLED THEM.
HE ASKED, "BY ANY CHANCE, IS THE OWNER OF YOUR STORE SCHEDULED TO TAKE A LONG TRAIN TRIP THAT WILL GO THROUGH A TUNNEL?"
IN THE STORY, THE OWNER OF THE ANTIQUE STORE IS SHOT TO DEATH ON A TRAIN.
WE FOUND OUT THAT THE OWNER WAS GOING TO RIDE THE NORTHERN STAR IN A WEEK.
BOOKER TRIED TO TALK HIM OUT OF IT, BUT HE WOULDN'T LISTEN.
Northern Star
SO WE HAD NO CHOICE BUT TO BUY TWO TRAIN TICKETS AND STOP THE MURDER!
BUT YOU ***DIDN'T*** STOP IT!
IT HAPPENED WHILE I WAS IN THE BATH-ROOM.
YOU SHOULD'VE WARNED ME IN ADVANCE!
BUT YOU WERE WITH RACHEL THE WHOLE TIME...
...AND WE STILL WEREN'T SURE IF IT WOULD REALLY HAPPEN.
BUT THERE MUST'VE BEEN ***SOME-THING*** YOU COULD HAVE DONE!

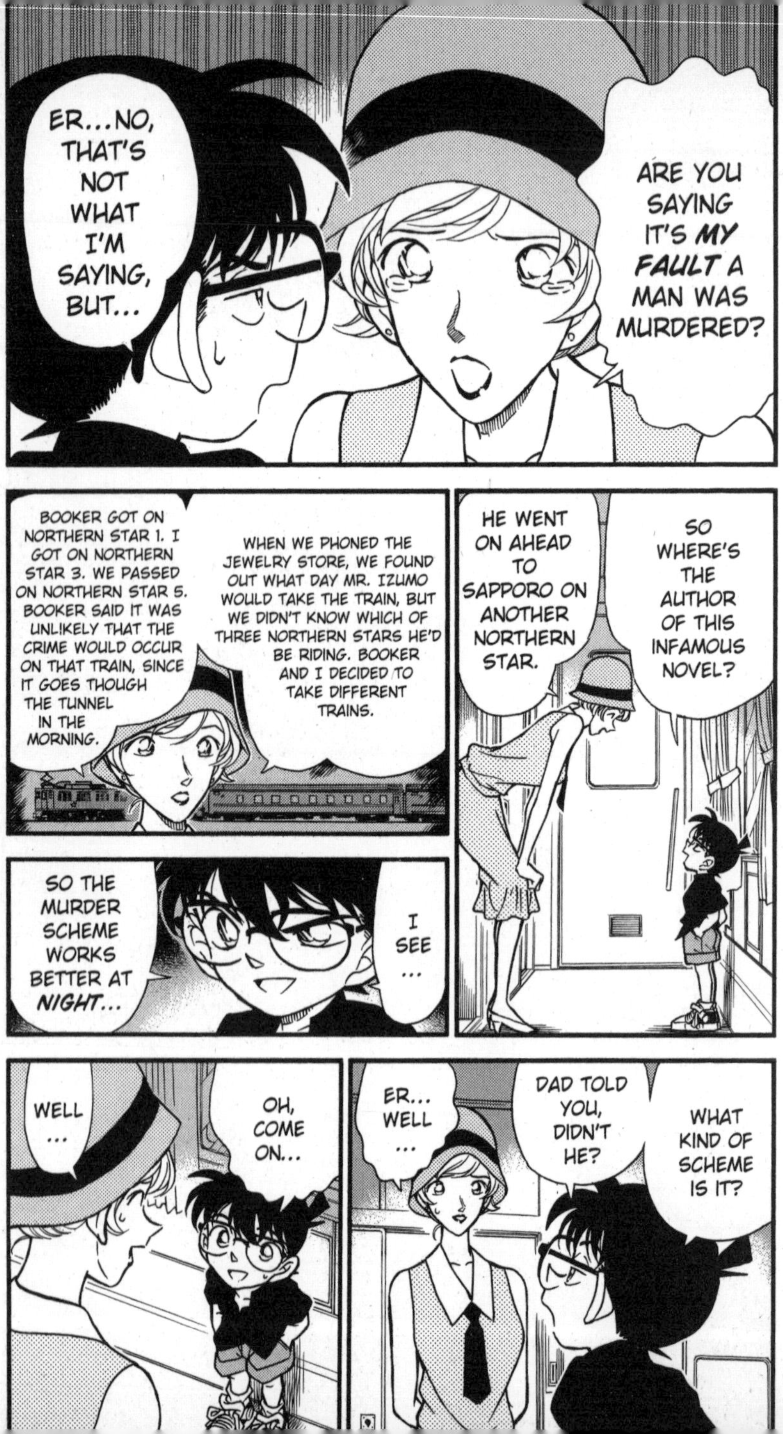
ARE YOU SAYING IT'S *MY FAULT* A MAN WAS MURDERED?
ER...NO, THAT'S NOT WHAT I'M SAYING, BUT...
SO WHERE'S THE AUTHOR OF THIS INFAMOUS NOVEL?
HE WENT ON AHEAD TO SAPPORO ON ANOTHER NORTHERN STAR.
WHEN WE PHONED THE JEWELRY STORE, WE FOUND OUT WHAT DAY MR. IZUMO WOULD TAKE THE TRAIN, BUT WE DIDN'T KNOW WHICH OF THREE NORTHERN STARS HE'D BE RIDING. BOOKER AND I DECIDED TO TAKE DIFFERENT TRAINS.
BOOKER GOT ON NORTHERN STAR 1. I GOT ON NORTHERN STAR 3. WE PASSED ON NORTHERN STAR 5. BOOKER SAID IT WAS UNLIKELY THAT THE CRIME WOULD OCCUR ON THAT TRAIN, SINCE IT GOES THOUGH THE TUNNEL IN THE MORNING.
I SEE...
SO THE MURDER SCHEME WORKS BETTER AT *NIGHT*...
WHAT KIND OF SCHEME IS IT?
DAD TOLD YOU, DIDN'T HE?
ER... WELL...
OH, COME ON...
WELL...

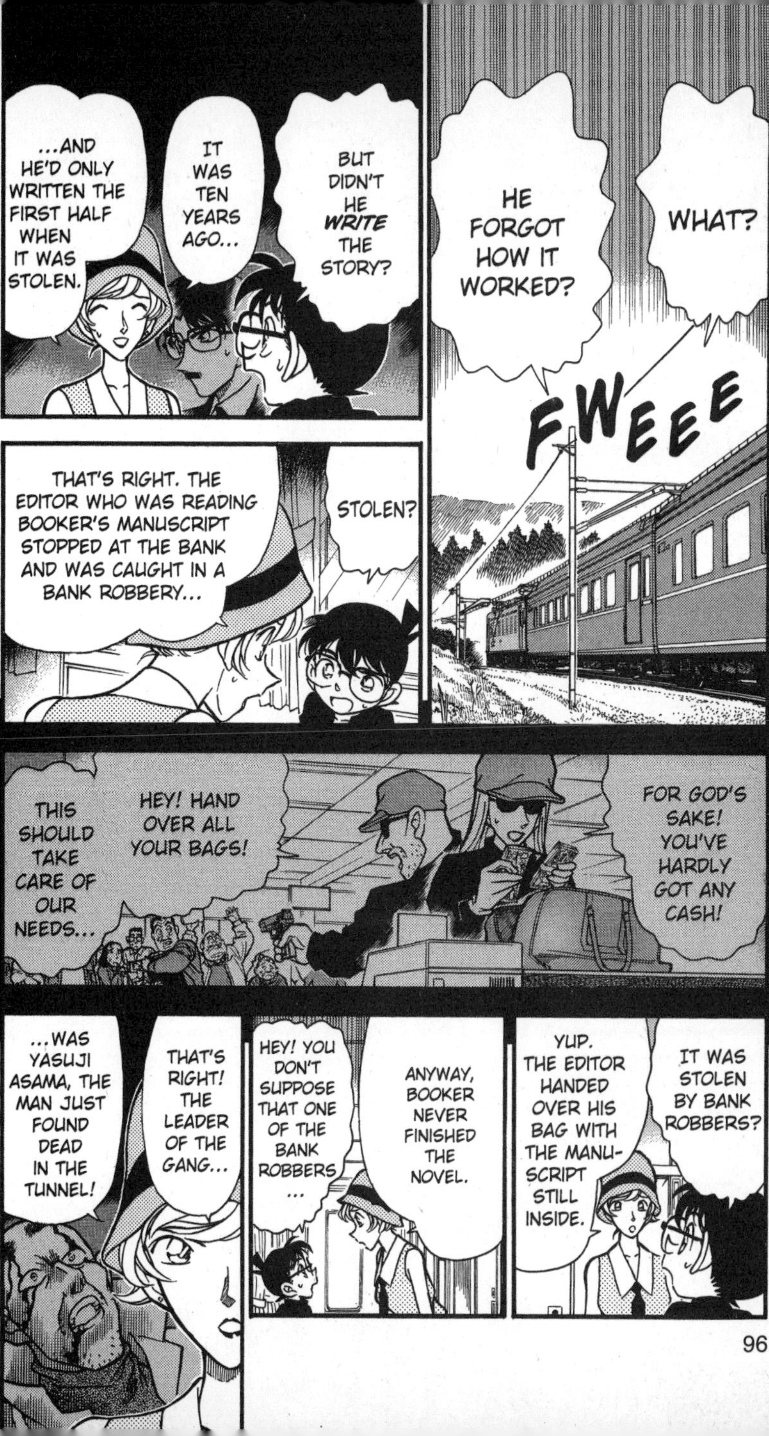
WHAT?
HE FORGOT HOW IT WORKED?
FWEEE
BUT DIDN'T HE *WRITE* THE STORY?
IT WAS TEN YEARS AGO...
...AND HE'D ONLY WRITTEN THE FIRST HALF WHEN IT WAS STOLEN.
STOLEN?
THAT'S RIGHT. THE EDITOR WHO WAS READING BOOKER'S MANUSCRIPT STOPPED AT THE BANK AND WAS CAUGHT IN A BANK ROBBERY...
FOR GOD'S SAKE! YOU'VE HARDLY GOT ANY CASH!
HEY! HAND OVER ALL YOUR BAGS!
THIS SHOULD TAKE CARE OF OUR NEEDS...
IT WAS STOLEN BY BANK ROBBERS?
YUP. THE EDITOR HANDED OVER HIS BAG WITH THE MANU-SCRIPT STILL INSIDE.
ANYWAY, BOOKER NEVER FINISHED THE NOVEL.
HEY! YOU DON'T SUPPOSE THAT ONE OF THE BANK ROBBERS ...
THAT'S RIGHT! THE LEADER OF THE GANG...
...WAS YASUJI ASAMA, THE MAN JUST FOUND DEAD IN THE TUNNEL!

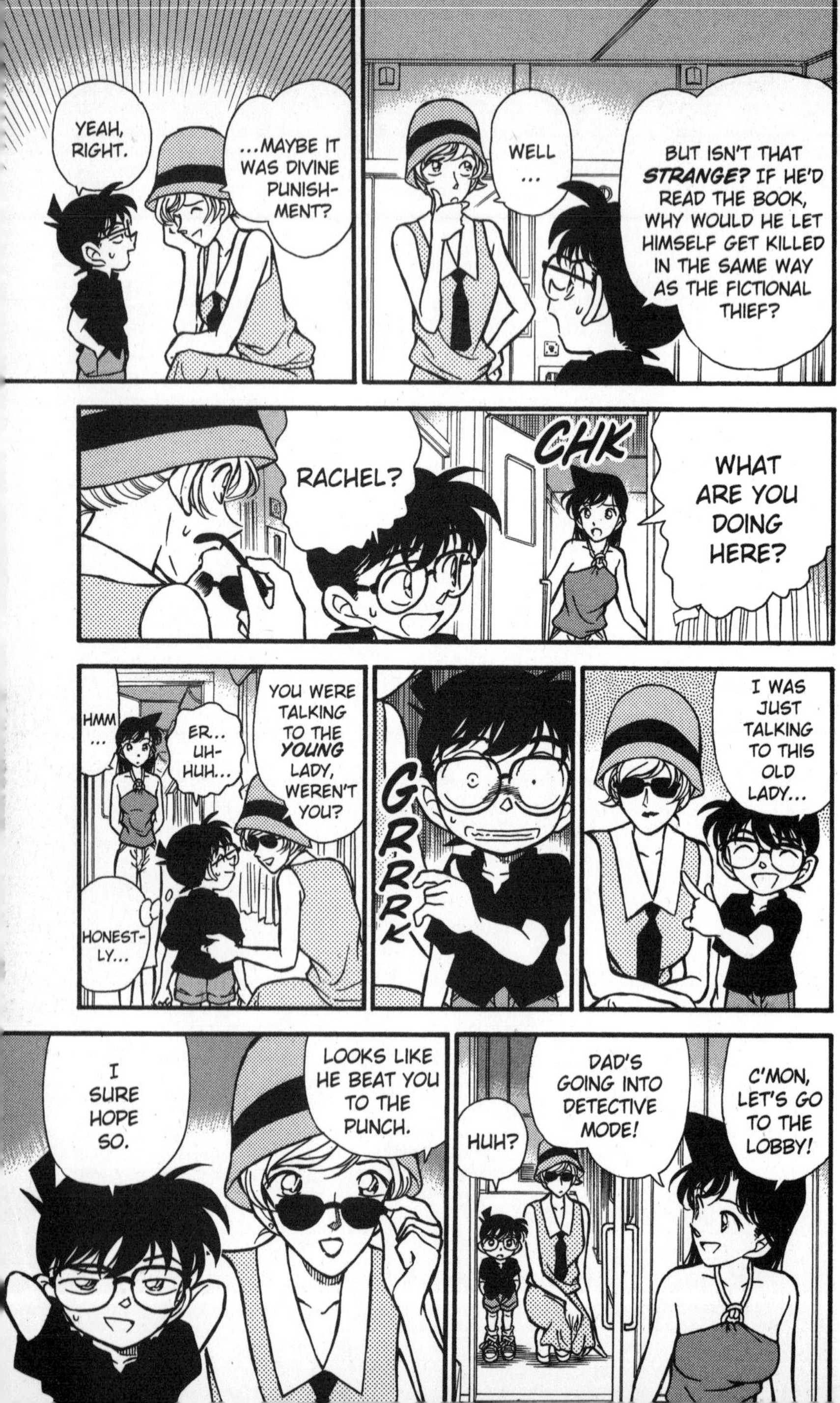
BUT ISN'T THAT STRANGE? IF HE'D READ THE BOOK, WHY WOULD HE LET HIMSELF GET KILLED IN THE SAME WAY AS THE FICTIONAL THIEF?
WELL ...
...MAYBE IT WAS DIVINE PUNISHMENT?
YEAH, RIGHT.
WHAT ARE YOU DOING HERE?
CHK
RACHEL?
I WAS JUST TALKING TO THIS OLD LADY...
GRRRRK
YOU WERE TALKING TO THE YOUNG LADY, WEREN'T YOU?
ER... UH-HUH...
HMM ...
HONESTLY...
C'MON, LET'S GO TO THE LOBBY!
DAD'S GOING INTO DETECTIVE MODE!
HUH?
LOOKS LIKE HE BEAT YOU TO THE PUNCH.
I SURE HOPE SO.

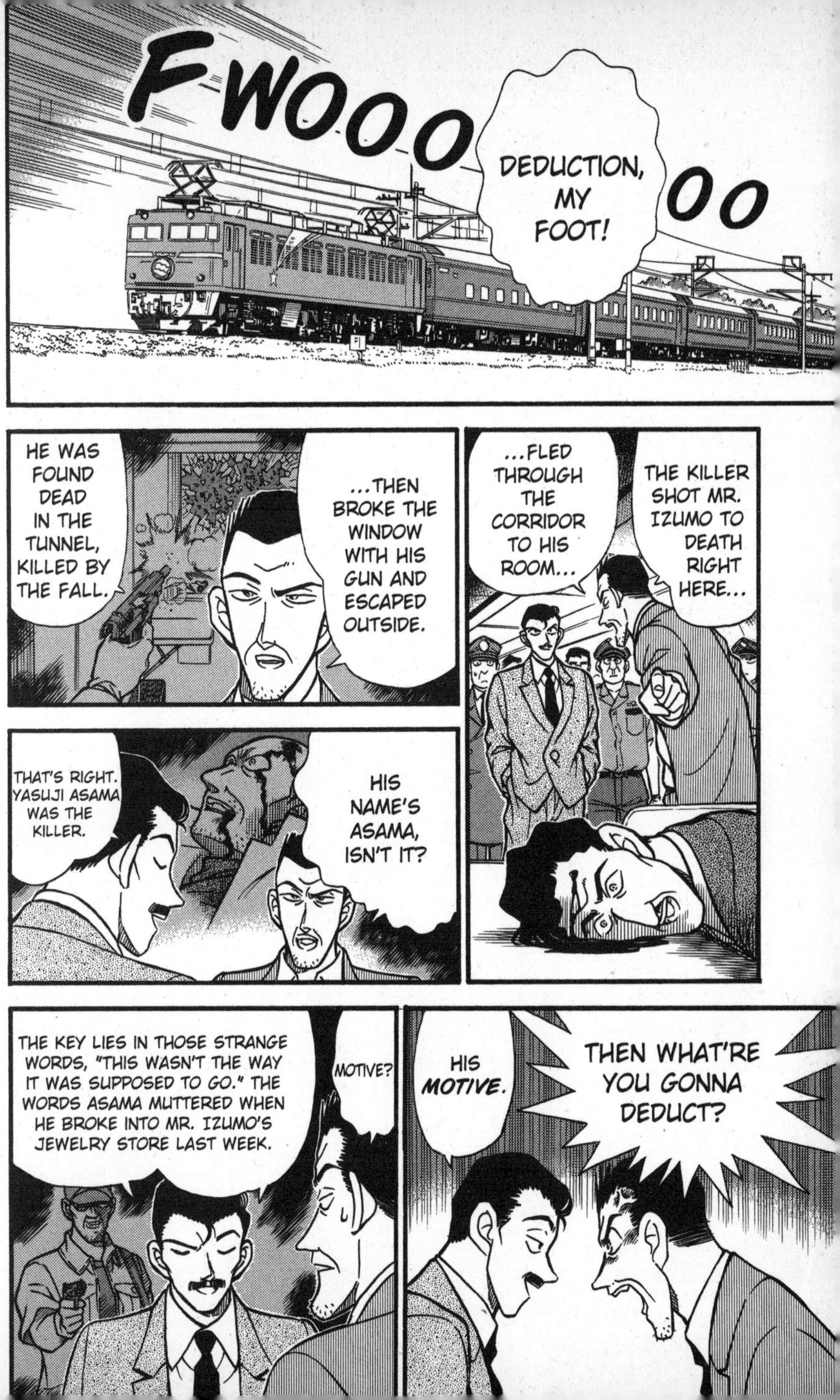
FWOOOOOO
DEDUCTION, MY FOOT!
THE KILLER SHOT MR. IZUMO TO DEATH RIGHT HERE...
...FLED THROUGH THE CORRIDOR TO HIS ROOM...
...THEN BROKE THE WINDOW WITH HIS GUN AND ESCAPED OUTSIDE.
HE WAS FOUND DEAD IN THE TUNNEL, KILLED BY THE FALL.
HIS NAME'S ASAMA, ISN'T IT?
THAT'S RIGHT. YASUJI ASAMA WAS THE KILLER.
THEN WHAT'RE YOU GONNA DEDUCT?
HIS *MOTIVE*.
MOTIVE?
THE KEY LIES IN THOSE STRANGE WORDS, "THIS WASN'T THE WAY IT WAS SUPPOSED TO GO." THE WORDS ASAMA MUTTERED WHEN HE BROKE INTO MR. IZUMO'S JEWELRY STORE LAST WEEK.

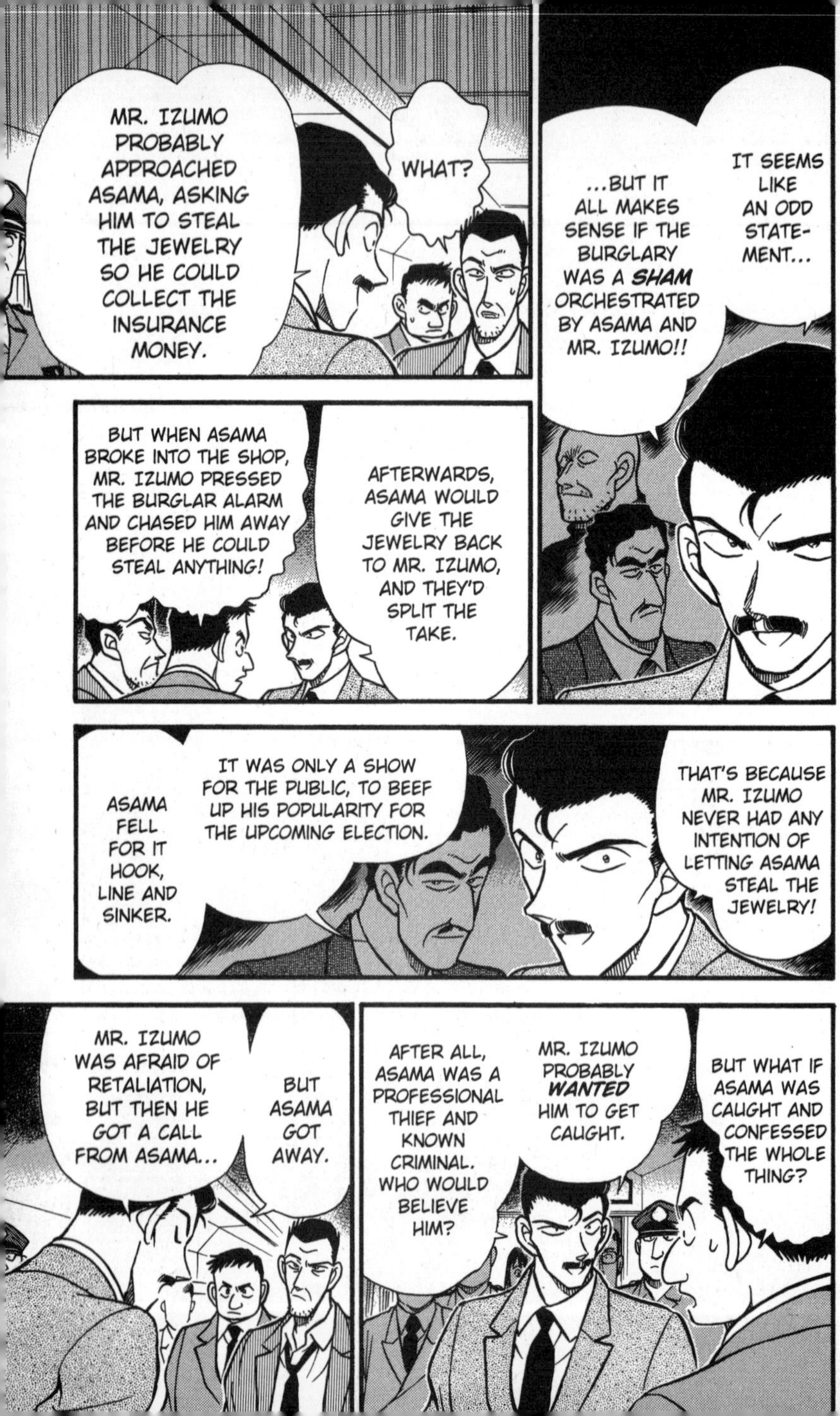
IT SEEMS LIKE AN ODD STATEMENT...
...BUT IT ALL MAKES SENSE IF THE BURGLARY WAS A **SHAM** ORCHESTRATED BY ASAMA AND MR. IZUMO!!
WHAT?
MR. IZUMO PROBABLY APPROACHED ASAMA, ASKING HIM TO STEAL THE JEWELRY SO HE COULD COLLECT THE INSURANCE MONEY.
AFTERWARDS, ASAMA WOULD GIVE THE JEWELRY BACK TO MR. IZUMO, AND THEY'D SPLIT THE TAKE.
BUT WHEN ASAMA BROKE INTO THE SHOP, MR. IZUMO PRESSED THE BURGLAR ALARM AND CHASED HIM AWAY BEFORE HE COULD STEAL ANYTHING!
THAT'S BECAUSE MR. IZUMO NEVER HAD ANY INTENTION OF LETTING ASAMA STEAL THE JEWELRY!
IT WAS ONLY A SHOW FOR THE PUBLIC, TO BEEF UP HIS POPULARITY FOR THE UPCOMING ELECTION.
ASAMA FELL FOR IT HOOK, LINE AND SINKER.
BUT WHAT IF ASAMA WAS CAUGHT AND CONFESSED THE WHOLE THING?
MR. IZUMO PROBABLY **WANTED** HIM TO GET CAUGHT.
AFTER ALL, ASAMA WAS A PROFESSIONAL THIEF AND KNOWN CRIMINAL. WHO WOULD BELIEVE HIM?
BUT ASAMA GOT AWAY.
MR. IZUMO WAS AFRAID OF RETALIATION, BUT THEN HE GOT A CALL FROM ASAMA...

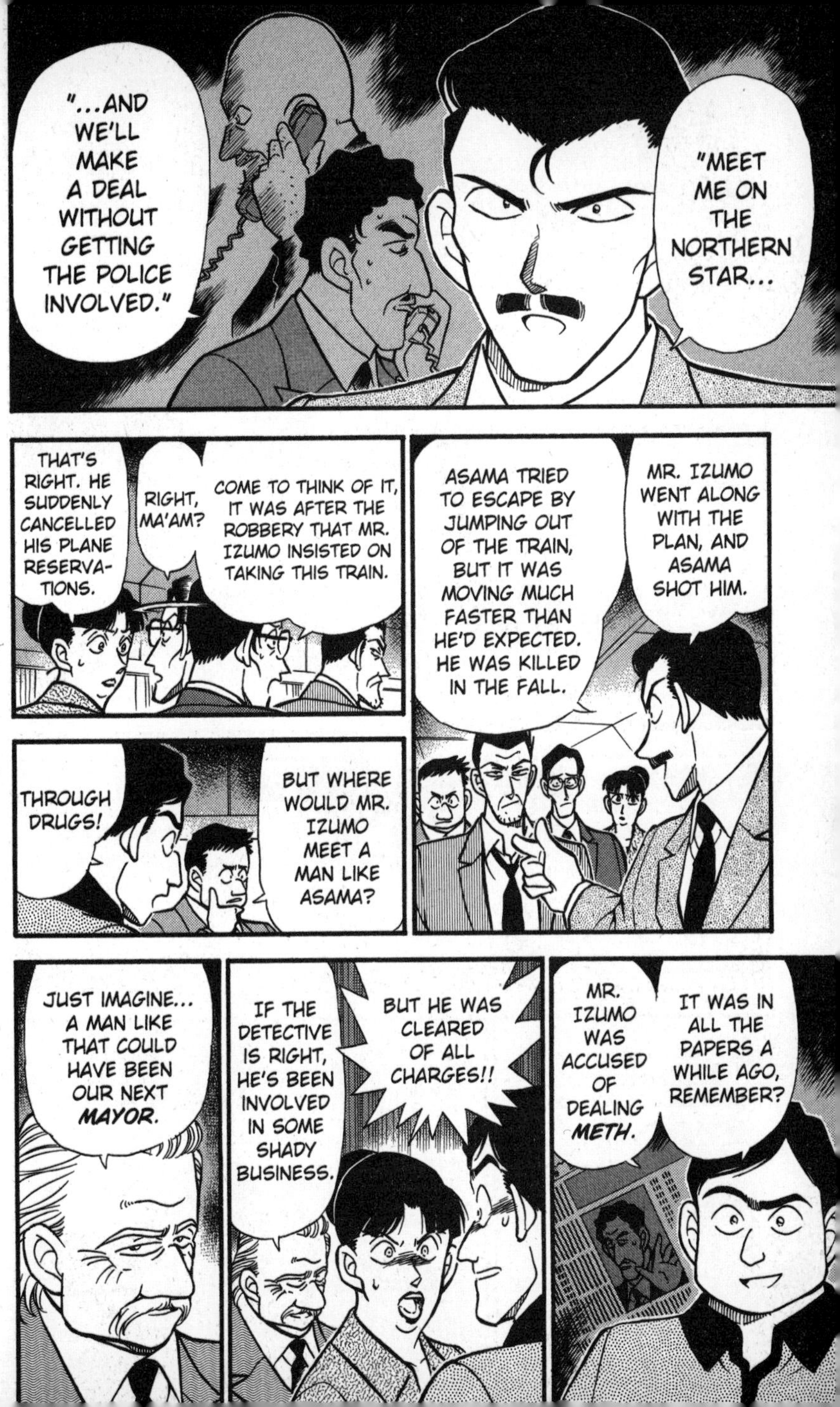

"MEET ME ON THE NORTHERN STAR...
"...AND WE'LL MAKE A DEAL WITHOUT GETTING THE POLICE INVOLVED."
MR. IZUMO WENT ALONG WITH THE PLAN, AND ASAMA SHOT HIM.
ASAMA TRIED TO ESCAPE BY JUMPING OUT OF THE TRAIN, BUT IT WAS MOVING MUCH FASTER THAN HE'D EXPECTED. HE WAS KILLED IN THE FALL.
COME TO THINK OF IT, IT WAS AFTER THE ROBBERY THAT MR. IZUMO INSISTED ON TAKING THIS TRAIN.
RIGHT, MA'AM?
THAT'S RIGHT. HE SUDDENLY CANCELLED HIS PLANE RESERVATIONS.
BUT WHERE WOULD MR. IZUMO MEET A MAN LIKE ASAMA?
THROUGH DRUGS!
IT WAS IN ALL THE PAPERS A WHILE AGO, REMEMBER?
MR. IZUMO WAS ACCUSED OF DEALING *METH*.
BUT HE WAS CLEARED OF ALL CHARGES!!
IF THE DETECTIVE IS RIGHT, HE'S BEEN INVOLVED IN SOME SHADY BUSINESS.
JUST IMAGINE... A MAN LIKE THAT COULD HAVE BEEN OUR NEXT *MAYOR*.

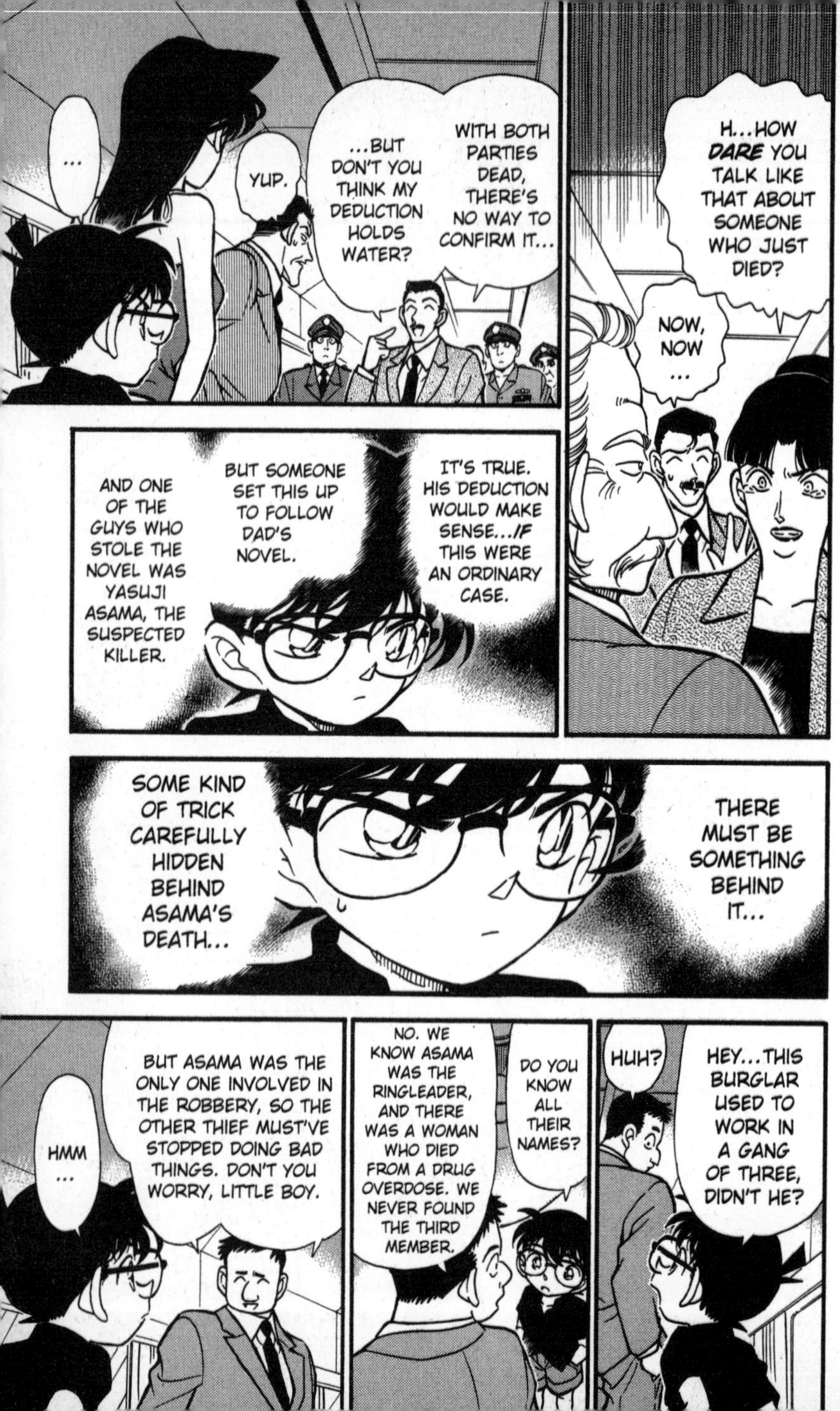
H...HOW DARE YOU TALK LIKE THAT ABOUT SOMEONE WHO JUST DIED?
NOW, NOW ...
WITH BOTH PARTIES DEAD, THERE'S NO WAY TO CONFIRM IT...
...BUT DON'T YOU THINK MY DEDUCTION HOLDS WATER?
YUP.
...
IT'S TRUE. HIS DEDUCTION WOULD MAKE SENSE...IF THIS WERE AN ORDINARY CASE.
BUT SOMEONE SET THIS UP TO FOLLOW DAD'S NOVEL.
AND ONE OF THE GUYS WHO STOLE THE NOVEL WAS YASUJI ASAMA, THE SUSPECTED KILLER.
THERE MUST BE SOMETHING BEHIND IT...
SOME KIND OF TRICK CAREFULLY HIDDEN BEHIND ASAMA'S DEATH...
HEY...THIS BURGLAR USED TO WORK IN A GANG OF THREE, DIDN'T HE?
HUH?
DO YOU KNOW ALL THEIR NAMES?
NO. WE KNOW ASAMA WAS THE RINGLEADER, AND THERE WAS A WOMAN WHO DIED FROM A DRUG OVERDOSE. WE NEVER FOUND THE THIRD MEMBER.
BUT ASAMA WAS THE ONLY ONE INVOLVED IN THE ROBBERY, SO THE OTHER THIEF MUST'VE STOPPED DOING BAD THINGS. DON'T YOU WORRY, LITTLE BOY.
HMM ...

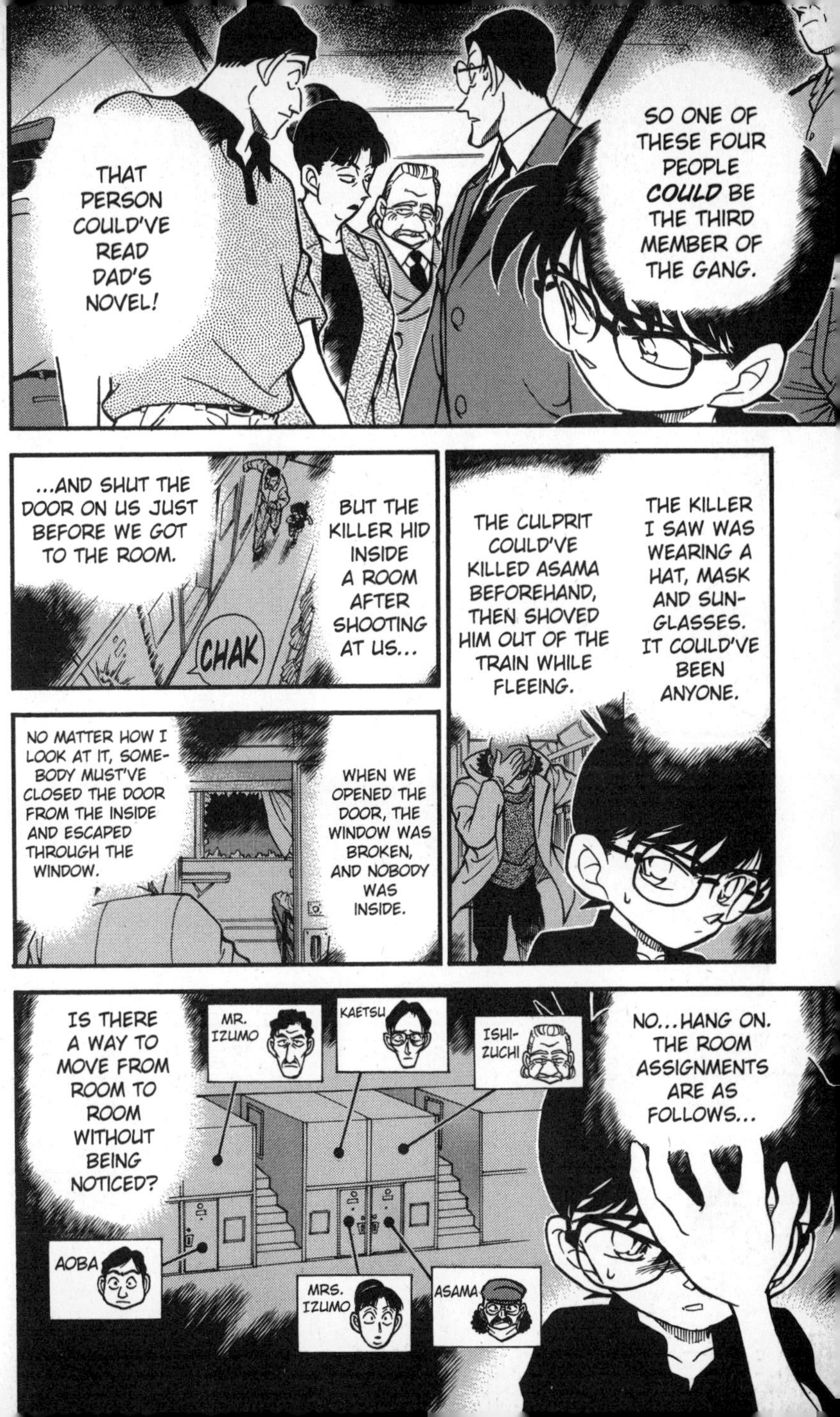

SO ONE OF THESE FOUR PEOPLE *COULD* BE THE THIRD MEMBER OF THE GANG.
THAT PERSON COULD'VE READ DAD'S NOVEL!
THE KILLER I SAW WAS WEARING A HAT, MASK AND SUN-GLASSES. IT COULD'VE BEEN ANYONE.
THE CULPRIT COULD'VE KILLED ASAMA BEFOREHAND, THEN SHOVED HIM OUT OF THE TRAIN WHILE FLEEING.
BUT THE KILLER HID INSIDE A ROOM AFTER SHOOTING AT US...
...AND SHUT THE DOOR ON US JUST BEFORE WE GOT TO THE ROOM.
CHAK
WHEN WE OPENED THE DOOR, THE WINDOW WAS BROKEN, AND NOBODY WAS INSIDE.
NO MATTER HOW I LOOK AT IT, SOME-BODY MUST'VE CLOSED THE DOOR FROM THE INSIDE AND ESCAPED THROUGH THE WINDOW.
NO...HANG ON. THE ROOM ASSIGNMENTS ARE AS FOLLOWS...
ISHI-ZUCHI
KAETSU
MR. IZUMO
ASAMA
MRS. IZUMO
AOBA
IS THERE A WAY TO MOVE FROM ROOM TO ROOM WITHOUT BEING NOTICED?

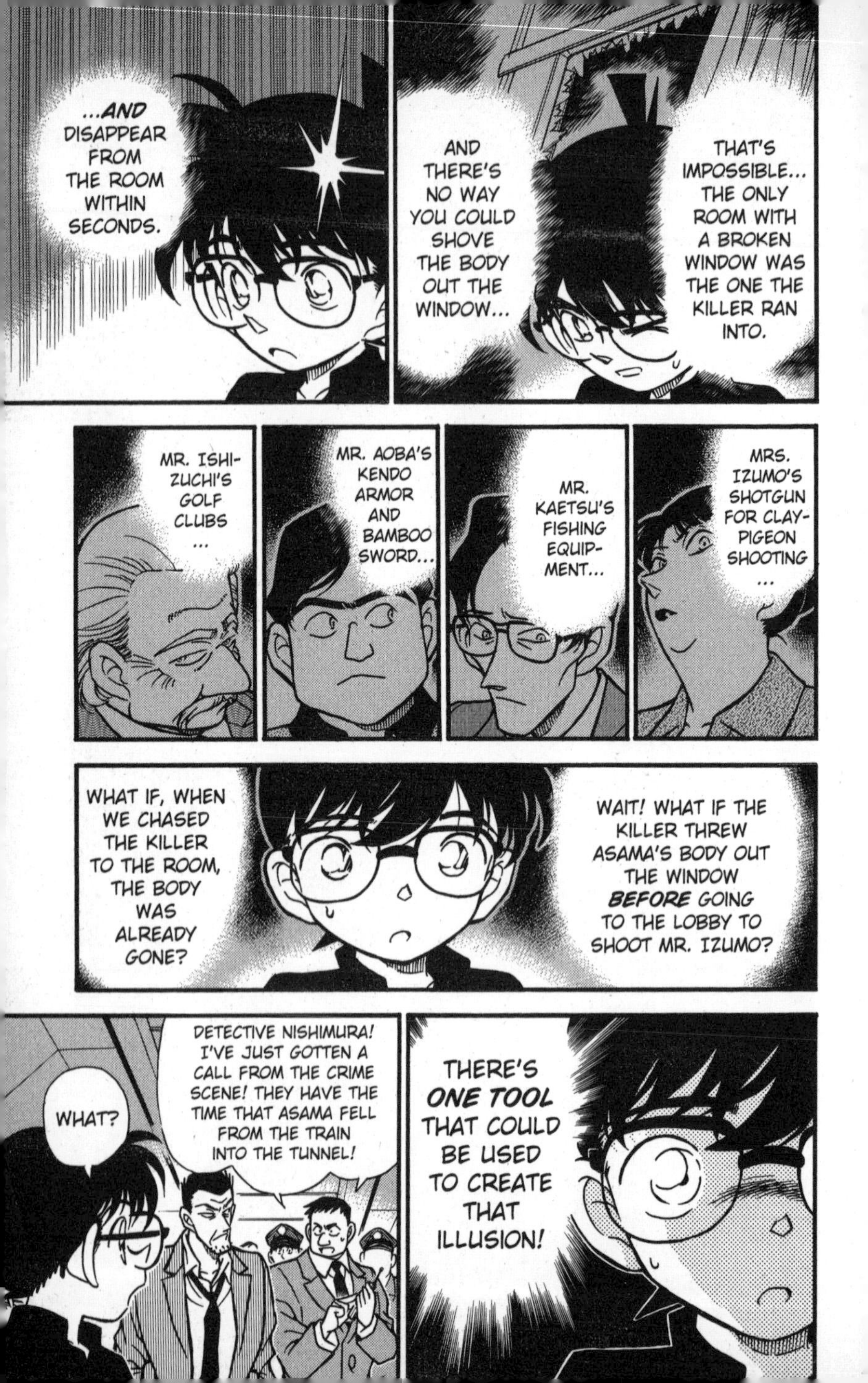
THAT'S IMPOSSIBLE... THE ONLY ROOM WITH A BROKEN WINDOW WAS THE ONE THE KILLER RAN INTO.
AND THERE'S NO WAY YOU COULD SHOVE THE BODY OUT THE WINDOW...
...AND DISAPPEAR FROM THE ROOM WITHIN SECONDS.
MRS. IZUMO'S SHOTGUN FOR CLAY-PIGEON SHOOTING ...
MR. KAETSU'S FISHING EQUIP-MENT...
MR. AOBA'S KENDO ARMOR AND BAMBOO SWORD...
MR. ISHI-ZUCHI'S GOLF CLUBS ...
WAIT! WHAT IF THE KILLER THREW ASAMA'S BODY OUT THE WINDOW BEFORE GOING TO THE LOBBY TO SHOOT MR. IZUMO?
WHAT IF, WHEN WE CHASED THE KILLER TO THE ROOM, THE BODY WAS ALREADY GONE?
THERE'S ONE TOOL THAT COULD BE USED TO CREATE THAT ILLUSION!
DETECTIVE NISHIMURA! I'VE JUST GOTTEN A CALL FROM THE CRIME SCENE! THEY HAVE THE TIME THAT ASAMA FELL FROM THE TRAIN INTO THE TUNNEL!
WHAT?

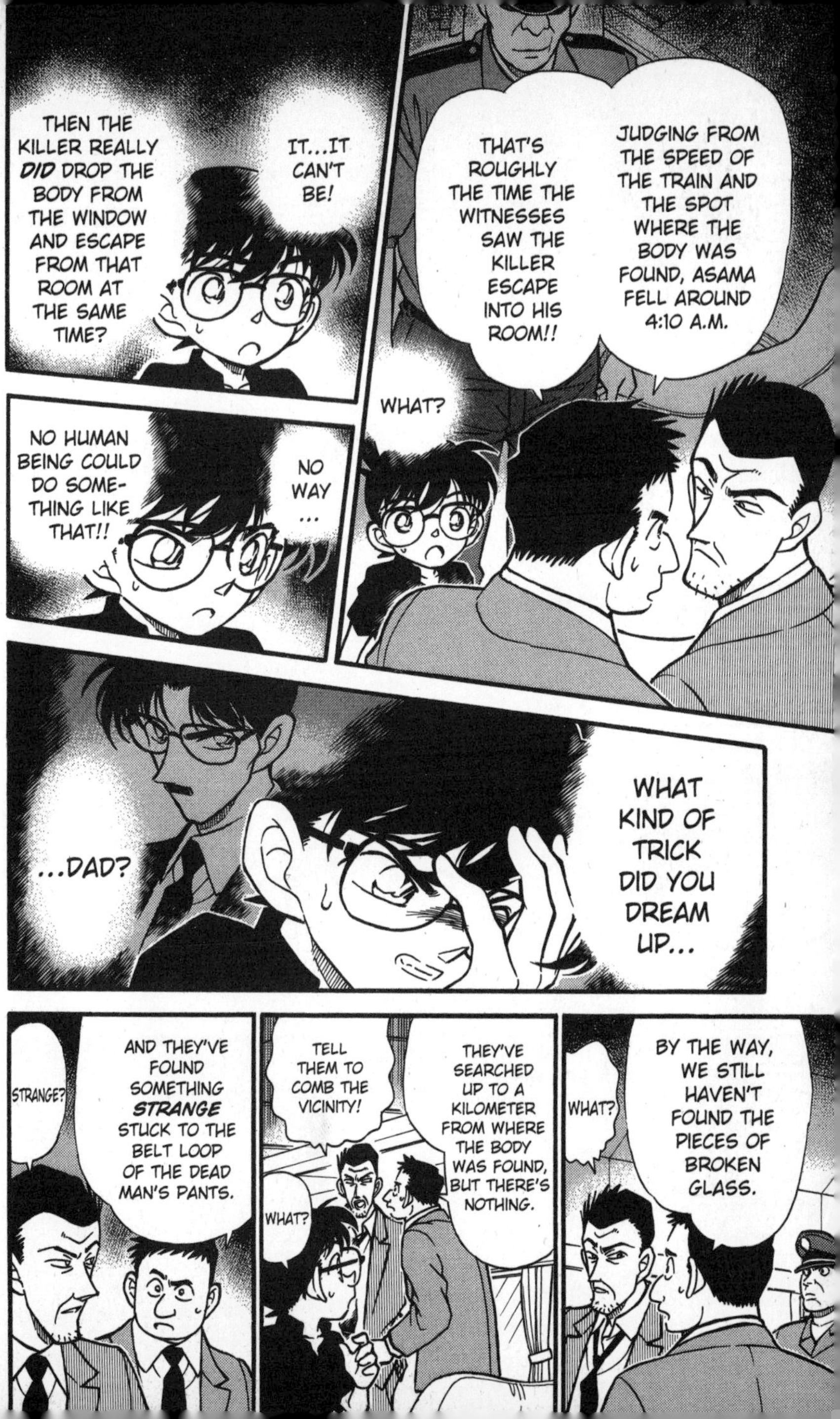
JUDGING FROM THE SPEED OF THE TRAIN AND THE SPOT WHERE THE BODY WAS FOUND, ASAMA FELL AROUND 4:10 A.M.
THAT'S ROUGHLY THE TIME THE WITNESSES SAW THE KILLER ESCAPE INTO HIS ROOM!!
WHAT?
IT...IT CAN'T BE!
THEN THE KILLER REALLY *DID* DROP THE BODY FROM THE WINDOW AND ESCAPE FROM THAT ROOM AT THE SAME TIME?
NO WAY ...
NO HUMAN BEING COULD DO SOME-THING LIKE THAT!!
WHAT KIND OF TRICK DID YOU DREAM UP...
...DAD?
BY THE WAY, WE STILL HAVEN'T FOUND THE PIECES OF BROKEN GLASS.
WHAT?
THEY'VE SEARCHED UP TO A KILOMETER FROM WHERE THE BODY WAS FOUND, BUT THERE'S NOTHING.
TELL THEM TO COMB THE VICINITY!
WHAT?
AND THEY'VE FOUND SOMETHING ***STRANGE*** STUCK TO THE BELT LOOP OF THE DEAD MAN'S PANTS.
STRANGE?

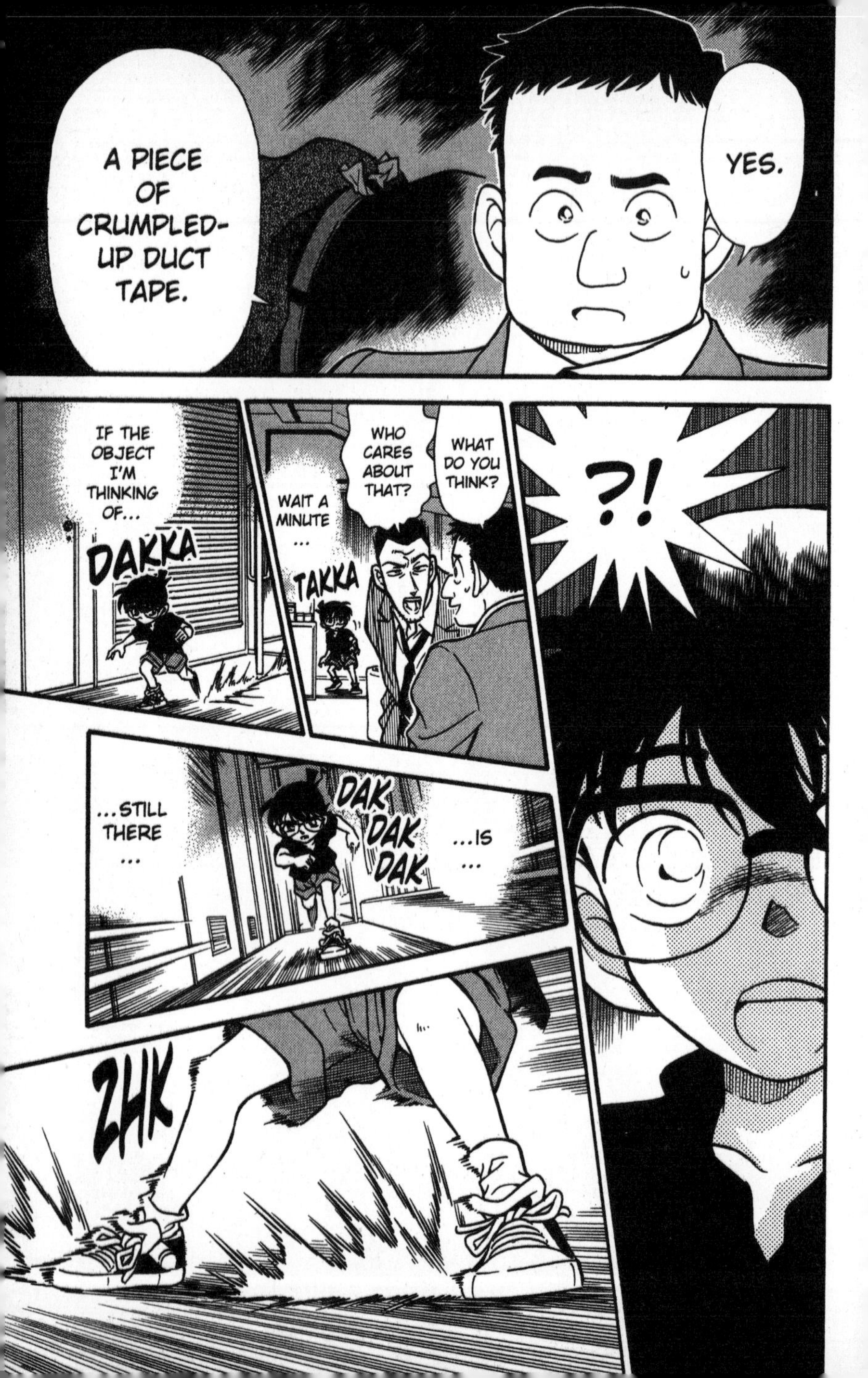
YES.
A PIECE OF CRUMPLED-UP DUCT TAPE.
?!
WHAT DO YOU THINK?
WHO CARES ABOUT THAT?
WAIT A MINUTE ...
TAKKA
IF THE OBJECT I'M THINKING OF...
DAKKA
...IS ...
DAK DAK DAK
...STILL THERE ...
ZHK

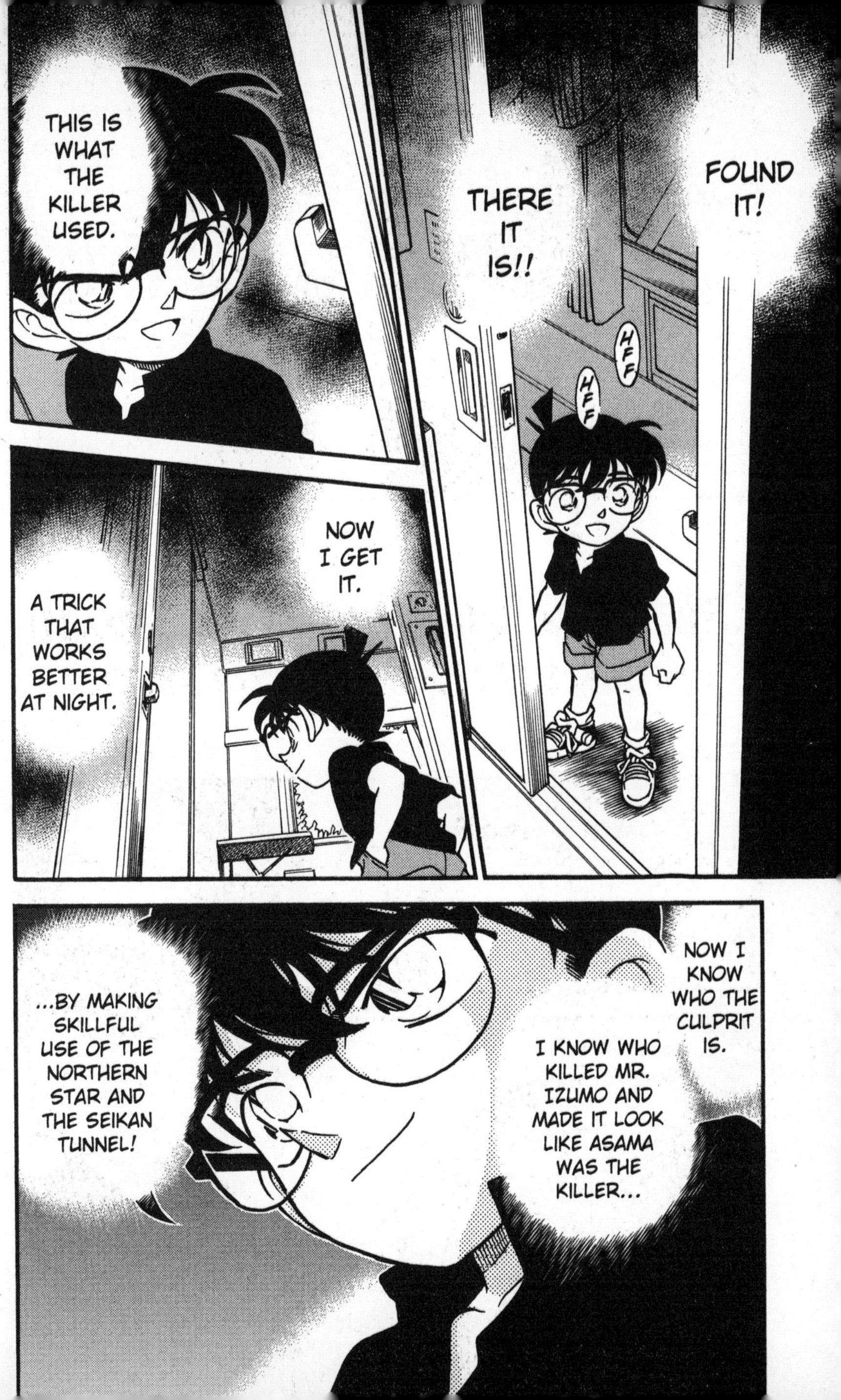

FOUND IT!
THERE IT IS!!
HFF
HFF
THIS IS WHAT THE KILLER USED.
NOW I GET IT.
A TRICK THAT WORKS BETTER AT NIGHT.
NOW I KNOW WHO THE CULPRIT IS.
I KNOW WHO KILLED MR. IZUMO AND MADE IT LOOK LIKE ASAMA WAS THE KILLER...
...BY MAKING SKILLFUL USE OF THE NORTHERN STAR AND THE SEIKAN TUNNEL!

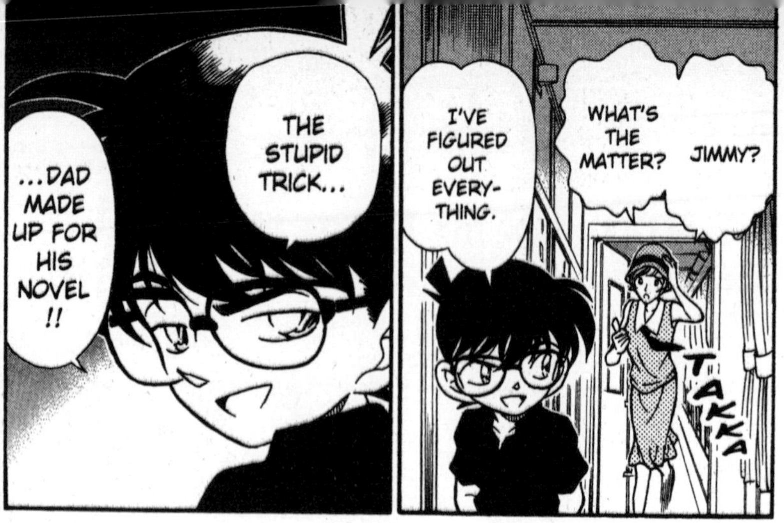
WHAT'S THE MATTER? JIMMY?
I'VE FIGURED OUT EVERY-THING.
TAKKA
THE STUPID TRICK...
...DAD MADE UP FOR HIS NOVEL !!

...THE YOUNG MAN IN THE BLACK-RIMMED GLASSES SNEERED TRIUMPHANTLY.

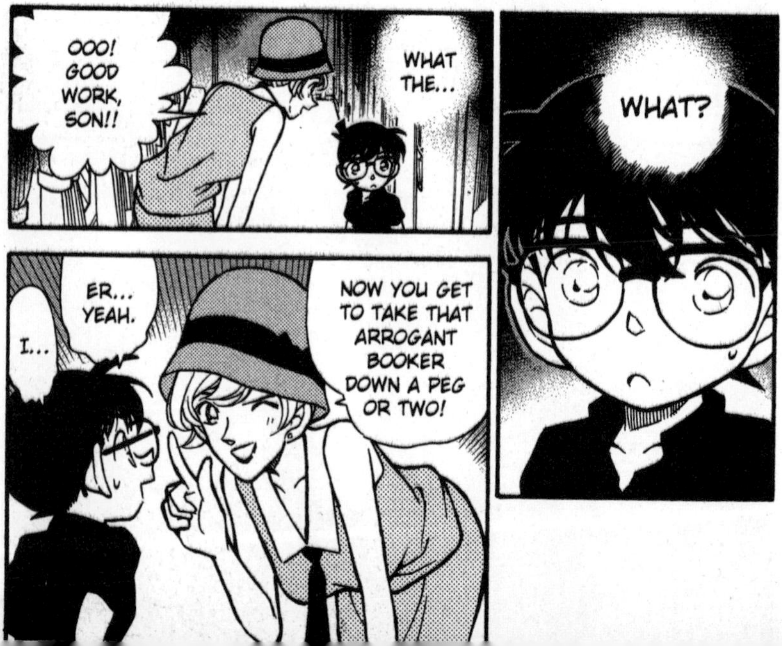
WHAT?
WHAT THE...
OOO! GOOD WORK, SON!!
NOW YOU GET TO TAKE THAT ARROGANT BOOKER DOWN A PEG OR TWO!
ER... YEAH.
I...

LITTLE DID HE KNOW THAT HE WOULD PAY FOR HIS CLEVERNESS WITH HIS OWN LIFE.

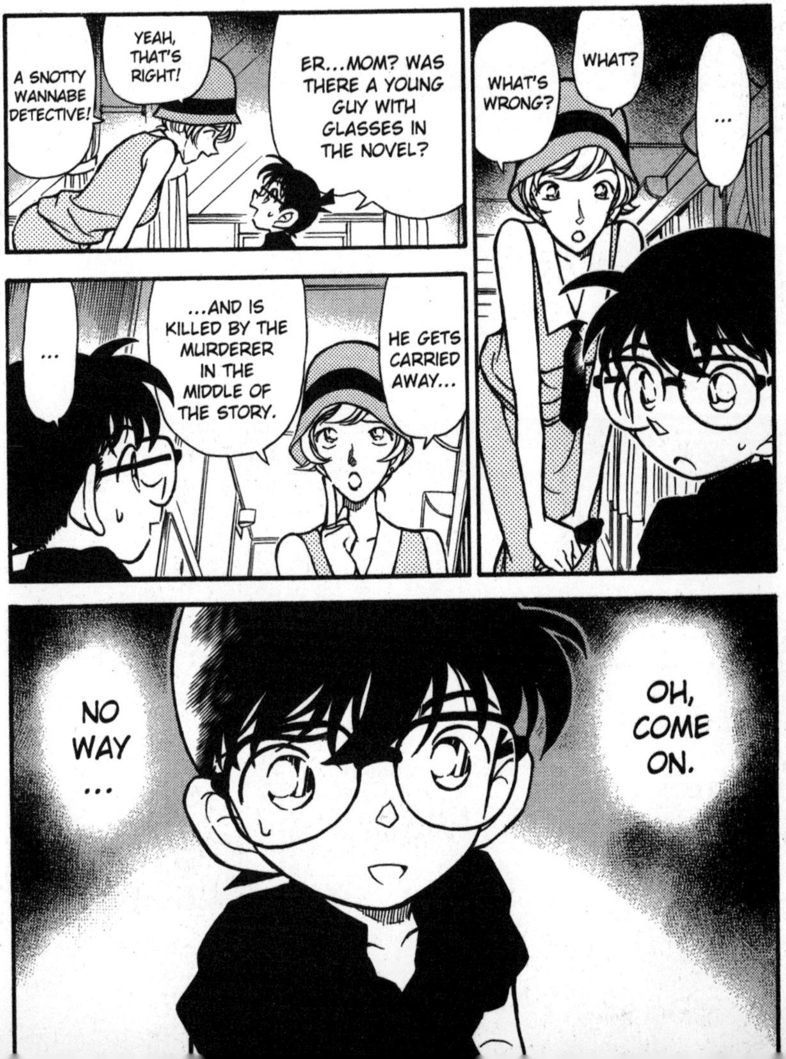
...
WHAT?
WHAT'S WRONG?
ER...MOM? WAS THERE A YOUNG GUY WITH GLASSES IN THE NOVEL?
YEAH, THAT'S RIGHT!
A SNOTTY WANNABE DETECTIVE!
HE GETS CARRIED AWAY...
...AND IS KILLED BY THE MURDERER IN THE MIDDLE OF THE STORY.
...
OH, COME ON.
NO WAY ...

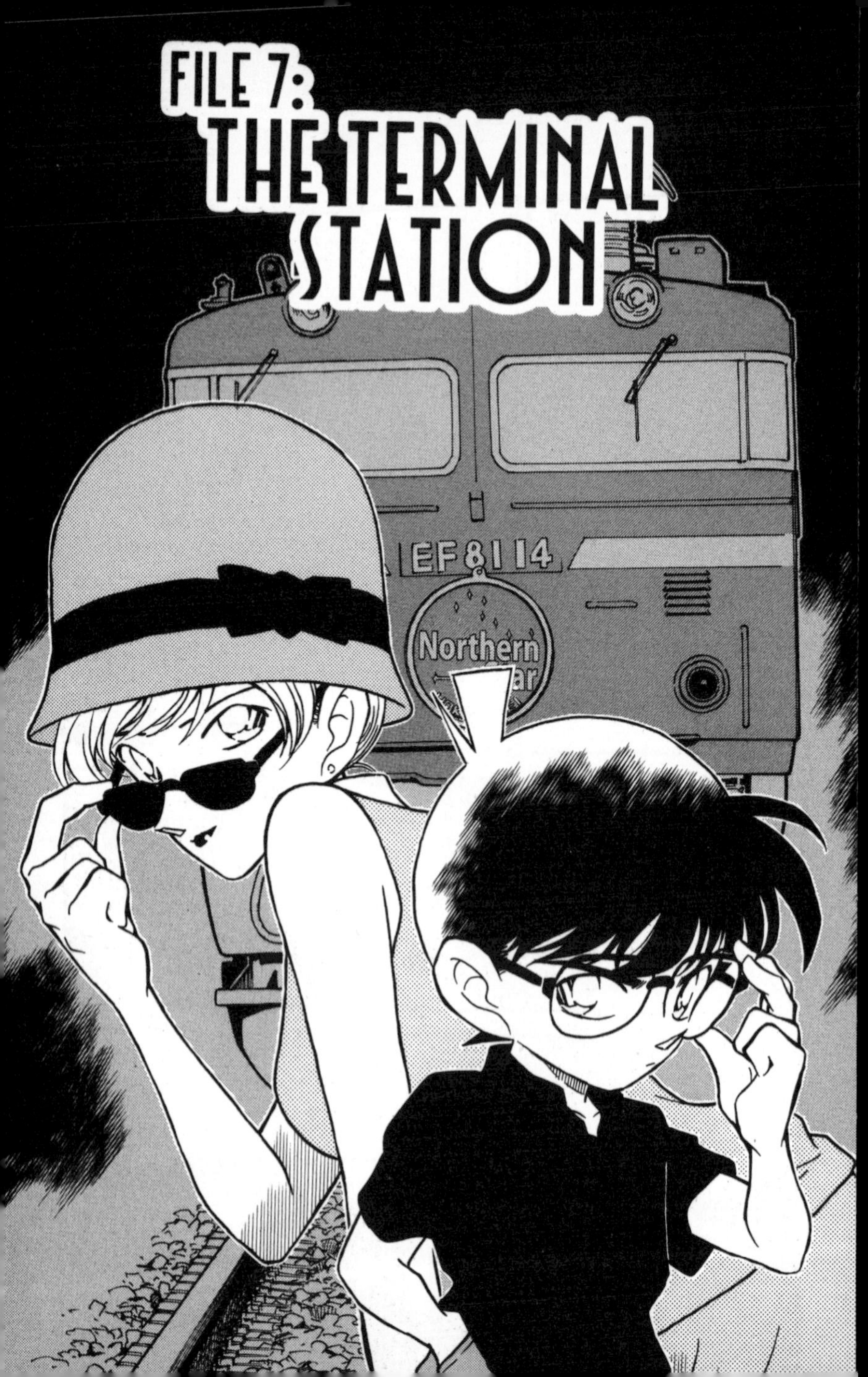
FILE 7:
THE TERMINAL STATION
EF81 14
Northern

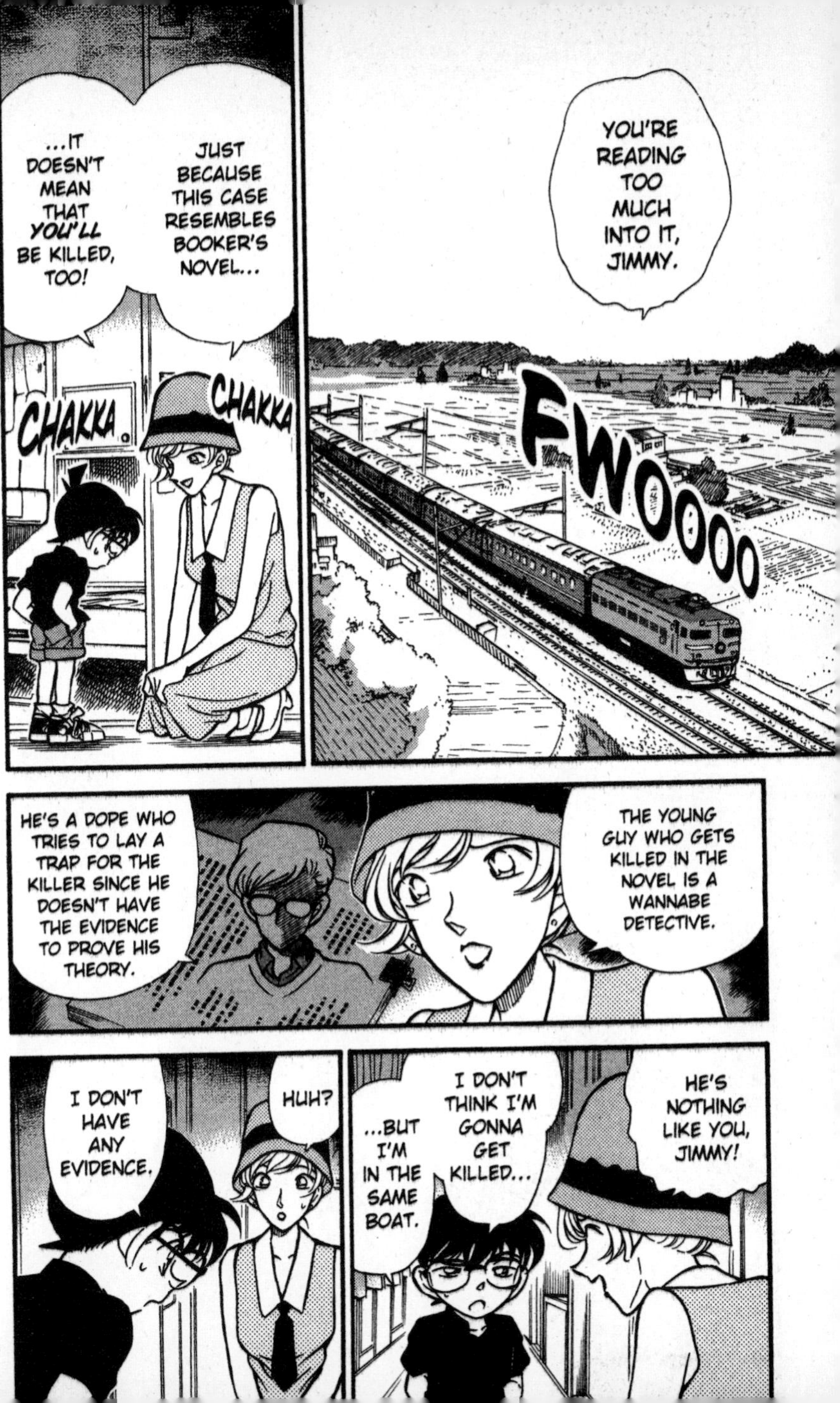
YOU'RE READING TOO MUCH INTO IT, JIMMY.
FWOOOO
CHAKKA
JUST BECAUSE THIS CASE RESEMBLES BOOKER'S NOVEL...
...IT DOESN'T MEAN THAT *YOU'LL* BE KILLED, TOO!
CHAKKA
THE YOUNG GUY WHO GETS KILLED IN THE NOVEL IS A WANNABE DETECTIVE.
HE'S A DOPE WHO TRIES TO LAY A TRAP FOR THE KILLER SINCE HE DOESN'T HAVE THE EVIDENCE TO PROVE HIS THEORY.
HE'S NOTHING LIKE YOU, JIMMY!
I DON'T THINK I'M GONNA GET KILLED...
...BUT I'M IN THE SAME BOAT.
HUH?
I DON'T HAVE ANY EVIDENCE.

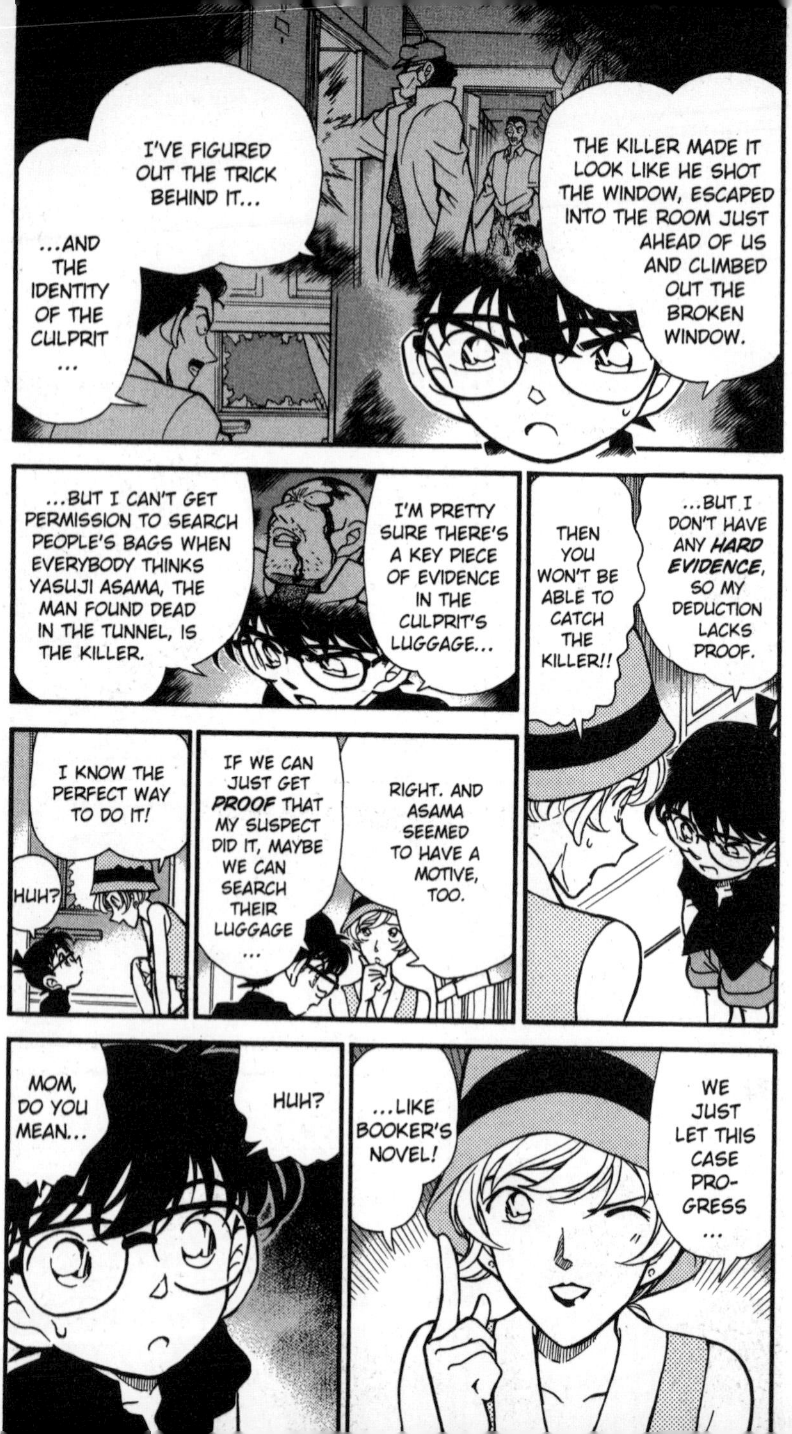
THE KILLER MADE IT LOOK LIKE HE SHOT THE WINDOW, ESCAPED INTO THE ROOM JUST AHEAD OF US AND CLIMBED OUT THE BROKEN WINDOW.
I'VE FIGURED OUT THE TRICK BEHIND IT...
...AND THE IDENTITY OF THE CULPRIT ...
...BUT I DON'T HAVE ANY HARD EVIDENCE, SO MY DEDUCTION LACKS PROOF.
THEN YOU WON'T BE ABLE TO CATCH THE KILLER!!
I'M PRETTY SURE THERE'S A KEY PIECE OF EVIDENCE IN THE CULPRIT'S LUGGAGE...
...BUT I CAN'T GET PERMISSION TO SEARCH PEOPLE'S BAGS WHEN EVERYBODY THINKS YASUJI ASAMA, THE MAN FOUND DEAD IN THE TUNNEL, IS THE KILLER.
RIGHT. AND ASAMA SEEMED TO HAVE A MOTIVE, TOO.
IF WE CAN JUST GET PROOF THAT MY SUSPECT DID IT, MAYBE WE CAN SEARCH THEIR LUGGAGE ...
I KNOW THE PERFECT WAY TO DO IT!
HUH?
WE JUST LET THIS CASE PROGRESS ...
...LIKE BOOKER'S NOVEL!
HUH?
MOM, DO YOU MEAN...

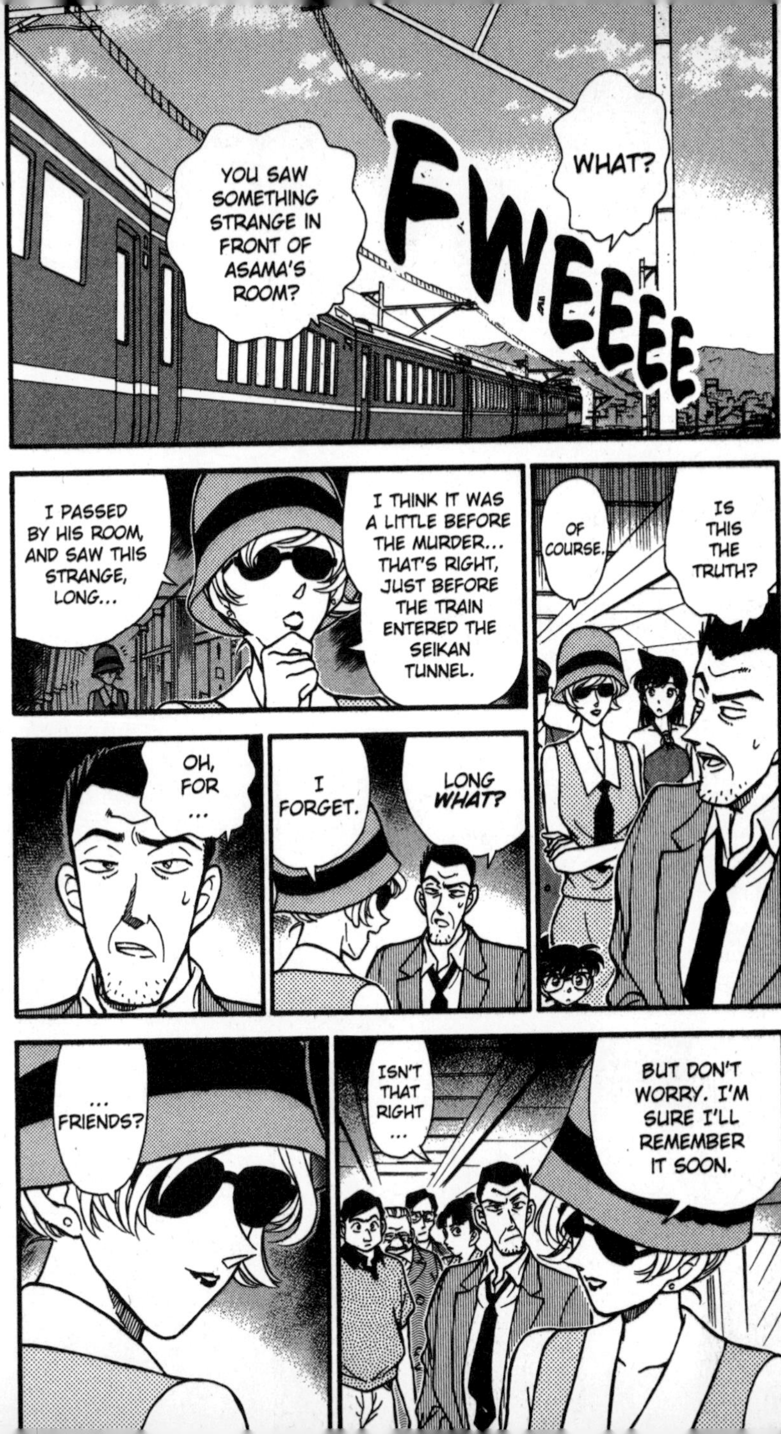
WHAT?
FWEEEEE
YOU SAW SOMETHING STRANGE IN FRONT OF ASAMA'S ROOM?
IS THIS THE TRUTH?
OF COURSE.
I THINK IT WAS A LITTLE BEFORE THE MURDER... THAT'S RIGHT, JUST BEFORE THE TRAIN ENTERED THE SEIKAN TUNNEL.
I PASSED BY HIS ROOM, AND SAW THIS STRANGE, LONG...
LONG *WHAT?*
I FORGET.
OH, FOR ...
BUT DON'T WORRY. I'M SURE I'LL REMEMBER IT SOON.
ISN'T THAT RIGHT ...
... FRIENDS?

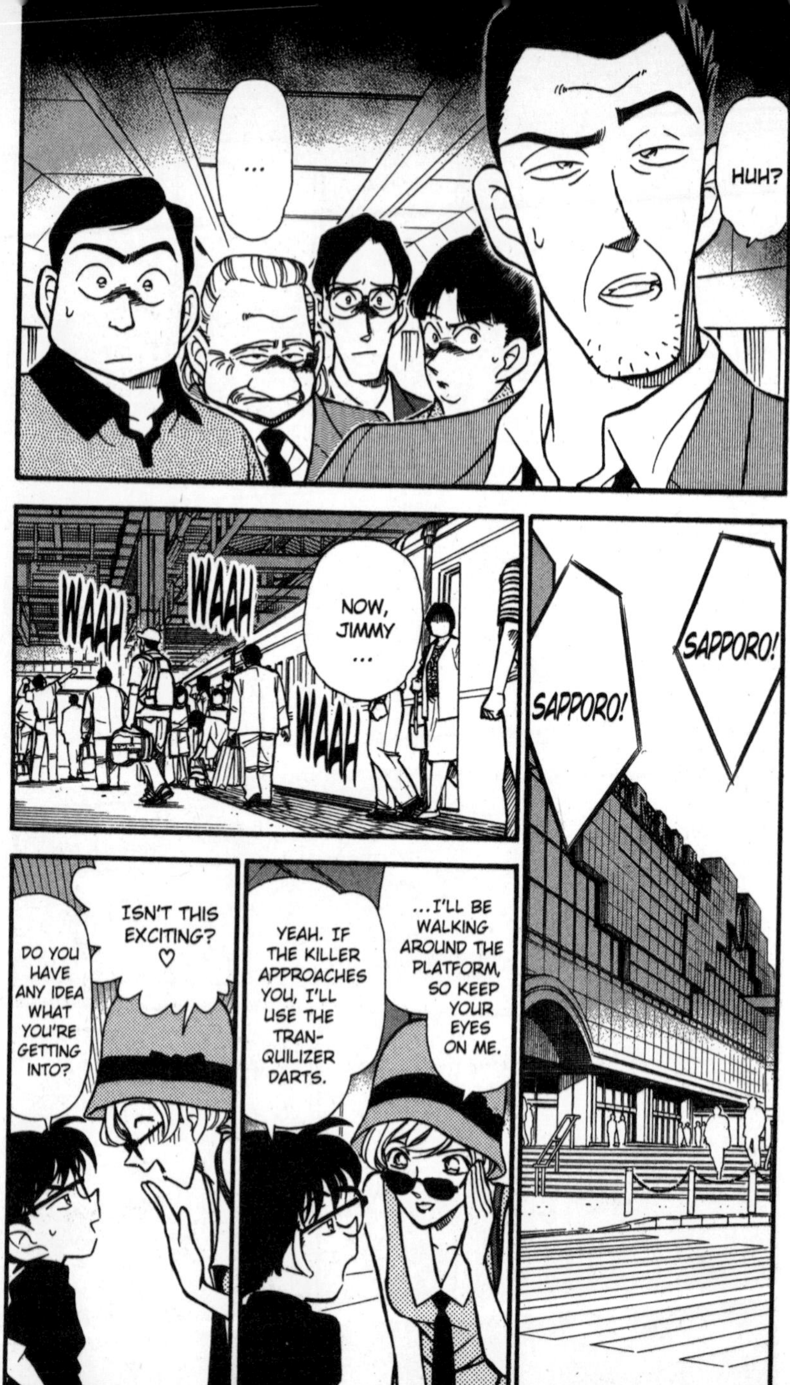
HUH?
...
SAPPORO!
SAPPORO!
WAAH
WAAH
NOW, JIMMY ...
WAAH
...I'LL BE WALKING AROUND THE PLATFORM, SO KEEP YOUR EYES ON ME.
YEAH. IF THE KILLER APPROACHES YOU, I'LL USE THE TRAN-QUILIZER DARTS.
ISN'T THIS EXCITING? ♡
DO YOU HAVE ANY IDEA WHAT YOU'RE GETTING INTO?

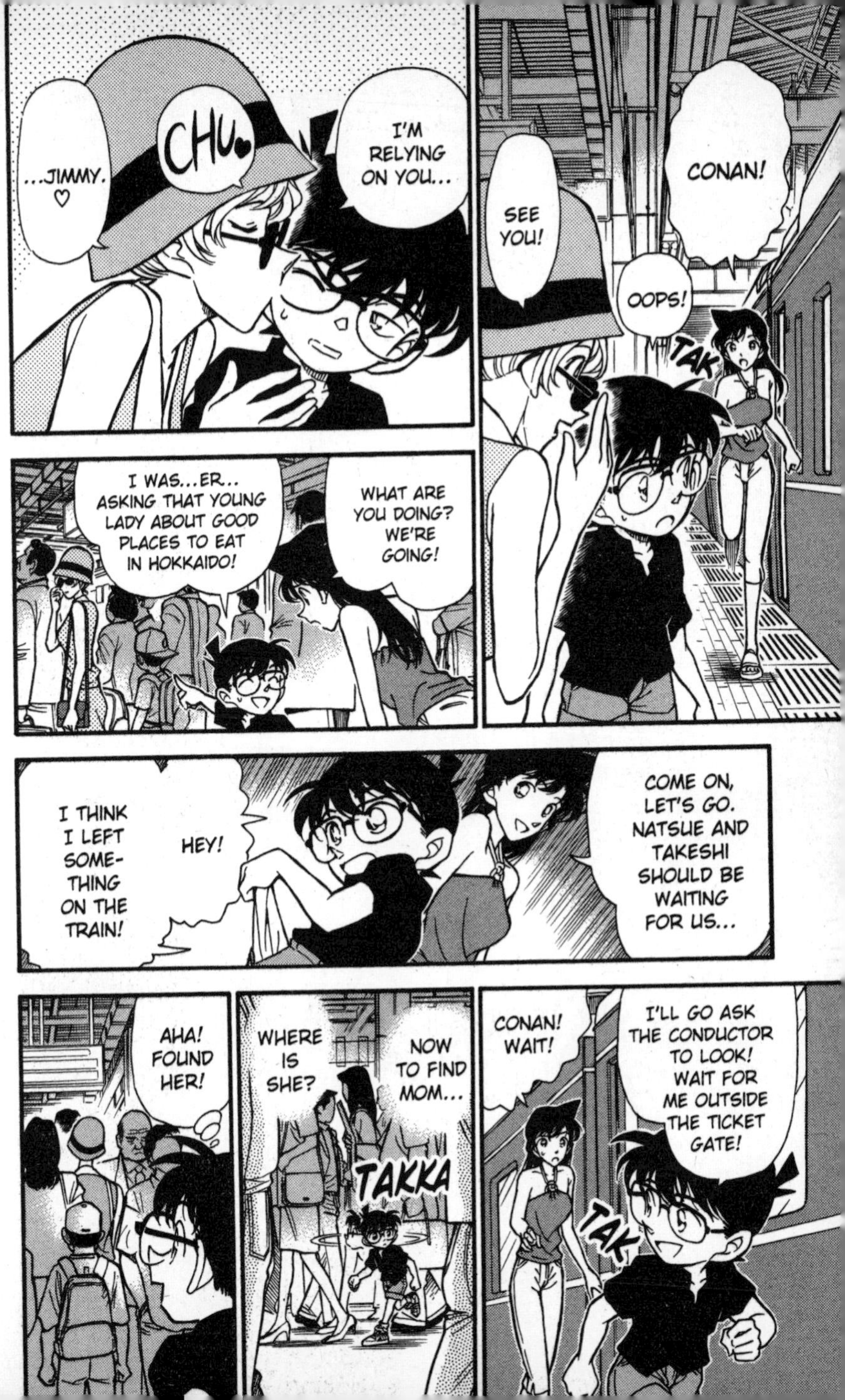
CONAN!
SEE YOU!
OOPS!
TAK
I'M RELYING ON YOU...
CHU
...JIMMY. ♡
WHAT ARE YOU DOING? WE'RE GOING!
I WAS...ER... ASKING THAT YOUNG LADY ABOUT GOOD PLACES TO EAT IN HOKKAIDO!
COME ON, LET'S GO. NATSUE AND TAKESHI SHOULD BE WAITING FOR US...
HEY!
I THINK I LEFT SOME-THING ON THE TRAIN!
I'LL GO ASK THE CONDUCTOR TO LOOK! WAIT FOR ME OUTSIDE THE TICKET GATE!
CONAN! WAIT!
TAK
NOW TO FIND MOM...
WHERE IS SHE?
TAKKA
AHA! FOUND HER!

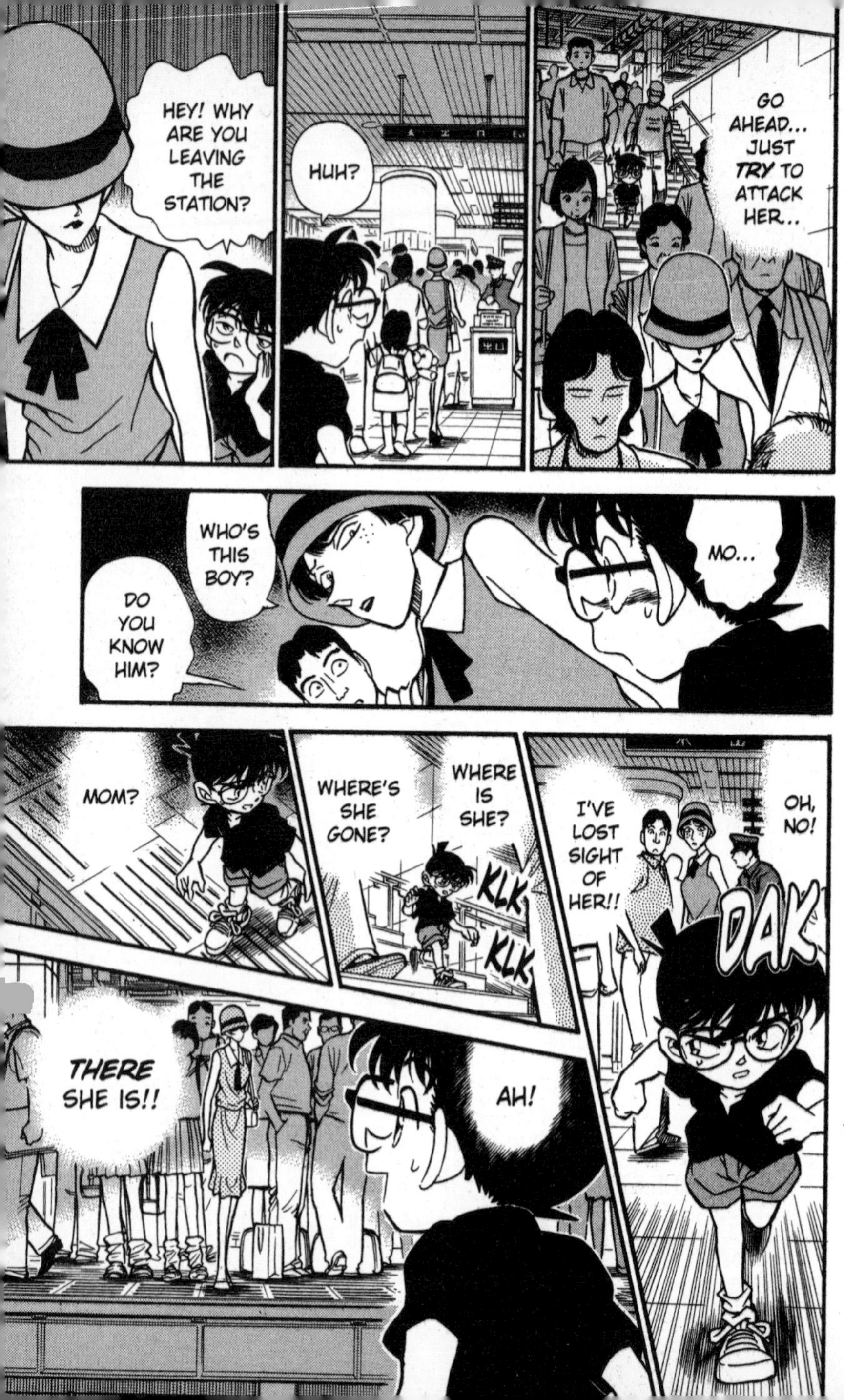
GO AHEAD... JUST TRY TO ATTACK HER...
HUH?
HEY! WHY ARE YOU LEAVING THE STATION?
NO...
WHO'S THIS BOY?
DO YOU KNOW HIM?
OH, NO!
I'VE LOST SIGHT OF HER!!
DAK
WHERE IS SHE?
WHERE'S SHE GONE?
KLK
KLK
MOM?
AH!
THERE SHE IS!!

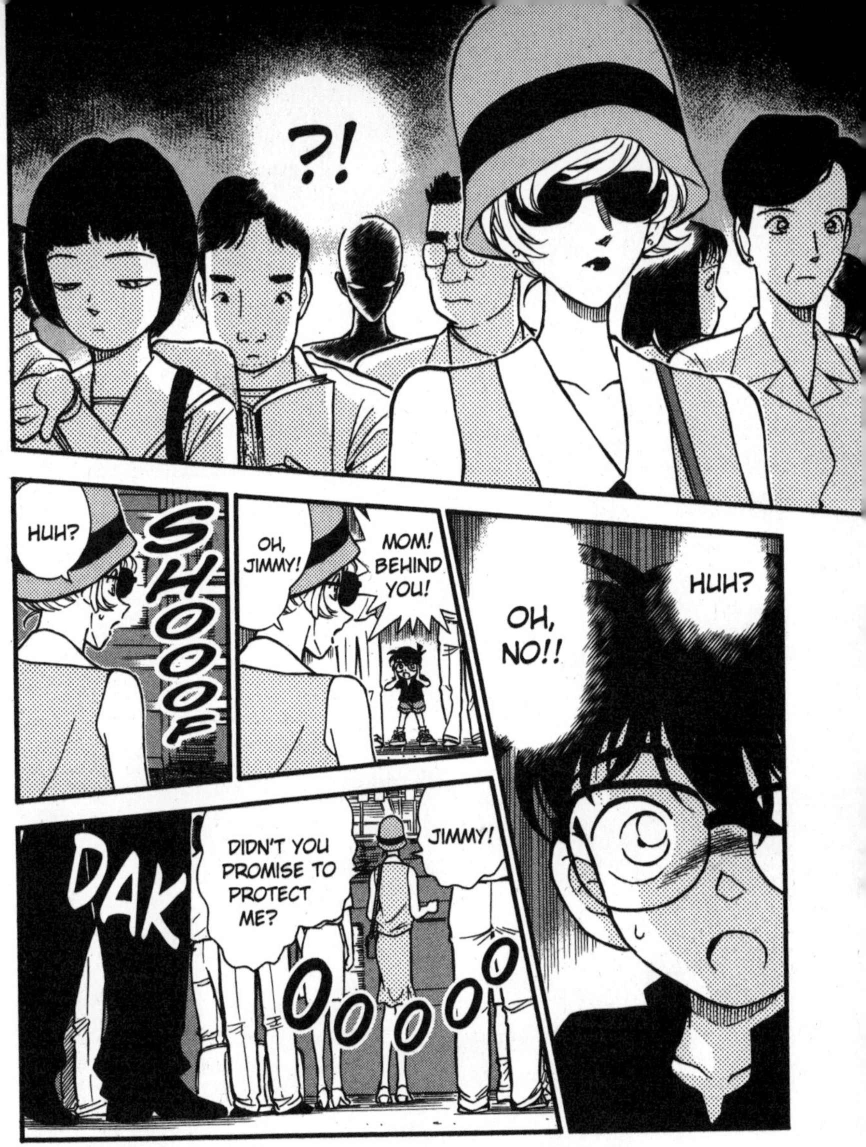
?!
HUH?
OH, NO!!
MOM! BEHIND YOU!
OH, JIMMY!
SHOOOOF
HUH?
JIMMY!
DIDN'T YOU PROMISE TO PROTECT ME?
OOOOO
DAK

THE CRIMINAL CREPT SOUNDLESSLY
BEHIND THE YOUNG DETECTIVE..

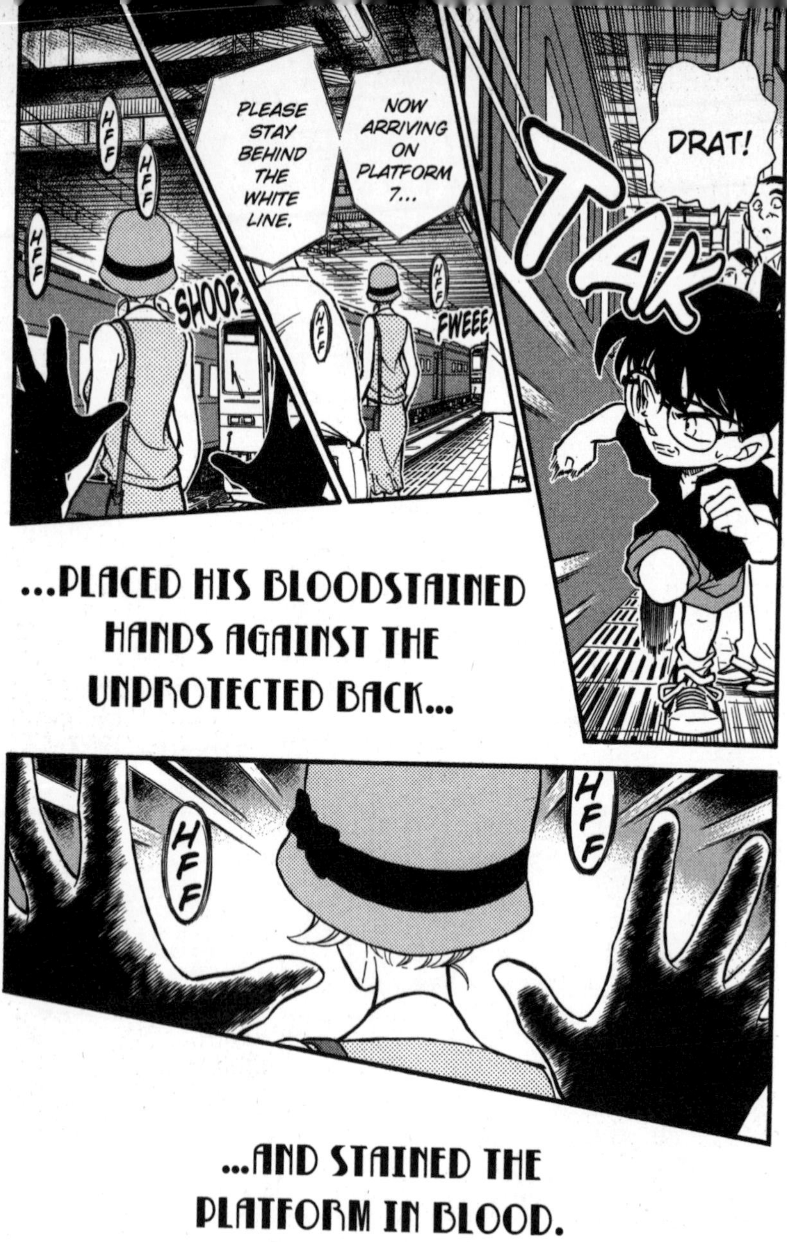
DRAT!
TAK
NOW ARRIVING ON PLATFORM 7...
PLEASE STAY BEHIND THE WHITE LINE.
HFF
FWEEE
HFF
HFF
HFF
HFF
SHOOF
...PLACED HIS BLOODSTAINED HANDS AGAINST THE UNPROTECTED BACK...
HFF
HFF
...AND STAINED THE PLATFORM IN BLOOD.

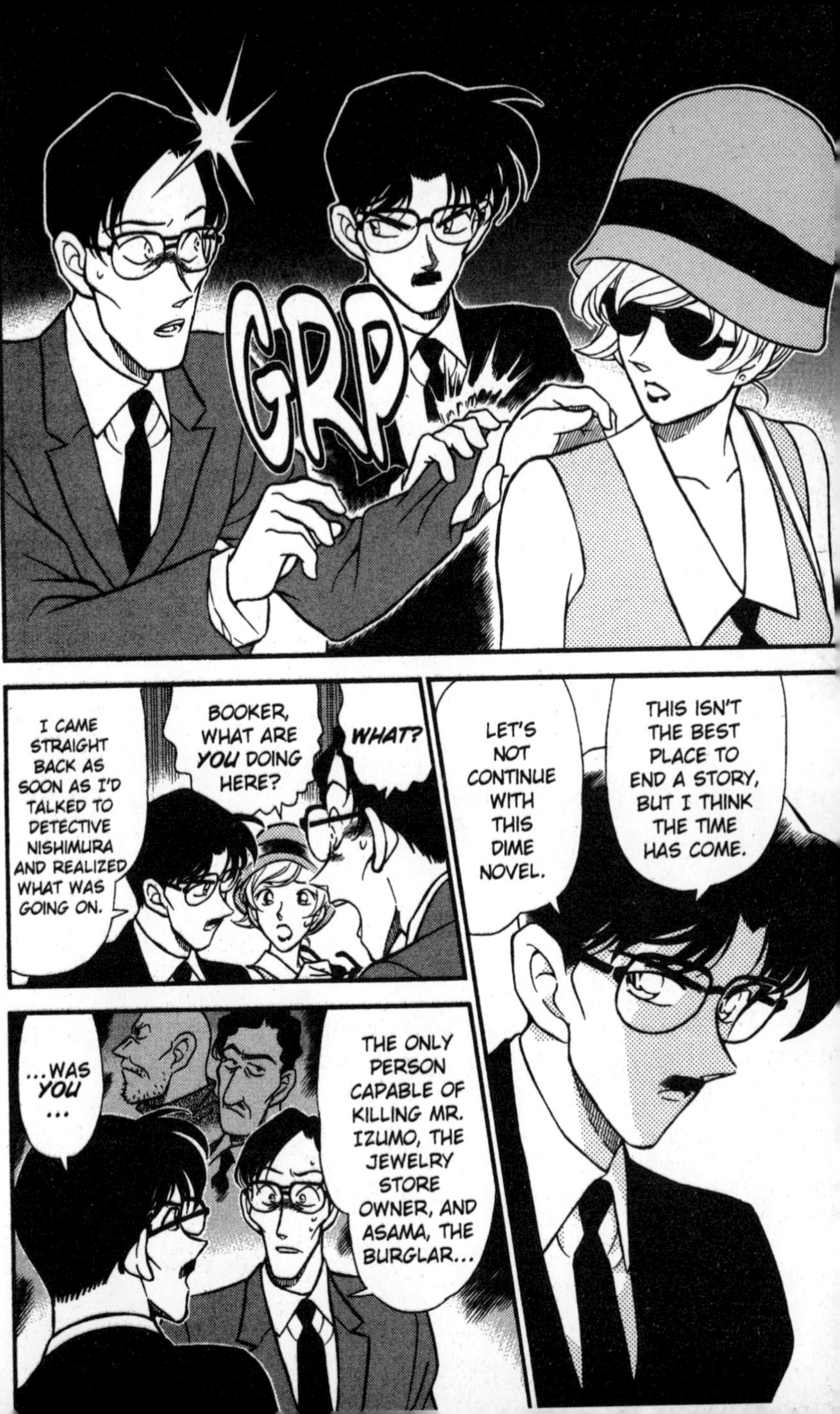
GRP
THIS ISN'T THE BEST PLACE TO END A STORY, BUT I THINK THE TIME HAS COME.
LET'S NOT CONTINUE WITH THIS DIME NOVEL.
WHAT?
BOOKER, WHAT ARE YOU DOING HERE?
I CAME STRAIGHT BACK AS SOON AS I'D TALKED TO DETECTIVE NISHIMURA AND REALIZED WHAT WAS GOING ON.
THE ONLY PERSON CAPABLE OF KILLING MR. IZUMO, THE JEWELRY STORE OWNER, AND ASAMA, THE BURGLAR...
...WAS YOU...

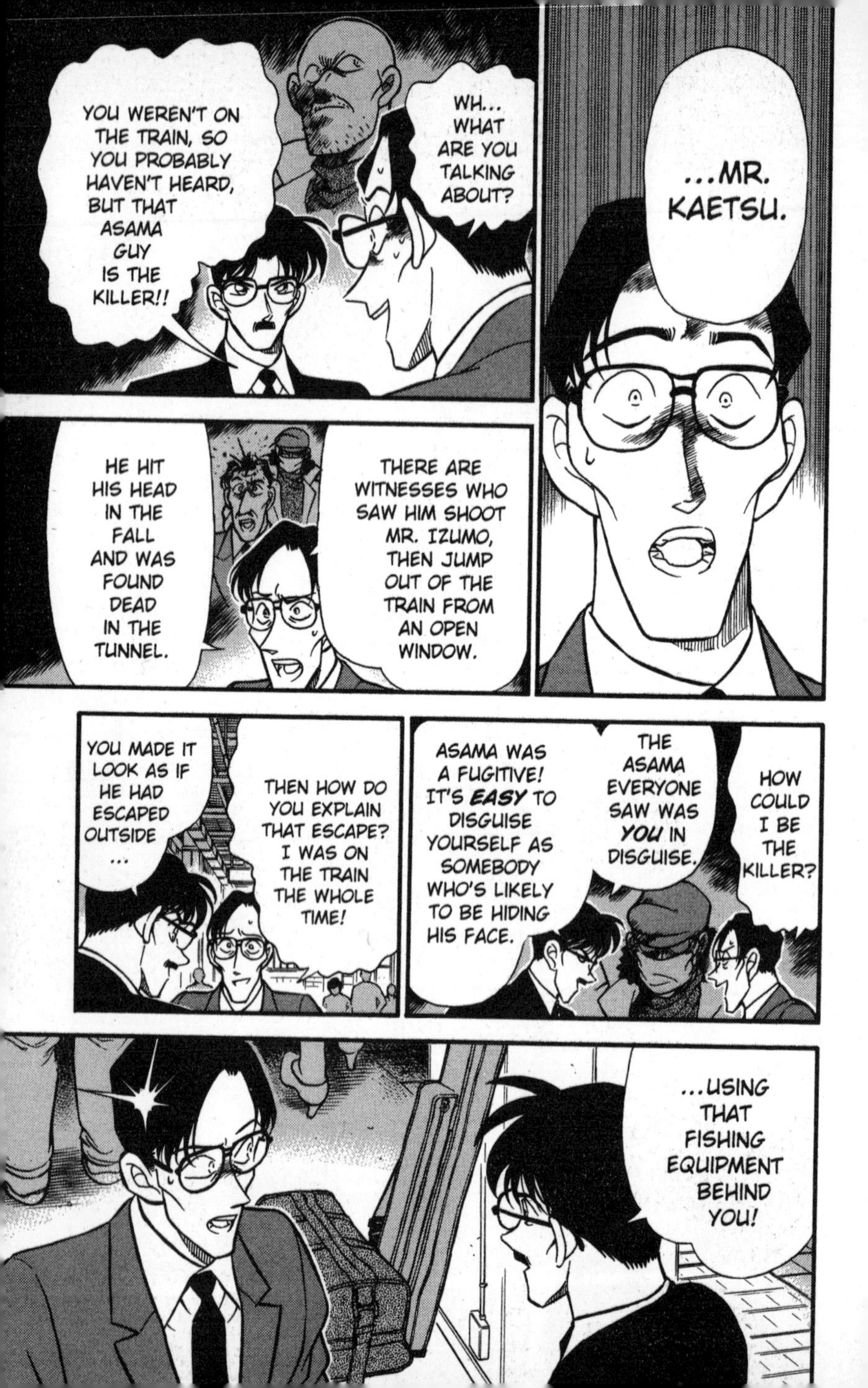
...MR. KAETSU.
WH... WHAT ARE YOU TALKING ABOUT?
YOU WEREN'T ON THE TRAIN, SO YOU PROBABLY HAVEN'T HEARD, BUT THAT ASAMA GUY IS THE KILLER!!
THERE ARE WITNESSES WHO SAW HIM SHOOT MR. IZUMO, THEN JUMP OUT OF THE TRAIN FROM AN OPEN WINDOW.
HE HIT HIS HEAD IN THE FALL AND WAS FOUND DEAD IN THE TUNNEL.
HOW COULD I BE THE KILLER?
THE ASAMA EVERYONE SAW WAS *YOU* IN DISGUISE.
ASAMA WAS A FUGITIVE! IT'S *EASY* TO DISGUISE YOURSELF AS SOMEBODY WHO'S LIKELY TO BE HIDING HIS FACE.
THEN HOW DO YOU EXPLAIN THAT ESCAPE? I WAS ON THE TRAIN THE WHOLE TIME!
YOU MADE IT LOOK AS IF HE HAD ESCAPED OUTSIDE ...
...USING THAT FISHING EQUIPMENT BEHIND YOU!

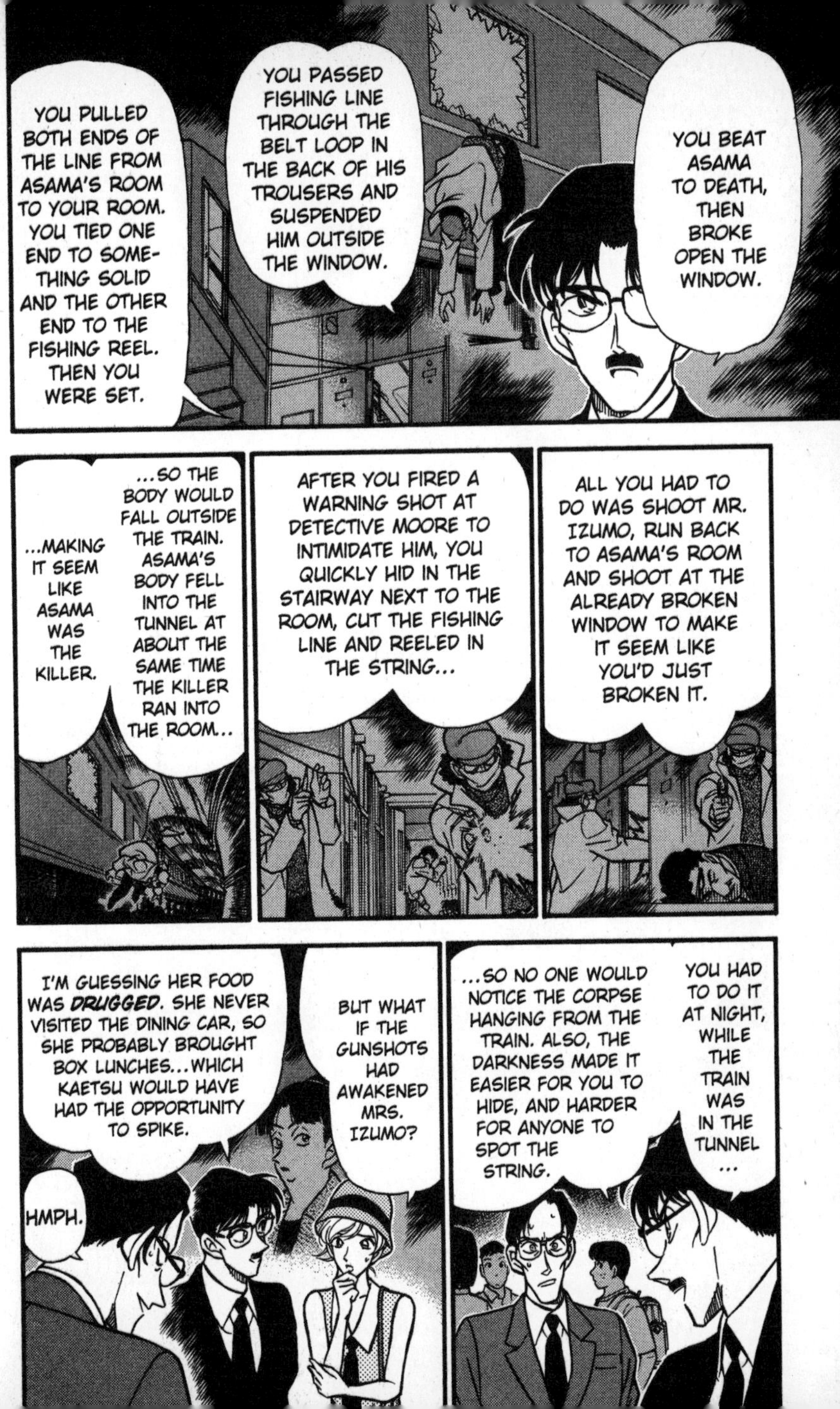
YOU BEAT ASAMA TO DEATH, THEN BROKE OPEN THE WINDOW.
YOU PASSED FISHING LINE THROUGH THE BELT LOOP IN THE BACK OF HIS TROUSERS AND SUSPENDED HIM OUTSIDE THE WINDOW.
YOU PULLED BOTH ENDS OF THE LINE FROM ASAMA'S ROOM TO YOUR ROOM. YOU TIED ONE END TO SOME-THING SOLID AND THE OTHER END TO THE FISHING REEL. THEN YOU WERE SET.
ALL YOU HAD TO DO WAS SHOOT MR. IZUMO, RUN BACK TO ASAMA'S ROOM AND SHOOT AT THE ALREADY BROKEN WINDOW TO MAKE IT SEEM LIKE YOU'D JUST BROKEN IT.
AFTER YOU FIRED A WARNING SHOT AT DETECTIVE MOORE TO INTIMIDATE HIM, YOU QUICKLY HID IN THE STAIRWAY NEXT TO THE ROOM, CUT THE FISHING LINE AND REELED IN THE STRING...
...SO THE BODY WOULD FALL OUTSIDE THE TRAIN. ASAMA'S BODY FELL INTO THE TUNNEL AT ABOUT THE SAME TIME THE KILLER RAN INTO THE ROOM...
...MAKING IT SEEM LIKE ASAMA WAS THE KILLER.
YOU HAD TO DO IT AT NIGHT, WHILE THE TRAIN WAS IN THE TUNNEL...
...SO NO ONE WOULD NOTICE THE CORPSE HANGING FROM THE TRAIN. ALSO, THE DARKNESS MADE IT EASIER FOR YOU TO HIDE, AND HARDER FOR ANYONE TO SPOT THE STRING.
BUT WHAT IF THE GUNSHOTS HAD AWAKENED MRS. IZUMO?
I'M GUESSING HER FOOD WAS **DRUGGED**. SHE NEVER VISITED THE DINING CAR, SO SHE PROBABLY BROUGHT BOX LUNCHES...WHICH KAETSU WOULD HAVE HAD THE OPPORTUNITY TO SPIKE.
HMPH.

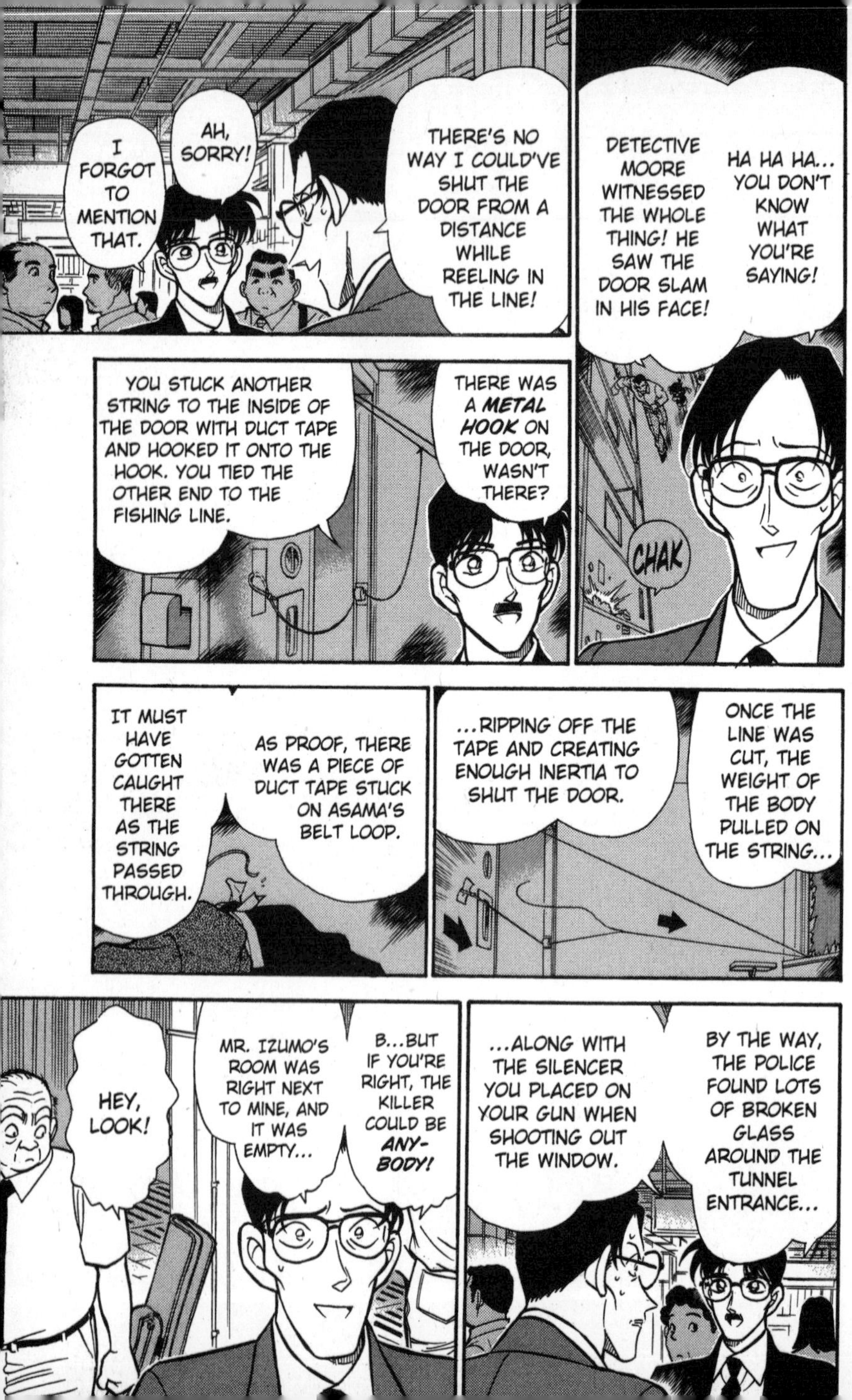
HA HA HA... YOU DON'T KNOW WHAT YOU'RE SAYING!
DETECTIVE MOORE WITNESSED THE WHOLE THING! HE SAW THE DOOR SLAM IN HIS FACE!
CHAK
THERE'S NO WAY I COULD'VE SHUT THE DOOR FROM A DISTANCE WHILE REELING IN THE LINE!
AH, SORRY!
I FORGOT TO MENTION THAT.
THERE WAS A METAL HOOK ON THE DOOR, WASN'T THERE?
YOU STUCK ANOTHER STRING TO THE INSIDE OF THE DOOR WITH DUCT TAPE AND HOOKED IT ONTO THE HOOK. YOU TIED THE OTHER END TO THE FISHING LINE.
ONCE THE LINE WAS CUT, THE WEIGHT OF THE BODY PULLED ON THE STRING...
...RIPPING OFF THE TAPE AND CREATING ENOUGH INERTIA TO SHUT THE DOOR.
AS PROOF, THERE WAS A PIECE OF DUCT TAPE STUCK ON ASAMA'S BELT LOOP.
IT MUST HAVE GOTTEN CAUGHT THERE AS THE STRING PASSED THROUGH.
BY THE WAY, THE POLICE FOUND LOTS OF BROKEN GLASS AROUND THE TUNNEL ENTRANCE...
...ALONG WITH THE SILENCER YOU PLACED ON YOUR GUN WHEN SHOOTING OUT THE WINDOW.
B...BUT IF YOU'RE RIGHT, THE KILLER COULD BE ANYBODY!
MR. IZUMO'S ROOM WAS RIGHT NEXT TO MINE, AND IT WAS EMPTY...
HEY, LOOK!

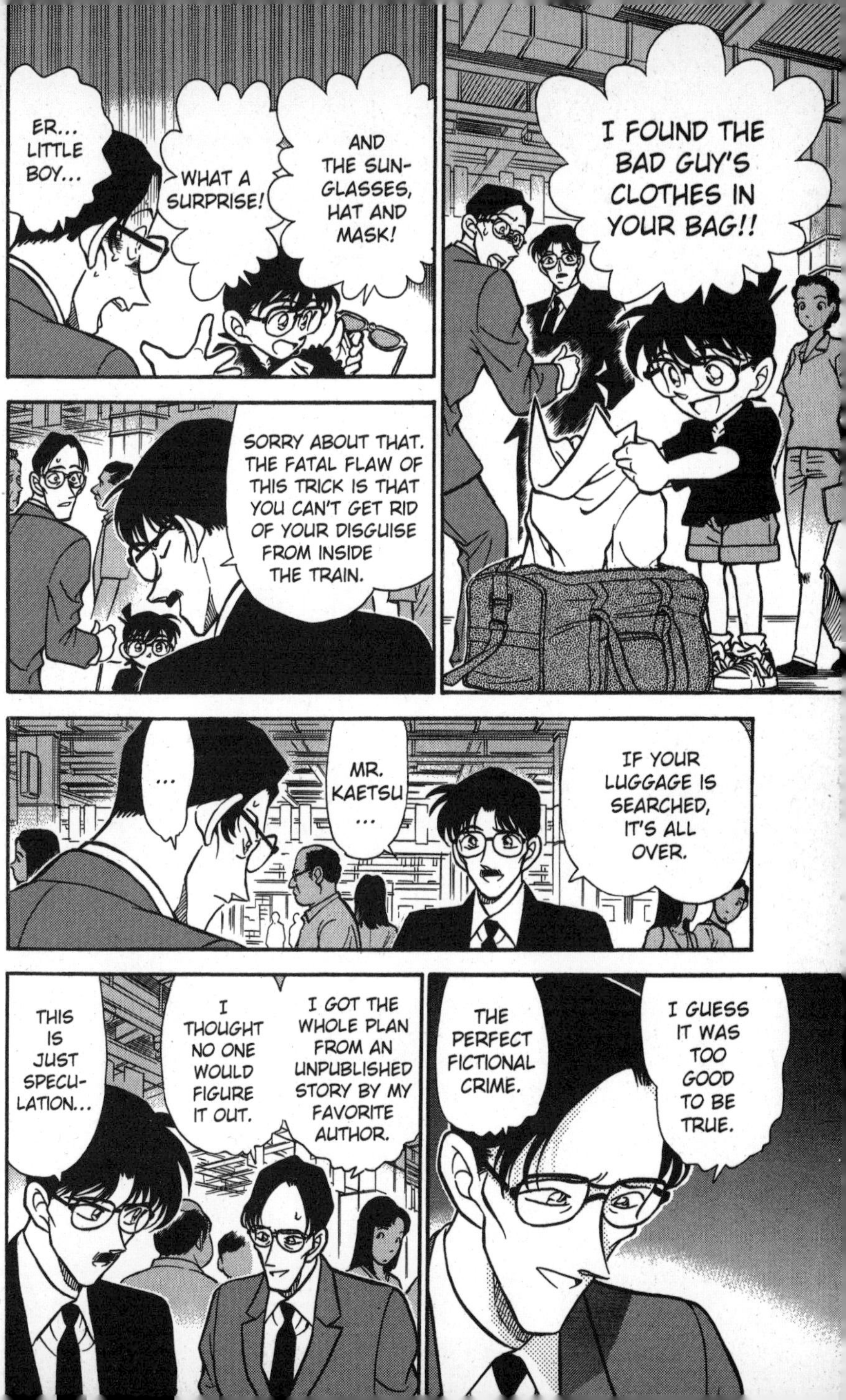
I FOUND THE BAD GUY'S CLOTHES IN YOUR BAG!!
AND THE SUN-GLASSES, HAT AND MASK!
WHAT A SURPRISE!
ER... LITTLE BOY...
SORRY ABOUT THAT. THE FATAL FLAW OF THIS TRICK IS THAT YOU CAN'T GET RID OF YOUR DISGUISE FROM INSIDE THE TRAIN.
IF YOUR LUGGAGE IS SEARCHED, IT'S ALL OVER.
MR. KAETSU...
...
I GUESS IT WAS TOO GOOD TO BE TRUE.
THE PERFECT FICTIONAL CRIME.
I GOT THE WHOLE PLAN FROM AN UNPUBLISHED STORY BY MY FAVORITE AUTHOR.
I THOUGHT NO ONE WOULD FIGURE IT OUT.
THIS IS JUST SPECULATION...

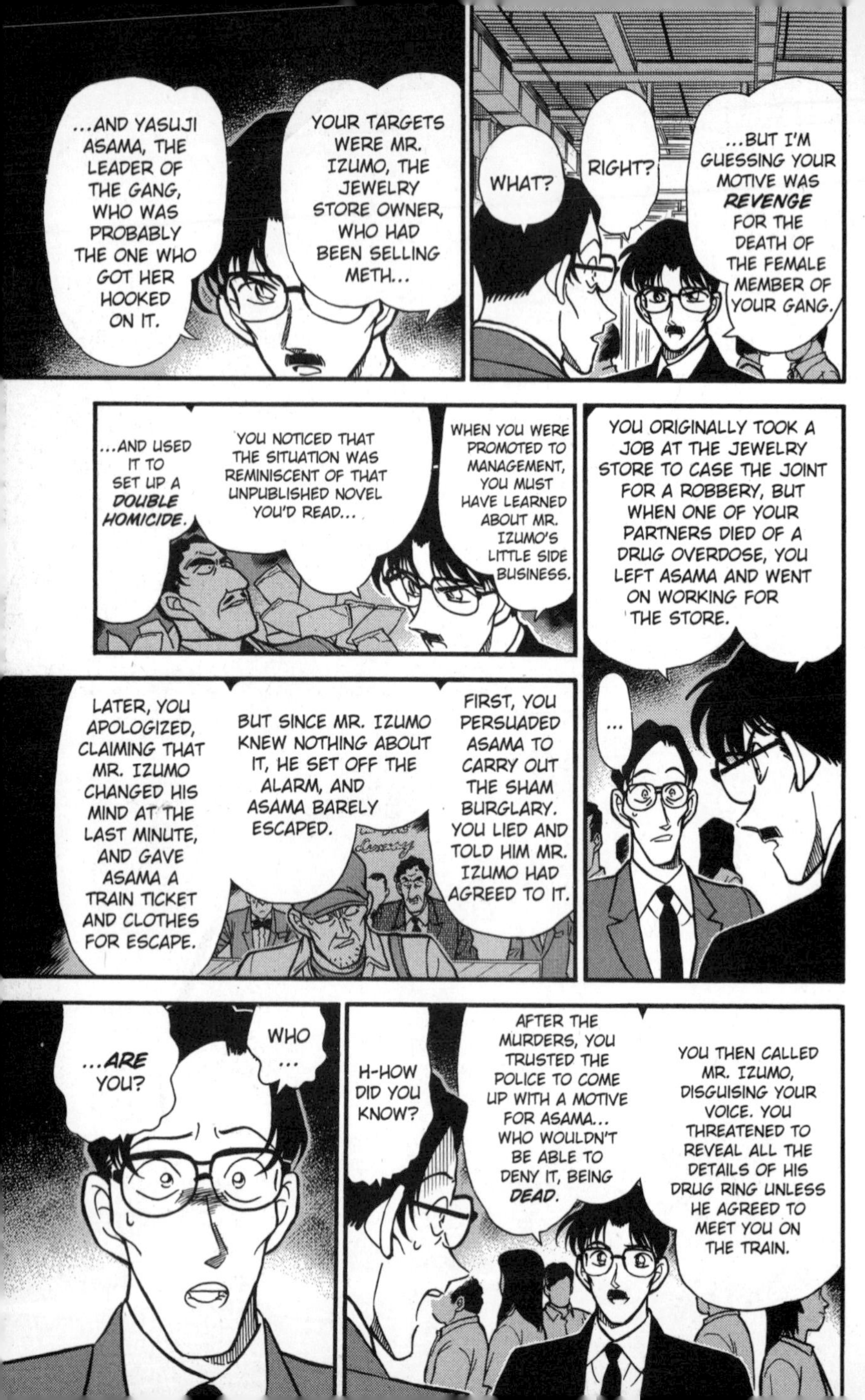
...BUT I'M GUESSING YOUR MOTIVE WAS **REVENGE** FOR THE DEATH OF THE FEMALE MEMBER OF YOUR GANG.
RIGHT?
WHAT?
YOUR TARGETS WERE MR. IZUMO, THE JEWELRY STORE OWNER, WHO HAD BEEN SELLING METH...
...AND YASUJI ASAMA, THE LEADER OF THE GANG, WHO WAS PROBABLY THE ONE WHO GOT HER HOOKED ON IT.
YOU ORIGINALLY TOOK A JOB AT THE JEWELRY STORE TO CASE THE JOINT FOR A ROBBERY, BUT WHEN ONE OF YOUR PARTNERS DIED OF A DRUG OVERDOSE, YOU LEFT ASAMA AND WENT ON WORKING FOR THE STORE.
...
WHEN YOU WERE PROMOTED TO MANAGEMENT, YOU MUST HAVE LEARNED ABOUT MR. IZUMO'S LITTLE SIDE BUSINESS.
YOU NOTICED THAT THE SITUATION WAS REMINISCENT OF THAT UNPUBLISHED NOVEL YOU'D READ...
...AND USED IT TO SET UP A ***DOUBLE HOMICIDE***.
FIRST, YOU PERSUADED ASAMA TO CARRY OUT THE SHAM BURGLARY. YOU LIED AND TOLD HIM MR. IZUMO HAD AGREED TO IT.
BUT SINCE MR. IZUMO KNEW NOTHING ABOUT IT, HE SET OFF THE ALARM, AND ASAMA BARELY ESCAPED.
LATER, YOU APOLOGIZED, CLAIMING THAT MR. IZUMO CHANGED HIS MIND AT THE LAST MINUTE, AND GAVE ASAMA A TRAIN TICKET AND CLOTHES FOR ESCAPE.
YOU THEN CALLED MR. IZUMO, DISGUISING YOUR VOICE. YOU THREATENED TO REVEAL ALL THE DETAILS OF HIS DRUG RING UNLESS HE AGREED TO MEET YOU ON THE TRAIN.
AFTER THE MURDERS, YOU TRUSTED THE POLICE TO COME UP WITH A MOTIVE FOR ASAMA... WHO WOULDN'T BE ABLE TO DENY IT, BEING ***DEAD***.
H-HOW DID YOU KNOW?
WHO...
...***ARE*** YOU?

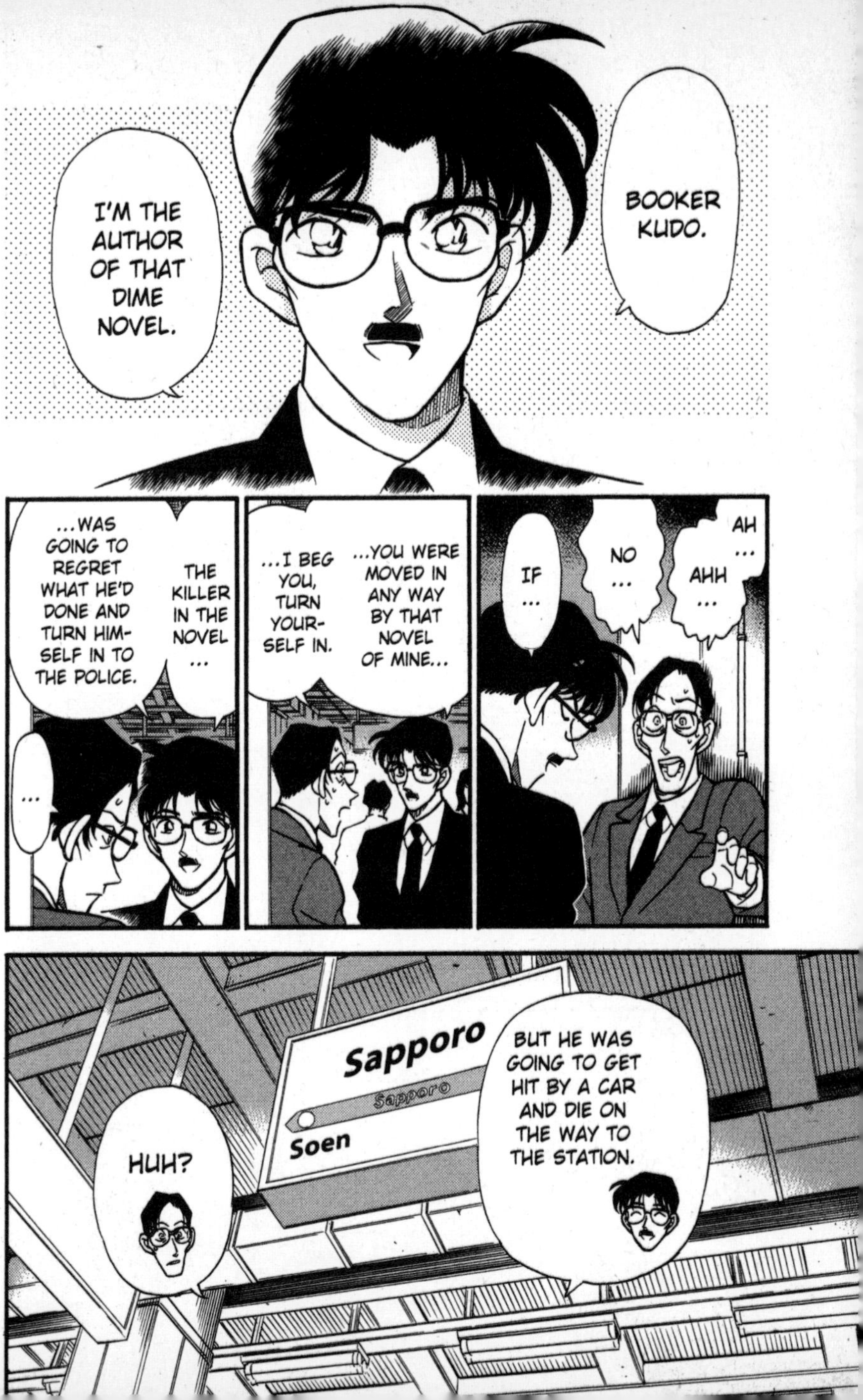
BOOKER KUDO.
I'M THE AUTHOR OF THAT DIME NOVEL.
AH... AHH...
NO...
IF...
...YOU WERE MOVED IN ANY WAY BY THAT NOVEL OF MINE...
...I BEG YOU, TURN YOURSELF IN.
THE KILLER IN THE NOVEL...
...WAS GOING TO REGRET WHAT HE'D DONE AND TURN HIMSELF IN TO THE POLICE.
...
Sapporo
Sapporo
Soen
BUT HE WAS GOING TO GET HIT BY A CAR AND DIE ON THE WAY TO THE STATION.
HUH?

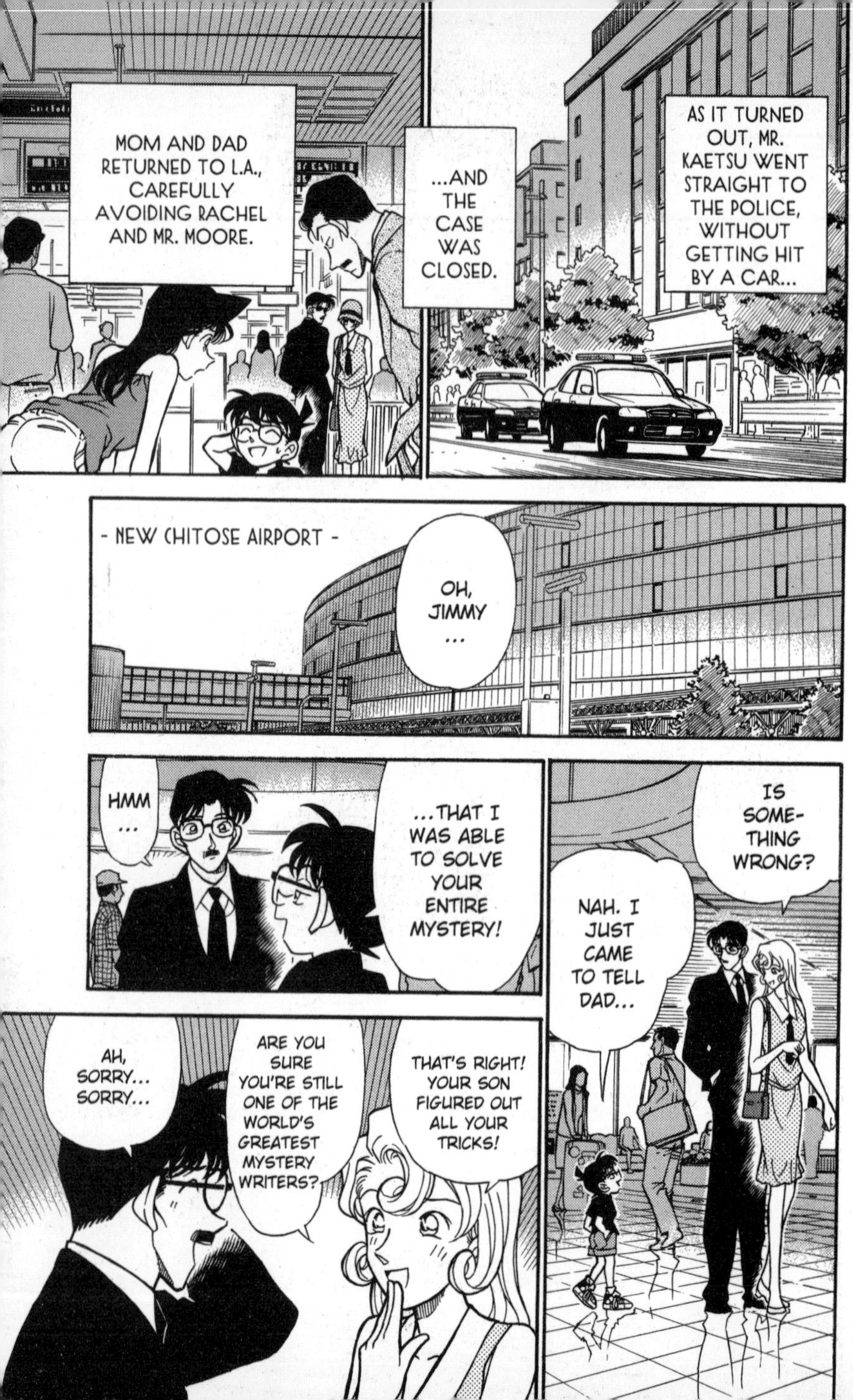
AS IT TURNED OUT, MR. KAETSU WENT STRAIGHT TO THE POLICE, WITHOUT GETTING HIT BY A CAR...
...AND THE CASE WAS CLOSED.
MOM AND DAD RETURNED TO L.A., CAREFULLY AVOIDING RACHEL AND MR. MOORE.
- NEW CHITOSE AIRPORT -
OH, JIMMY ...
IS SOME-THING WRONG?
NAH. I JUST CAME TO TELL DAD...
...THAT I WAS ABLE TO SOLVE YOUR ENTIRE MYSTERY!
HMM ...
THAT'S RIGHT! YOUR SON FIGURED OUT ALL YOUR TRICKS!
ARE YOU SURE YOU'RE STILL ONE OF THE WORLD'S GREATEST MYSTERY WRITERS?
AH, SORRY... SORRY...

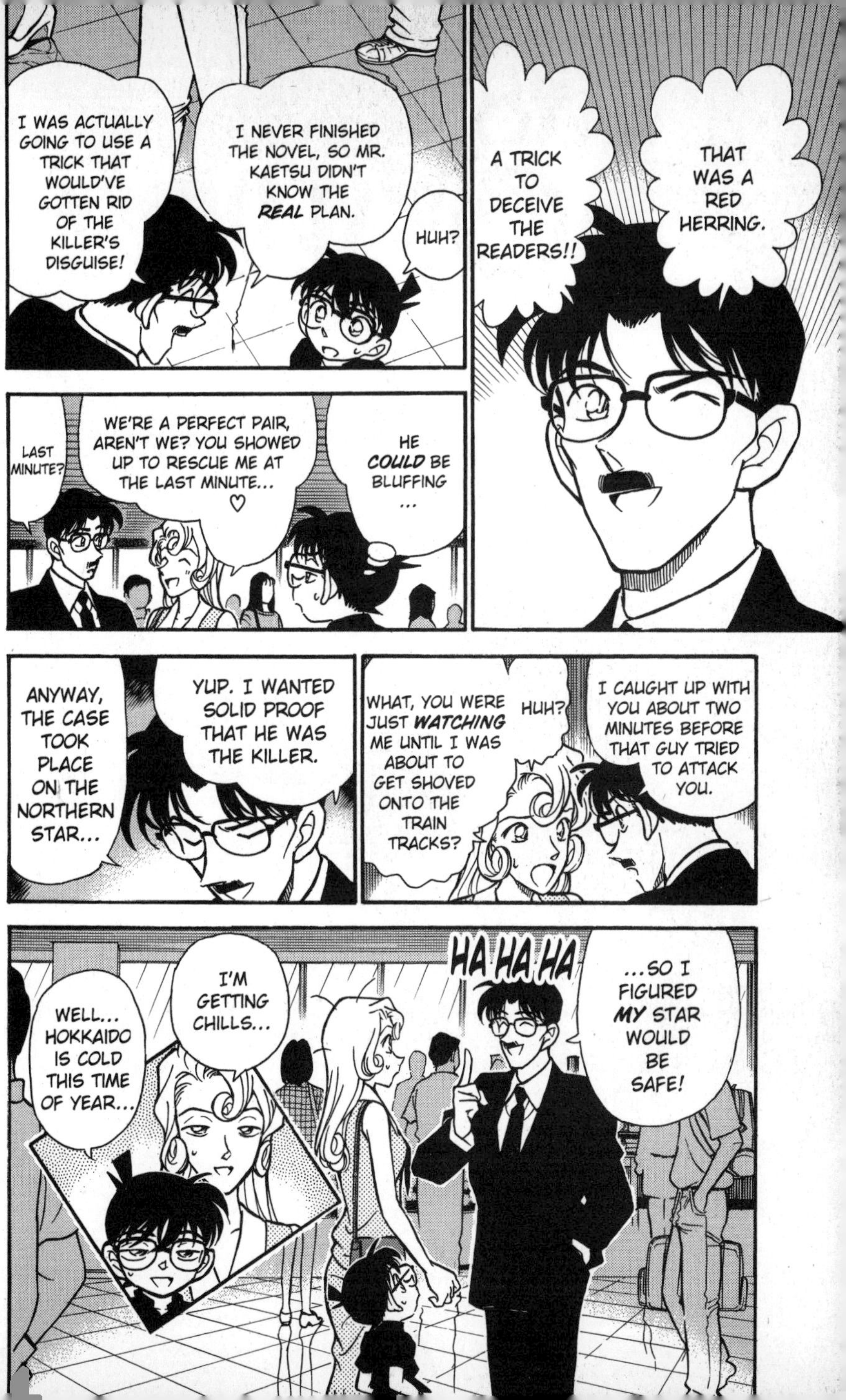
THAT WAS A RED HERRING.
A TRICK TO DECEIVE THE READERS!!
I NEVER FINISHED THE NOVEL, SO MR. KAETSU DIDN'T KNOW THE *REAL* PLAN.
HUH?
I WAS ACTUALLY GOING TO USE A TRICK THAT WOULD'VE GOTTEN RID OF THE KILLER'S DISGUISE!
HE *COULD* BE BLUFFING...
WE'RE A PERFECT PAIR, AREN'T WE? YOU SHOWED UP TO RESCUE ME AT THE LAST MINUTE... ♡
LAST MINUTE?
I CAUGHT UP WITH YOU ABOUT TWO MINUTES BEFORE THAT GUY TRIED TO ATTACK YOU.
HUH?
WHAT, YOU WERE JUST *WATCHING* ME UNTIL I WAS ABOUT TO GET SHOVED ONTO THE TRAIN TRACKS?
YUP. I WANTED SOLID PROOF THAT HE WAS THE KILLER.
ANYWAY, THE CASE TOOK PLACE ON THE NORTHERN STAR...
...SO I FIGURED *MY* STAR WOULD BE SAFE!
HA HA HA
I'M GETTING CHILLS...
WELL... HOKKAIDO IS COLD THIS TIME OF YEAR...

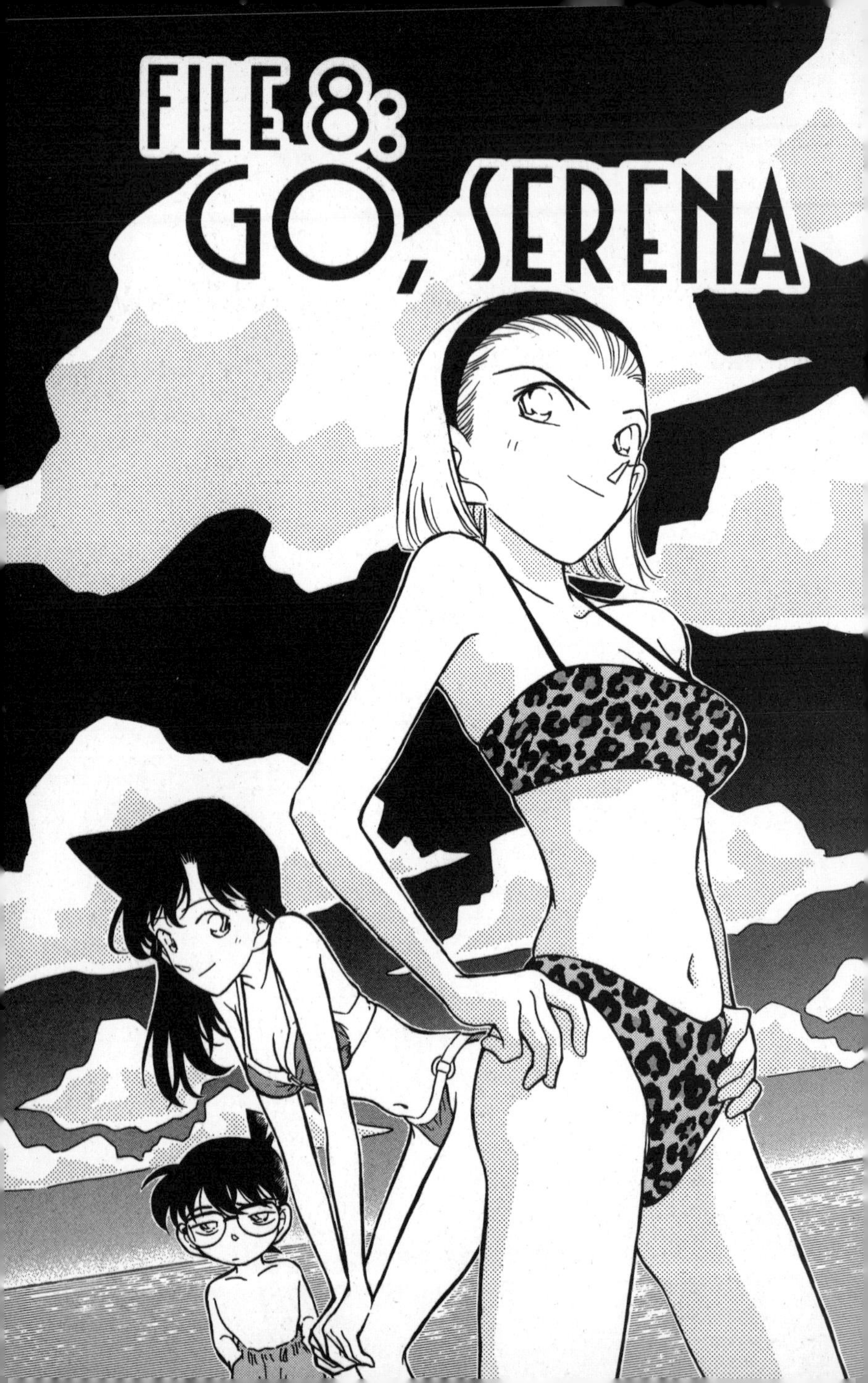
FILE 8:
GO, SERENA

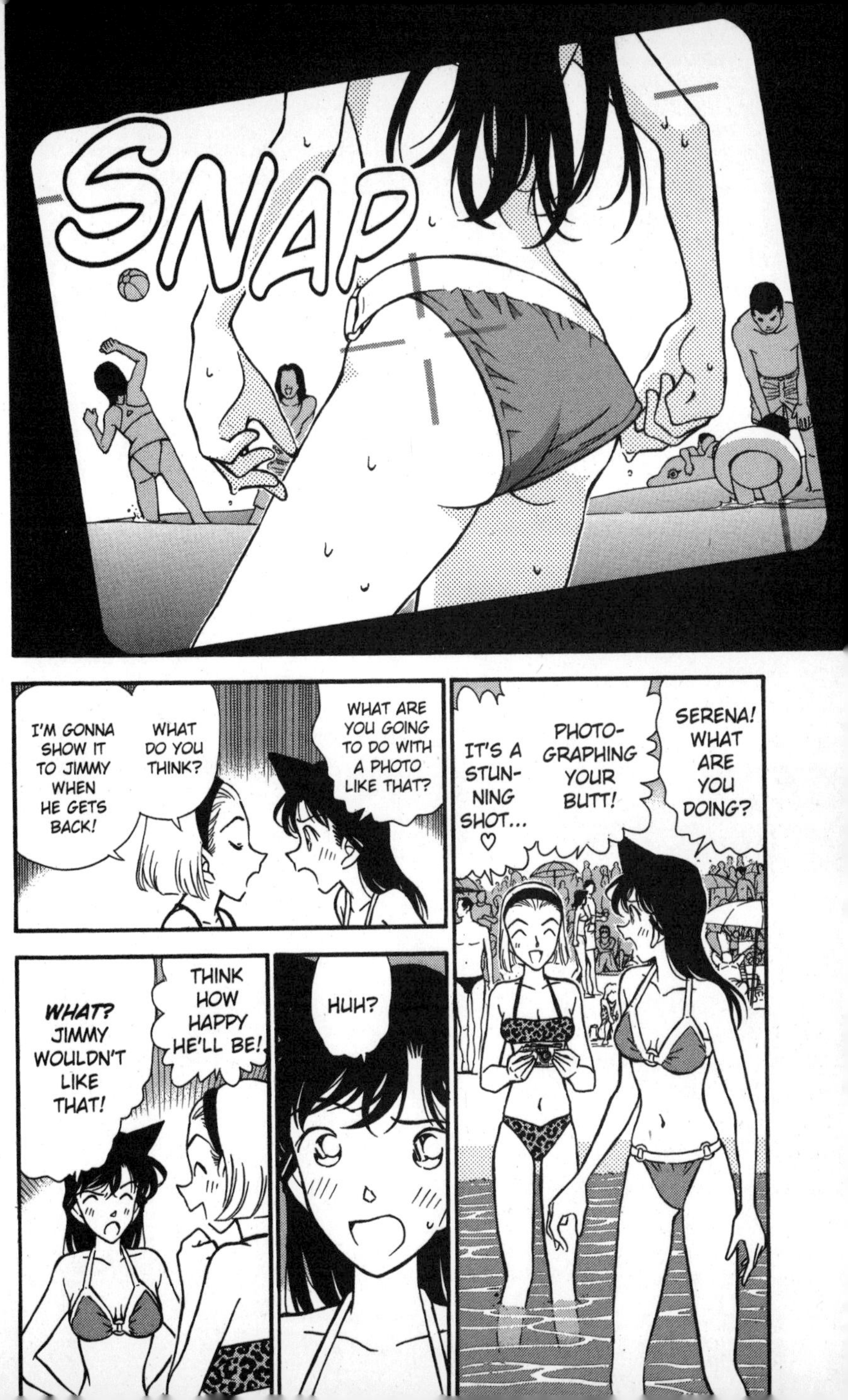
SNAP
SERENA! WHAT ARE YOU DOING?
PHOTO-GRAPHING YOUR BUTT!
IT'S A STUN-NING SHOT... ♡
WHAT ARE YOU GOING TO DO WITH A PHOTO LIKE THAT?
WHAT DO YOU THINK?
I'M GONNA SHOW IT TO JIMMY WHEN HE GETS BACK!
HUH?
THINK HOW HAPPY HE'LL BE!
WHAT? JIMMY WOULDN'T LIKE THAT!

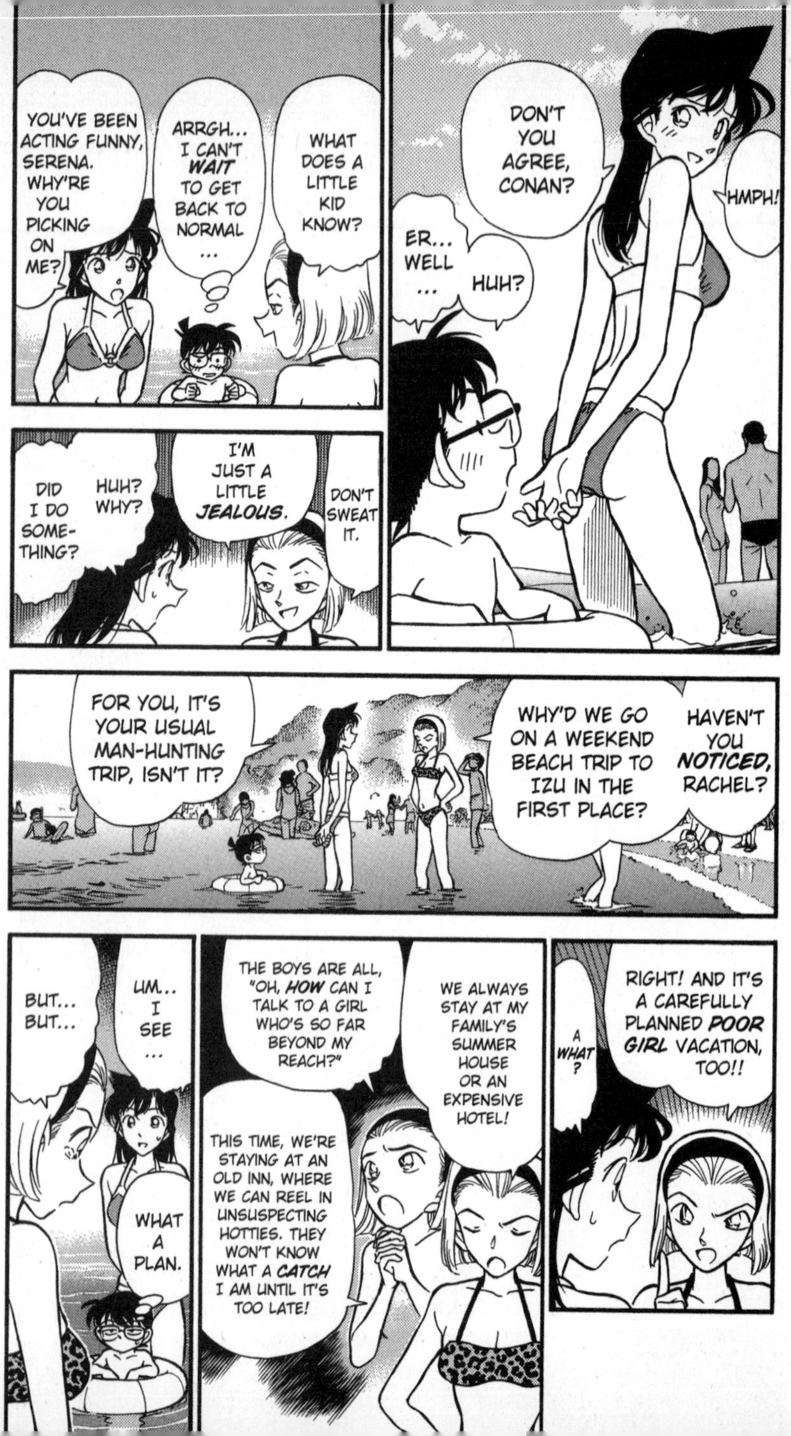
DON'T YOU AGREE, CONAN?
HMPH!
HUH?
ER... WELL...
WHAT DOES A LITTLE KID KNOW?
ARRGH... I CAN'T *WAIT* TO GET BACK TO NORMAL...
YOU'VE BEEN ACTING FUNNY, SERENA. WHY'RE YOU PICKING ON ME?
DON'T SWEAT IT.
I'M JUST A LITTLE *JEALOUS*.
HUH? WHY?
DID I DO SOME-THING?
HAVEN'T YOU *NOTICED*, RACHEL?
WHY'D WE GO ON A WEEKEND BEACH TRIP TO IZU IN THE FIRST PLACE?
FOR YOU, IT'S YOUR USUAL MAN-HUNTING TRIP, ISN'T IT?
RIGHT! AND IT'S A CAREFULLY PLANNED *POOR GIRL* VACATION, TOO!!
A *WHAT*?
WE ALWAYS STAY AT MY FAMILY'S SUMMER HOUSE OR AN EXPENSIVE HOTEL!
THE BOYS ARE ALL, "OH, *HOW* CAN I TALK TO A GIRL WHO'S SO FAR BEYOND MY REACH?"
THIS TIME, WE'RE STAYING AT AN OLD INN, WHERE WE CAN REEL IN UNSUSPECTING HOTTIES. THEY WON'T KNOW WHAT A *CATCH* I AM UNTIL IT'S TOO LATE!
UM... I SEE...
BUT... BUT...
WHAT A PLAN.

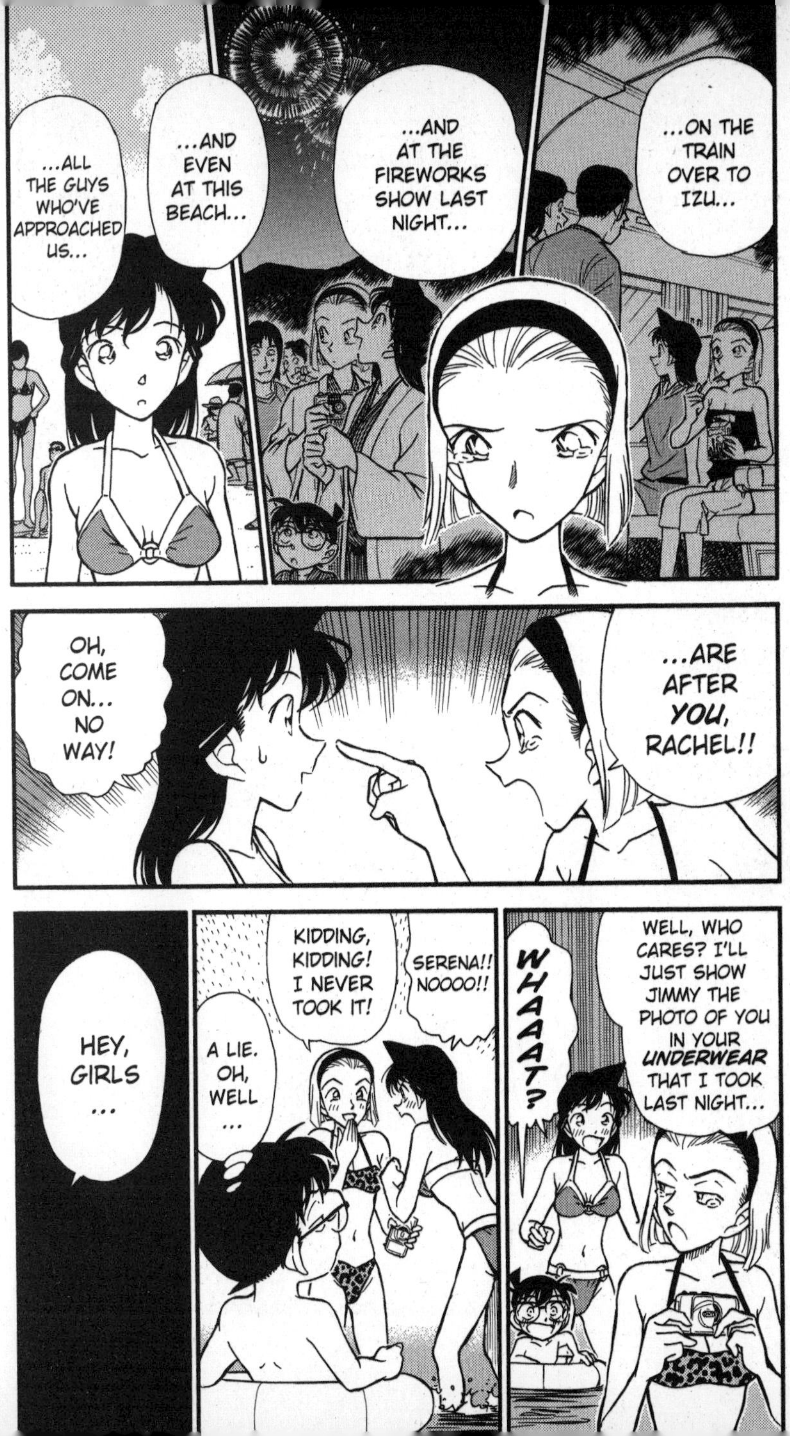
...ON THE TRAIN OVER TO IZU...
...AND AT THE FIREWORKS SHOW LAST NIGHT...
...AND EVEN AT THIS BEACH...
...ALL THE GUYS WHO'VE APPROACHED US...
...ARE AFTER *YOU*, RACHEL!!
OH, COME ON... NO WAY!
WELL, WHO CARES? I'LL JUST SHOW JIMMY THE PHOTO OF YOU IN YOUR *UNDERWEAR* THAT I TOOK LAST NIGHT...
WHAAAAT?
SERENA!! NOOOO!!
KIDDING, KIDDING! I NEVER TOOK IT!
A LIE. OH, WELL ...
HEY, GIRLS ...

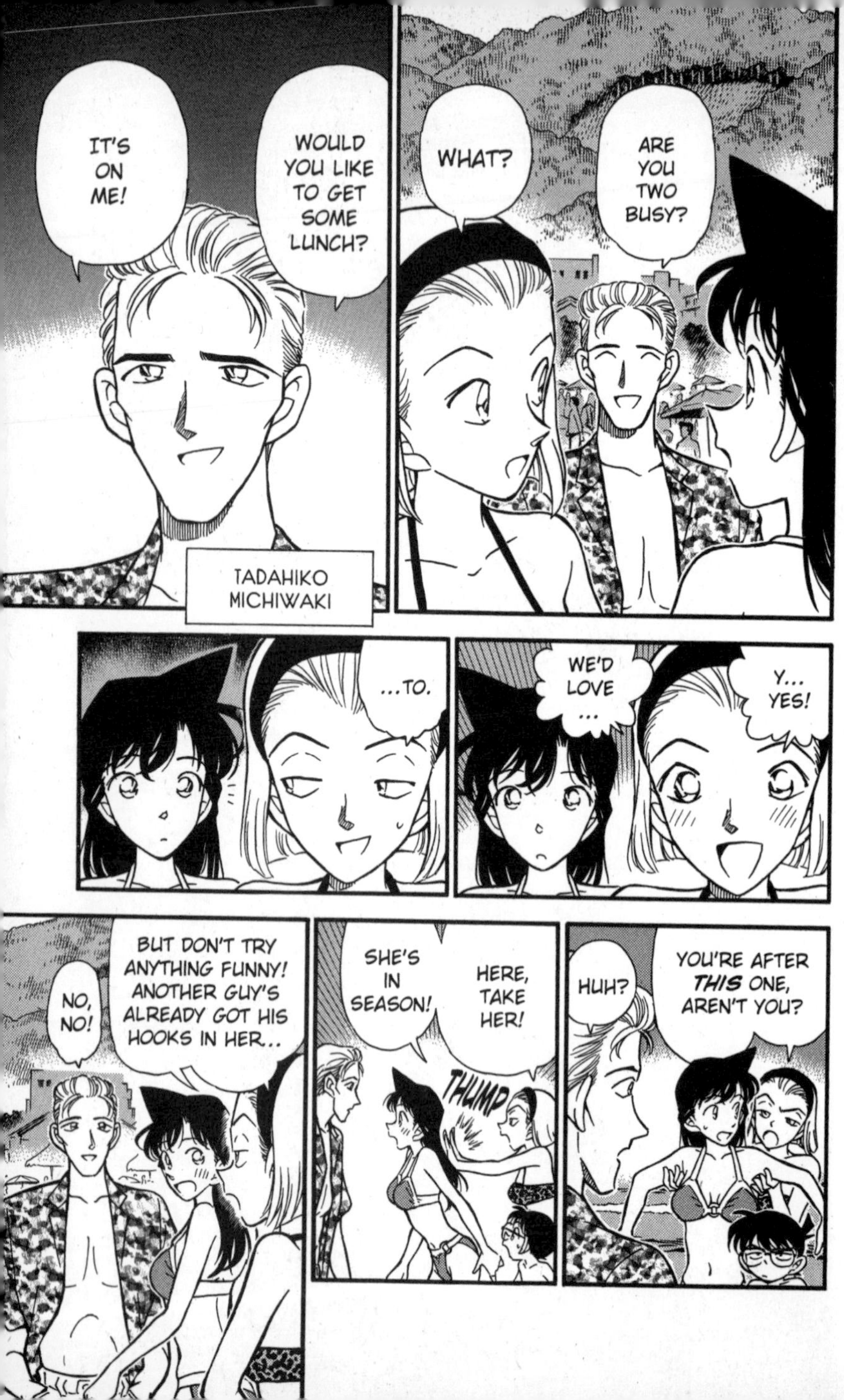
ARE YOU TWO BUSY?
WHAT?
WOULD YOU LIKE TO GET SOME LUNCH?
IT'S ON ME!
TADAHIKO MICHIWAKI
Y... YES!
WE'D LOVE ...
...TO.
YOU'RE AFTER *THIS* ONE, AREN'T YOU?
HUH?
HERE, TAKE HER!
SHE'S IN SEASON!
THUMP
BUT DON'T TRY ANYTHING FUNNY! ANOTHER GUY'S ALREADY GOT HIS HOOKS IN HER...
NO, NO!

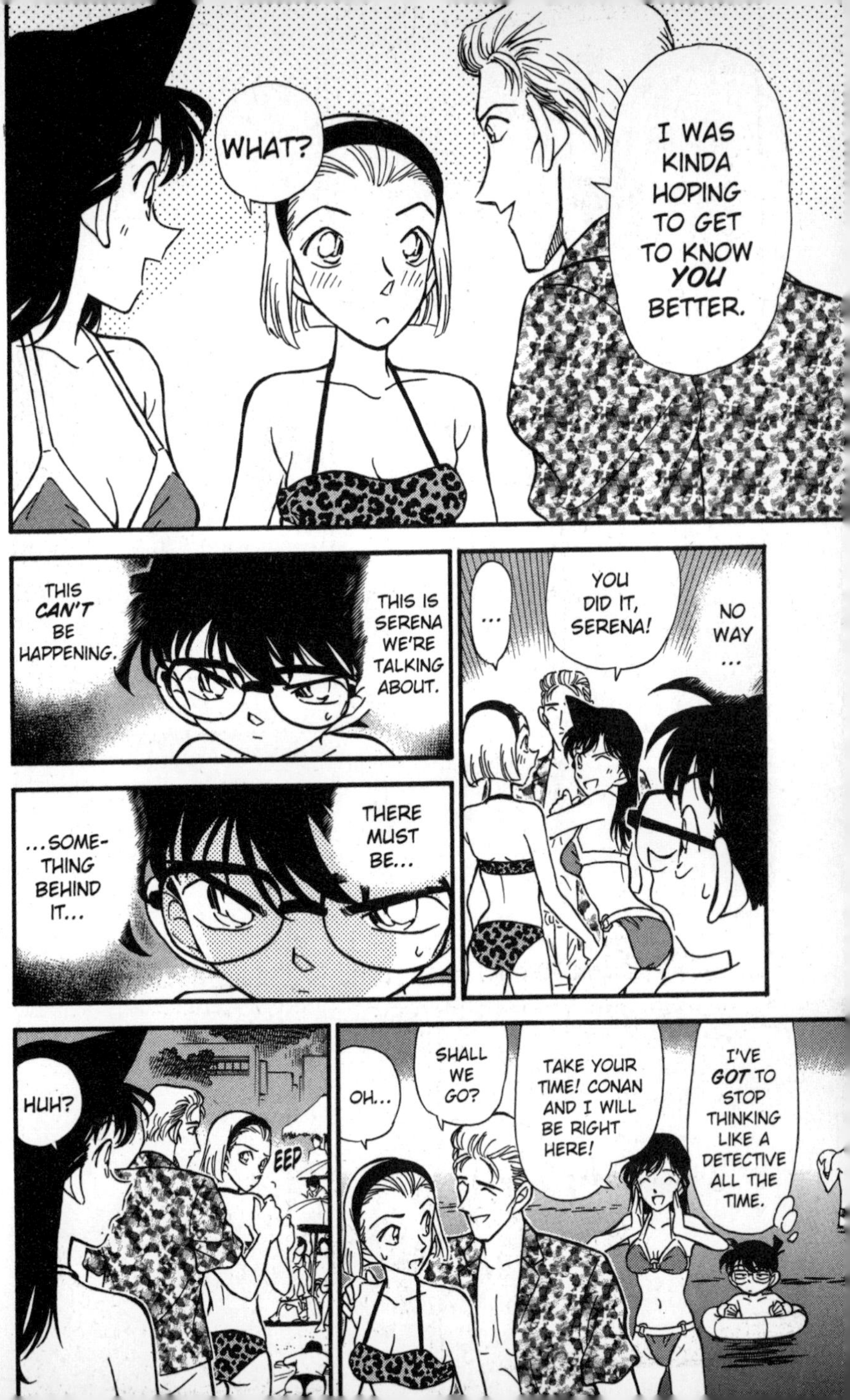
I WAS KINDA HOPING TO GET TO KNOW *YOU* BETTER.
WHAT?
NO WAY ...
YOU DID IT, SERENA!
...
THIS IS SERENA WE'RE TALKING ABOUT.
THIS *CAN'T* BE HAPPENING.
THERE MUST BE...
...SOME-THING BEHIND IT...
I'VE *GOT* TO STOP THINKING LIKE A DETECTIVE ALL THE TIME.
TAKE YOUR TIME! CONAN AND I WILL BE RIGHT HERE!
SHALL WE GO?
OH...
EEP
HUH?

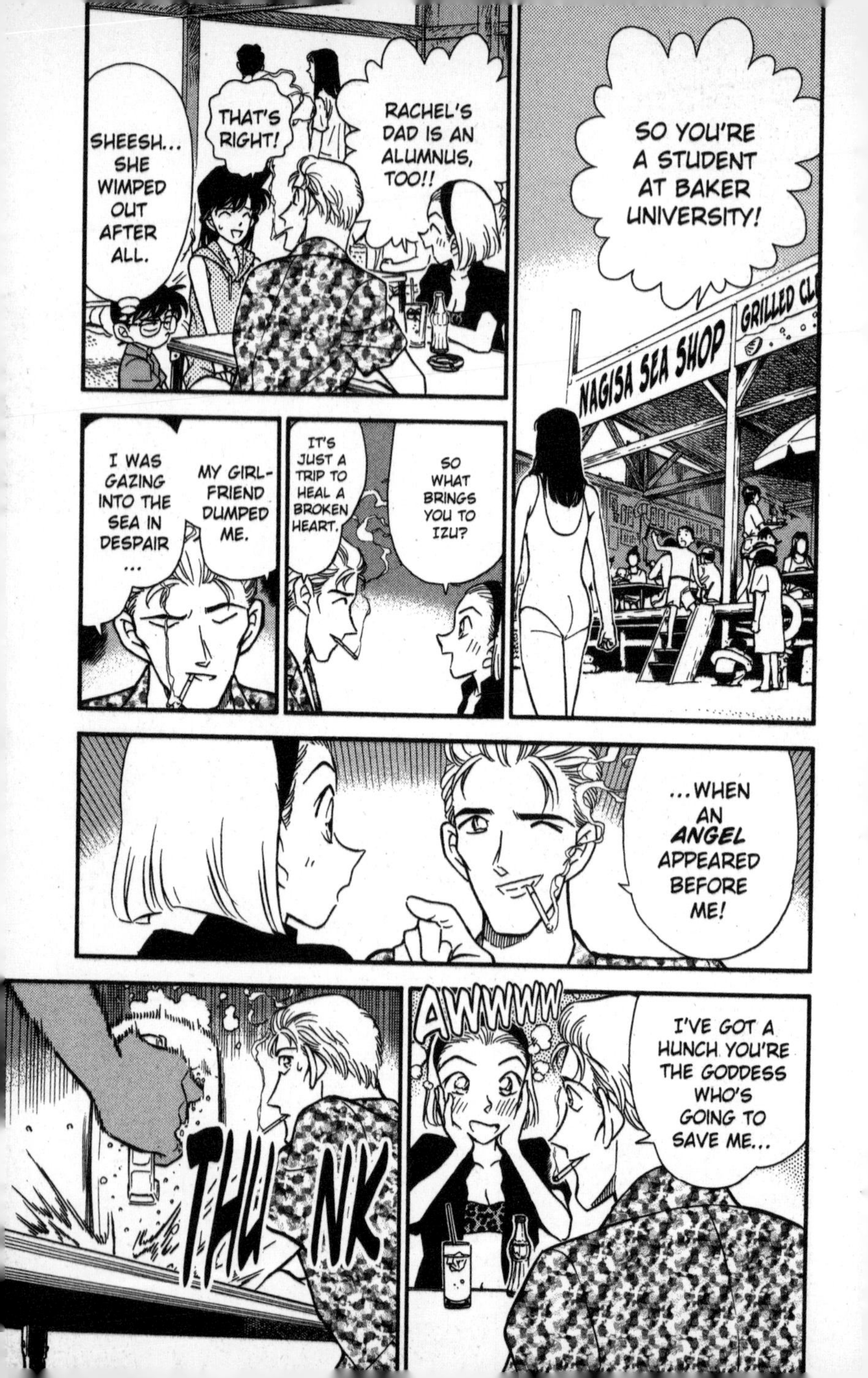
SO YOU'RE A STUDENT AT BAKER UNIVERSITY!
NAGISA SEA SHOP
RACHEL'S DAD IS AN ALUMNUS, TOO!!
THAT'S RIGHT!
SHEESH... SHE WIMPED OUT AFTER ALL.
SO WHAT BRINGS YOU TO IZU?
IT'S JUST A TRIP TO HEAL A BROKEN HEART.
MY GIRL-FRIEND DUMPED ME.
I WAS GAZING INTO THE SEA IN DESPAIR...
...WHEN AN ANGEL APPEARED BEFORE ME!
AWWWW
I'VE GOT A HUNCH YOU'RE THE GODDESS WHO'S GOING TO SAVE ME...
THUNK

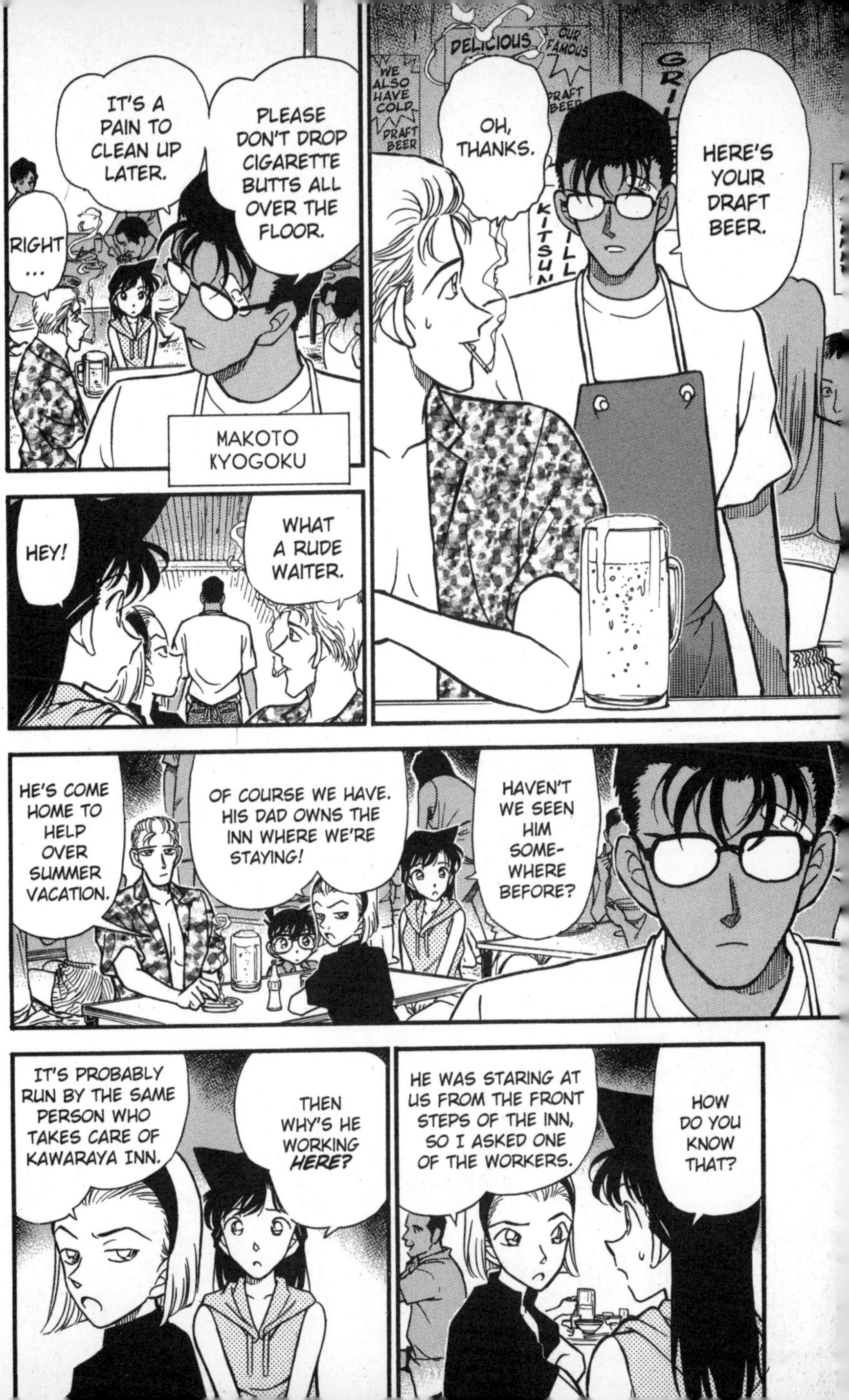
DELICIOUS
OUR FAMOUS
WE ALSO HAVE COLD DRAFT BEER
HERE'S YOUR DRAFT BEER.
OH, THANKS.
PLEASE DON'T DROP CIGARETTE BUTTS ALL OVER THE FLOOR.
IT'S A PAIN TO CLEAN UP LATER.
RIGHT ...
MAKOTO KYOGOKU
WHAT A RUDE WAITER.
HEY!
HAVEN'T WE SEEN HIM SOME-WHERE BEFORE?
OF COURSE WE HAVE. HIS DAD OWNS THE INN WHERE WE'RE STAYING!
HE'S COME HOME TO HELP OVER SUMMER VACATION.
HOW DO YOU KNOW THAT?
HE WAS STARING AT US FROM THE FRONT STEPS OF THE INN, SO I ASKED ONE OF THE WORKERS.
THEN WHY'S HE WORKING *HERE*?
IT'S PROBABLY RUN BY THE SAME PERSON WHO TAKES CARE OF KAWARAYA INN.

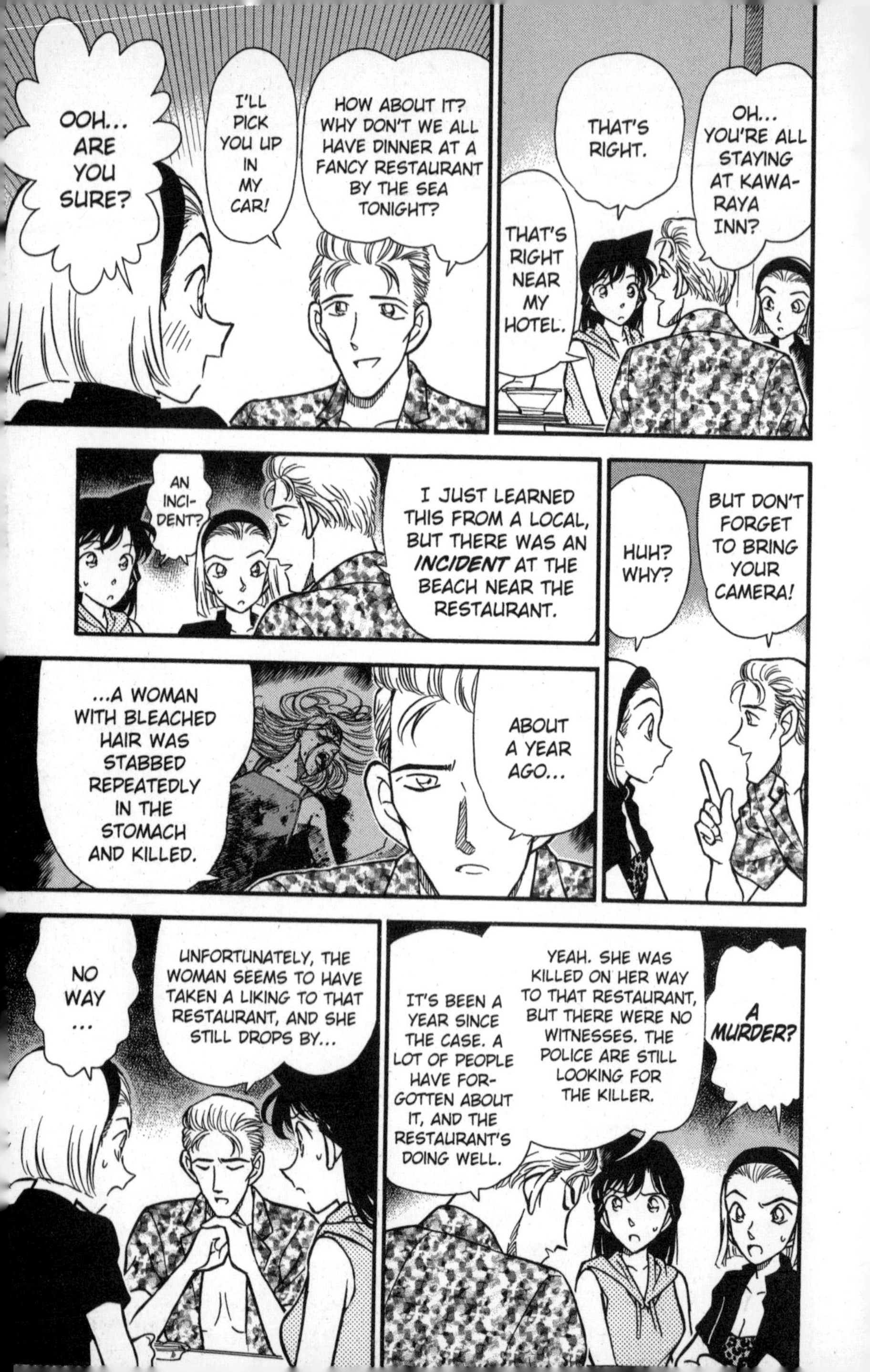
OH... YOU'RE ALL STAYING AT KAWA-RAYA INN?
THAT'S RIGHT.
THAT'S RIGHT NEAR MY HOTEL.
HOW ABOUT IT? WHY DON'T WE ALL HAVE DINNER AT A FANCY RESTAURANT BY THE SEA TONIGHT?
I'LL PICK YOU UP IN MY CAR!
OOH... ARE YOU SURE?
BUT DON'T FORGET TO BRING YOUR CAMERA!
HUH? WHY?
I JUST LEARNED THIS FROM A LOCAL, BUT THERE WAS AN *INCIDENT* AT THE BEACH NEAR THE RESTAURANT.
AN INCI-DENT?
ABOUT A YEAR AGO...
...A WOMAN WITH BLEACHED HAIR WAS STABBED REPEATEDLY IN THE STOMACH AND KILLED.
A *MURDER?*
YEAH. SHE WAS KILLED ON HER WAY TO THAT RESTAURANT, BUT THERE WERE NO WITNESSES. THE POLICE ARE STILL LOOKING FOR THE KILLER.
IT'S BEEN A YEAR SINCE THE CASE. A LOT OF PEOPLE HAVE FOR-GOTTEN ABOUT IT, AND THE RESTAURANT'S DOING WELL.
UNFORTUNATELY, THE WOMAN SEEMS TO HAVE TAKEN A LIKING TO THAT RESTAURANT, AND SHE STILL DROPS BY...
NO WAY ...

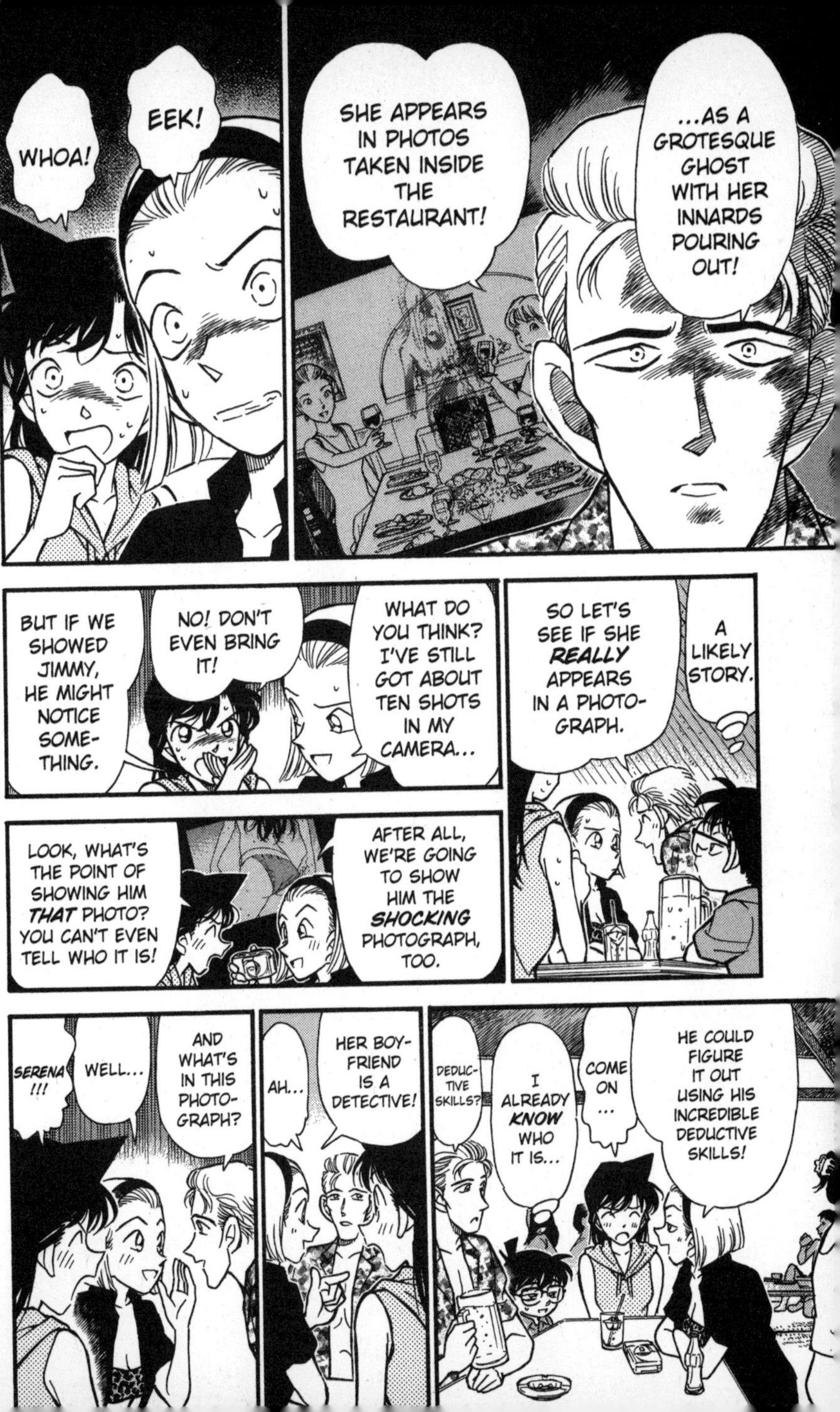
SHE APPEARS IN PHOTOS TAKEN INSIDE THE RESTAURANT!
...AS A GROTESQUE GHOST WITH HER INNARDS POURING OUT!
EEK!
WHOA!
A LIKELY STORY.
SO LET'S SEE IF SHE *REALLY* APPEARS IN A PHOTO-GRAPH.
WHAT DO YOU THINK? I'VE STILL GOT ABOUT TEN SHOTS IN MY CAMERA...
NO! DON'T EVEN BRING IT!
BUT IF WE SHOWED JIMMY, HE MIGHT NOTICE SOME-THING.
AFTER ALL, WE'RE GOING TO SHOW HIM THE *SHOCKING* PHOTOGRAPH, TOO.
LOOK, WHAT'S THE POINT OF SHOWING HIM *THAT* PHOTO? YOU CAN'T EVEN TELL WHO IT IS!
HE COULD FIGURE IT OUT USING HIS INCREDIBLE DEDUCTIVE SKILLS!
COME ON ...
I ALREADY *KNOW* WHO IT IS...
DEDUC-TIVE SKILLS?
HER BOY-FRIEND IS A DETECTIVE!
AH...
AND WHAT'S IN THIS PHOTO-GRAPH?
WELL...
SERENA!!!

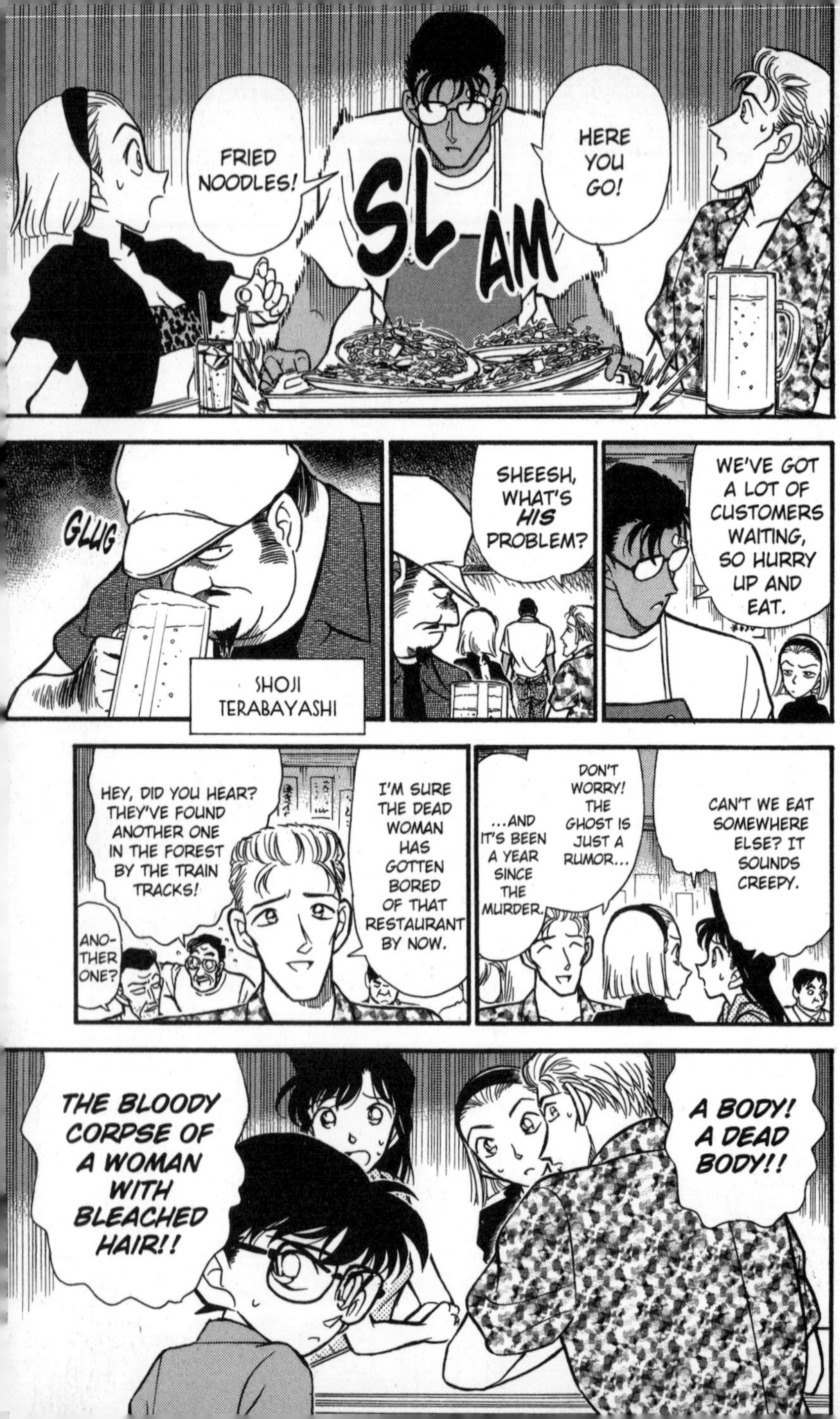
HERE YOU GO!
FRIED NOODLES!
SLAM
WE'VE GOT A LOT OF CUSTOMERS WAITING, SO HURRY UP AND EAT.
SHEESH, WHAT'S HIS PROBLEM?
GLUG
SHOJI TERABAYASHI
CAN'T WE EAT SOMEWHERE ELSE? IT SOUNDS CREEPY.
DON'T WORRY! THE GHOST IS JUST A RUMOR...
...AND IT'S BEEN A YEAR SINCE THE MURDER.
I'M SURE THE DEAD WOMAN HAS GOTTEN BORED OF THAT RESTAURANT BY NOW.
HEY, DID YOU HEAR? THEY'VE FOUND ANOTHER ONE IN THE FOREST BY THE TRAIN TRACKS!
ANOTHER ONE?
A BODY! A DEAD BODY!!
THE BLOODY CORPSE OF A WOMAN WITH BLEACHED HAIR!!

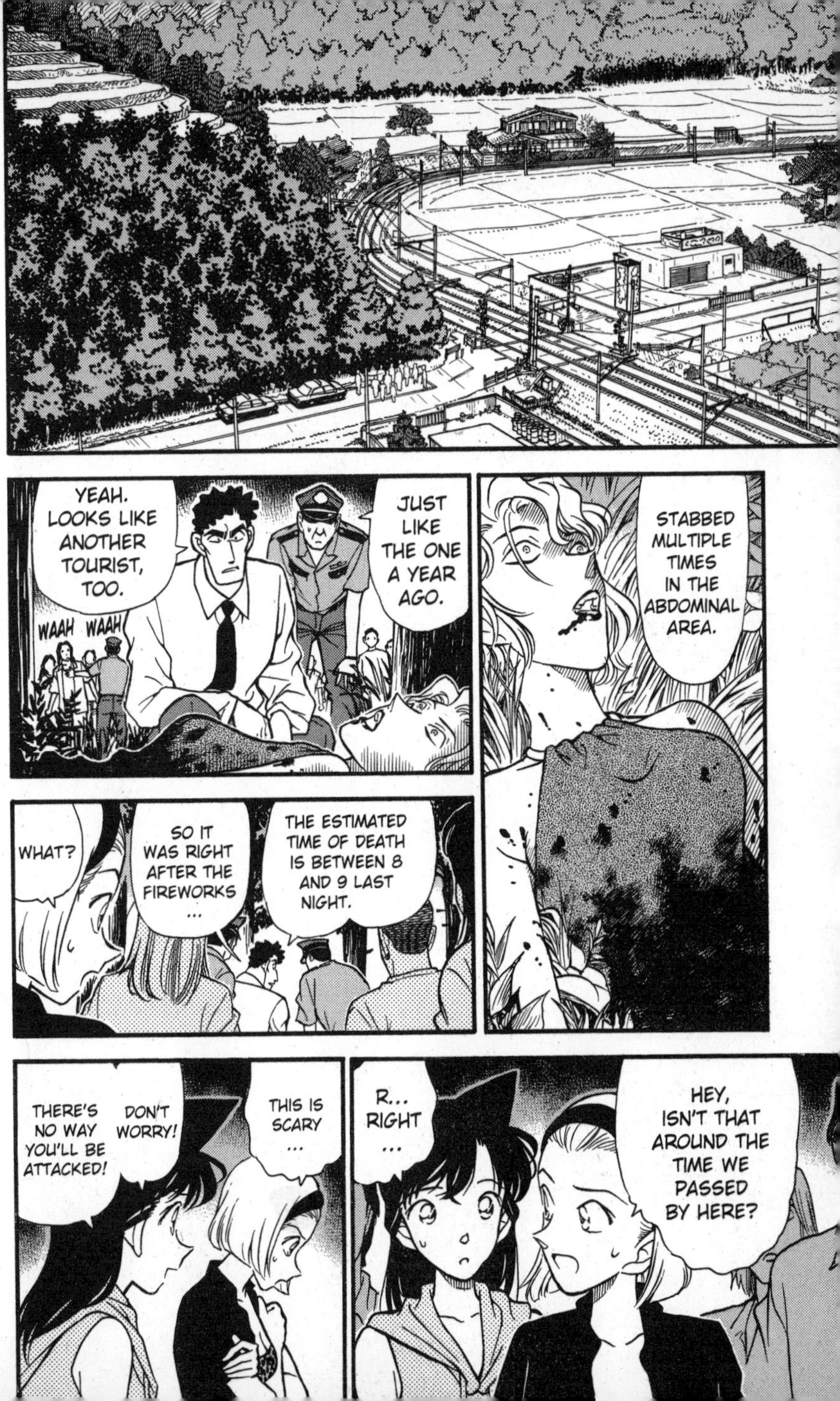
STABBED MULTIPLE TIMES IN THE ABDOMINAL AREA.
JUST LIKE THE ONE A YEAR AGO.
YEAH. LOOKS LIKE ANOTHER TOURIST, TOO.
WAAH WAAH
THE ESTIMATED TIME OF DEATH IS BETWEEN 8 AND 9 LAST NIGHT.
SO IT WAS RIGHT AFTER THE FIREWORKS ...
WHAT?
HEY, ISN'T THAT AROUND THE TIME WE PASSED BY HERE?
R... RIGHT ...
THIS IS SCARY ...
DON'T WORRY!
THERE'S NO WAY YOU'LL BE ATTACKED!

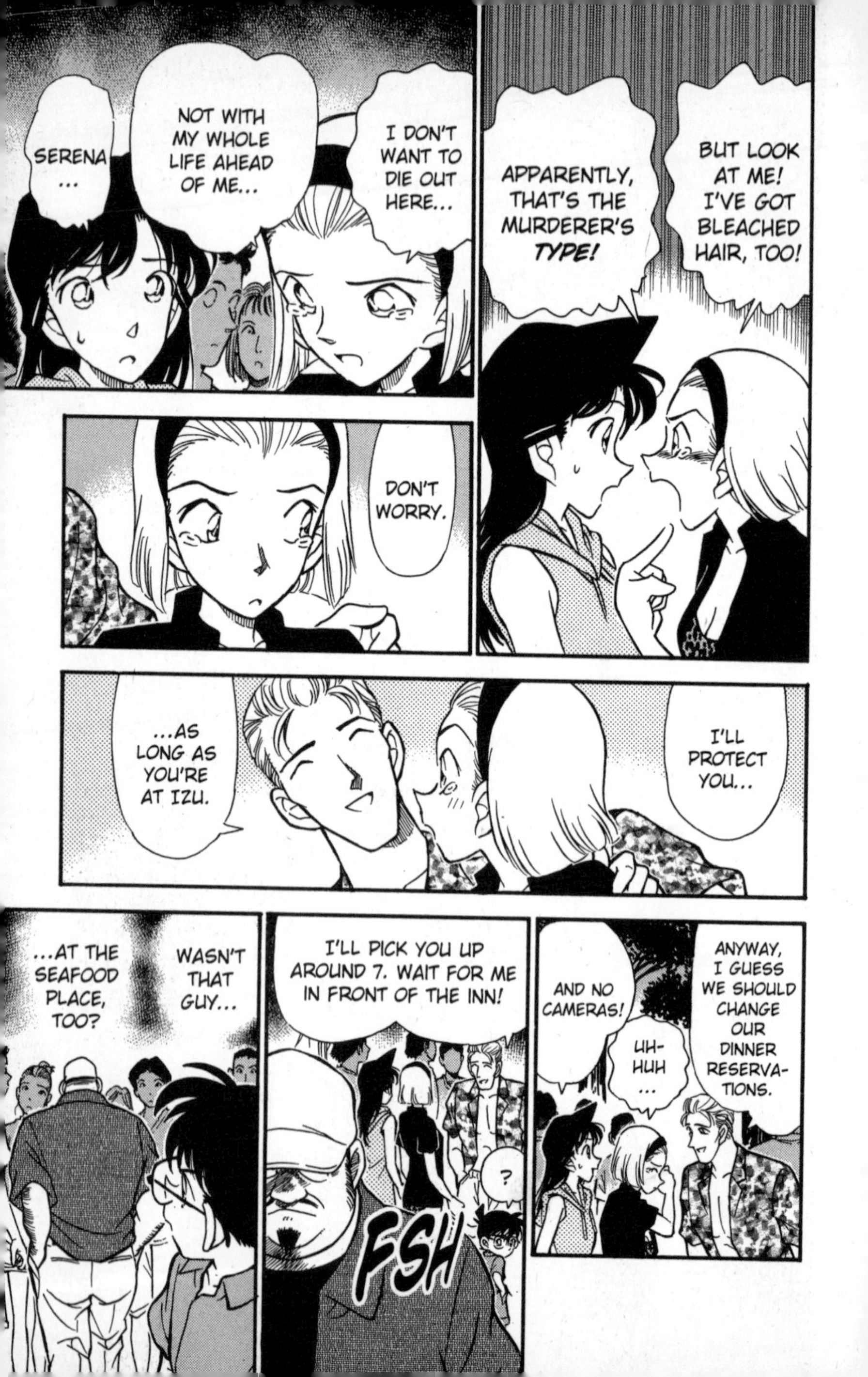
BUT LOOK AT ME! I'VE GOT BLEACHED HAIR, TOO!
APPARENTLY, THAT'S THE MURDERER'S *TYPE!*
I DON'T WANT TO DIE OUT HERE...
NOT WITH MY WHOLE LIFE AHEAD OF ME...
SERENA ...
DON'T WORRY.
I'LL PROTECT YOU...
...AS LONG AS YOU'RE AT IZU.
ANYWAY, I GUESS WE SHOULD CHANGE OUR DINNER RESERVATIONS.
UH-HUH ...
AND NO CAMERAS!
I'LL PICK YOU UP AROUND 7. WAIT FOR ME IN FRONT OF THE INN!
?
FSH
WASN'T THAT GUY...
...AT THE SEAFOOD PLACE, TOO?

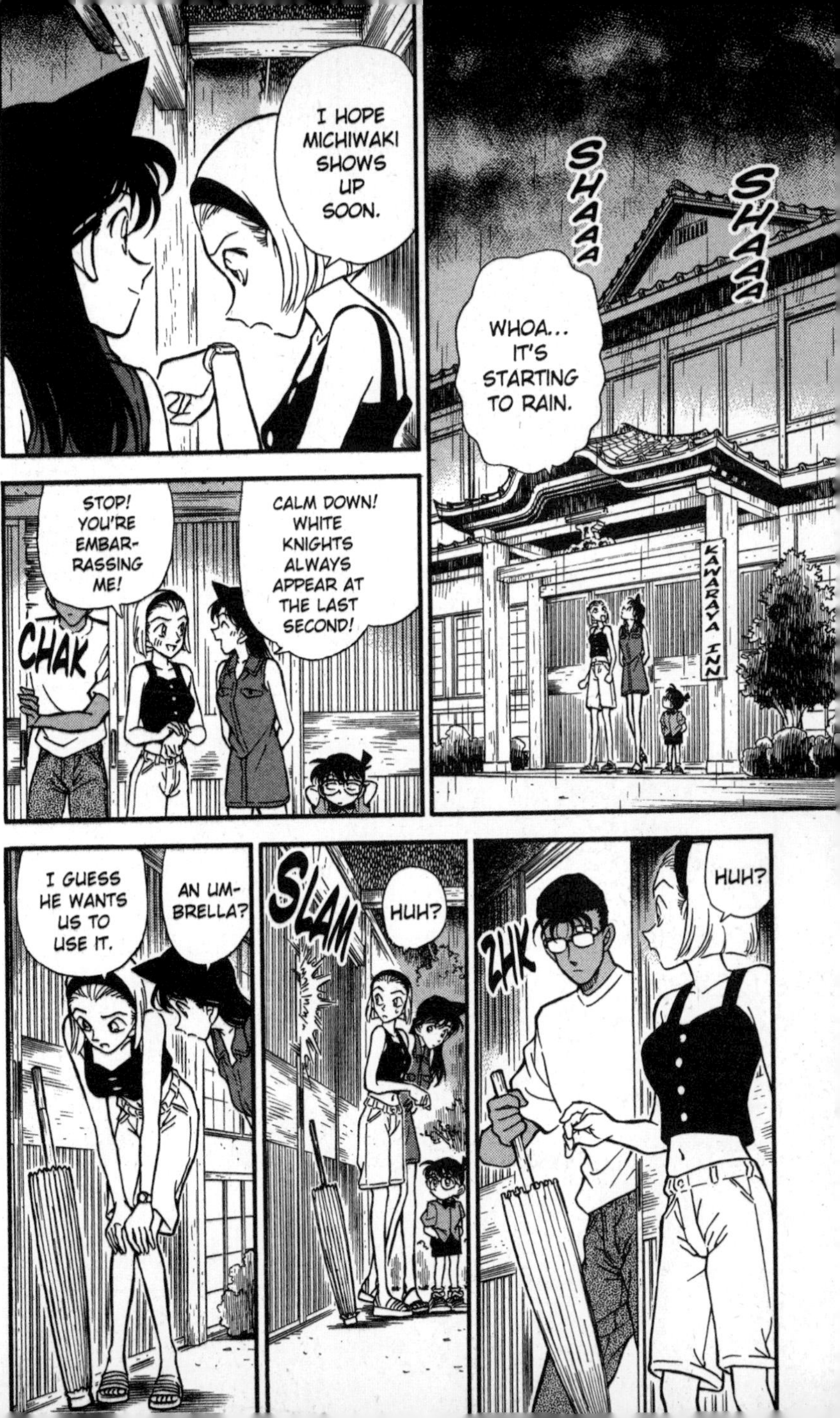
SHAAA
SHAAA
WHOA... IT'S STARTING TO RAIN.
KAWARAYA INN
I HOPE MICHIWAKI SHOWS UP SOON.
CALM DOWN! WHITE KNIGHTS ALWAYS APPEAR AT THE LAST SECOND!
STOP! YOU'RE EMBAR-RASSING ME!
CHAK
HUH?
ZHK
HUH?
SLAM
AN UM-BRELLA?
I GUESS HE WANTS US TO USE IT.

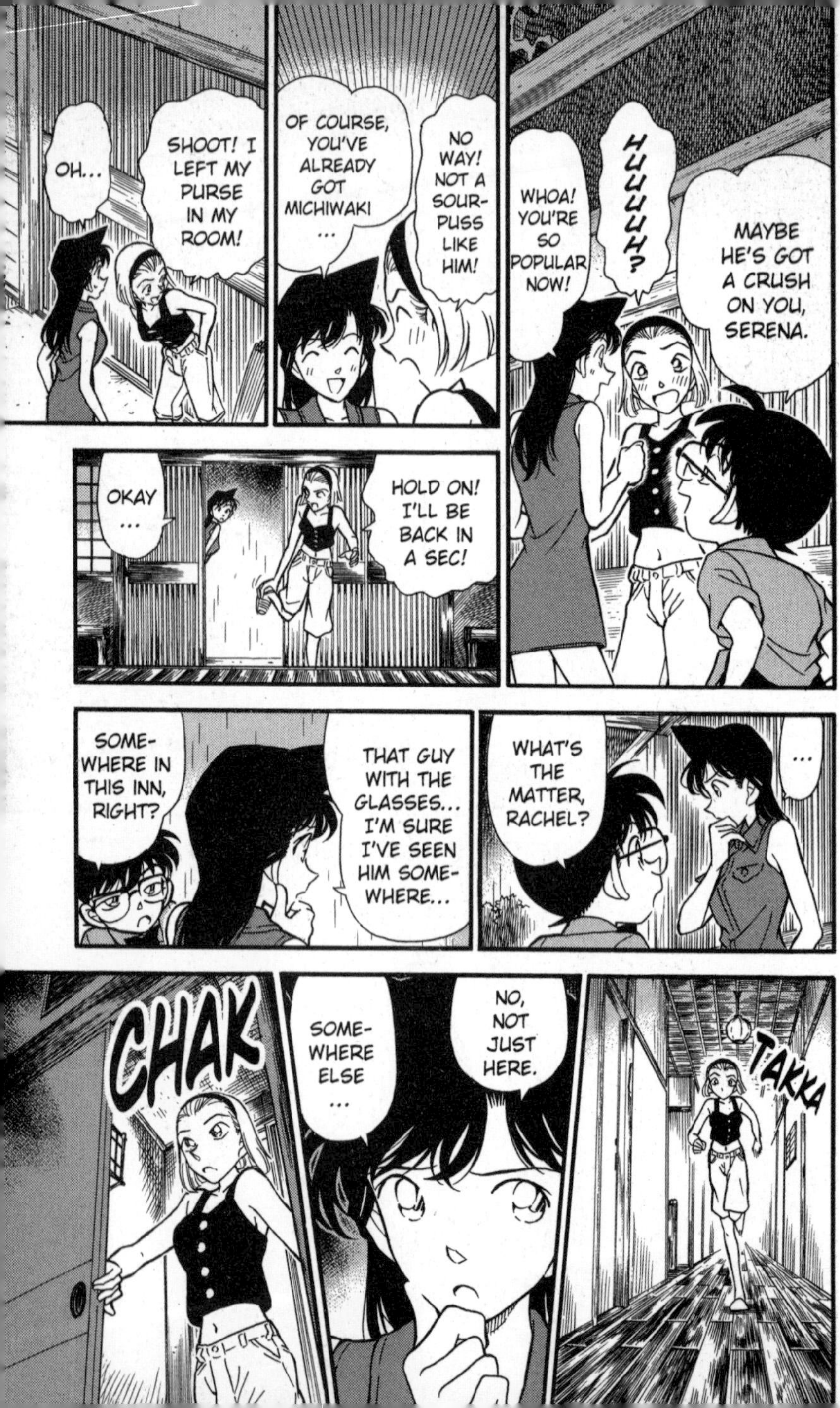
MAYBE HE'S GOT A CRUSH ON YOU, SERENA.
HUUUUH?
WHOA! YOU'RE SO POPULAR NOW!
NO WAY! NOT A SOUR-PUSS LIKE HIM!
OF COURSE, YOU'VE ALREADY GOT MICHIWAKI ...
SHOOT! I LEFT MY PURSE IN MY ROOM!
OH...
HOLD ON! I'LL BE BACK IN A SEC!
OKAY ...
...
WHAT'S THE MATTER, RACHEL?
THAT GUY WITH THE GLASSES... I'M SURE I'VE SEEN HIM SOME-WHERE...
SOME-WHERE IN THIS INN, RIGHT?
TAKKA
NO, NOT JUST HERE.
SOME-WHERE ELSE ...
CHAK

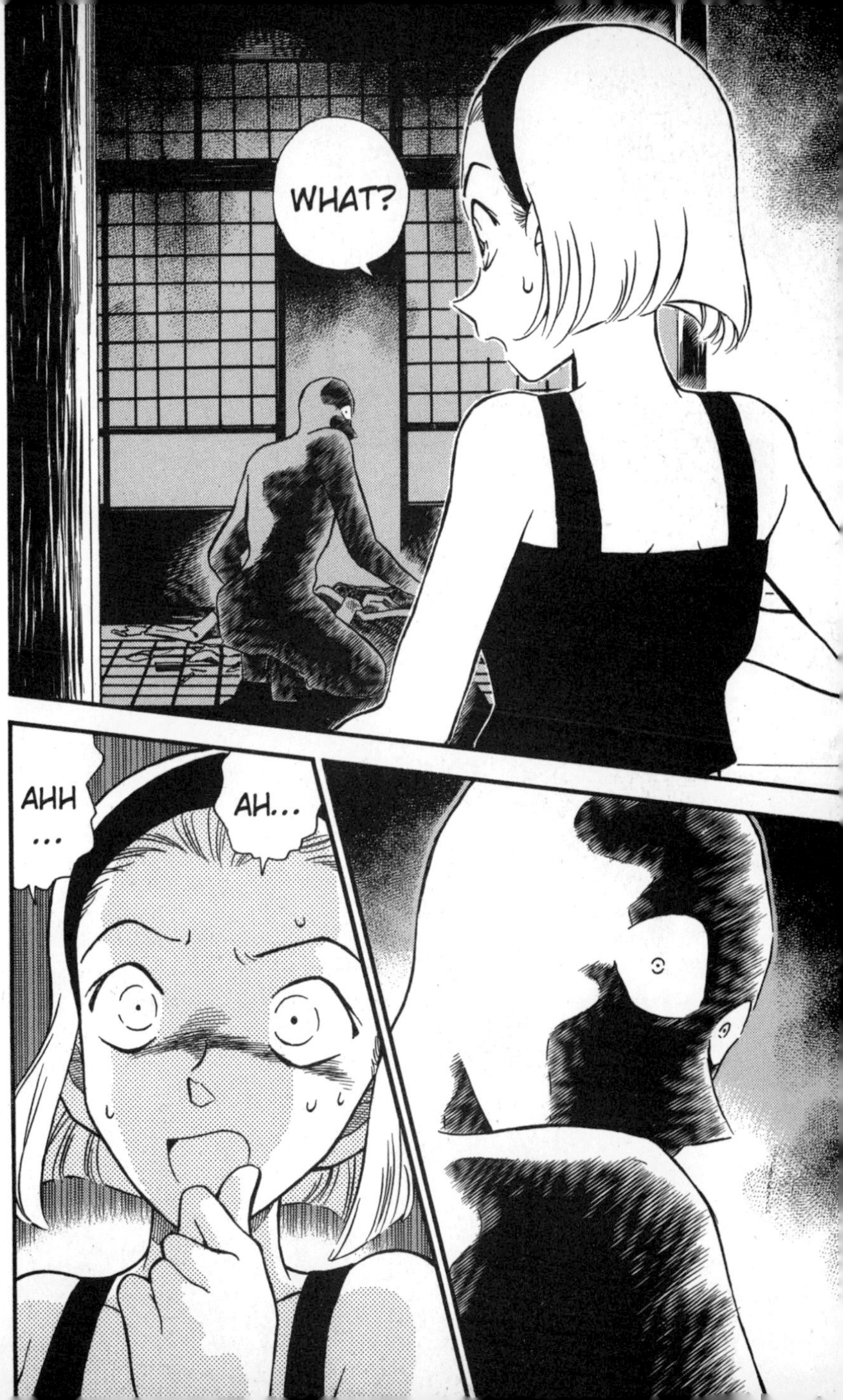
WHAT?
AH...
AHH ...

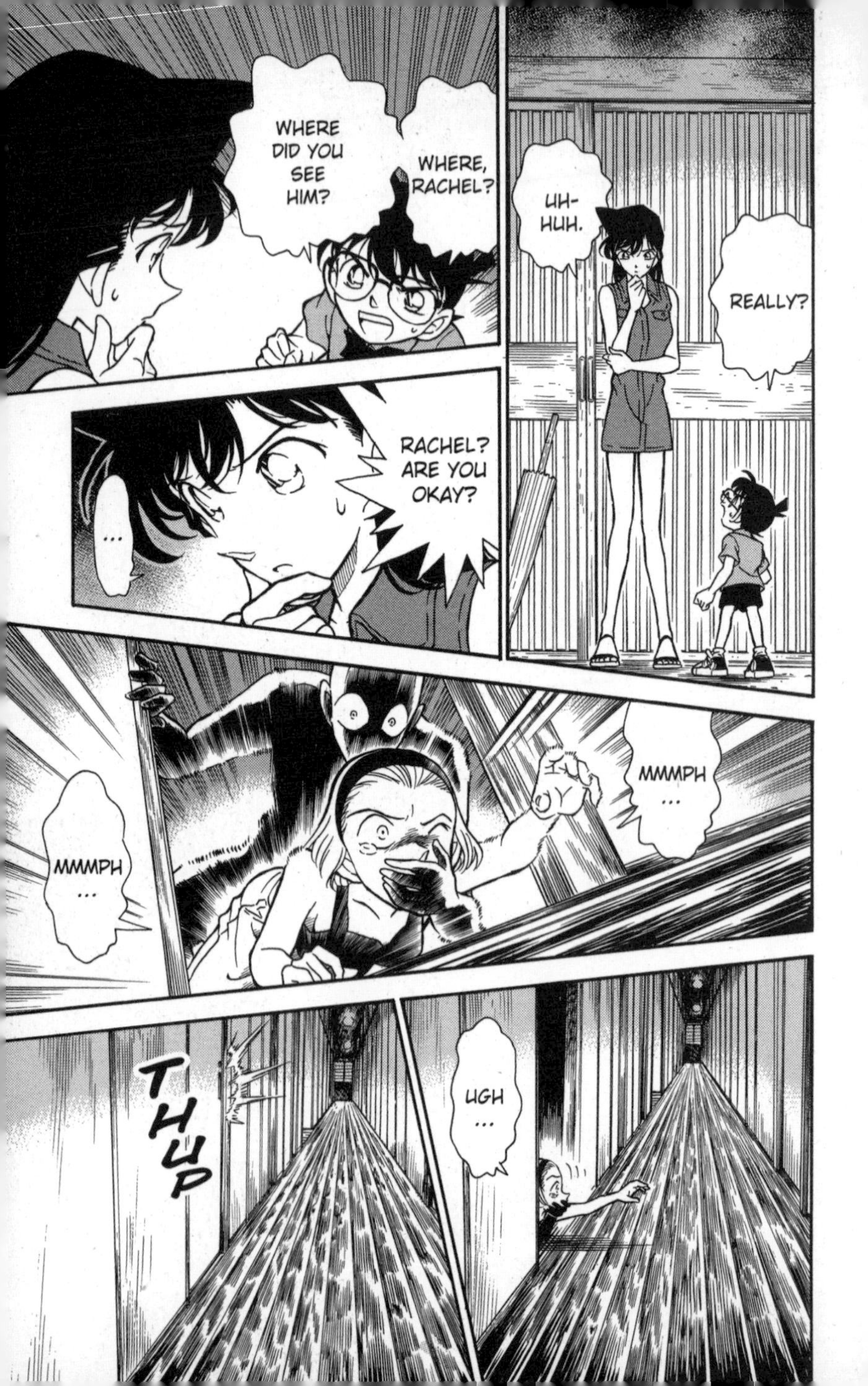

UH-HUH.
REALLY?
WHERE, RACHEL?
WHERE DID YOU SEE HIM?
RACHEL? ARE YOU OKAY?
...
MMMPH ...
MMMPH ...
UGH ...
THUP

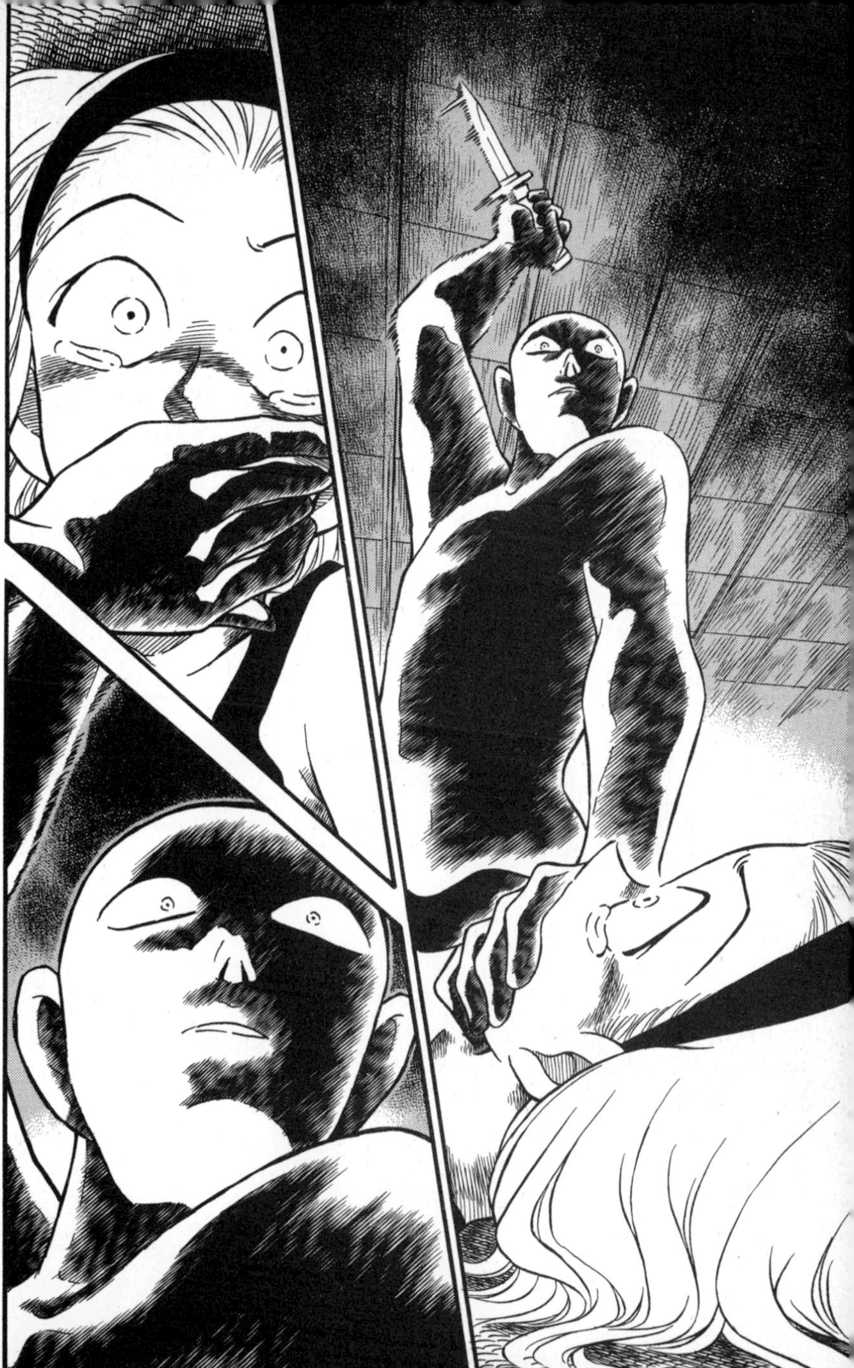

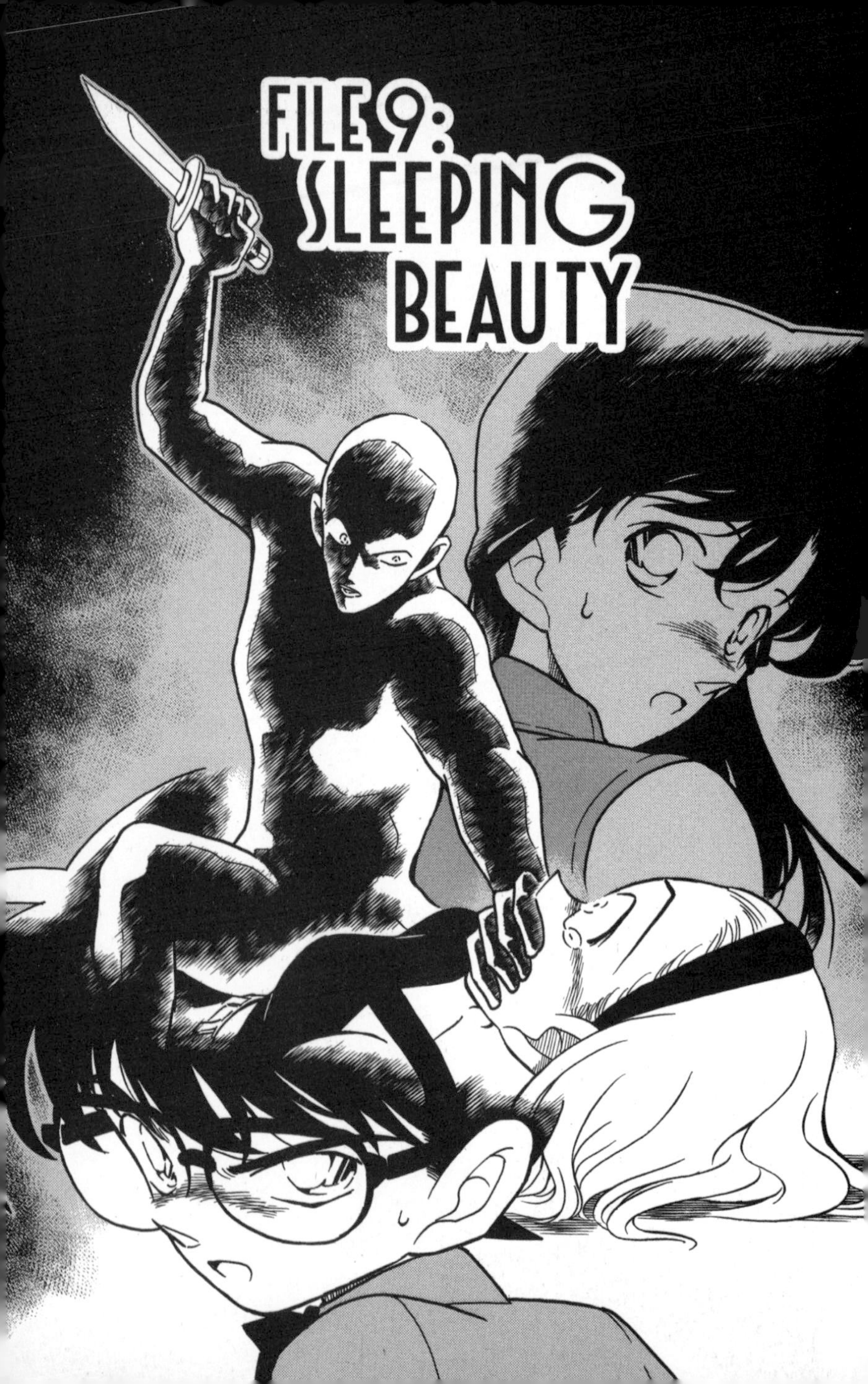
FILE 9:
SLEEPING
BEAUTY

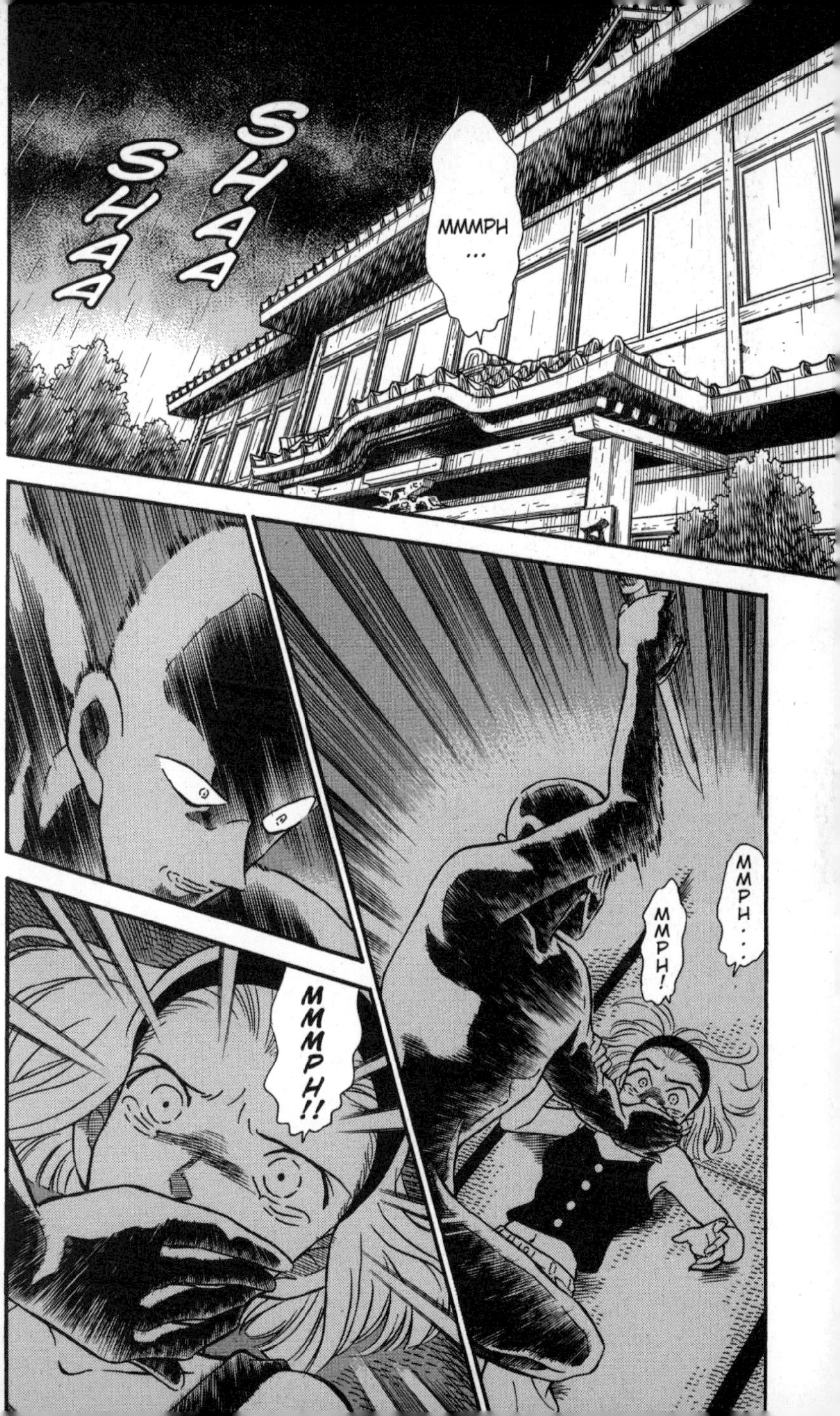
SHAA
SHAAA
MMMPH ...
MMPH...
MMPH!
MMMPH!!

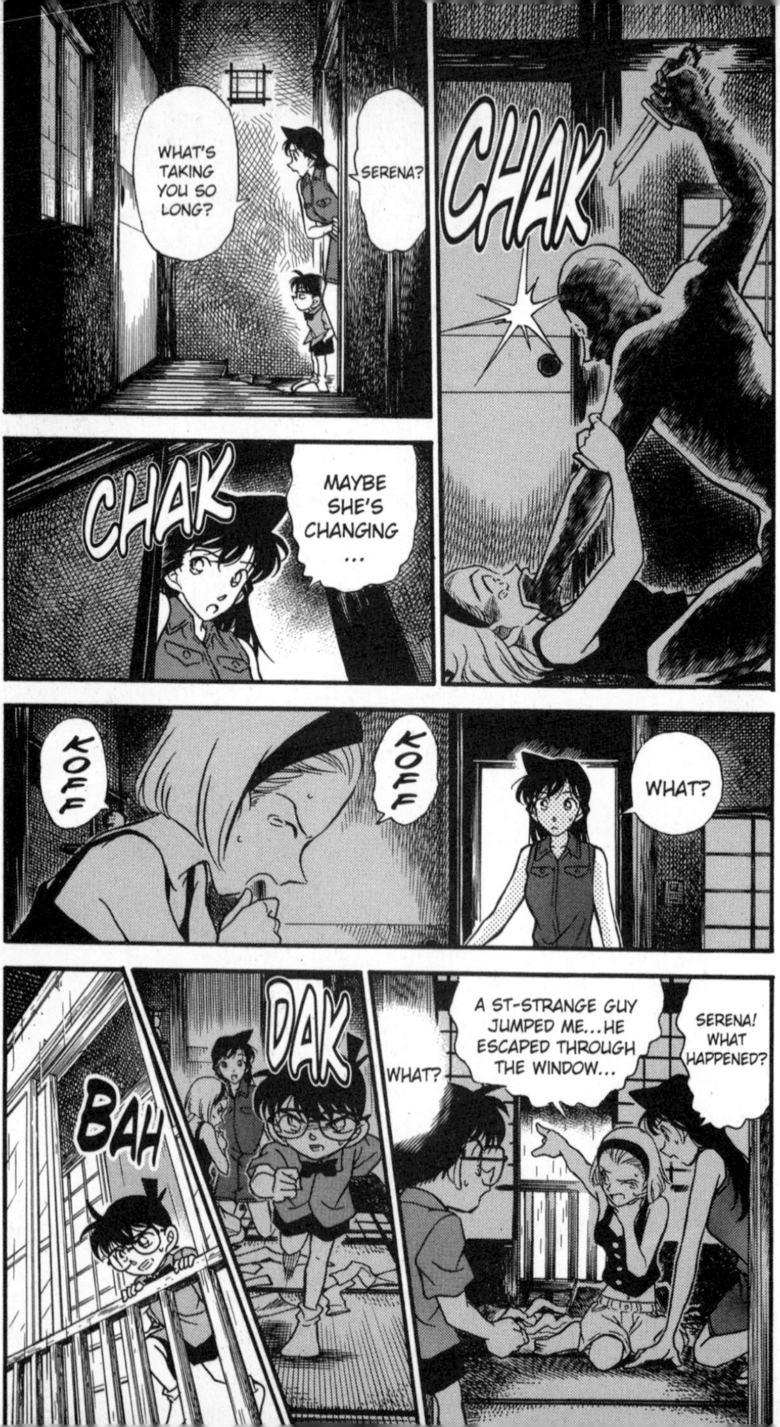
CHAK
SERENA?
WHAT'S TAKING YOU SO LONG?
MAYBE SHE'S CHANGING ...
CHAK
WHAT?
KOFF
KOFF
SERENA! WHAT HAPPENED?
A ST-STRANGE GUY JUMPED ME... HE ESCAPED THROUGH THE WINDOW...
WHAT?
DAK
BAH

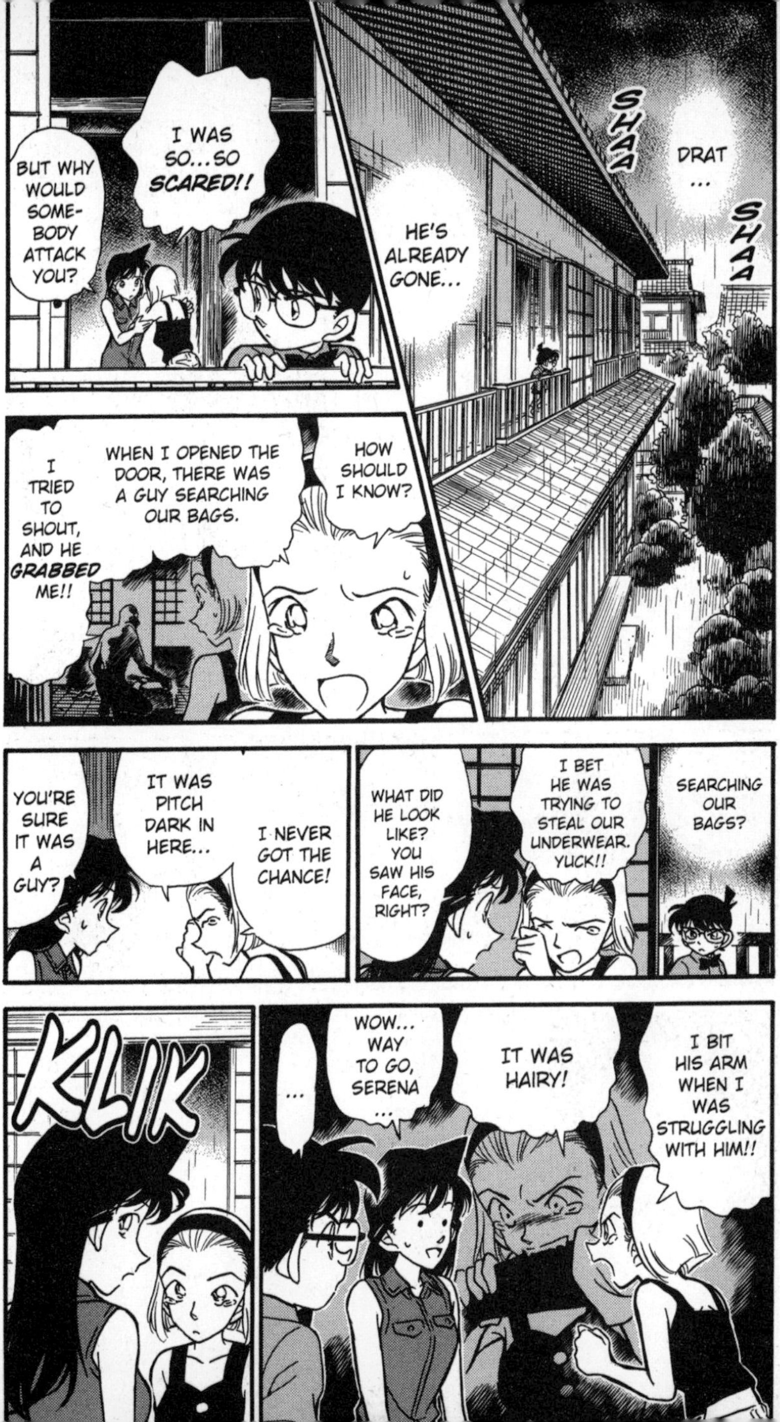
SHAA
DRAT ...
SHAA
HE'S ALREADY GONE...
I WAS SO...SO SCARED!!
BUT WHY WOULD SOMEBODY ATTACK YOU?
HOW SHOULD I KNOW?
WHEN I OPENED THE DOOR, THERE WAS A GUY SEARCHING OUR BAGS.
I TRIED TO SHOUT, AND HE GRABBED ME!!
SEARCHING OUR BAGS?
I BET HE WAS TRYING TO STEAL OUR UNDERWEAR. YUCK!!
WHAT DID HE LOOK LIKE? YOU SAW HIS FACE, RIGHT?
I NEVER GOT THE CHANCE!
IT WAS PITCH DARK IN HERE...
YOU'RE SURE IT WAS A GUY?
I BIT HIS ARM WHEN I WAS STRUGGLING WITH HIM!!
IT WAS HAIRY!
WOW... WAY TO GO, SERENA ...
...
KLIK

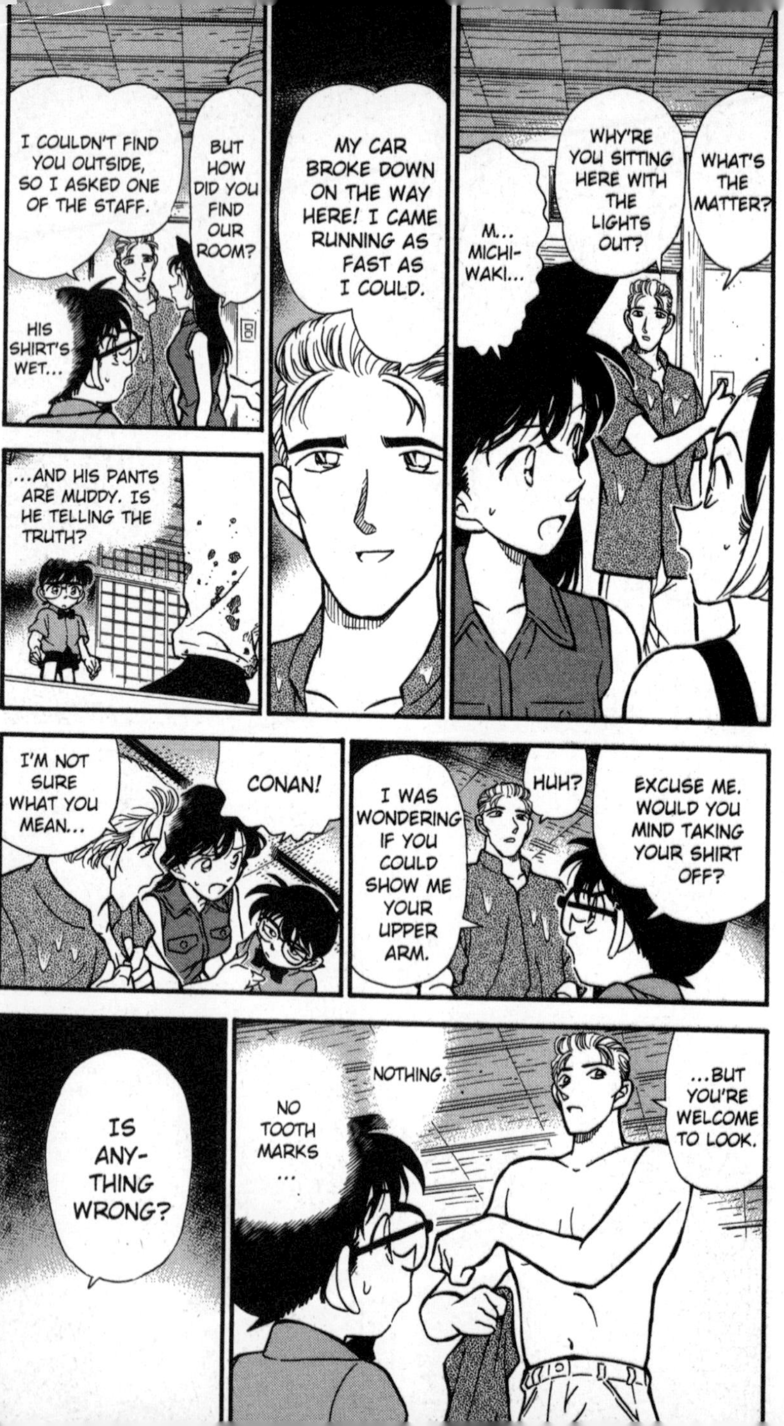
WHAT'S THE MATTER?
WHY'RE YOU SITTING HERE WITH THE LIGHTS OUT?
M... MICHI-WAKI...
MY CAR BROKE DOWN ON THE WAY HERE! I CAME RUNNING AS FAST AS I COULD.
BUT HOW DID YOU FIND OUR ROOM?
I COULDN'T FIND YOU OUTSIDE, SO I ASKED ONE OF THE STAFF.
HIS SHIRT'S WET...
...AND HIS PANTS ARE MUDDY. IS HE TELLING THE TRUTH?
EXCUSE ME. WOULD YOU MIND TAKING YOUR SHIRT OFF?
HUH?
I WAS WONDERING IF YOU COULD SHOW ME YOUR UPPER ARM.
CONAN!
I'M NOT SURE WHAT YOU MEAN...
...BUT YOU'RE WELCOME TO LOOK.
NOTHING.
NO TOOTH MARKS ...
IS ANY-THING WRONG?

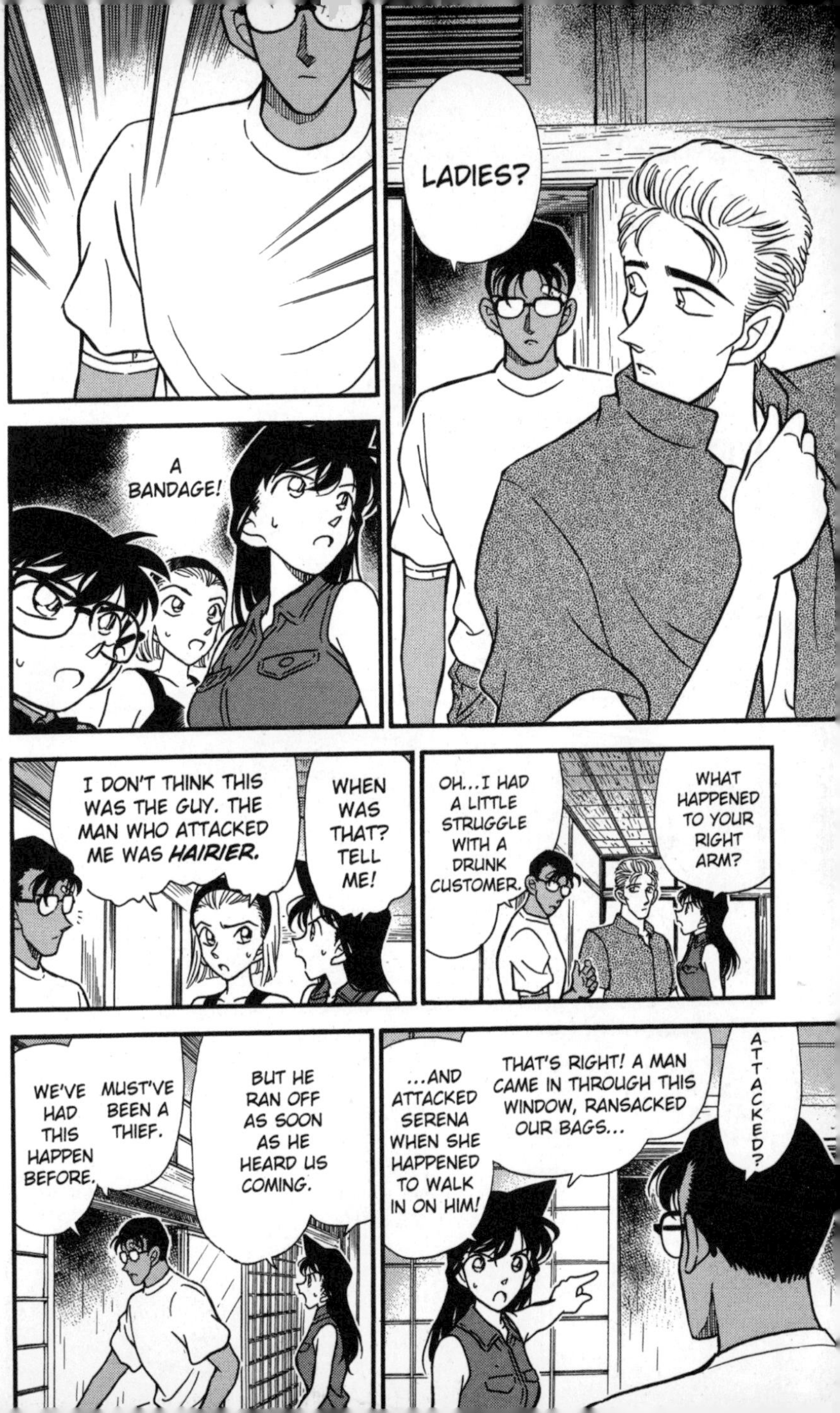
LADIES?
A BANDAGE!
WHAT HAPPENED TO YOUR RIGHT ARM?
OH...I HAD A LITTLE STRUGGLE WITH A DRUNK CUSTOMER.
WHEN WAS THAT? TELL ME!
I DON'T THINK THIS WAS THE GUY. THE MAN WHO ATTACKED ME WAS *HAIRIER.*
ATTACKED?
THAT'S RIGHT! A MAN CAME IN THROUGH THIS WINDOW, RANSACKED OUR BAGS...
...AND ATTACKED SERENA WHEN SHE HAPPENED TO WALK IN ON HIM!
BUT HE RAN OFF AS SOON AS HE HEARD US COMING.
MUST'VE BEEN A THIEF.
WE'VE HAD THIS HAPPEN BEFORE.

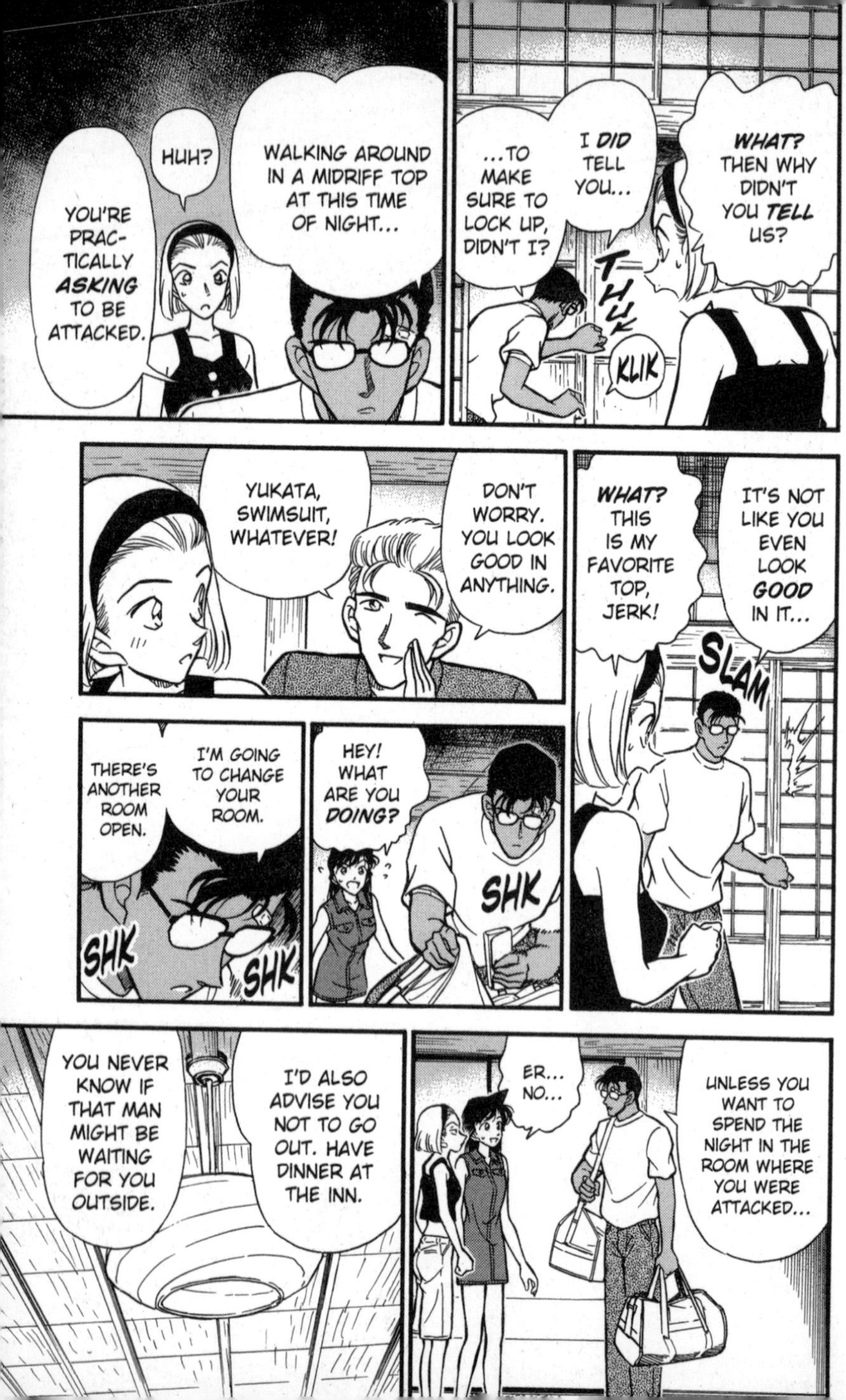
WHAT? THEN WHY DIDN'T YOU TELL US?
I DID TELL YOU...
...TO MAKE SURE TO LOCK UP, DIDN'T I?
THUK
KLIK
WALKING AROUND IN A MIDRIFF TOP AT THIS TIME OF NIGHT...
HUH?
YOU'RE PRACTICALLY ASKING TO BE ATTACKED.
IT'S NOT LIKE YOU EVEN LOOK GOOD IN IT...
WHAT? THIS IS MY FAVORITE TOP, JERK!
SLAM
DON'T WORRY. YOU LOOK GOOD IN ANYTHING.
YUKATA, SWIMSUIT, WHATEVER!
HEY! WHAT ARE YOU DOING?
SHK
I'M GOING TO CHANGE YOUR ROOM.
THERE'S ANOTHER ROOM OPEN.
SHK
SHK
UNLESS YOU WANT TO SPEND THE NIGHT IN THE ROOM WHERE YOU WERE ATTACKED...
ER... NO...
I'D ALSO ADVISE YOU NOT TO GO OUT. HAVE DINNER AT THE INN.
YOU NEVER KNOW IF THAT MAN MIGHT BE WAITING FOR YOU OUTSIDE.

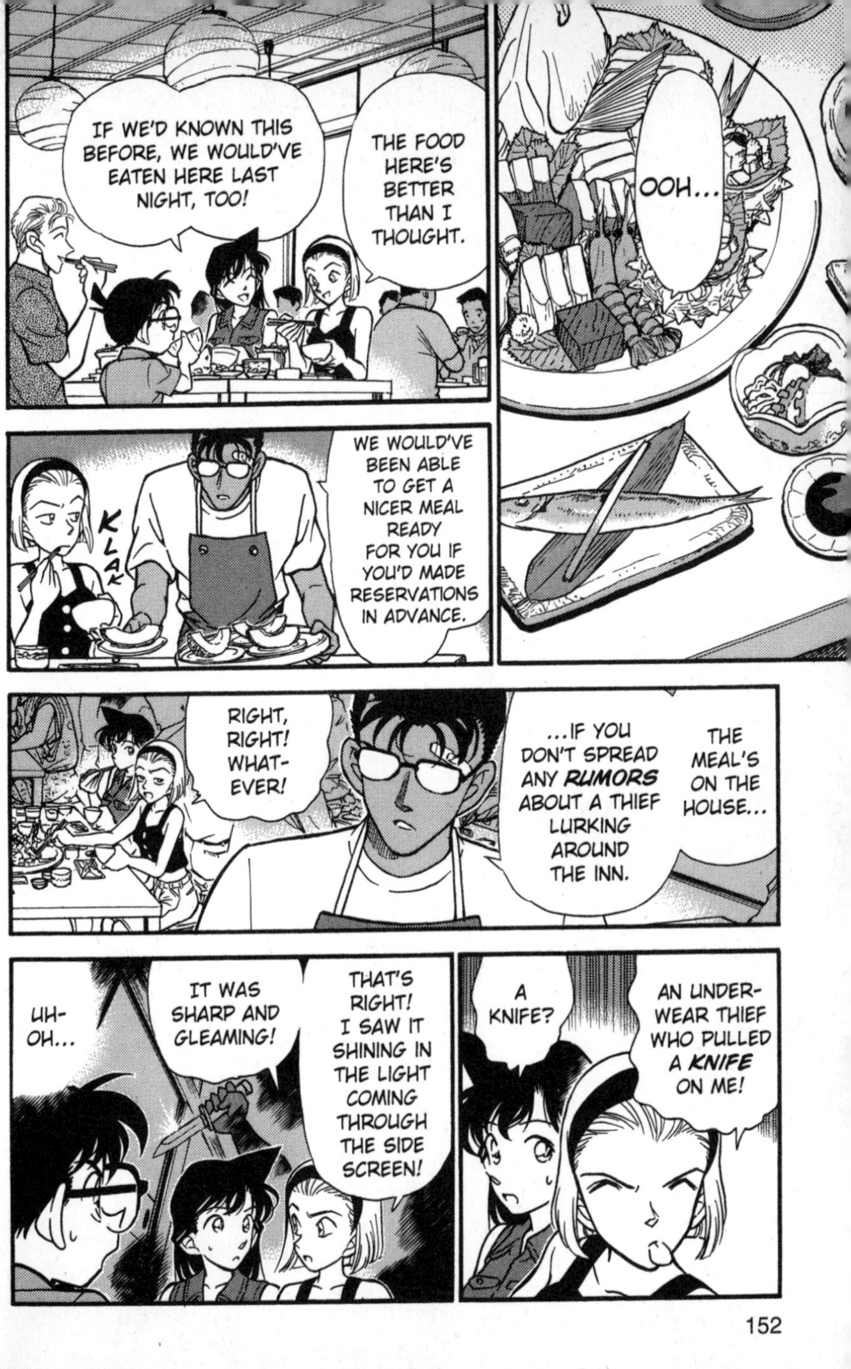
OOH...
THE FOOD HERE'S BETTER THAN I THOUGHT.
IF WE'D KNOWN THIS BEFORE, WE WOULD'VE EATEN HERE LAST NIGHT, TOO!
WE WOULD'VE BEEN ABLE TO GET A NICER MEAL READY FOR YOU IF YOU'D MADE RESERVATIONS IN ADVANCE.
KLAK
THE MEAL'S ON THE HOUSE...
...IF YOU DON'T SPREAD ANY **RUMORS** ABOUT A THIEF LURKING AROUND THE INN.
RIGHT, RIGHT! WHAT-EVER!
AN UNDER-WEAR THIEF WHO PULLED A **KNIFE** ON ME!
A KNIFE?
THAT'S RIGHT! I SAW IT SHINING IN THE LIGHT COMING THROUGH THE SIDE SCREEN!
IT WAS SHARP AND GLEAMING!
UH-OH...

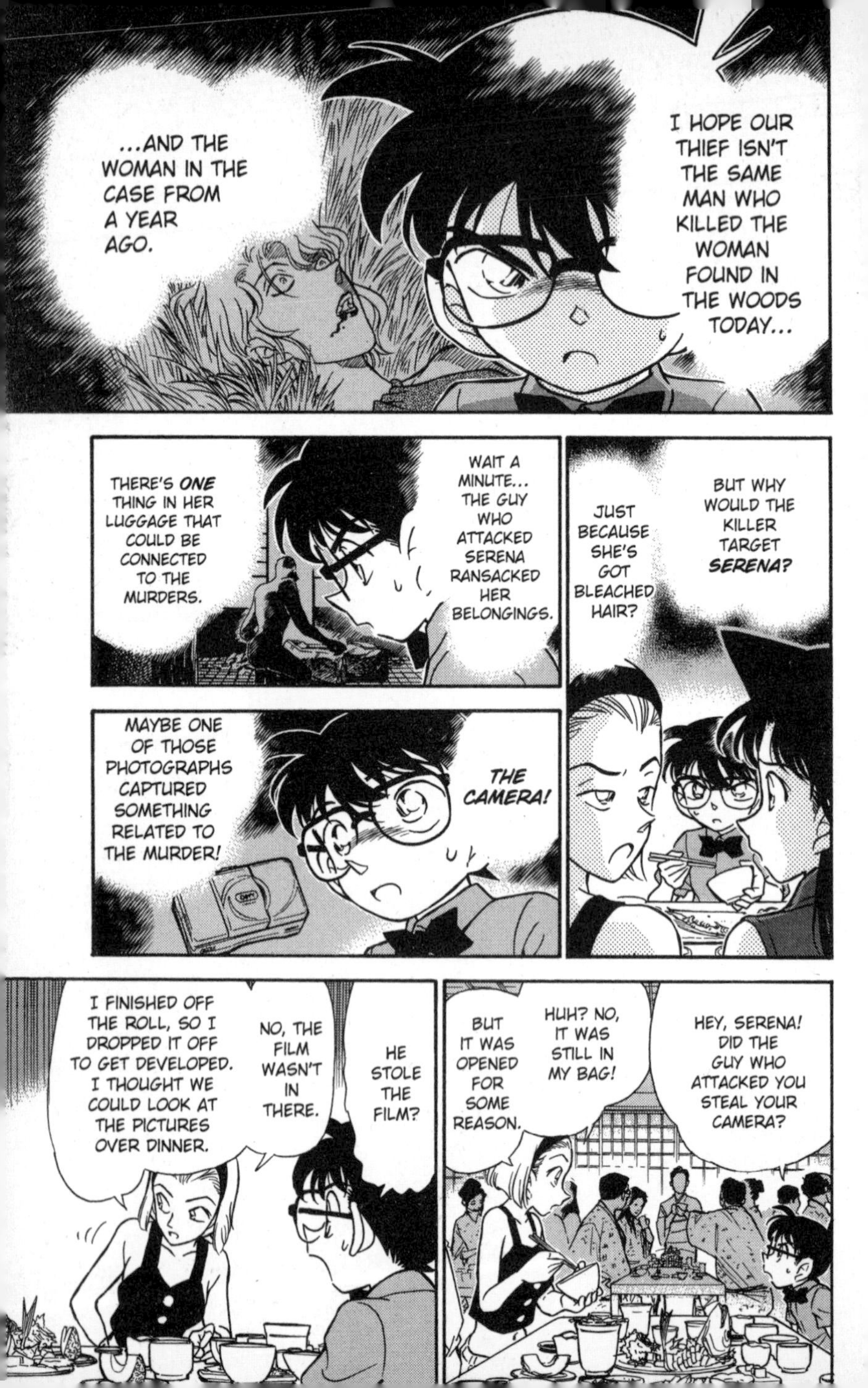
I HOPE OUR THIEF ISN'T THE SAME MAN WHO KILLED THE WOMAN FOUND IN THE WOODS TODAY...
...AND THE WOMAN IN THE CASE FROM A YEAR AGO.
BUT WHY WOULD THE KILLER TARGET ***SERENA?***
JUST BECAUSE SHE'S GOT BLEACHED HAIR?
WAIT A MINUTE... THE GUY WHO ATTACKED SERENA RANSACKED HER BELONGINGS.
THERE'S ***ONE*** THING IN HER LUGGAGE THAT COULD BE CONNECTED TO THE MURDERS.
THE CAMERA!
MAYBE ONE OF THOSE PHOTOGRAPHS CAPTURED SOMETHING RELATED TO THE MURDER!
HEY, SERENA! DID THE GUY WHO ATTACKED YOU STEAL YOUR CAMERA?
HUH? NO, IT WAS STILL IN MY BAG!
BUT IT WAS OPENED FOR SOME REASON.
HE STOLE THE FILM?
NO, THE FILM WASN'T IN THERE.
I FINISHED OFF THE ROLL, SO I DROPPED IT OFF TO GET DEVELOPED. I THOUGHT WE COULD LOOK AT THE PICTURES OVER DINNER.

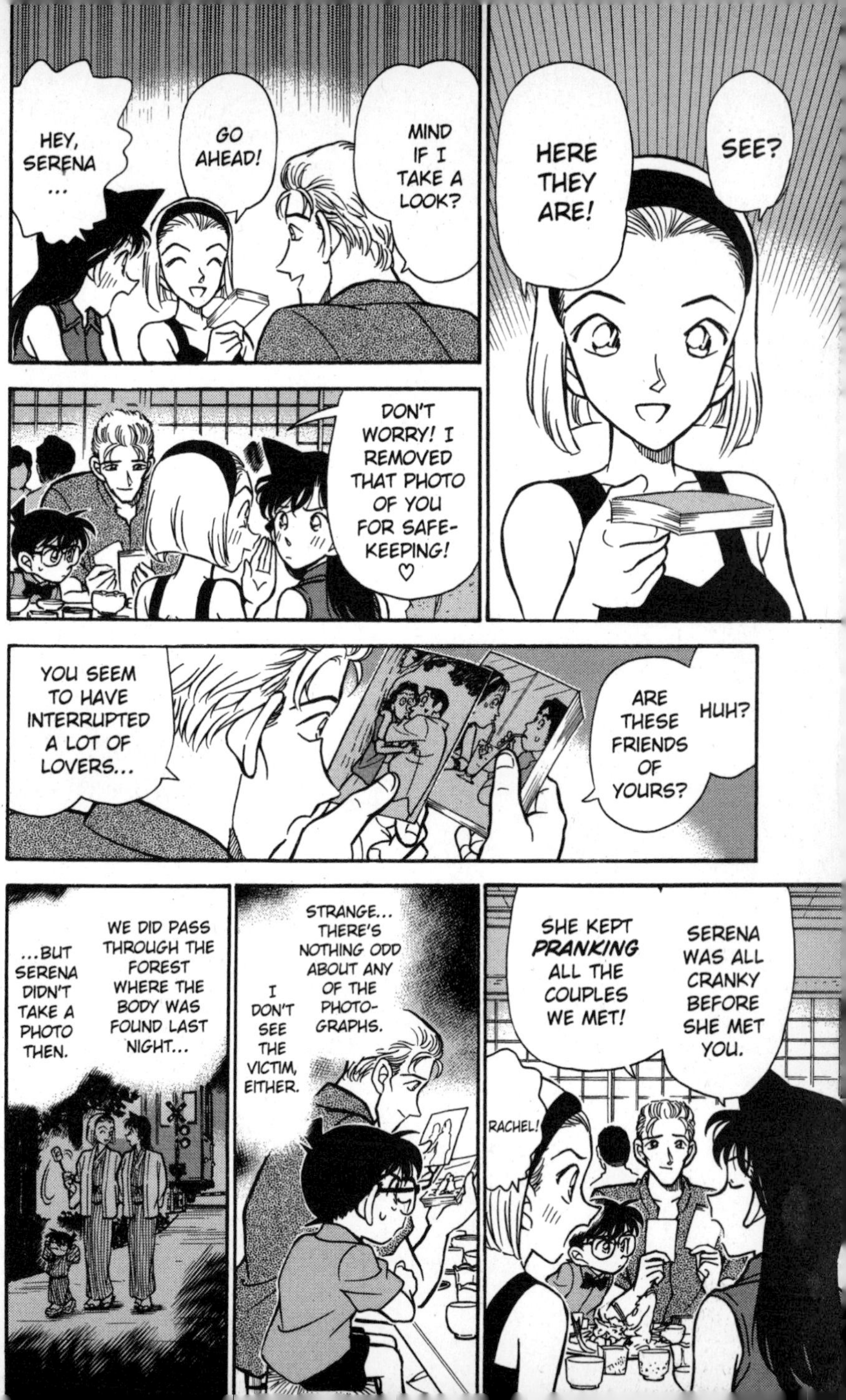
SEE?
HERE THEY ARE!
MIND IF I TAKE A LOOK?
GO AHEAD!
HEY, SERENA ...
DON'T WORRY! I REMOVED THAT PHOTO OF YOU FOR SAFE-KEEPING! ♡
HUH?
ARE THESE FRIENDS OF YOURS?
YOU SEEM TO HAVE INTERRUPTED A LOT OF LOVERS...
SERENA WAS ALL CRANKY BEFORE SHE MET YOU.
SHE KEPT **PRANKING** ALL THE COUPLES WE MET!
RACHEL!
STRANGE... THERE'S NOTHING ODD ABOUT ANY OF THE PHOTO-GRAPHS.
I DON'T SEE THE VICTIM, EITHER.
WE DID PASS THROUGH THE FOREST WHERE THE BODY WAS FOUND LAST NIGHT...
...BUT SERENA DIDN'T TAKE A PHOTO THEN.

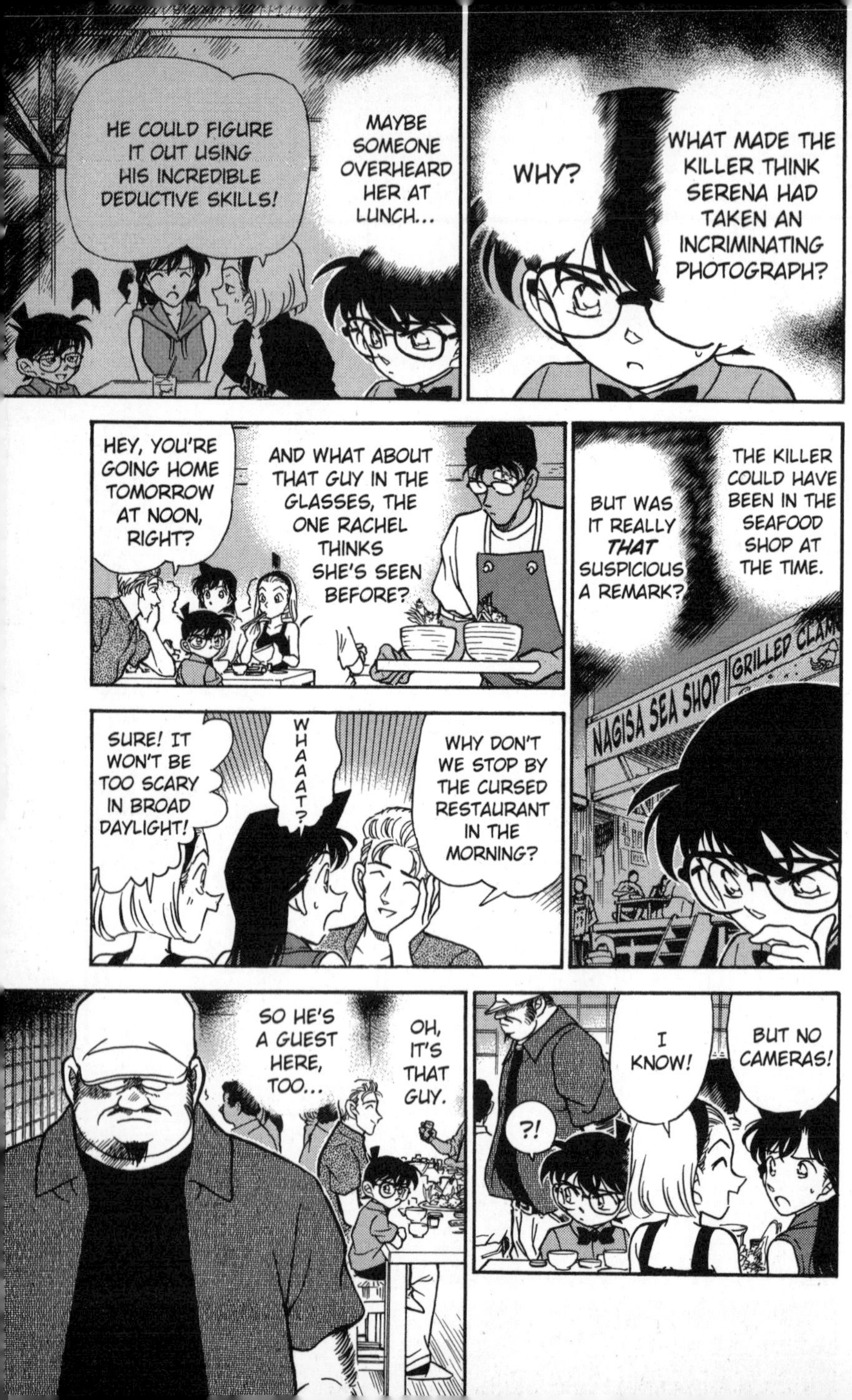
WHY?
WHAT MADE THE KILLER THINK SERENA HAD TAKEN AN INCRIMINATING PHOTOGRAPH?
MAYBE SOMEONE OVERHEARD HER AT LUNCH...
HE COULD FIGURE IT OUT USING HIS INCREDIBLE DEDUCTIVE SKILLS!
THE KILLER COULD HAVE BEEN IN THE SEAFOOD SHOP AT THE TIME.
BUT WAS IT REALLY *THAT* SUSPICIOUS A REMARK?
GRILLED CLAM
NAGISA SEA SHOP
AND WHAT ABOUT THAT GUY IN THE GLASSES, THE ONE RACHEL THINKS SHE'S SEEN BEFORE?
HEY, YOU'RE GOING HOME TOMORROW AT NOON, RIGHT?
WHY DON'T WE STOP BY THE CURSED RESTAURANT IN THE MORNING?
WHAAAAT?
SURE! IT WON'T BE TOO SCARY IN BROAD DAYLIGHT!
BUT NO CAMERAS!
I KNOW!
?!
OH, IT'S THAT GUY.
SO HE'S A GUEST HERE, TOO...

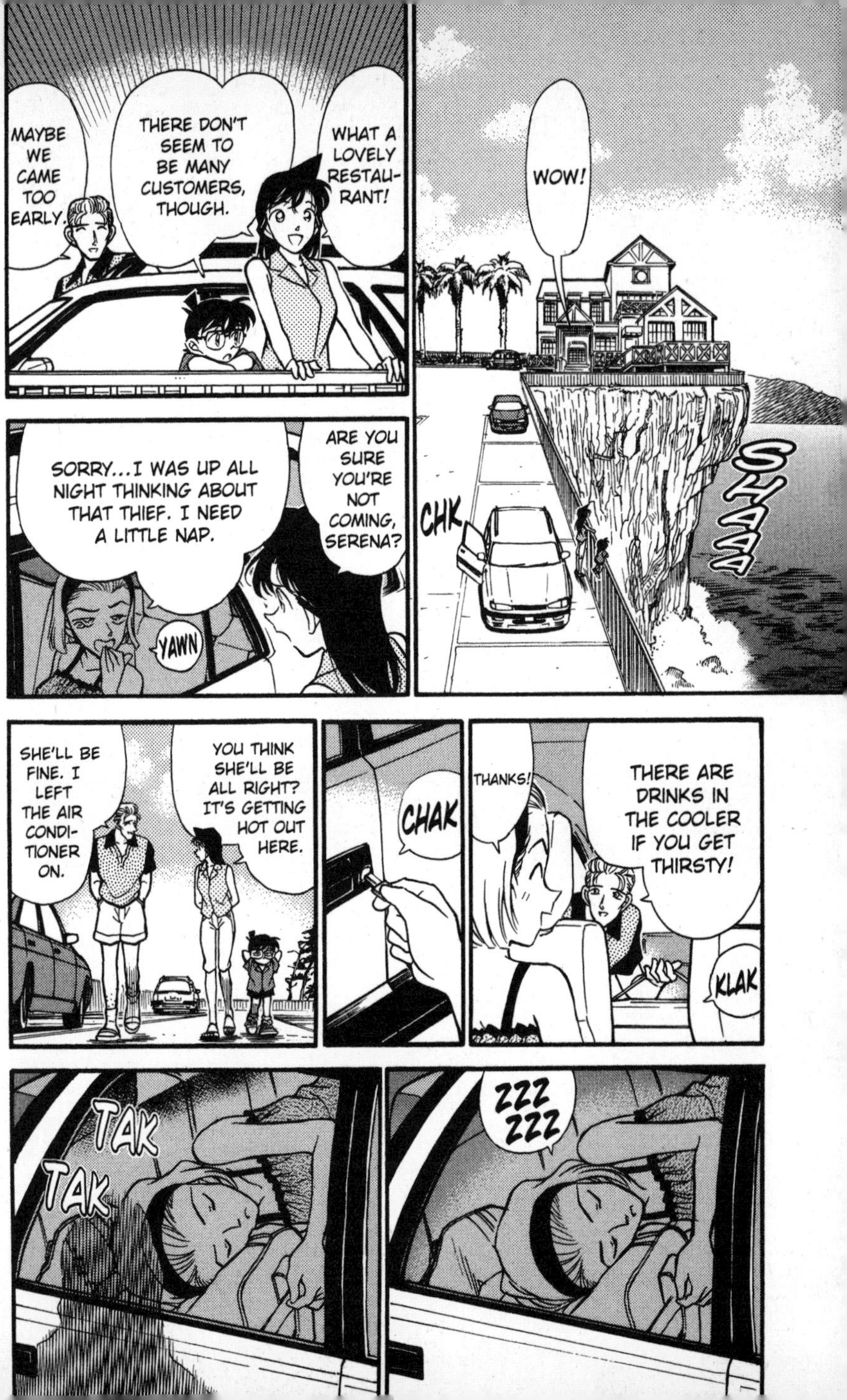
WOW!
CHK
SHAAAA
WHAT A LOVELY RESTAU-RANT!
THERE DON'T SEEM TO BE MANY CUSTOMERS, THOUGH.
MAYBE WE CAME TOO EARLY.
ARE YOU SURE YOU'RE NOT COMING, SERENA?
SORRY...I WAS UP ALL NIGHT THINKING ABOUT THAT THIEF. I NEED A LITTLE NAP.
YAWN
THERE ARE DRINKS IN THE COOLER IF YOU GET THIRSTY!
THANKS!
KLAK
CHAK
YOU THINK SHE'LL BE ALL RIGHT? IT'S GETTING HOT OUT HERE.
SHE'LL BE FINE. I LEFT THE AIR CONDI-TIONER ON.
ZZZ ZZZ
TAK
TAK

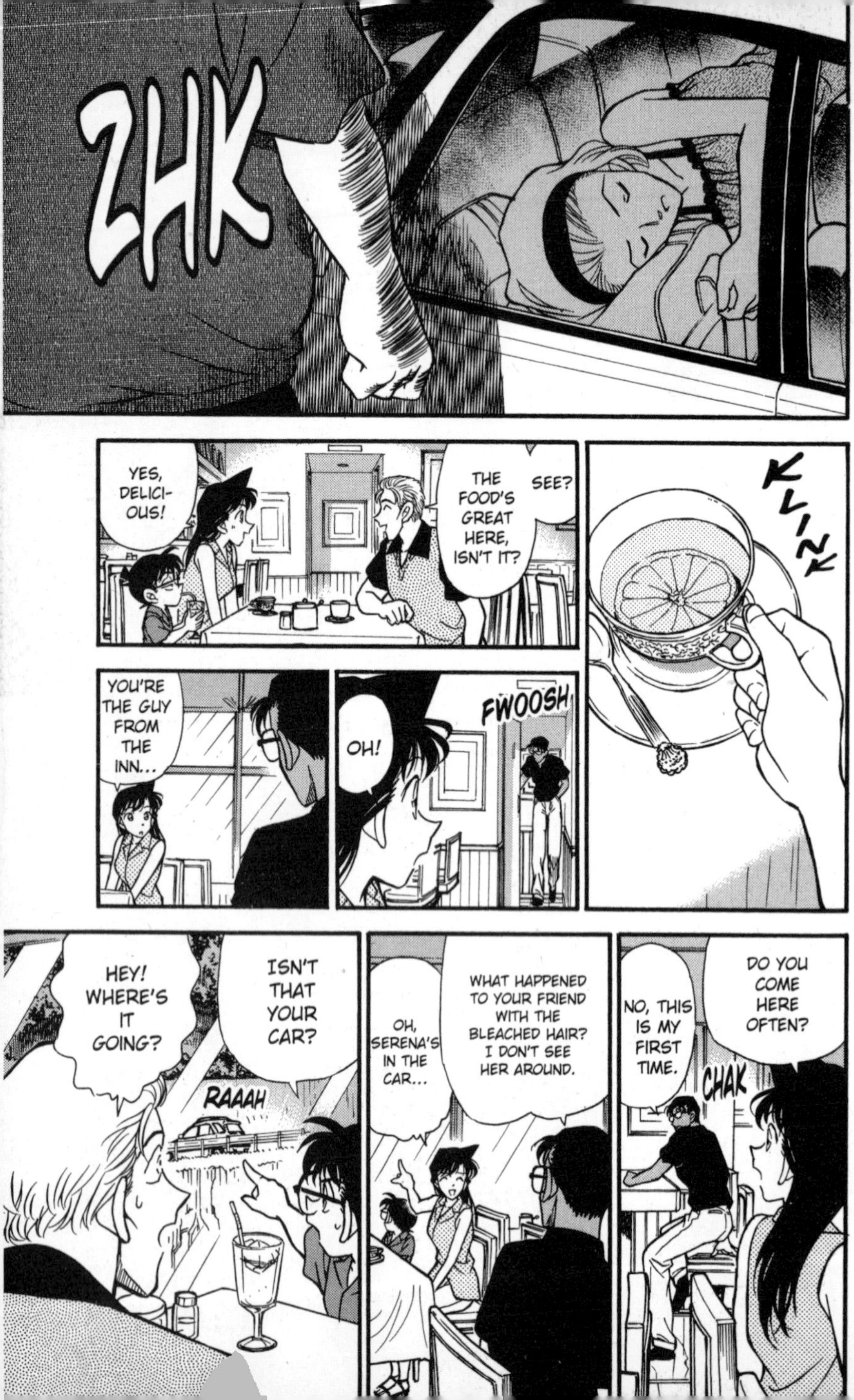
ZHK
KLINK
SEE?
THE FOOD'S GREAT HERE, ISN'T IT?
YES, DELICIOUS!
FWOOSH
OH!
YOU'RE THE GUY FROM THE INN...
DO YOU COME HERE OFTEN?
CHAK
NO, THIS IS MY FIRST TIME.
WHAT HAPPENED TO YOUR FRIEND WITH THE BLEACHED HAIR? I DON'T SEE HER AROUND.
OH, SERENA'S IN THE CAR...
ISN'T THAT YOUR CAR?
HEY! WHERE'S IT GOING?
RAAAH

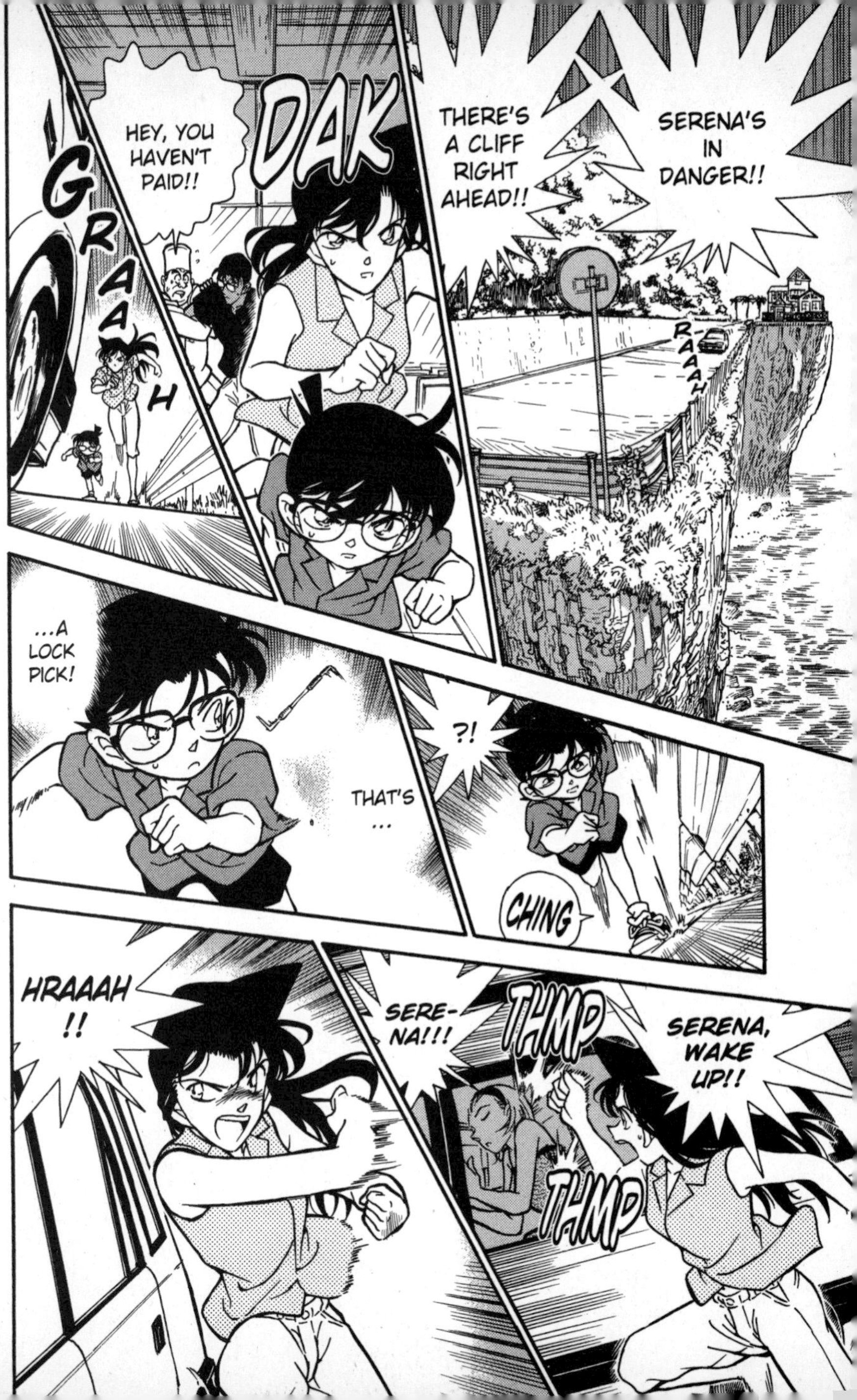
SERENA'S IN DANGER!!
THERE'S A CLIFF RIGHT AHEAD!!
R-RAAAH
DAK
HEY, YOU HAVEN'T PAID!!
GRAAAH
?!
CHING
THAT'S ...
...A LOCK PICK!
SERENA, WAKE UP!!
THMP
SERE-NA!!!
THMP
HRAAAH !!

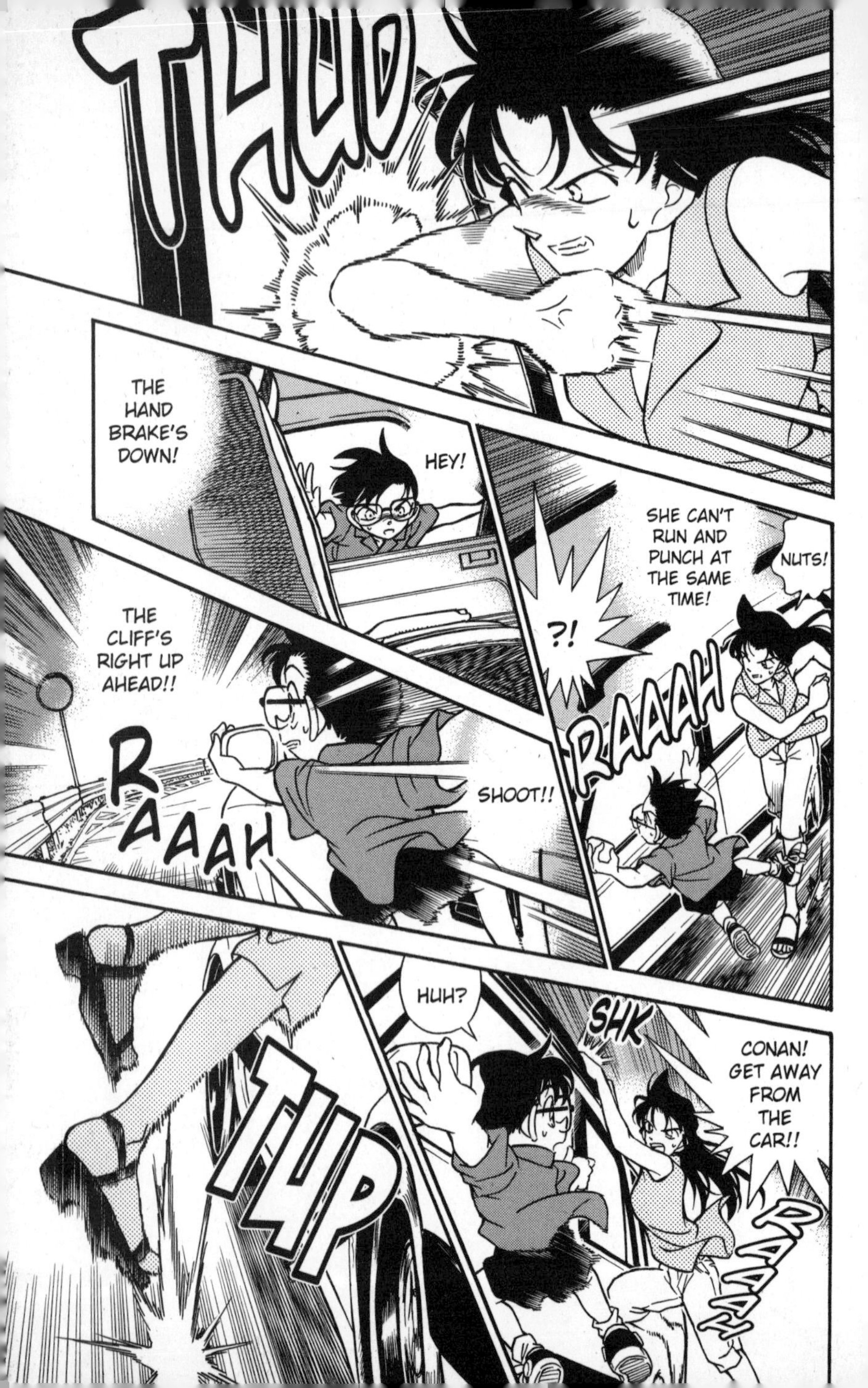
THUD
NUTS!
SHE CAN'T RUN AND PUNCH AT THE SAME TIME!
?!
RAAAH
THE HAND BRAKE'S DOWN!
HEY!
THE CLIFF'S RIGHT UP AHEAD!!
SHOOT!!
RAAAH
CONAN! GET AWAY FROM THE CAR!!
SHK
HUH?
RAAAAH
THUP

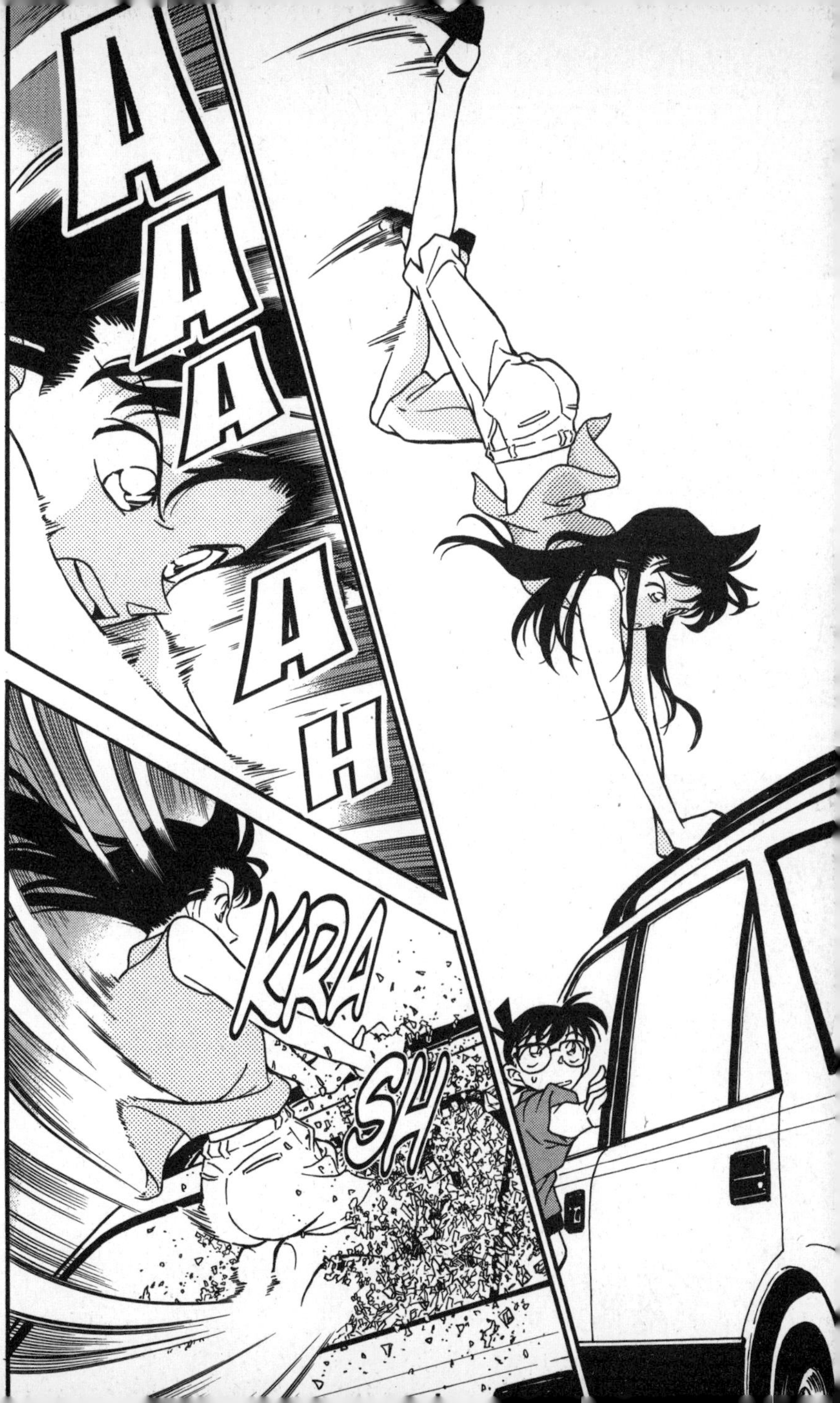
AAAAAAH
KRASH

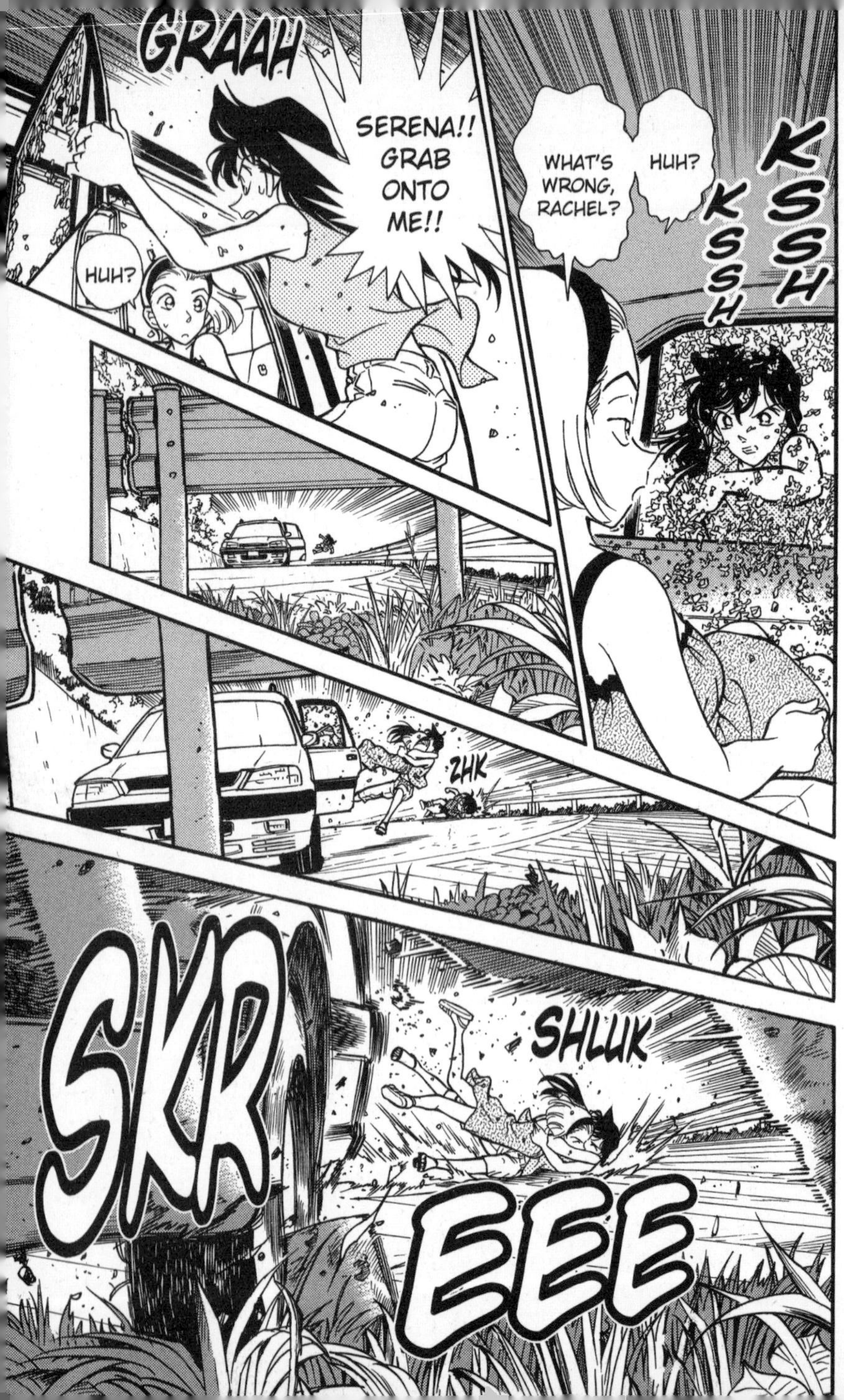
KSSH
KSSH
HUH?
WHAT'S WRONG, RACHEL?
GRAAH
SERENA!! GRAB ONTO ME!!
HUH?
ZHK
SHLUK
SKR
EEE

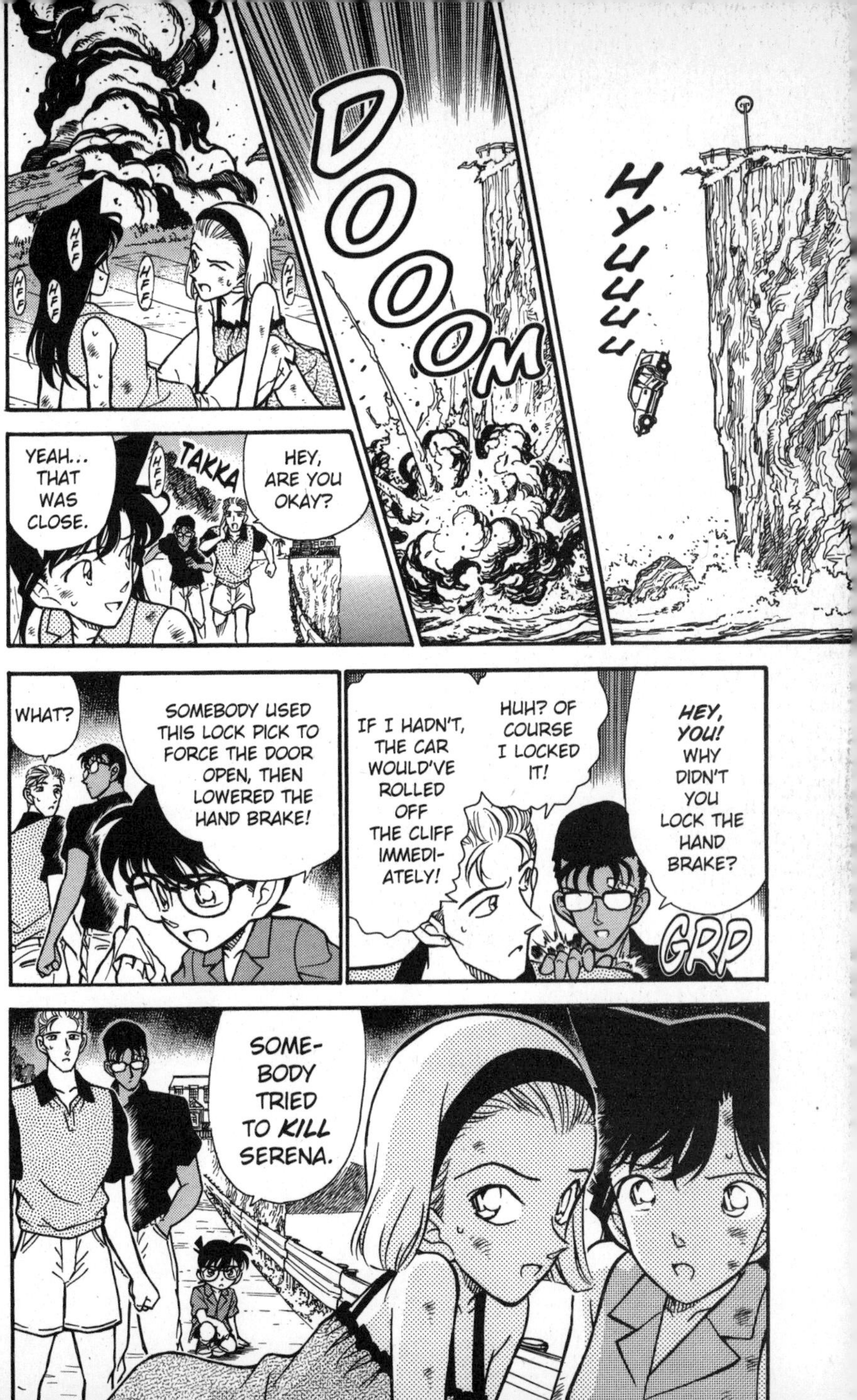
HYUUUUU
DOOOOM
HFF
HFF
HFF
HFF
HEY, ARE YOU OKAY?
TAKKA
HFF
YEAH... THAT WAS CLOSE.
HEY, YOU! WHY DIDN'T YOU LOCK THE HAND BRAKE?
GRP
HUH? OF COURSE I LOCKED IT!
IF I HADN'T, THE CAR WOULD'VE ROLLED OFF THE CLIFF IMMEDI-ATELY!
SOMEBODY USED THIS LOCK PICK TO FORCE THE DOOR OPEN, THEN LOWERED THE HAND BRAKE!
WHAT?
SOME-BODY TRIED TO ***KILL*** SERENA.

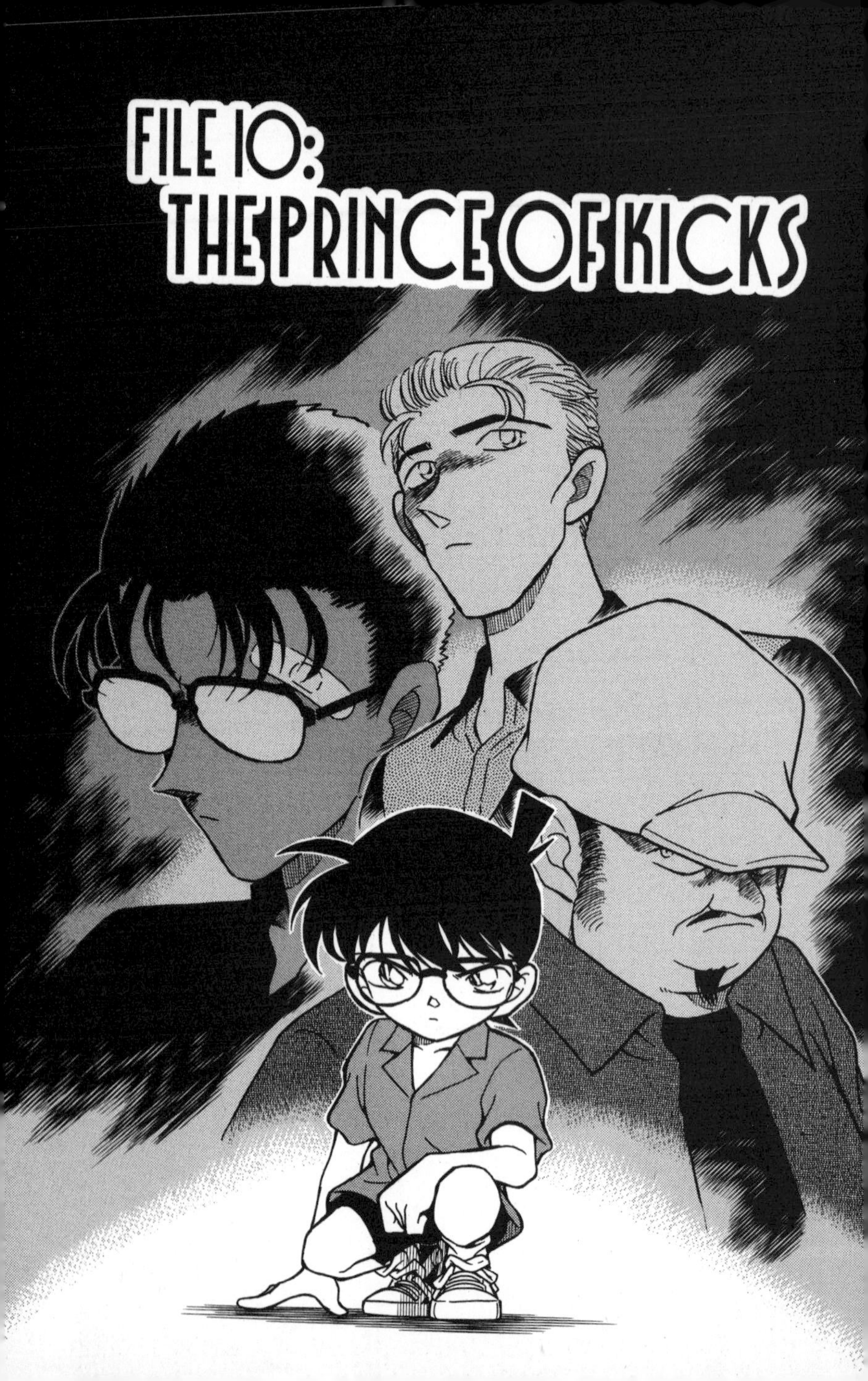
FILE 10:
THE PRINCE OF KICKS

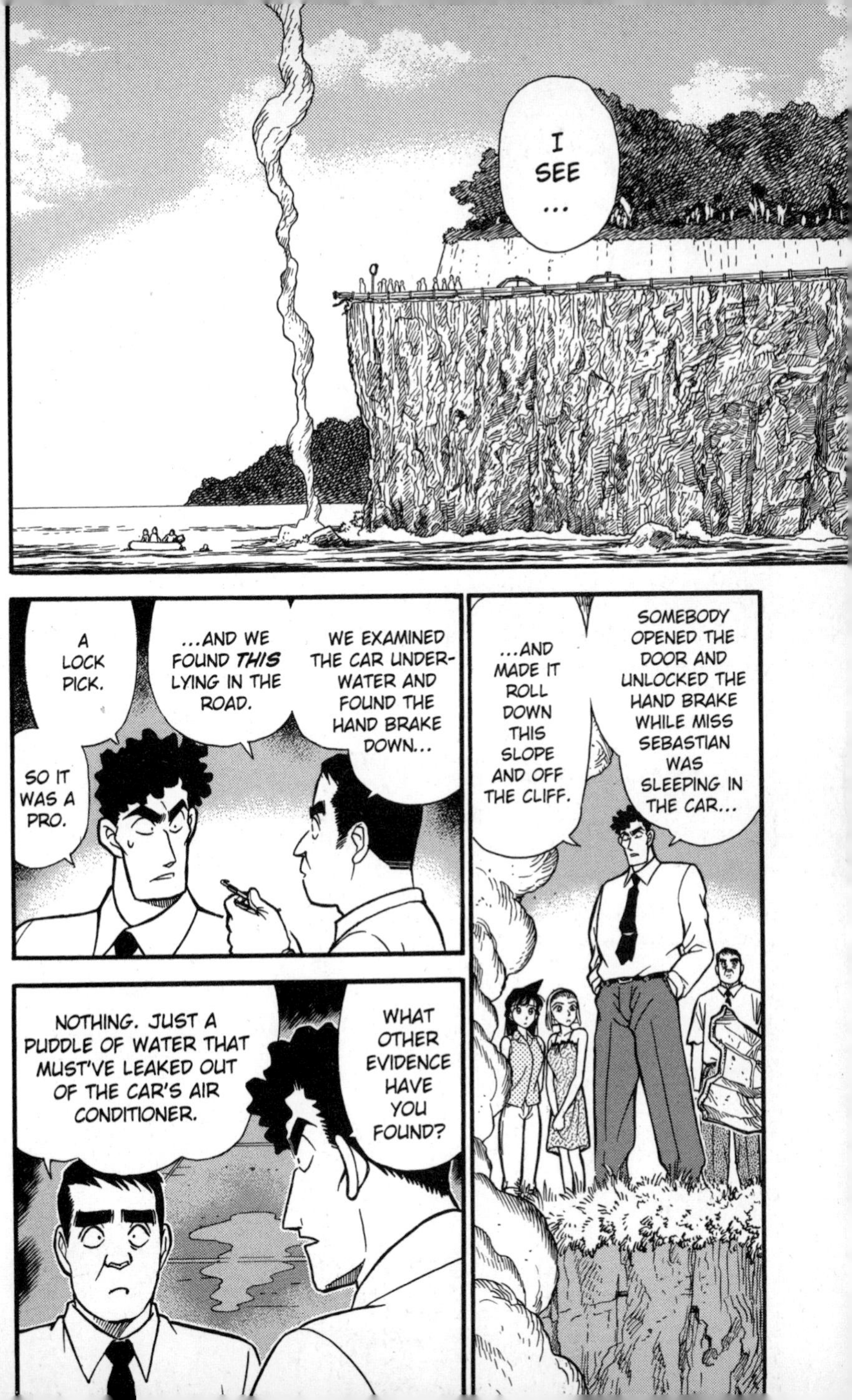
I SEE...
SOMEBODY OPENED THE DOOR AND UNLOCKED THE HAND BRAKE WHILE MISS SEBASTIAN WAS SLEEPING IN THE CAR...
...AND MADE IT ROLL DOWN THIS SLOPE AND OFF THE CLIFF.
WE EXAMINED THE CAR UNDERWATER AND FOUND THE HAND BRAKE DOWN...
...AND WE FOUND *THIS* LYING IN THE ROAD.
A LOCK PICK.
SO IT WAS A PRO.
WHAT OTHER EVIDENCE HAVE YOU FOUND?
NOTHING. JUST A PUDDLE OF WATER THAT MUST'VE LEAKED OUT OF THE CAR'S AIR CONDITIONER.

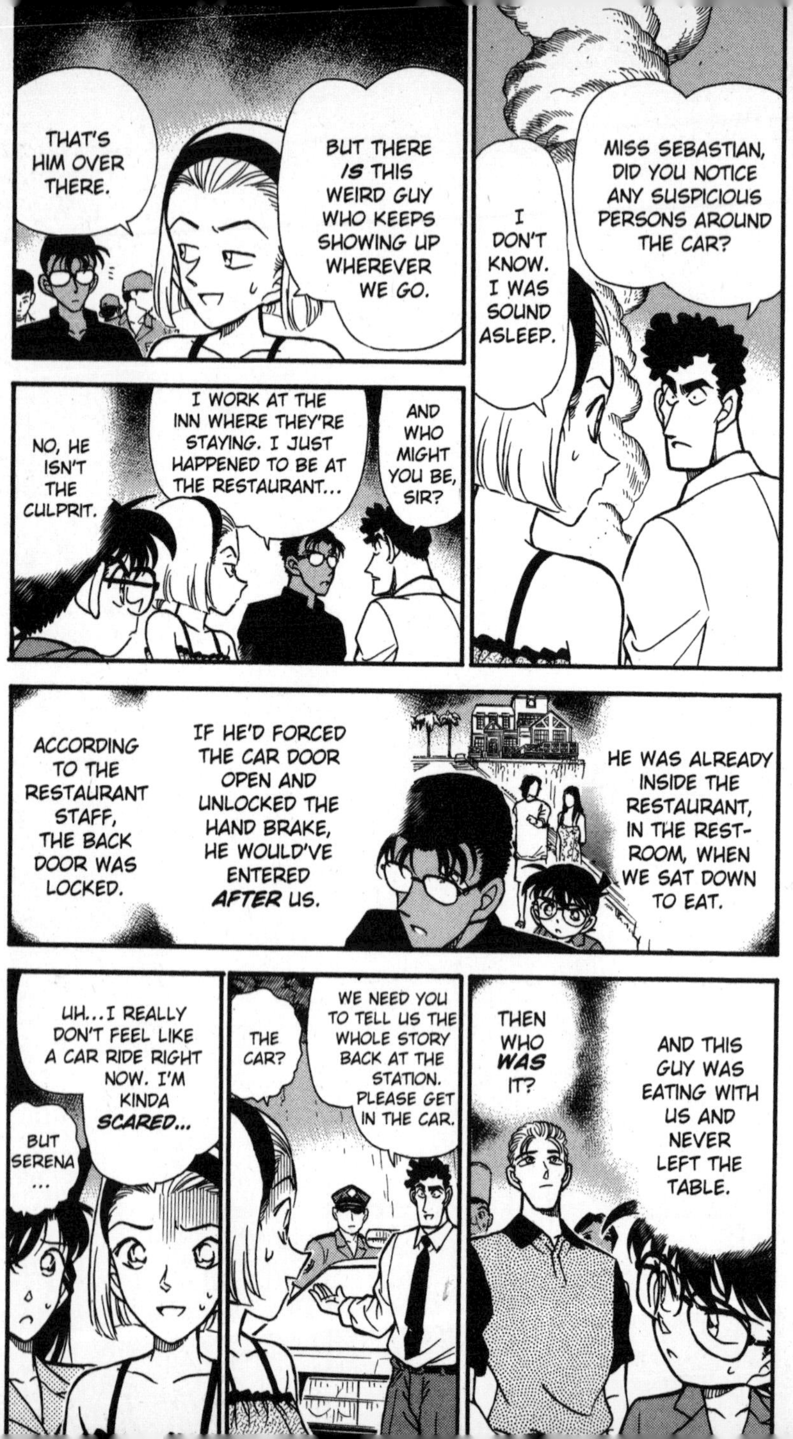
MISS SEBASTIAN, DID YOU NOTICE ANY SUSPICIOUS PERSONS AROUND THE CAR?
I DON'T KNOW. I WAS SOUND ASLEEP.
BUT THERE *IS* THIS WEIRD GUY WHO KEEPS SHOWING UP WHEREVER WE GO.
THAT'S HIM OVER THERE.
AND WHO MIGHT YOU BE, SIR?
I WORK AT THE INN WHERE THEY'RE STAYING. I JUST HAPPENED TO BE AT THE RESTAURANT...
NO, HE ISN'T THE CULPRIT.
HE WAS ALREADY INSIDE THE RESTAURANT, IN THE REST-ROOM, WHEN WE SAT DOWN TO EAT.
IF HE'D FORCED THE CAR DOOR OPEN AND UNLOCKED THE HAND BRAKE, HE WOULD'VE ENTERED **AFTER** US.
ACCORDING TO THE RESTAURANT STAFF, THE BACK DOOR WAS LOCKED.
AND THIS GUY WAS EATING WITH US AND NEVER LEFT THE TABLE.
THEN WHO **WAS** IT?
WE NEED YOU TO TELL US THE WHOLE STORY BACK AT THE STATION. PLEASE GET IN THE CAR.
THE CAR?
UH...I REALLY DON'T FEEL LIKE A CAR RIDE RIGHT NOW. I'M KINDA **SCARED...**
BUT SERENA...

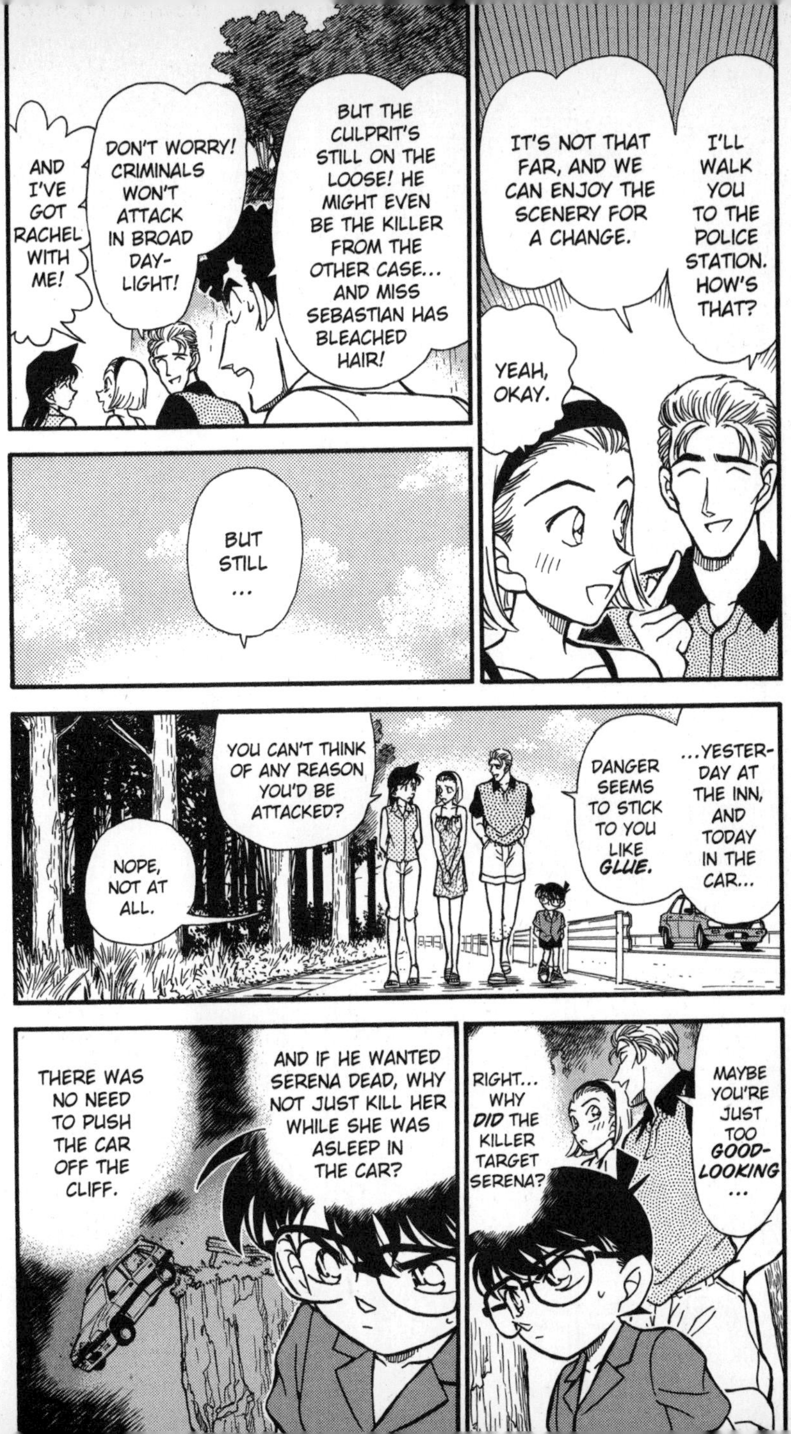
I'LL WALK YOU TO THE POLICE STATION. HOW'S THAT?
IT'S NOT THAT FAR, AND WE CAN ENJOY THE SCENERY FOR A CHANGE.
YEAH, OKAY.
BUT THE CULPRIT'S STILL ON THE LOOSE! HE MIGHT EVEN BE THE KILLER FROM THE OTHER CASE... AND MISS SEBASTIAN HAS BLEACHED HAIR!
DON'T WORRY! CRIMINALS WON'T ATTACK IN BROAD DAY-LIGHT!
AND I'VE GOT RACHEL WITH ME!
BUT STILL ...
...YESTER-DAY AT THE INN, AND TODAY IN THE CAR...
DANGER SEEMS TO STICK TO YOU LIKE *GLUE.*
YOU CAN'T THINK OF ANY REASON YOU'D BE ATTACKED?
NOPE, NOT AT ALL.
MAYBE YOU'RE JUST TOO *GOOD-LOOKING* ...
RIGHT... WHY *DID* THE KILLER TARGET SERENA?
AND IF HE WANTED SERENA DEAD, WHY NOT JUST KILL HER WHILE SHE WAS ASLEEP IN THE CAR?
THERE WAS NO NEED TO PUSH THE CAR OFF THE CLIFF.

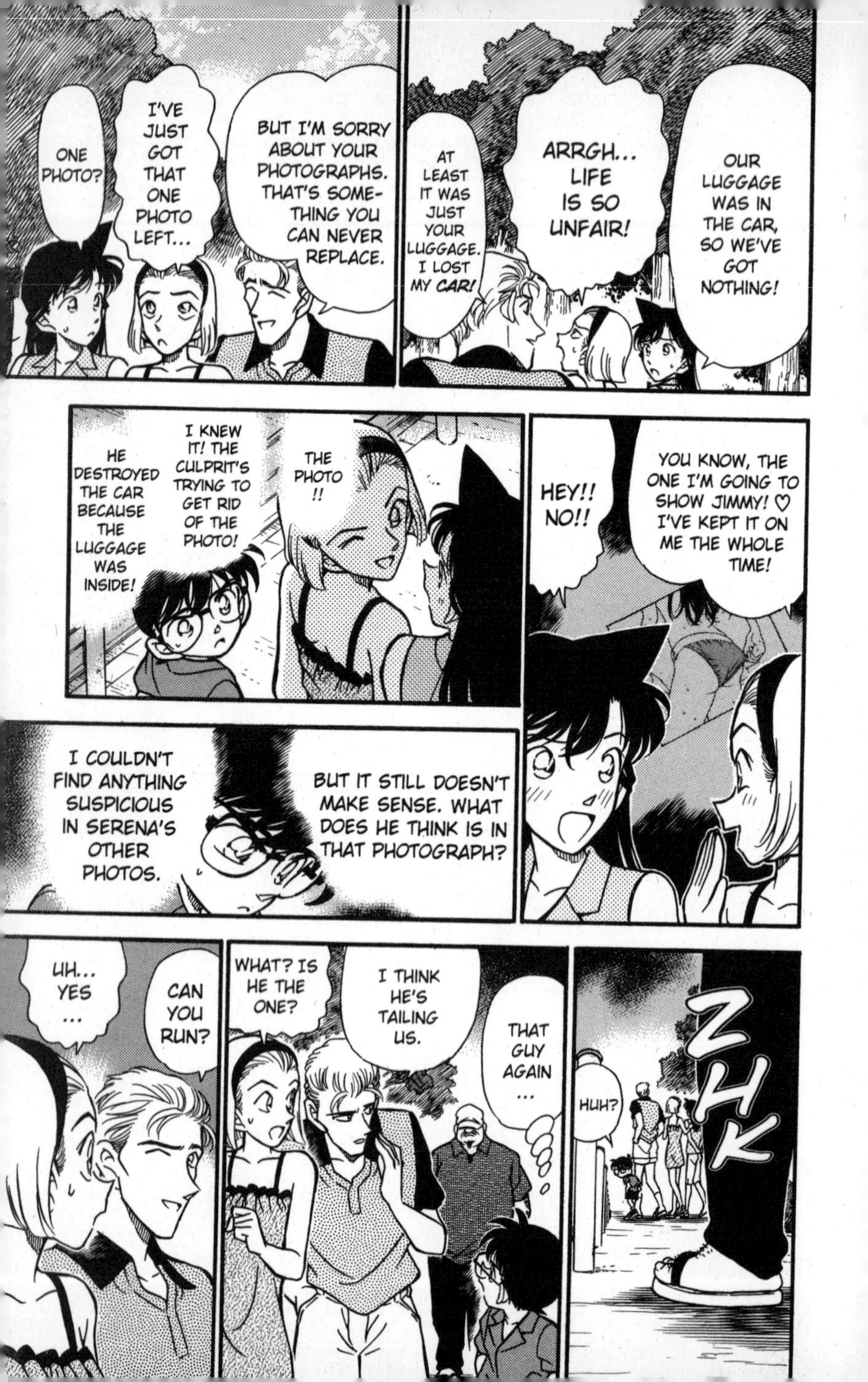
OUR LUGGAGE WAS IN THE CAR, SO WE'VE GOT NOTHING!
ARRGH... LIFE IS SO UNFAIR!
AT LEAST IT WAS JUST YOUR LUGGAGE. I LOST MY *CAR!*
BUT I'M SORRY ABOUT YOUR PHOTOGRAPHS. THAT'S SOMETHING YOU CAN NEVER REPLACE.
I'VE JUST GOT THAT ONE PHOTO LEFT...
ONE PHOTO?
YOU KNOW, THE ONE I'M GOING TO SHOW JIMMY! ♡ I'VE KEPT IT ON ME THE WHOLE TIME!
HEY!! NO!!
THE PHOTO !!
I KNEW IT! THE CULPRIT'S TRYING TO GET RID OF THE PHOTO!
HE DESTROYED THE CAR BECAUSE THE LUGGAGE WAS INSIDE!
I COULDN'T FIND ANYTHING SUSPICIOUS IN SERENA'S OTHER PHOTOS.
BUT IT STILL DOESN'T MAKE SENSE. WHAT DOES HE THINK IS IN THAT PHOTOGRAPH?
ZHK
HUH?
THAT GUY AGAIN ...
I THINK HE'S TAILING US.
WHAT? IS HE THE ONE?
CAN YOU RUN?
UH... YES ...

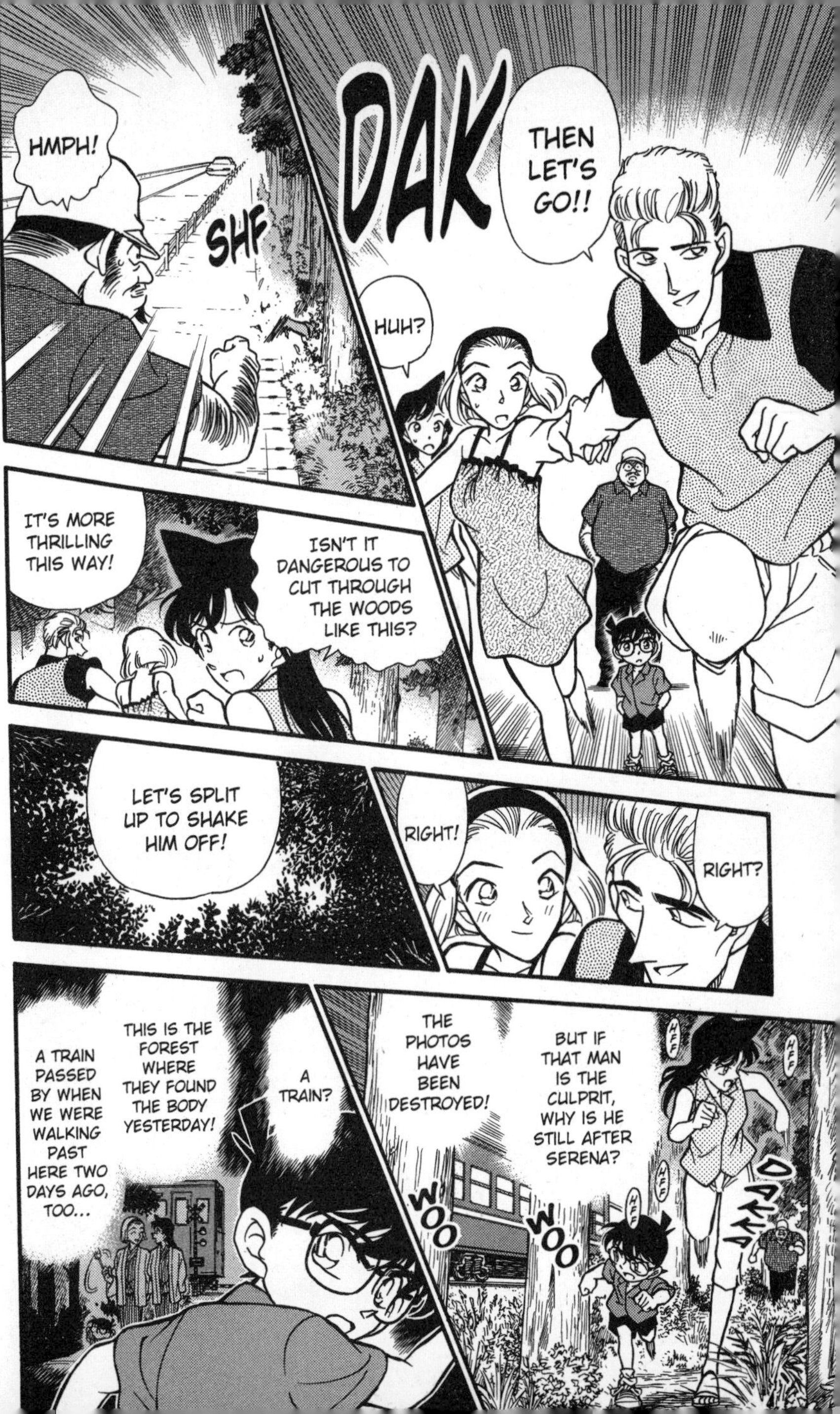
DAK
THEN LET'S GO!!
HUH?
HMPH!
SHF
ISN'T IT DANGEROUS TO CUT THROUGH THE WOODS LIKE THIS?
IT'S MORE THRILLING THIS WAY!
RIGHT?
RIGHT!
LET'S SPLIT UP TO SHAKE HIM OFF!
HFF
HFF
BUT IF THAT MAN IS THE CULPRIT, WHY IS HE STILL AFTER SERENA?
THE PHOTOS HAVE BEEN DESTROYED!
DAKKA
HFF
HFF
WOO
WOO
A TRAIN?
THIS IS THE FOREST WHERE THEY FOUND THE BODY YESTERDAY!
A TRAIN PASSED BY WHEN WE WERE WALKING PAST HERE TWO DAYS AGO, TOO...

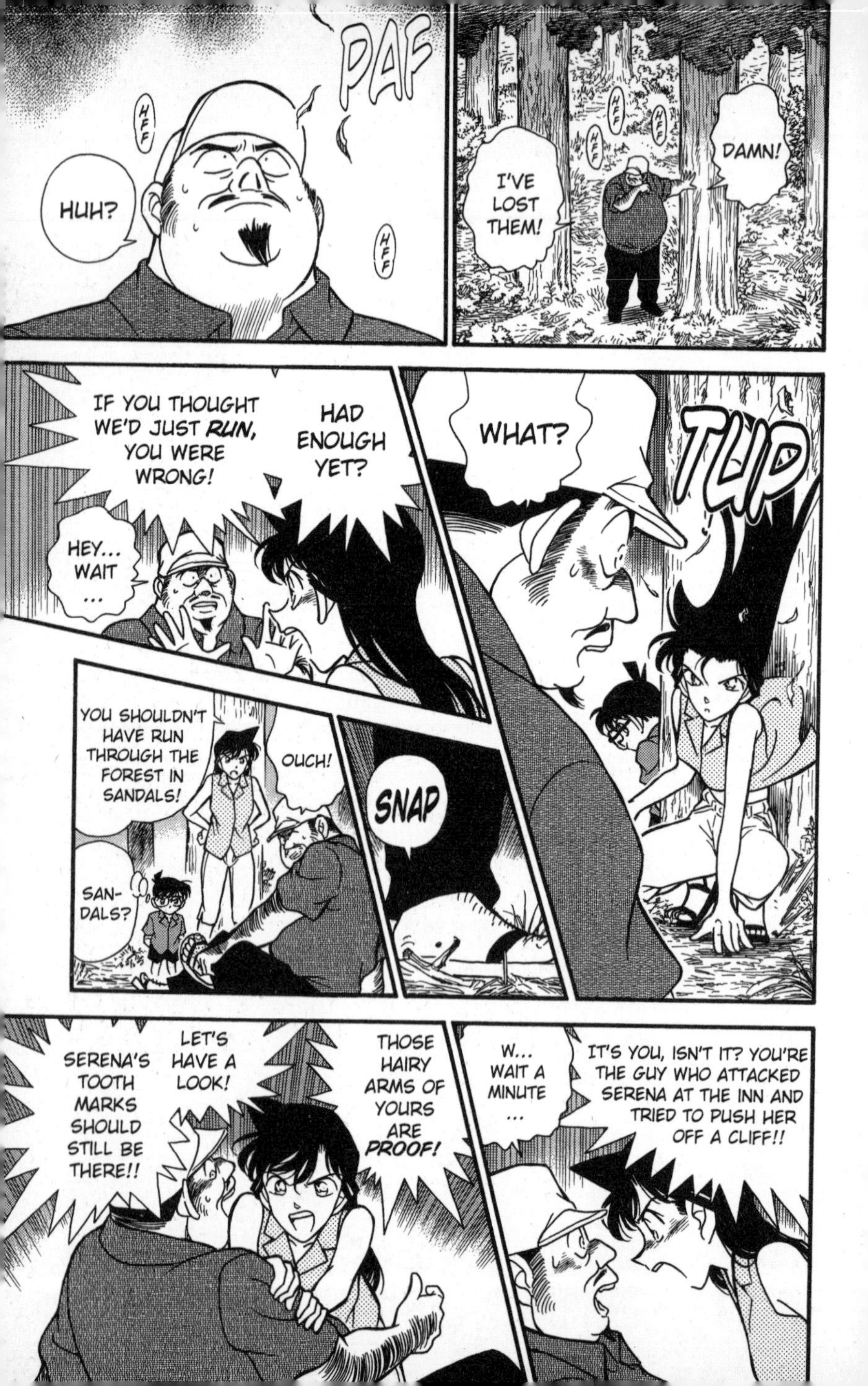
DAMN!
HFF HFF HFF
I'VE LOST THEM!
PAF
HFF
HUH?
HFF
TUP
WHAT?
HAD ENOUGH YET?
IF YOU THOUGHT WE'D JUST *RUN*, YOU WERE WRONG!
HEY... WAIT ...
SNAP
OUCH!
YOU SHOULDN'T HAVE RUN THROUGH THE FOREST IN SANDALS!
SAN-DALS?
IT'S YOU, ISN'T IT? YOU'RE THE GUY WHO ATTACKED SERENA AT THE INN AND TRIED TO PUSH HER OFF A CLIFF!!
W... WAIT A MINUTE ...
THOSE HAIRY ARMS OF YOURS ARE *PROOF!*
LET'S HAVE A LOOK!
SERENA'S TOOTH MARKS SHOULD STILL BE THERE!!

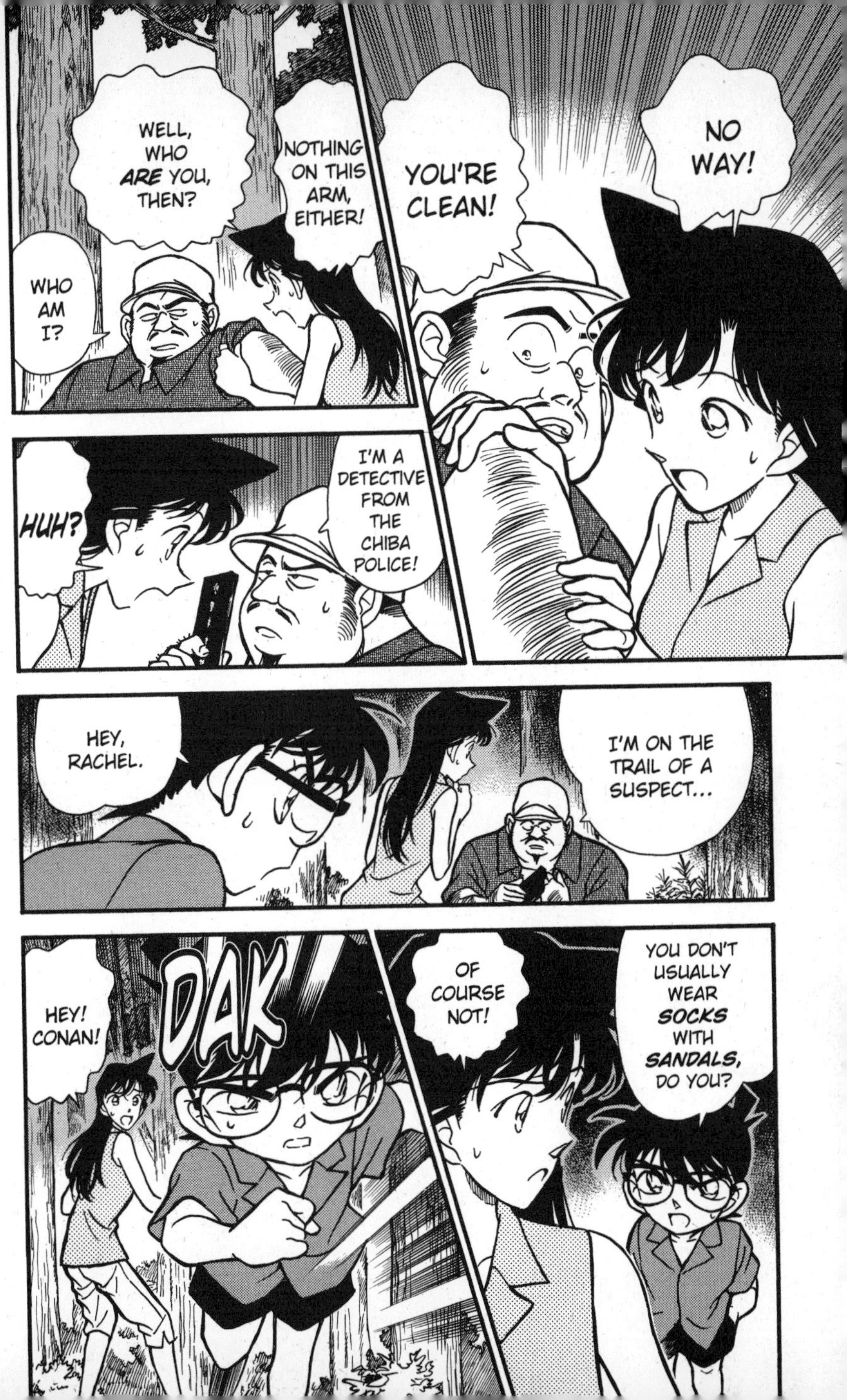
NO WAY!
YOU'RE CLEAN!
NOTHING ON THIS ARM, EITHER!
WELL, WHO ARE YOU, THEN?
WHO AM I?
I'M A DETECTIVE FROM THE CHIBA POLICE!
HUH?
I'M ON THE TRAIL OF A SUSPECT...
HEY, RACHEL.
YOU DON'T USUALLY WEAR SOCKS WITH SANDALS, DO YOU?
OF COURSE NOT!
DAK
HEY! CONAN!

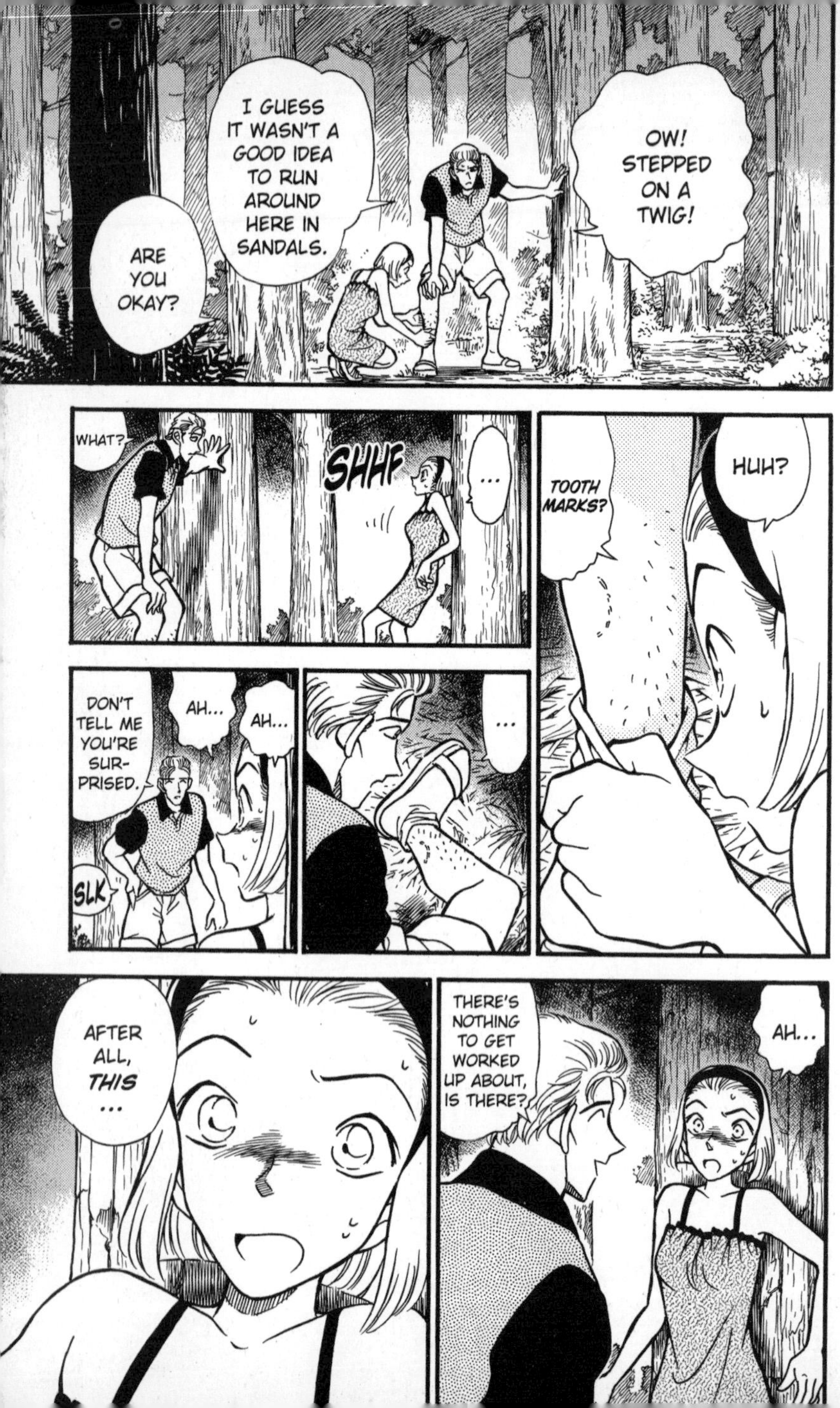
OW! STEPPED ON A TWIG!
I GUESS IT WASN'T A GOOD IDEA TO RUN AROUND HERE IN SANDALS.
ARE YOU OKAY?
HUH?
TOOTH MARKS?
...
SHHF
WHAT?
...
AH...
AH...
DON'T TELL ME YOU'RE SUR-PRISED.
SLK
AH...
THERE'S NOTHING TO GET WORKED UP ABOUT, IS THERE?
AFTER ALL, *THIS* ...

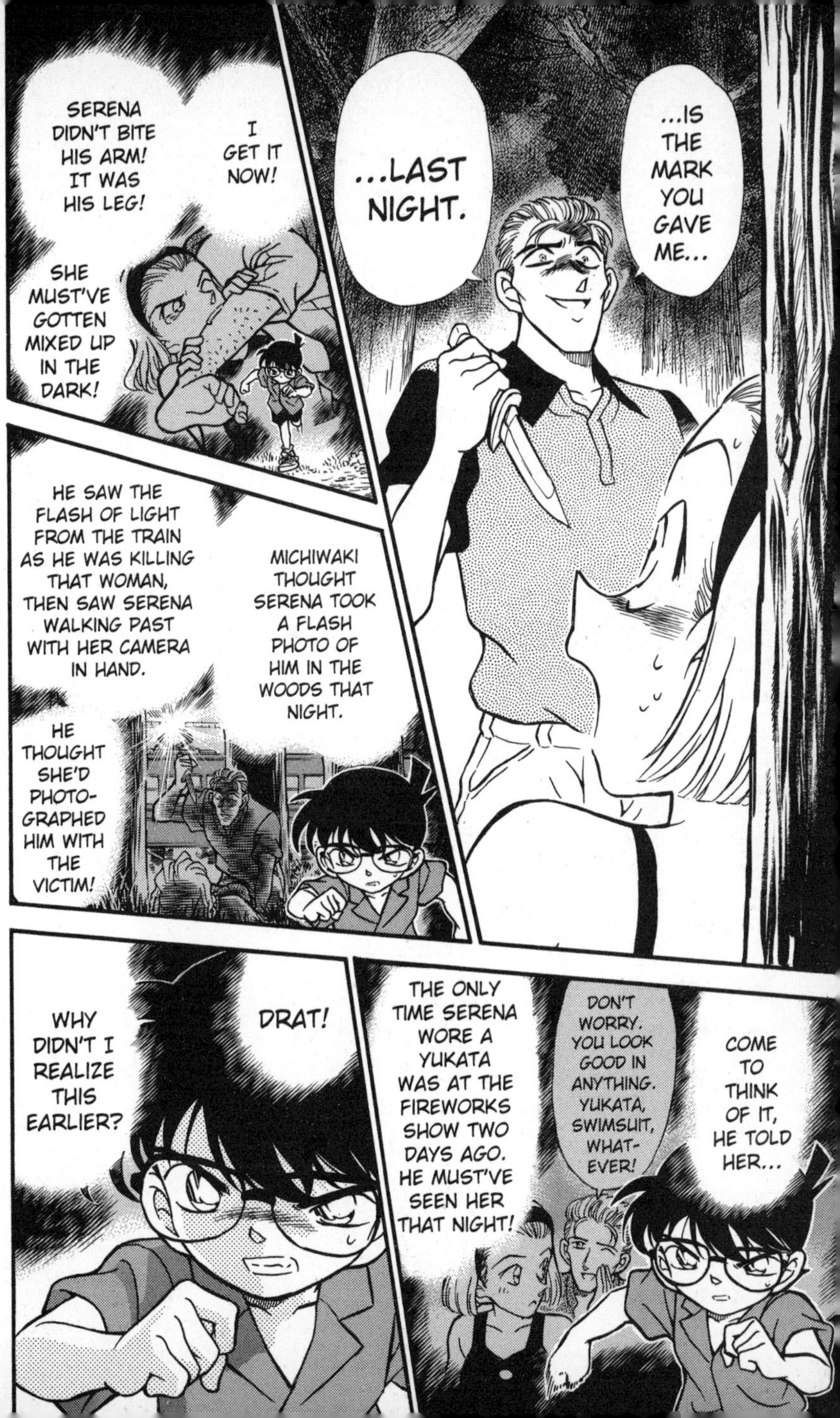
...IS THE MARK YOU GAVE ME...
...LAST NIGHT.
I GET IT NOW!
SERENA DIDN'T BITE HIS ARM! IT WAS HIS LEG!
SHE MUST'VE GOTTEN MIXED UP IN THE DARK!
MICHIWAKI THOUGHT SERENA TOOK A FLASH PHOTO OF HIM IN THE WOODS THAT NIGHT.
HE SAW THE FLASH OF LIGHT FROM THE TRAIN AS HE WAS KILLING THAT WOMAN, THEN SAW SERENA WALKING PAST WITH HER CAMERA IN HAND.
HE THOUGHT SHE'D PHOTO-GRAPHED HIM WITH THE VICTIM!
COME TO THINK OF IT, HE TOLD HER...
DON'T WORRY. YOU LOOK GOOD IN ANYTHING. YUKATA, SWIMSUIT, WHAT-EVER!
THE ONLY TIME SERENA WORE A YUKATA WAS AT THE FIREWORKS SHOW TWO DAYS AGO. HE MUST'VE SEEN HER THAT NIGHT!
DRAT!
WHY DIDN'T I REALIZE THIS EARLIER?

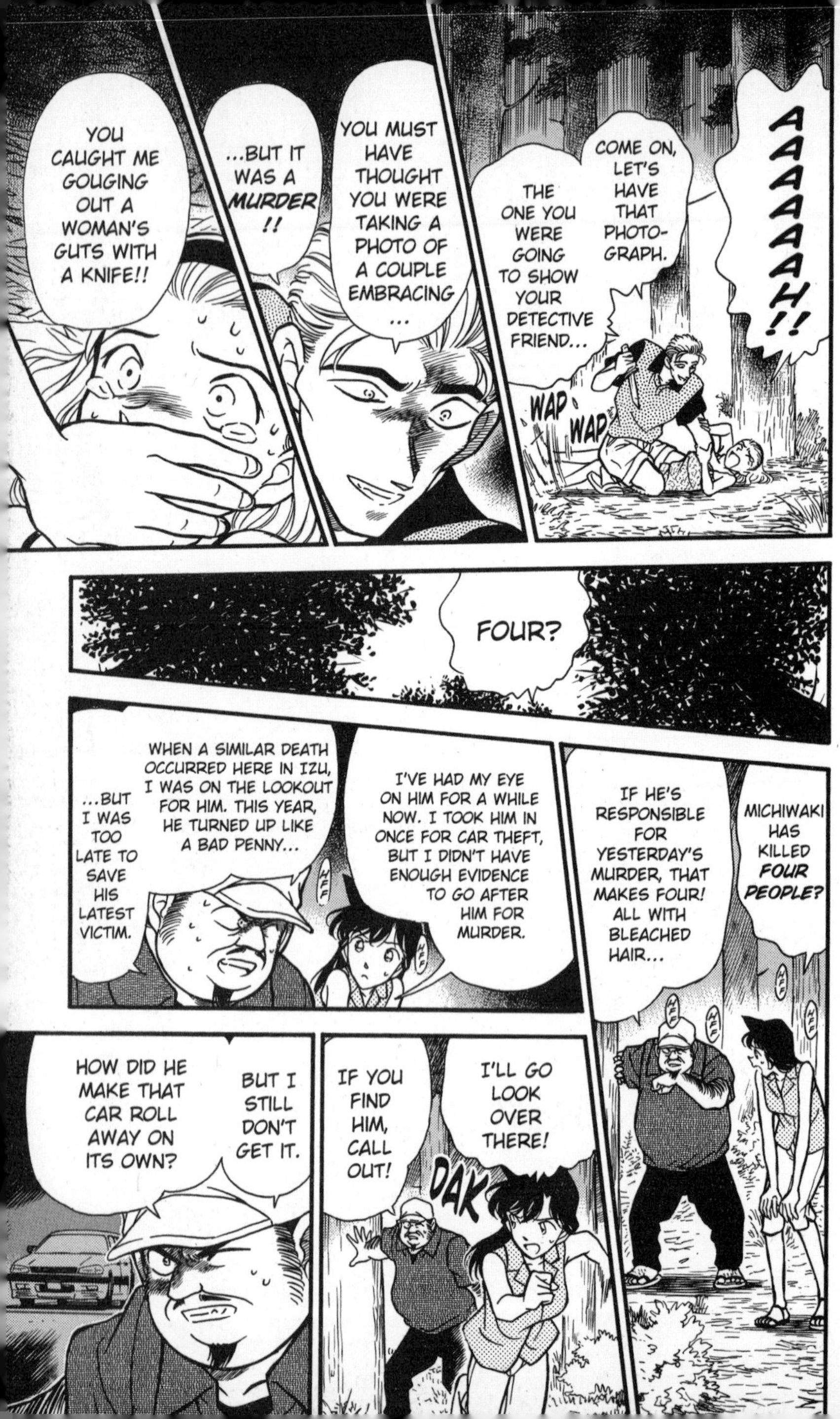
AAAAAAAH!!
COME ON, LET'S HAVE THAT PHOTOGRAPH.
THE ONE YOU WERE GOING TO SHOW YOUR DETECTIVE FRIEND...
WAP
WAP
YOU MUST HAVE THOUGHT YOU WERE TAKING A PHOTO OF A COUPLE EMBRACING...
...BUT IT WAS A *MURDER*!!
YOU CAUGHT ME GOUGING OUT A WOMAN'S GUTS WITH A KNIFE!!
FOUR?
MICHIWAKI HAS KILLED *FOUR PEOPLE?*
IF HE'S RESPONSIBLE FOR YESTERDAY'S MURDER, THAT MAKES FOUR! ALL WITH BLEACHED HAIR...
I'VE HAD MY EYE ON HIM FOR A WHILE NOW. I TOOK HIM IN ONCE FOR CAR THEFT, BUT I DIDN'T HAVE ENOUGH EVIDENCE TO GO AFTER HIM FOR MURDER.
WHEN A SIMILAR DEATH OCCURRED HERE IN IZU, I WAS ON THE LOOKOUT FOR HIM. THIS YEAR, HE TURNED UP LIKE A BAD PENNY...
...BUT I WAS TOO LATE TO SAVE HIS LATEST VICTIM.
I'LL GO LOOK OVER THERE!
IF YOU FIND HIM, CALL OUT!
DAK
BUT I STILL DON'T GET IT.
HOW DID HE MAKE THAT CAR ROLL AWAY ON ITS OWN?

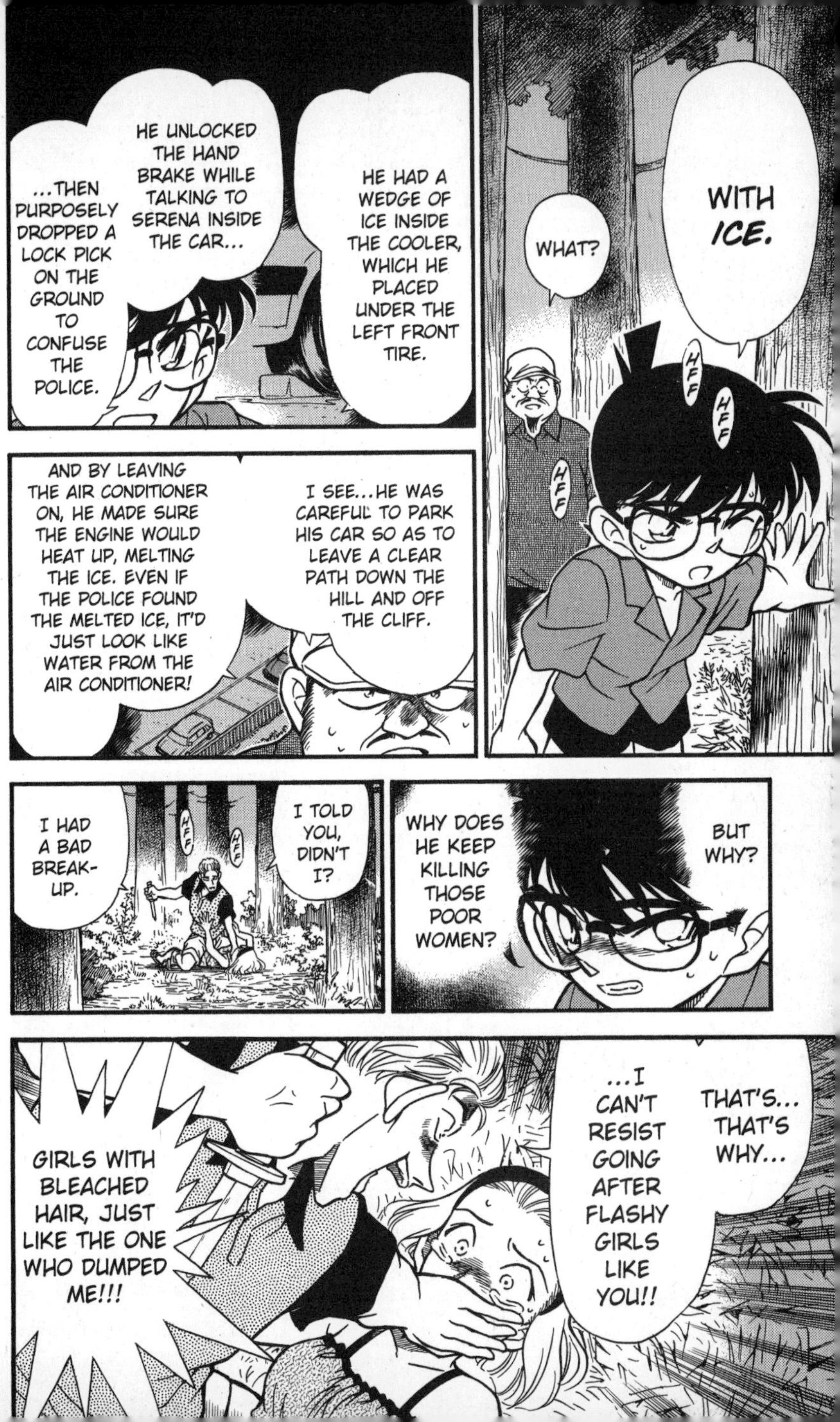
WITH ICE.
WHAT?
HFF HFF
HFF
HE HAD A WEDGE OF ICE INSIDE THE COOLER, WHICH HE PLACED UNDER THE LEFT FRONT TIRE.
HE UNLOCKED THE HAND BRAKE WHILE TALKING TO SERENA INSIDE THE CAR...
...THEN PURPOSELY DROPPED A LOCK PICK ON THE GROUND TO CONFUSE THE POLICE.
I SEE... HE WAS CAREFUL TO PARK HIS CAR SO AS TO LEAVE A CLEAR PATH DOWN THE HILL AND OFF THE CLIFF.
AND BY LEAVING THE AIR CONDITIONER ON, HE MADE SURE THE ENGINE WOULD HEAT UP, MELTING THE ICE. EVEN IF THE POLICE FOUND THE MELTED ICE, IT'D JUST LOOK LIKE WATER FROM THE AIR CONDITIONER!
BUT WHY?
WHY DOES HE KEEP KILLING THOSE POOR WOMEN?
HFF
HFF
I TOLD YOU, DIDN'T I?
I HAD A BAD BREAK-UP.
THAT'S... THAT'S WHY...
...I CAN'T RESIST GOING AFTER FLASHY GIRLS LIKE YOU!!
GIRLS WITH BLEACHED HAIR, JUST LIKE THE ONE WHO DUMPED ME!!!

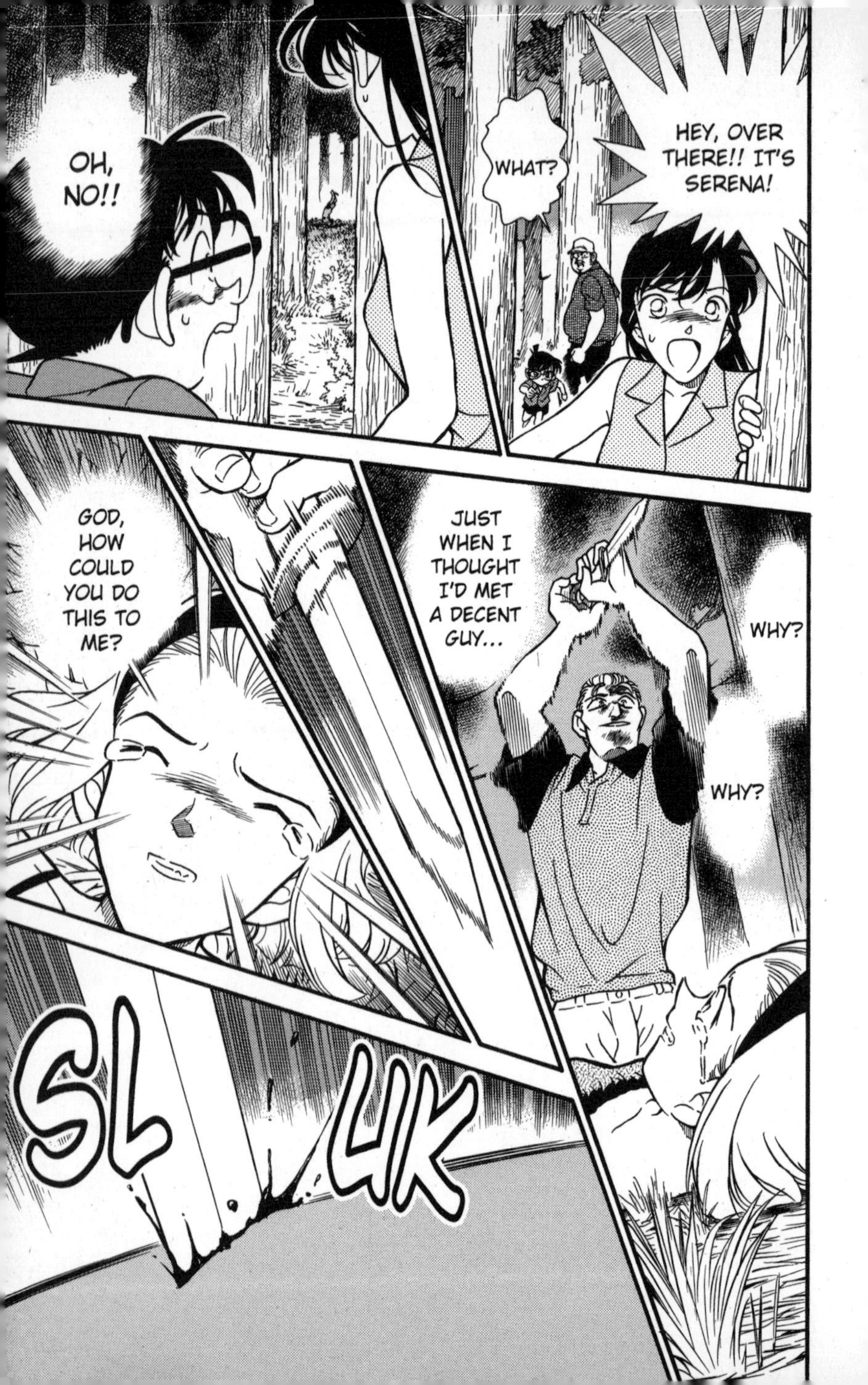

HEY, OVER THERE!! IT'S SERENA!
WHAT?
OH, NO!!
WHY?
WHY?
JUST WHEN I THOUGHT I'D MET A DECENT GUY...
GOD, HOW COULD YOU DO THIS TO ME?
SLUK

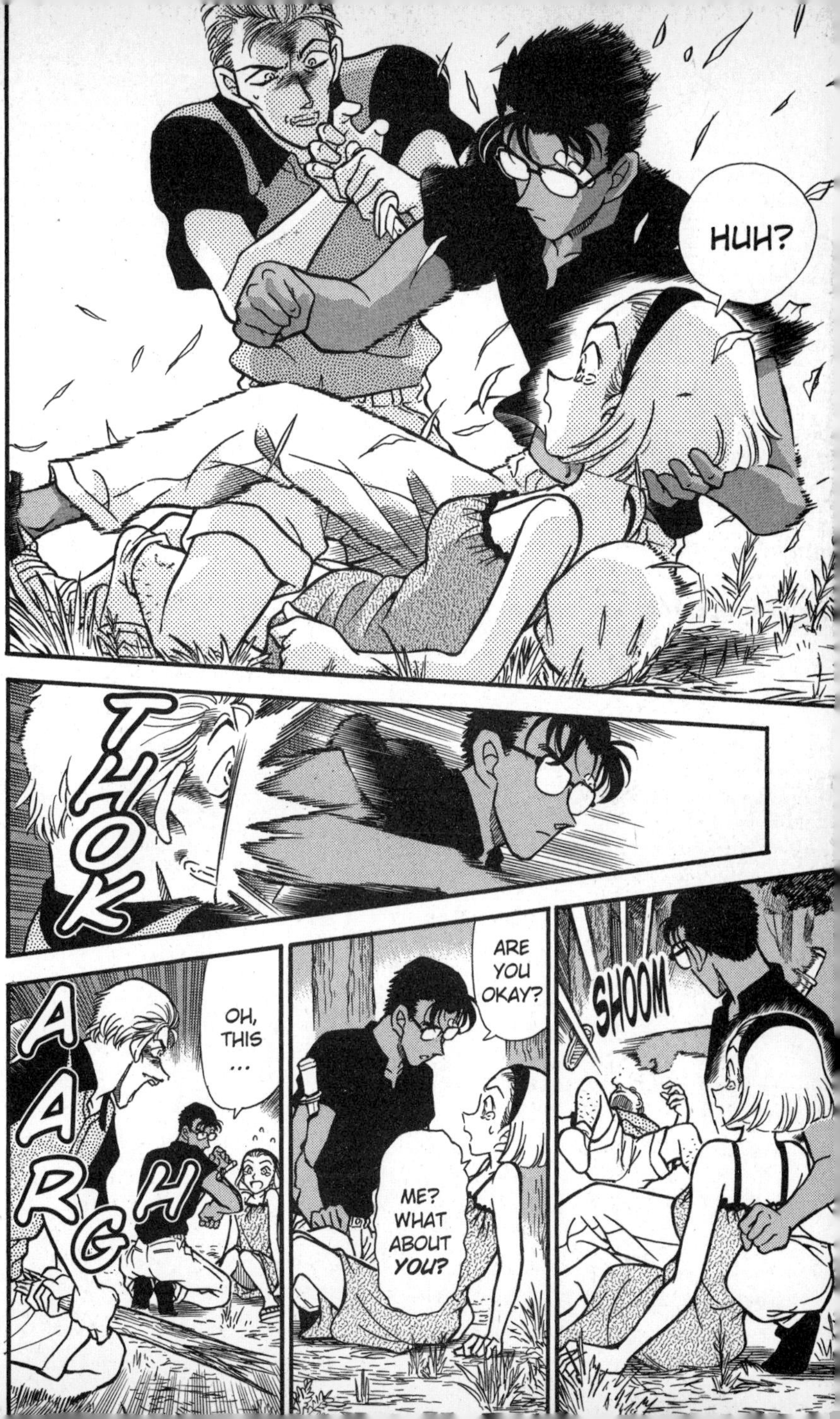
HUH?
THOK
SHOOM
ARE YOU OKAY?
ME? WHAT ABOUT YOU?
OH, THIS ...
AARGH

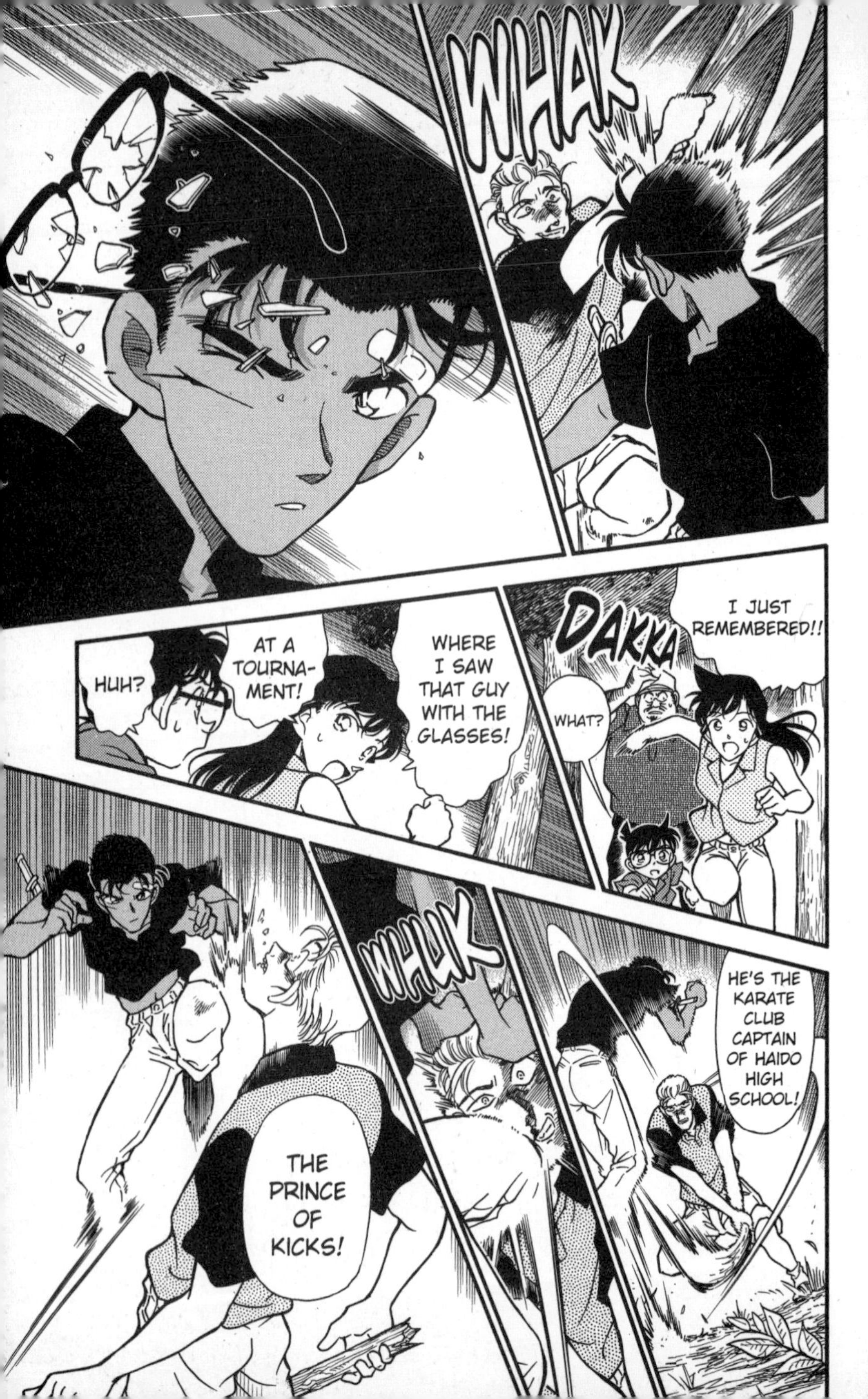
WHAK
I JUST REMEMBERED!!
DAKKA
WHAT?
WHERE I SAW THAT GUY WITH THE GLASSES!
AT A TOURNAMENT!
HUH?
HE'S THE KARATE CLUB CAPTAIN OF HAIDO HIGH SCHOOL!
WHUK
THE PRINCE OF KICKS!

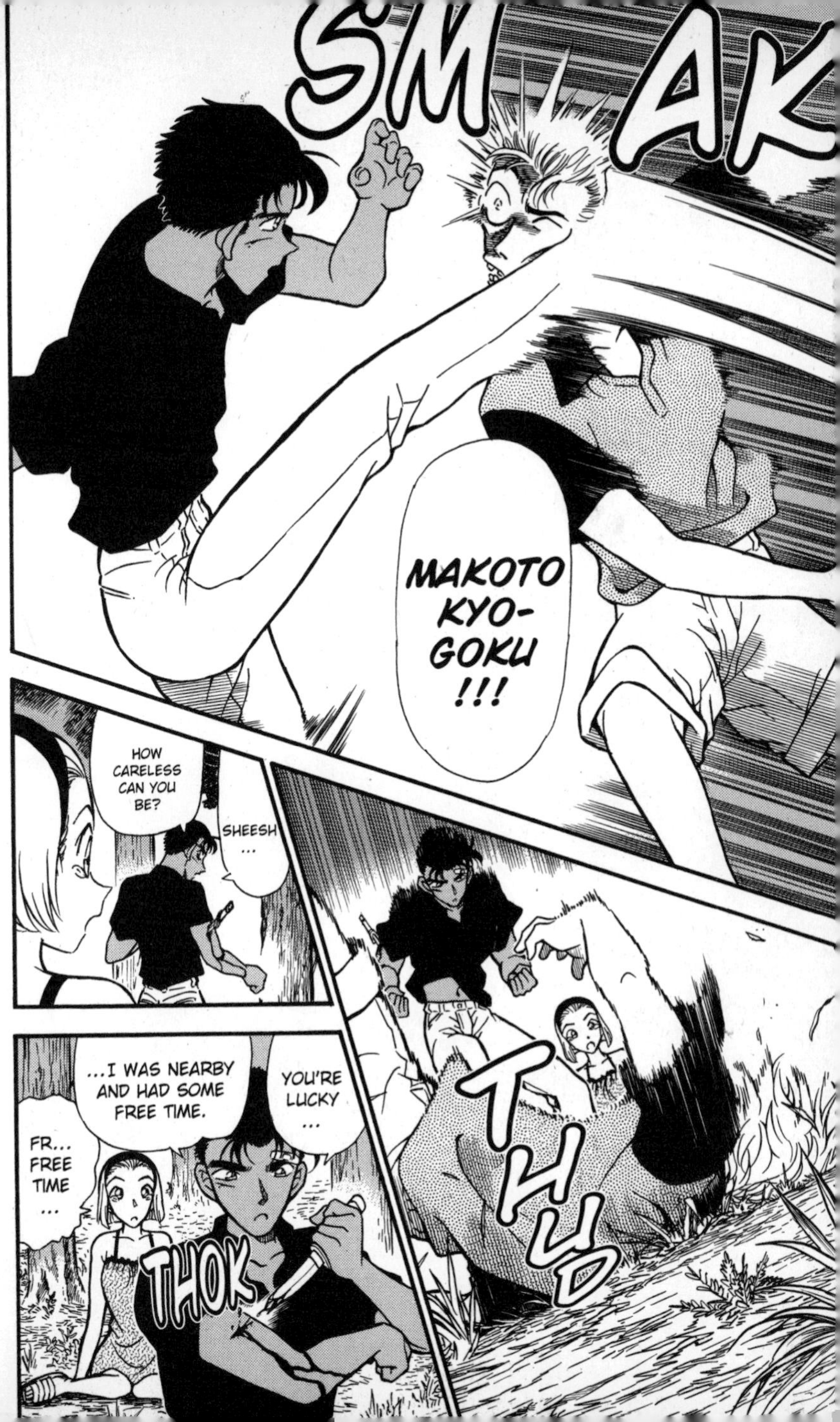
SMAK
MAKOTO KYO-GOKU !!!
THUD
SHEESH ...
HOW CARELESS CAN YOU BE?
YOU'RE LUCKY ...
...I WAS NEARBY AND HAD SOME FREE TIME.
FR... FREE TIME ...
THOK

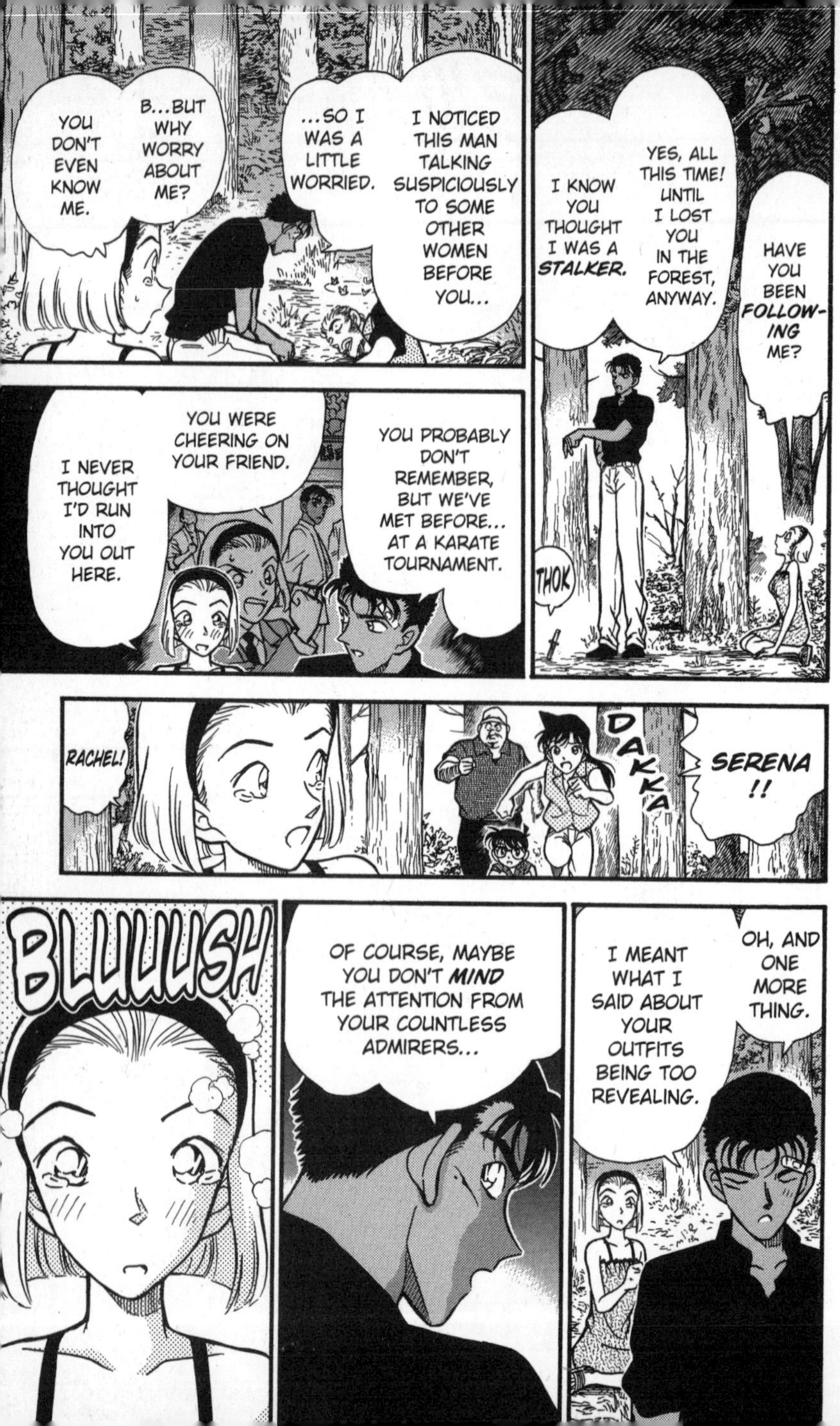
HAVE YOU BEEN FOLLOWING ME?
YES, ALL THIS TIME! UNTIL I LOST YOU IN THE FOREST, ANYWAY.
I KNOW YOU THOUGHT I WAS A STALKER.
THOK
I NOTICED THIS MAN TALKING SUSPICIOUSLY TO SOME OTHER WOMEN BEFORE YOU...
...SO I WAS A LITTLE WORRIED.
B...BUT WHY WORRY ABOUT ME?
YOU DON'T EVEN KNOW ME.
YOU PROBABLY DON'T REMEMBER, BUT WE'VE MET BEFORE... AT A KARATE TOURNAMENT.
YOU WERE CHEERING ON YOUR FRIEND.
I NEVER THOUGHT I'D RUN INTO YOU OUT HERE.
SERENA!!
DAKKA
RACHEL!
OH, AND ONE MORE THING.
I MEANT WHAT I SAID ABOUT YOUR OUTFITS BEING TOO REVEALING.
OF COURSE, MAYBE YOU DON'T MIND THE ATTENTION FROM YOUR COUNTLESS ADMIRERS...
BLUUUSH

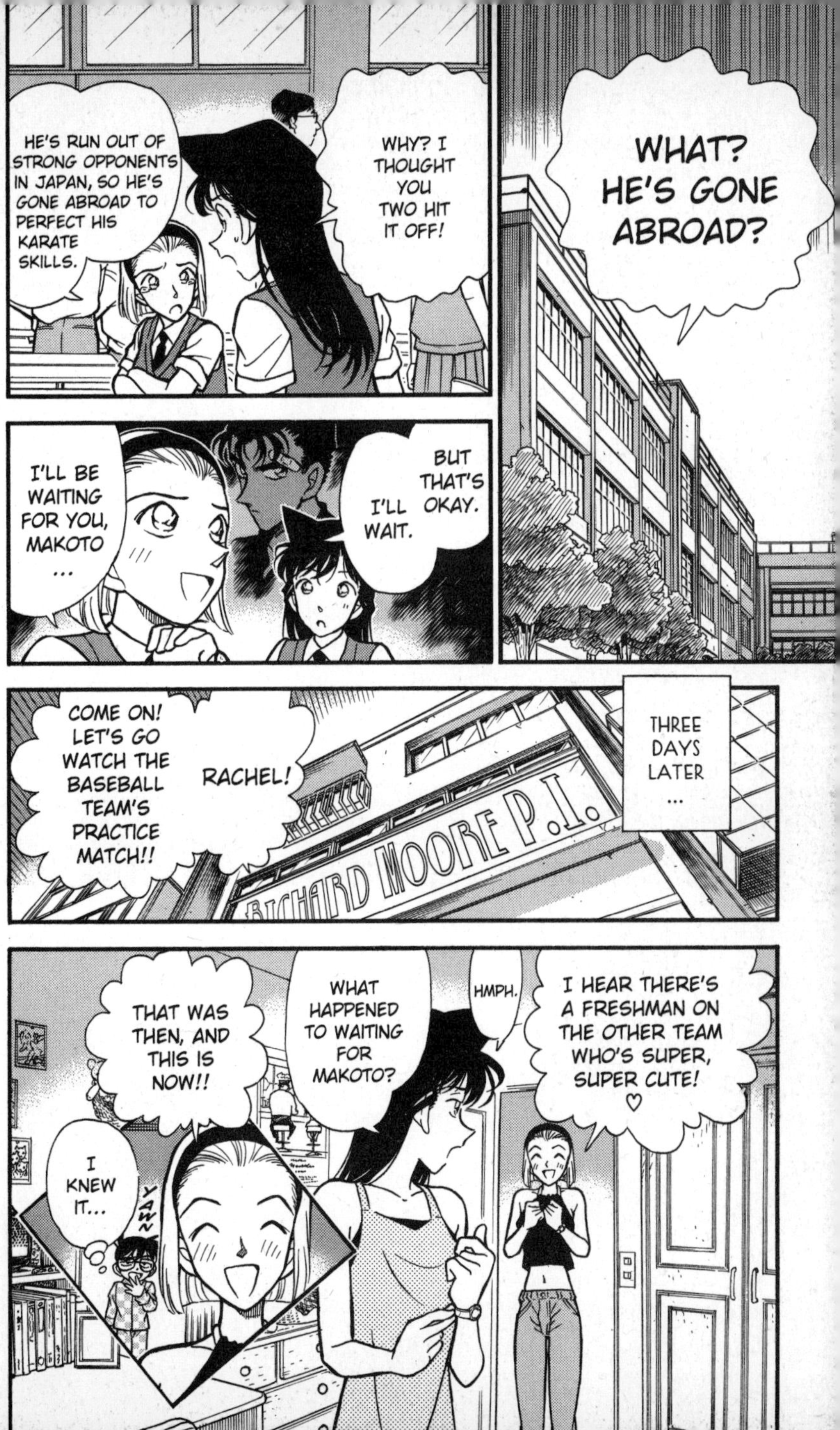
WHAT? HE'S GONE ABROAD?
WHY? I THOUGHT YOU TWO HIT IT OFF!
HE'S RUN OUT OF STRONG OPPONENTS IN JAPAN, SO HE'S GONE ABROAD TO PERFECT HIS KARATE SKILLS.
BUT THAT'S OKAY.
I'LL WAIT.
I'LL BE WAITING FOR YOU, MAKOTO ...
THREE DAYS LATER ...
RICHARD MOORE P.I.
RACHEL!
COME ON! LET'S GO WATCH THE BASEBALL TEAM'S PRACTICE MATCH!!
I HEAR THERE'S A FRESHMAN ON THE OTHER TEAM WHO'S SUPER, SUPER CUTE! ♡
HMPH.
WHAT HAPPENED TO WAITING FOR MAKOTO?
THAT WAS THEN, AND THIS IS NOW!!
YAWN
I KNEW IT...

Hello, Aoyama here.

Whoaaaa!

I've just received a baseball bat autographed by Matsui of the Giants! It even says "to Gosho Aoyama" on it!! I guess all my hard work and no play have paid off!

From now on, swinging this bat around should help cheer me up whenever I'm in a slump. Whoosh! Whoosh! Whoosh!

(Hmm...now I feel like playing baseball...)

*Editor's Note: At the time Aoyama wrote this, Hideki Matsui was on the Yomiuri Giants, one of Japan's top baseball teams. He now plays for the New York Yankees.

Gosho Aoyama's Mystery Library

22

SHOZO TOTSUGAWA

When you're on vacation and faced with a crime, the greatest sleuth to rely on is Inspector Shozo Totsugawa, created by Kyotaro Nishimura! He's 40 and slightly rotund, giving him the nickname "Tanuki." He loves to smoke, doesn't have a head for alcohol, and seems to be an ordinary middle-aged man. But he's a master detective when it comes to cases involving trains. He's a member of the Homicide Investigation Department of the Metropolitan Police, but he works pretty much all over Japan. He'll go anywhere for an investigation, as long as it can be reached by rail. Even when the suspect has an airtight alibi, he makes use of every mode of transportation imaginable to reach a deduction! His partner is veteran detective Kamei, who is five years older than Totsugawa. They make a great pair, with Totsugawa claiming, "You make the best instant coffee, Kamei!" ♥ But with the trouble they run into, they're not a pair you'd like to meet on your journey...

I recommend *Taminaru Satsujin Jiken* (The Terminal Station Murder Case).

[Editor's Note: Tanuki are animals native to Japan. They look a bit like a cross between a raccoon and a badger.]

LOVE MANGA?
LET US KNOW WHA

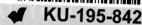
OUR MANGA SURVEY IS NOW
AVAILABLE ONLINE. PLEASE VISIT:
VIZ.COM/MANGASURVEY

HELP US MAKE THE MANGA
YOU LOVE BETTER!